PHILOSOPHY AND THE
HUMAN SCIENCES

PHILOSOPHICAL PAPERS
2

PHILOSOPHY AND THE HUMAN SCIENCES

PHILOSOPHICAL PAPERS
2

CHARLES TAYLOR

Professor of Philosophy and Political Science
McGill University, Montreal

CAMBRIDGE
UNIVERSITY PRESS

Published by the Press Syndicate of the University of Cambridge
The Pitt Building, Trumpington Street, Cambridge CB2 1RP
40 West 20th Street, New York, NY 10011-4211, USA
10 Stamford Road, Oakleigh, Melbourne 3166, Australia

First published 1985
Reprinted 1986, 1988, 1990, 1992, 1993

Printed in the United States of America

Library of Congress Cataloging in Publication data is available

A catalogue record for this book is available from the British Library

ISBN 0-521-31749-5 paperback

CONTENTS

ACKNOWLEDGEMENTS

1. 'Interpretation and the sciences of man', from *The Review of Metaphysics*, 25:1 (Sept. 1971), pp. 3–51.

2. 'Neutrality in political science', from P. Laslett and G. Runciman, *Philosophy, Politics and Society*, 3rd ser. (Oxford, Blackwell, 1967), pp. 25–57; reprinted in Alan Ryan (ed.), *The Philosophy of Social Explanation* (Oxford, Oxford University Press, 1973), pp. 139–70.

3. 'Social theory as practice', from *Social Theory as Practice*, The B. N. Ganguli Memorial Lectures 1981 (Delhi, Oxford University Press, 1983), pp. 1–27.

4. 'Understanding and ethnocentricity', from *Social Theory as Practice*, The B. N. Ganguli Memorial Lectures 1981 (Delhi, Oxford University Press, 1983), pp. 28–47.

5. 'Rationality', from Martin Hollis and Steven Lukes (eds.) *Rationality and Relativism* (Oxford, Blackwell, 1982), pp. 87–105.

6. 'Foucault on freedom and truth', from *Political Theory*, 12:2 (May 1984), pp. 152–83.

7. 'Atomism', from Alkis Kontos (ed.), *Powers, Possessions and Freedom* (Toronto, University of Toronto Press, 1979), pp. 39–61.

8. 'What's wrong with negative liberty', from A. Ryan (ed.), *The Idea of Freedom* (Oxford, Oxford University Press, 1979), pp. 175–93.

9. 'The diversity of goods', from Amartya Sen and Bernard Williams (eds.), *Utilitarianism and Beyond* (Cambridge, Cambridge University Press, 1982), pp. 129–44.

10. 'Legitimation crisis?'; a shorter version of this paper was published as 'Growth, legitimacy and the modern identity' in *Praxis*, 1:2 (July 1981), pp. 111–25.

11. 'The nature and scope of distributive justice', Summer 1976, unpublished.

12. 'Kant's theory of freedom', from J. N. Gray and Z. Pelczynski (eds.), *Conceptions of Liberty in Political Theory* (London, Athlone Press, 1984), pp. 100–21.

INTRODUCTION

Despite the appearance of variety in the papers published in this collection, they are the work of a monomaniac; or perhaps better, what Isaiah Berlin has called a hedgehog. If not a single idea, then at least a single rather tightly related agenda underlies all of them. If one had to find a name for where this agenda falls in the geography of philosophical domains, the term 'philosophical anthropology' would perhaps be best, although this term seems to make English-speaking philosophers uneasy.

I started on it with a polemical concern. I wanted to argue against the understanding of human life and action implicit in an influential family of theories in the sciences of man. The common feature of this family is the ambition to model the study of man on the natural sciences. Theories of this kind seem to me to be terribly implausible. They lead to very bad science: either they end up in wordy elaborations of the obvious, or they fail altogether to address the interesting questions, or their practitioners end up squandering their talents and ingenuity in the attempt to show that they can after all recapture the insights of ordinary life in their manifestly reductive explanatory languages.

Indeed, one could argue that the second and third pitfalls should rather be seen as the horns of a dilemma: either these inadequate theories avoid the interesting questions, or they show themselves up, and hence have to expend more and more energy defending themselves against the charge of irrelevancy. Behaviourism offers the classical example. The original popular experimental design, running rats in mazes, in fact screened out the interesting phenomena of insightful learning. Once these are put on the agenda, behaviourism enters its long decline, moving through phase after phase of special pleading. Something similar seems to be emerging with theories purporting to explain intelligent performance on a model based on the digital computer. Artificial Intelligence programs tend to do rather well on very explicitly structured tasks, like playing chess, and even more checkers, and become more and more manifestly inadequate the more they call on implicit know-how. (I have tried to draw the boundary between the areas where a mechanistic psychology can be useful and those where it must fail in volume 1 chapter 5.)

What is striking about this family of theories is their reductive nature; they are all trying to avoid recognizing some important and obtrusive aspect of human life, and purport to explain the phenomena we normally understand in terms of this aspect by other factors. Behaviourism, which was the target of my *Explanation of Behaviour*,[1] tried to ignore purpose and intentionality, indeed, even to side-step consciousness. Computer-influenced theories ignore what I call 'significance' in volume 1 chapter 8, the fact that we are beings to whom things matter. The atomist theories which I discuss in volume 2 chapter 1 have no place for the common meanings which are embedded in our institutions and practices; they see political culture as a question of the 'orientations' of individuals.

But this diversity in the aspect ignored raises the question whether my targets really form a family. The theories I want to attack take issue explicitly with each other on this matter of reduction. For instance, the theories of cognitive psychology were partly devised to cope with the manifest inadequacies of behaviourism. One of their strongest talking points was that they could cope with the phenomena of intelligence which behaviourism was committed to deny.

But I think that for all the diversity of these reductionisms they form a family nonetheless. What they have in common is a certain metaphysical motivation. Defining this has been in a sense the next item on my agenda after the polemic against them. In fact the motivation is many-faceted, but one way of defining it is via the paradigm status accorded to the natural sciences as the models for the sciences of man. In a certain sense of the term, this family of theories shares an allegiance to 'naturalism', by which I mean not just the view that man can be seen as part of nature – in one sense or other this would surely be accepted by everyone – but that the nature of which he is a part is to be understood according to the canons which emerged in the seventeenth-century revolution in natural science. One of the most important of these is that we must avoid anthropocentric properties (what I call in the first section of volume 1 chapter 2 'subjective' properties), and give an account of things in absolute terms. 'Anthropocentric' properties are those which things have only within the experience of agents of a certain kind – the classical example in the seventeenth-century discussion are the 'secondary' qualities; while 'absolute' properties (I borrow the term from Bernard Williams in his *Descartes*)[2]

---

[1] London and New York, 1964.   [2] Harmondsworth, 1978.

are supposedly free of any such relativity. This requirement can be more or less stringently interpreted and can be applied at different levels, which accounts, I believe, for the variety of reductionist views, but it underlies all of them.

But naturalism is more than a view about the language of science. It ramifies also into an understanding of agency. This too can be described first negatively, in terms of what its reductionist temper ignores. What it fails to recognize is a crucial feature of our ordinary understanding of human agency, of a person or self.

One way of getting at this feature is in terms of the notion of self-interpretation. A fully competent human agent not only has some understanding (which may be also more or less *mis*understanding) of himself, but is partly constituted by this understanding. This is a thesis of a post-Heideggerian hermeneutics, which I have tried to develop in a number of papers (especially volume 1 chapter 1 and volume 2 chapter 1). But it still does not capture the crucial point. This is that our self-understanding essentially incorporates our seeing ourselves against a background of what I have called 'strong evaluation'. I mean by that a background of distinctions between things which are recognized as of categoric or unconditioned or higher importance or worth, and things which lack this or are of lesser value. I discuss what is involved in this kind of distinction in volume 1 chapter 1 and 2.

In other terms, to be a full human agent, to be a person or a self in the ordinary meaning, is to exist in a space defined by distinctions of worth. A self is a being for whom certain questions of categoric value have arisen, and received at least partial answers. Perhaps these have been given authoritatively by the culture more than they have been elaborated in the deliberation of the person concerned, but they are his in the sense that they are incorporated into his self-understanding, in some degree and fashion. My claim is that this is not just a contingent fact about human agents, but is essential to what we would understand and recognize as full, normal human agency.

But if this is so, then the programme of naturalism as I define it above is severely limited in principle. For there can be no absolute understanding of what we are as persons, and this in two obvious respects. A being who exists only in self-interpretation cannot be understood absolutely; and one who can only be understood against the background of distinctions of worth cannot be captured by a scientific language which essentially aspires to neutrality. Our personhood cannot be treated scientifically in exactly the same way we approach our organic being. What it is to possess a liver or a heart is something I can define quite independently of the space of questions in which I exist for myself, but not what it is to have a self or be a person.

In any case, it is this thesis about the self that I aspire to make clearly and convincingly. I wish I could flatter myself that I had already done so, but it is something I am still working on. It is, however, what I am struggling towards in the papers that make up the first section of volume 1. While the second section of the first volume, and the first of the second volume, are largely taken up with the polemic against naturalistic theories in different domains, it is in this section on agency and the self that I have tried to move further in my agenda towards the underlying views of the nature of agency itself.

But this involves more than just making the negative point above, that naturalism cannot cope with our understanding of the self. A critic of naturalism from a hermeneutical standpoint, like myself, owes his opponent more. He has to give an account of his adversary's motivation in hermeneutical terms. It is not just that the final challenge that this kind of account ought to meet is to explain the opponent's error, that is, to explain why people are attracted by naturalism. It is also that the very nature of the claim I am putting forward, that we all as human agents define ourselves against a background of distinctions of worth, requires that we explain in these terms what people are doing who espouse a naturalist outlook. For it surely could not be that naturalists are somehow exceptions to this rule, just because they do not *recognize* that they are constituted by strongly evaluative self-interpretations. If the theory is right, we ought to be able to give an account of what tempts naturalists to adopt their thin theory of the self in terms of our richer theory.

Now I believe not only that this requirement can be met, but that it is very illuminating to meet it. Because behind and supporting the impetus to naturalism I mentioned above, viz. the understandable prestige of the natural science model, stands an attachment to a certain picture of the agent. This picture is deeply attractive to moderns, both flattering and inspiring. It shows us as capable of achieving a kind of disengagement from our world by objectifying it. We objectify our situation to the extent that we can overcome a sense of it as what determines for us our paradigm purposes and ends, and can come to see it and function in it as a neutral environment, within which we can effect the purposes which we determine out of ourselves. In a sense, the great shift in cosmology which occurred in the seventeenth century, from a picture of the world-order based on the Ideas to one of the universe as mechanism, was the founding objectification, the source and inspiration for the continuing development of a disengaged modern consciousness.

The ideal of disengagement defines a certain – typically modern – notion of freedom, as the ability to act on one's own, without outside interference or subordination to outside authority. It defines its own peculiar notion of human dignity, closely connected to freedom. And these in turn are linked to ideals of efficacy, power, unperturbability, which for all their links with earlier ideals are original with modern culture.

The great attraction of these ideals, all the more powerful in that this understanding of the agent is woven into a host of modern practices – economic, scientific, technological, psycho-therapeutic, and so on – lends great weight and credence to the disengaged image of the self. The liberation through objectification wrought by the cosmological revolution of the seventeenth century has become for many the model of the agent's relation to the world, and hence sets the very definition of what is to be an agent.

My claim is that it is this image of agency which offers crucial support to the naturalist world-view. Despite its own pretensions, naturalism is not mainly powered by epistemological or scientific considerations. Looked at dispassionately, the scientific theories it encourages us to espouse are extremely implausible, in the ways I described above. In the papers in volume 1, section II, and volume 2, section I, as well as in a host of other writings, I have been trying to make this case. But after engaging long and hard in the debate within any one of the sciences of man, there comes a moment when one is led to stand back and question the significance of it all. Why is one spending this immense effort to show the inadequacy of what in the end is a wildly implausible view?

To take what is admittedly an extreme case, once one has broken out from the world-view of a very narrow form of naturalism, it seems almost unbelievable that anyone could ever have taken a theory like behaviourism seriously. It takes a very powerful metaphysical set of preconceptions for one to ignore or over-ride so much that is so intuitively obvious about human life, for no valid scientific or explanatory reason. Behaviourism is out of fashion, so many readers may agree with my sentiments on this case. But I think that the situation is not all that different with the contemporary fashion of computer-modelled explanations. Their neglect of what I call (in volume 1 chapter 8) the 'significance feature' is so flagrant, and so bizarre, that only very strong preconceptions could mask it.

What generates these preconceptions? If the scientific and epistemological arguments are so poor, what gives them their strength? I believe that they derive their force from the underlying image of the self, and that this exercises its hold on us because of the ideal of disengagement and the images of freedom, dignity and power which attach to it. More specifically, the claim is that the more we are led to interpret ourselves in the light of the disengaged picture, to define our identity by this, the more the connected epistemology of naturalism will seem right and proper to us. Or otherwise put, a commitment to this identity generates powerful resistances against any challenges to the naturalist outlook. In short, its epistemological weaknesses are more than made up for by its moral appeal.

But what I am offering here is an account of the appeal of naturalism within the terms of the hermeneutical theory. I am saying that it is the hold of a particular set of background distinctions of worth, those of the disengaged identity, which leads people to espouse what are ultimately rather implausible epistemological doctrines. And this explanation is flagrantly at odds with the one naturalism offers of itself. For it does not allow any account at all in terms of identity and self-interpretation, and it deems its epistemological grounds sufficient. To be able to make this hermeneutical account plausible would thus be to make the final refutation of naturalism, to show that its opponents understand it better than it does itself, that indeed the phenomenon of people believing in naturalism was only adequately explicable in terms of a rival, incompatible theory.

And so my own agenda draws me on, as it were, to try a proof of this kind, partly because the very nature of the hermeneutical theory seems to make this demand of me, as I said above; and partly because the long experience of polemic against naturalist views on the epistemological level of the philosophy of science, the sense of futility when one fails to carry conviction against what seem ultimately absurd views, convinces me that the real issue lies elsewhere.

Of course, this is not at all uncharted terrain. A number of influential accounts have been put forth explaining the hold of the scientific outlook in terms of the appeal of a certain moral self-understanding. The most famous, or notorious, author of such a theory was Nietzsche, and in a sense all those in the twentieth century who have developed such have been influenced to some degree by him. These include Scheler, Heidegger, the writers of the Frankfurt school, Foucault, and various varieties of French 'post-structuralism', to mention the best known. But I confess to being very dissatisfied with most of these theories. They generally share two great drawbacks: they are often under-demonstrated, indeed, rather impressionistically argued for; and they also tend to be hostile and dismissive towards the scientific outlook and the disengaged identity. But this latter stance is both uncalled for, and in the end inauthentic. That is, the disengaged identity is far from being simply wrong and misguided, and besides, we are all too deeply imbued with it to be able really and authentically to repudiate it. The kind of critique we need is one that can free it of its illusory pretensions to define the totality of our lives as agents, without attempting the futile and ultimately self-destructive task of rejecting it altogether.

So for all these reasons the case for the ultimately moral grounding of modern naturalism needs to be made again, with more convincing argument and with finer moral discrimination. Having said this, I cannot claim to be very advanced in this task. Some beginnings of it are made in volume 1 chapter 4, but only the very first moves. But I think I see better than in the past what such a case would involve.

Apart from the negative side of the argument, the case that naturalism makes a bad philosophy of science (which I think has been very powerfully made), the positive thesis can only be established in an historical account. This would have to show how, through the whole course of the development of the modern identity, the moral motivation has been intertwined with the epistemological, how the latter has never been a sufficient motive force but has always been seconded by the former, but how paradoxically the very nature of this modern identity has tended to make us reluctant to acknowledge this moral dimension. The very ideal of disengagement militates against it. This would mean placing the history of our scientific and philosophical consciousness in relation to the whole development of modern culture, and particularly of the underlying interpretations of agency and the self. What would ultimately carry conviction would be an account of this development which illuminated it and made more sense of it than its rivals, and particularly than naturalistic ones. As for any hermeneutic explanation, interpretive plausibility is the ultimate criterion.

Michel Foucault has in a sense been engaged in an account of this kind, and I touch on some of the things it would require in my paper on his work (volume 2 chapter 6); I also sketch some of the themes it would have to deal with in the discussion of contemporary 'legitimation crisis' (volume 2 chapter 10). But I am basically at the beginning. I am now trying to write a larger work which will come to grips with this kind of historical account, and do at least something to meet this demand which I see as weighing on a position like mine, to explain plausibly the spiritual roots of naturalism.

So what I have to offer here is, alas, mainly promissory notes. But there are yet further items on my tightly knit agenda where I have some modest progress to report. I mentioned above that the ideal account of the spiritual basis of modern naturalism should not only be very convincing as interpretation, but should also allow us to discriminate sensitively what we want to affirm and what we want to reject. But even before such an account has been worked out we can try to define more clearly the features of the modern identity, and the ideals which help constitute it, and offer a critique of them.

One of the most negative of these features is atomism. The disengaged identity and its attendant notion of freedom tend to generate an understanding of the individual as metaphysically independent of society. Of course, it can allow for views which see the individual as shaped by his social environment; and these are the views generally espoused today – the early atomism of the seventeenth century seems incredible to us. But what it hides from view is the way in which an individual is constituted by the language and culture which can only be maintained and renewed in the communities he is part of. The community is not simply an aggregation of individuals; nor is there simply a causal interaction between the two. The community is also constitutive of the individual, in the sense that the self-interpretations which define him are drawn from the interchange which the community carries on. A human being alone is an impossibility, not just *de facto*, but as it were *de jure*. Outside of the continuing conversation of a community, which provides the language by which we draw our background distinctions, human agency of the kind I describe above would be not just impossible, but inconceivable. As organisms we are separable from society – though it may be hard in fact to survive as a lone being; but as humans this separation is unthinkable. On our own, as Aristotle says, we would be either beasts or Gods.

Because of the ascendancy of the modern identity, this dimension of our existence is constantly being lost from sight. It is not that moderns are attracted to theories which really portray human beings as independent of society, in the manner of seventeenth-century contract theory. It is rather that, however tightly the dependence is conceived, it is seen in causal terms, and not as touching our very identity. Bringing this back into view is therefore a perpetually necessary philosophical task, both in order to attain a more valid conception of the nature of social science, and in order to purge our key normative notions – freedom, justice, rights – of their atomist distortions.

I have tried to do something to the first purpose in some of the papers in volume 2, section I (notably chapter 1); and something to the second in the papers of volume 2, section II (especially chapters 7, 8 and 11).

Obviously, from here my 'agenda' ramifies in a number of directions, some of which I have followed up. For instance, once one accepts a hermeneutical conception of the sciences of man, a number of further questions arise. I have tried to deal with some of the more insistent, such as: the nature of the contrast between human and natural sciences (volume 2 chapter 3); what is involved in explaining/understanding a quite different culture (volume 2 chapter 4); and the issue of relativism (volume 2 chapter 5).

But I would like to say something here about a rather different direction, which is in a way more fundamental. That is the philosophy of language. Obviously a view of human life as constituted by self-understanding is one in which the philosophy of language will play a central role. Heidegger's philosophical development illustrates this strikingly. And obviously, too, the conception of language will be rather different from those which develop out of naturalist views. This will emerge, among other places, in their theories of meaning. A number of views on linguistic meaning have been put forward during the history of modern philosophy from the standpoint of what I have been calling the disengaged modern identity. The earlier views, those of Hobbes or Locke for instance, saw language as an instrument, and understood meaning in terms of designation. Discovering the meaning of words is finding what ideas or things they stood for. We are much more sophisticated in the twentieth century, and especially in the English-speaking philosophical world, which has been through the Fregean revolution. But some of the basic ideas of that Hobbes–Locke tradition still survive in transposed form. With truth-conditional theories of meaning, for instance, we still have the basic notion that meaning is to be understood in terms of the things language is used to talk about. The crucial unit is now the sentence and not the word, and relations like 'making true' and 'satisfying' replace the earlier emphasis on designation (or 'signifying', in seventeenth-century parlance), but meaning is still being explicated by some notion of representation: the meaning of a word is to be explained by the way it can be used to *depict* the world.

By contrast, a hermeneutical view requires a very different conception. If we are partly constituted by our self-understanding, and this in turn can be very different according to the various languages which articulate for us a background of distinctions of worth, then language does not only serve to *depict* ourselves and the world, it also helps *constitute* our lives.

Certain ways of being, of feeling, of relating to each other are only possible given certain linguistic resources. Without a certain articulation of oneself and of the highest, it is neither possible to *be* a Christian ascetic, nor to *feel* that combination of one's own lack of worth and high calling (the 'grandeur at misère' of Pascal), not to be *part* of, say, a monastic order.

In order to understand this, we need a rather different theory of meaning, more in line with those developed in the Romantic period, which explore how language not only depicts, but also articulates and makes things manifest, and in so doing helps shape our form of life. The original figures in this expressive-constitutive line of thought are, I believe, Herder and Humboldt. Their work contains seminal insights which need further development. This is what I am trying to argue in the papers in volume 1, section III. In volume 1 chapter 9 I sketch the historical development of both the designative and expressive views on meaning, and try to define the contrast between them; in volume 1 chapter 10 I explore some of the features of the Herder–Humboldt view by showing the kind of critique one can make of truth-conditional theories from their standpoint.

Of course, here again one seems to be trespassing on terrain that is already well occupied. Structuralist and especially 'post-Structuralist' thinkers have already allegedly made the critique of purely designative views. The latter seem to have gone Frege one better; while he shifted the crucial unit of meaning from the word to the sentence, they have gone further and identified the text as an indissociable whole. And their rejection of depictive theories seems all the more radical in that they refuse to allow any relation to a reality outside the text to serve as our key to understanding it.

There is, of course, an important line of historical filiation between Herder and Humboldt and twentieth-century structuralist theories. For instance, Saussure's privileging of the code over the individual item within it is prefigured in Humboldt's image of language as a web. But nevertheless it seems to me that the current vogue, say, of Derrida's later writings (admittedly largely outside philosophical circles) is something close to an unmitigated disaster for this tradition. A good case is being discredited by obscurity, posturing and dramatic over-statement.

A critique of what can be called 'subjectivism' is, indeed, one of the central themes of the Herder–Humboldt line of thought. They saw that the disengaged identity and the designative account of meaning it gravitates toward centres everything on the subject, and exalts a quite unreal model of self-clarity and control. The ultimate absurdity into which the designative view can fall is the voluntarism parodied in Lewis Carroll's Humpty Dumpty. The speaking agent is in fact enmeshed in two kinds of larger order, which he can never fully oversee, and can only punctually and marginally refashion. For he is only a speaking agent at all as part of a language community, as I argued above, and the meanings and illocutionary forces activated in any speech act are only what they are against the background of a whole language and way of life. In the light of this, certain models of transparent consciousness and clairvoyant control are shown to be not only unrealizable but destructive.

But this point is more parodied than articulated by playful rhetoric about the end of subjectivity, or about texts with nothing outside to relate to. If any general position emerges from all this, it points to a view of the code as ultimate, dominating the supposedly autonomous agent. But this makes just as much sense as, and no more than, the equal and opposite error of Humpty Dumpty subjectivism. A position like this can only make itself remotely plausible by claiming that the only alternative to it is some such wildly extreme subjectivism. And so it has a vested interest in muddying the waters, and obscuring all the interesting insights which must necessarily lie in the space between these two absurd theses. Like a debate between, say, an orthodox Cartesian and a vulgar Marxist, this one will be rich in histrionics, but a waste-land intellectually.

This is the more to be regretted in that there is a genuinely interesting frontier to be explored beyond modern subjectivism through the philosophy of language. Heidegger, and later Gadamer, have tried to open this up. I do not know how clear I can be about this at the present stage, but perhaps I can gesture towards the question in this way: if one of the fundamental uses of language is to articulate or make manifest the background of distinctions of worth we define ourselves by, how should we understand *what* is being manifested here? Is what we are articulating ultimately to be understood as our human response to our condition? Or is our articulation striving rather to be faithful to something beyond us, not explicable simply in terms of human response? In the philosophy of the late Heidegger, the first alternative is seen as the quintessential expression of modern subjectivism. It belongs to the 'humanism' he is trying to get beyond. He seemed to be exploring variations of the second answer. Which shows how far removed he is from the contemporary theories of self-enclosed texts for all their immense debt to him.

I would dearly like to be able to cut through the clutter and confusion that we all labour under so as to be able to explore this question, but I have to admit that I am far away from this at present. I need, among other things, to be much clearer about language and meaning. Once more, in these last paragraphs, my discussion has been leading up to another promissory note (this one with a rather remote maturity).

But if this question could be tackled, it would greatly help with another issue, which stands more urgently on the agenda. Let my definition of this be my last promissory note. If, as I said above, the ultimate basis of naturalism turns out to be a certain definition of agency and the background of worth, does the critique terminate with the proof that this is so (supposing I finally bring it off), or is there a way we can go on and rationally assess this and other definitions of worth? This is, in fact, a particular way of putting the general question: what are the capacities of practical reason? Is it quite helpless before such basic differences in spiritual outlook, like that between the disengaged identity and its opponents? Or is there, at least in principle, a way in which this kind of question can be rationally arbitrated? I am fiercely committed to the latter view, and I recognize that the onus is on me to come up with a good argument. I am working on it, and I hope at not too remote a date to be able to publish something convincing (at least to some) on this.

But for the moment, let this collection serve as a kind of fragmentary and provisional exploration of aspects of this much more ambitious project.

PART I

PHILOSOPHY AND SOCIAL
SCIENCE

CHAPTER ONE

INTERPRETATION AND THE SCIENCES OF MAN*

I

1

Is there a sense in which interpretation is essential to explanation in the sciences of man? The view that it is, that there is an unavoidably 'hermeneutical' component in the sciences of man, goes back to Dilthey. But recently the question has come again to the fore, for instance, in the work of Gadamer,[1] in Ricoeur's interpretation of Freud,[2] and in the writings of Habermas.[3]

Interpretation, in the sense relevant to hermeneutics, is an attempt to make clear, to make sense of, an object of study. This object must, therefore, be a text, or a text-analogue, which in some way is confused, incomplete, cloudy, seemingly contradictory – in one way or another, unclear. The interpretation aims to bring to light an underlying coherence or sense.

This means that any science which can be called 'hermeneutical', even in an extended sense, must be dealing with one or another of the confusingly interrelated forms of meaning. Let us try to see a little more clearly what this involves.

We need, first, an object or field of objects, about which we can speak in terms of coherence or its absence, of making sense or nonsense.

Second, we need to be able to make a distinction, even if only a relative one, between the sense or coherence made, and its embodiment in a particular field of carriers or signifiers. For otherwise the task of making clear what is fragmentary or confused would be radically impossible. No

---

* I have greatly benefited in preparing this paper from discussions held under the auspices of the Study Group for the Unity of Knowledge, whose meetings were supported by the Ford Foundation.
[1] E.g., H. G. Gadamer, *Wahrheit und Methode* (Tübingen, 1960).
[2] Paul Ricoeur, *De l'interprétation* (Paris, 1965).
[3] E.g., J. Habermas, *Erkenntnis und Interesse* (Frankfurt, 1968).

sense could be given to this idea. We have to be able to make for our interpretations claims of the order: the meaning confusedly present in this text or text-analogue is clearly expressed here. The meaning, in other words, is one which admits of more than one expression, and, in this sense, a distinction must be possible between meaning and expression.

The point of the above qualification, that this distinction may be only relative, is that there are cases where no clear, unambiguous, non-arbitrary line can be drawn between what is said and its expression. It can be plausibly argued (I think convincingly, although there is no space to go into it here) that this is the normal and fundamental condition of meaningful expression, that exact synonymy, or equivalence of meaning, is a rare and localized achievement of specialized languages or uses of civilization. But this, if true (and I think it is), does not do away with the distinction between meaning and expression. Even if there is an important sense in which a meaning re-expressed in a new medium cannot be declared identical, this by no means entails that we can give no sense to the project of expressing a meaning in a new way. It does of course raise an interesting and difficult question about what can be meant by expressing it in a clearer way: what is the 'it' which is clarified if equivalence is denied? I hope to return to this in examining interpretation in the sciences of man.

Hence the object of a science of interpretation must be describable in terms of sense and nonsense, coherence and its absence; and must admit of a distinction between meaning and its expression.

There is also a third condition it must meet. We can speak of sense or coherence, and of their different embodiments, in connection with such phenomena as gestalts, or patterns in rock formations, or snow crystals, where the notion of expression has no real warrant. What is lacking here is the notion of a subject for whom these meanings are. Without such a subject, the choice of criteria of sameness and difference, the choice among the different forms of coherence which can be identified in a given pattern, among the different conceptual fields in which it can be seen, is arbitrary.

In a text or text-analogue, on the other hand, we are trying to make explicit the meaning expressed, and this means expressed by or for a subject or subjects. The notion of expression refers us to that of a subject. The identification of the subject is by no means necessarily unproblematical, as we shall see further on; it may be one of the most difficult problems, an area in which prevailing epistemological prejudice may blind us to the nature of our object of study. I think this has been the case, as I will show below. And moreover, the identification of a subject does not assure us of a clear and absolute distinction between meaning and expression, as we saw above. But any such distinction, even a relative one, is without any anchor at all, is totally arbitrary, without appeal to a subject.

The object of a science of interpretation must thus have: sense, distinguishable from its expression, which is for or by a subject.

2

Before going on to see in what way, if any, these conditions are realized in the sciences of man, I think it would be useful to set out more clearly what rides on this question, why it matters whether or not we think of the sciences of man as hermeneutical, what the issue is at stake here.

The issue here is at root an epistemological one. But it is inextricable from an ontological one, and, hence, cannot but be relevant to our notions of science and of the proper conduct of enquiry. We might say that it is an ontological issue which has been argued ever since the seventeenth century in terms of epistemological considerations which have appeared to some to be unanswerable.

The case could be put in these terms: what are the criteria of judgement in a hermeneutical science? A successful interpretation is one which makes clear the meaning originally present in a confused, fragmentary, cloudy form. But how does one know that this interpretation is correct? Presumably because it makes sense of the original text: what is strange, mystifying, puzzling, contradictory is no longer so, is accounted for. The interpretation appeals throughout to our understanding of the 'language' of expression, which understanding allows us to see that this expression is puzzling, that it is in contradiction to that other, and so on, and that these difficulties are cleared up when the meaning is expressed in a new way.

But this appeal to our understanding seems to be crucially inadequate. What if someone does not 'see' the adequacy of our interpretation, does not accept our reading? We try to show him how it makes sense of the original nonsense or partial sense. But for him to follow us he must read the original language as we do, he must recognize these expressions as puzzling in a certain way, and hence be looking for a solution to our problem. If he does not, what can we do? The answer, it would seem, can only be more of the same. We have to show him through the reading of other expressions why this expression must be read in the way we propose. But success here requires that he follow us in these other readings, and so on, it would seem, potentially forever. We cannot escape an ultimate appeal to a common understanding of the expressions, of the 'language' involved.

This is one way of trying to express what has been called the 'hermeneutical circle'. What we are trying to establish is a certain reading of text or expressions, and what we appeal to as our grounds for this reading can only be other readings. The circle can also be put in terms of part–whole relations: we are trying to establish a reading for the whole text, and for this we appeal to readings of its partial expressions; and yet because we are dealing with meaning, with making sense, where expressions only make sense or not in relation to others, the readings of partial expressions depend on those of others, and ultimately of the whole.

Put in forensic terms, as we started to do above, we can only convince an interlocutor if at some point he shares our understanding of the language concerned. If he does not, there is no further step to take in rational argument; we can try to awaken these intuitions in him, or we can simply give up; argument will advance us no further. But of course the forensic predicament can be transferred into my own judging: if I am this ill-equipped to convince a stubborn interlocutor, how can I convince myself? How can I be sure? Maybe my intuitions are wrong or distorted, maybe I am locked into a circle of illusion.

Now one, and perhaps the only, sane response to this would be to say that such uncertainty is an ineradicable part of our epistemological predicament; that even to characterize it as 'uncertainty' is to adopt an absurdly severe criterion of 'certainty', which deprives the concept of any sensible use. But this has not been the only or even the main response of our philosophical tradition. And it is another response which has had an important and far-reaching effect on the sciences of man. The demand has been for a level of certainty which can only be attained by breaking beyond the circle.

There are two ways in which this break-out has been envisaged. The first might be called the 'rationalist' one and could be thought to reach a culmination in Hegel. It does not involve a negation of intuition, or of our understanding of meaning, but rather aspires to attainment of an understanding of such clarity that it would carry with it the certainty of the undeniable. In Hegel's case, for instance, our full understanding of the whole in 'thought' carries with it a grasp of its inner necessity, such that we see how it could not be otherwise. No higher grade of certainty is conceivable. For this aspiration the word 'break-out' is badly chosen; the aim is rather to bring understanding to an inner clarity which is absolute.

The other way, which we can call 'empiricist', is a genuine attempt to go beyond the circle of our own interpretations, to get beyond subjectivity. The attempt is to reconstruct knowledge in such a way that there is no need to make final appeal to readings or judgements which cannot be checked further. That is why the basic building block of knowledge on this view is the impression, or sense-datum; a unit of information which is not the deliverance of a judgement, which has by definition no element in it of reading or interpretation, which is a brute datum. The highest ambition would be to build our knowledge from such building blocks by judgements which could be anchored in a certainty beyond subjective intuition. This is what underlies the attraction of the notion of the association of ideas, or if the same procedure is viewed as a method, induction. If the original acquisition of the units of information is not the fruit of judgement or interpretation, then the constatation that two such elements occur together need not be the fruit of interpretation either, of a reading or intuition which cannot be checked. For if the occurrence of a single element is a brute datum, then so is the co-occurrence of two such elements. The path to true knowledge would then repose crucially on the correct recording of such co-occurrences.

This is what lies behind an ideal of verification which is central to an important tradition in the philosophy of science, whose main contemporary protagonists are the logical empiricists. Verification must be grounded ultimately in the acquisition of brute data. By 'brute data' I mean here and throughout data whose validity cannot be questioned by offering another interpretation or reading, data whose credibility cannot be founded or undetermined by further reasoning.[4] If such a difference of interpretation can arise over given data, then it must be possible to structure the argument so as to distinguish the basic, brute data from the inferences made on the basis of them.

· The inferences themselves, of course, to be valid, must similarly be beyond the challenge of a rival interpretation. Here the logical empiricists added to the armoury of traditional empiricism, which set great store by the method of induction, the whole domain of logical and mathematical inference which had been central to the rationalist

---

[4] The notion of brute data here has some relation to, but is not at all the same as, the 'brute facts' discussed by Elizabeth Anscombe, 'On brute facts', *Analysis*, 18 (1957–58), pp. 69–72, and John Searle, *Speech Acts* (Cambridge, 1969), pp. 50–3. For Anscombe and Searle, brute facts are contrasted to what may be called 'institutional facts', to use Searle's term, i.e., facts which presuppose the existence of certain institutions. Voting would be an example. But, as we shall see below in section II, some institutional facts, such as X's having voted Liberal, can be verified as brute data in the sense used here, and thus find a place in the category of political behaviour. What cannot as easily be described in terms of brute data are the institutions themselves. Cf. the discussion below in section II.

position (with Leibniz at least, although not with Hegel), and which offered another brand of unquestionable certainty.

Of course, mathematical inference and empirical verification were combined in such a way that two theories or more could be verified of the same domain of facts. But this was a consequence to which logical empiricism was willing to accommodate itself. As for the surplus meaning in a theory which could not be rigorously co-ordinated with brute data, it was considered to be quite outside the logic of verification.

As a theory of perception, this epistemology gave rise to all sorts of problems, not least of which was the perpetual threat of scepticism and solipsism inseparable from a conception of the basic data of knowledge as brute data, beyond investigation. As a theory of perception, however, it seems largely a thing of the past, in spite of a surprising recrudescence in the Anglo-Saxon world in the 1930s and 1940s. But there is no doubt that it goes marching on, among other places, as a theory of how the human mind and human knowledge actually function.

In a sense, the contemporary period has seen a better, more rigorous statement of what this epistemology is about in the form of computer-influenced theories of intelligence. These try to model intelligence as consisting of operations on machine-recognizable input which could themselves be matched by programs which could be run on machines. The machine criterion provides us with our assurance against an appeal to intuition or interpretations which cannot be understood by fully explicit procedures operating on brute data – the input.[5]

The progress of natural science has lent great credibility to this epistemology, since it can be plausibly reconstructed on this model, as for instance has been done by the logical empiricists. And, of course, the temptation has been overwhelming to reconstruct the sciences of man on the same model; or rather to launch them in lines of enquiry that fit this paradigm, since they are constantly said to be in their 'infancy'. Psychology, where an earlier vogue of behaviourism is being replaced by a boom of computer-based models, is far from the only case.

The form this epistemological bias – one might say obsession – takes is different for different sciences. Later I would like to look at a particular case, the study of politics, where the issue can be followed out. But in general, the empiricist orientation must be hostile to a conduct of enquiry

[5] Cf. discussion in M. Minsky, *Computation* (Englewood Cliffs, NJ, 1967), pp. 104–7, where Minsky explicitly argues that an effective procedure, which no longer requires intuition or interpretation, is one which can be realized by a machine.

which is based on interpretation, and which encounters the hermeneutical circle as this was characterized above. This cannot meet the requirements of intersubjective, non-arbitrary verification which it considers essential to science. And along with the epistemological stance goes the ontological belief that reality must be susceptible to understanding and explanation by science so understood. From this follows a certain set of notions of what the sciences of man must be.

On the other hand, many, including myself, would like to argue that these notions about the sciences of man are sterile, that we cannot come to understand important dimensions of human life within the bounds set by this epistemological orientation. This dispute is of course familiar to all in at least some of its ramifications. What I want to claim is that the issue can be fruitfully posed in terms of the notion of interpretation as I began to outline it above.

I think this way of putting the question is useful because it allows us at once to bring to the surface the powerful epistemological beliefs which underlie the orthodox view of the sciences of man in our academy, and to make explicit the notion of our epistemological predicament implicit in the opposing thesis. This is in fact rather more way-out and shocking to the tradition of scientific thought than is often admitted or realized by the opponents of narrow scientism. It may not strengthen the case of the opposition to bring out fully what is involved in a hermeneutical science as far as convincing waverers is concerned, but a gain in clarity is surely worth a thinning of the ranks – at least in philosophy.

3

Before going on to look at the case of political science, it might be worth asking another question: why should we even pose the question whether the sciences of man are hermeneutical? What gives us the idea in the first place that men and their actions constitute an object or a series of objects which meet the conditions outlined above?

The answer is that on the phenomenological level or that of ordinary speech (and the two converge for the purposes of this argument) a certain notion of meaning has an essential place in the characterization of human behaviour. This is the sense in which we speak of a situation, an action, a demand, a prospect having a certain meaning for a person.

Now it is frequently thought that 'meaning' is used here in a sense which is a kind of illegitimate extension from the notion of linguistic meaning. Whether it can be considered an extension or not is another matter; it certainly differs from linguistic meaning. But it would be very hard to argue that it is an illegitimate use of the term.

When we speak of the 'meaning' of a given predicament, we are using a concept which has the following articulation. (1) Meaning is for a subject: it is not the meaning of the situation *in vacuo*, but its meaning for a subject, a specific subject, a group of subjects, or perhaps what its meaning is for the human subject as such (even though particular humans might be reproached with not admitting or realizing this). (2) Meaning is of something; that is, we can distinguish between a given element – situation, action, or whatever – and its meaning. But this is not to say that they are physically separable. Rather we are dealing with two descriptions of the element, in one of which it is characterized in terms of its meaning for the subject. But the relations between the two descriptions are not symmetrical. For, on the one hand, the description in terms of meaning cannot be, unless descriptions of the other kind apply as well; or put differently, there can be no meaning without a substrate. But on the other hand, it may be that the same meaning may be borne by another substrate – for instance, a situation with the same meaning may be realized in different physical conditions. There is a necessary role for a potentially substitutable substrate; or all meanings are of something.

(3) Things only have meaning in a field, that is, in relation to the meanings of other things. This means that there is no such thing as a single, unrelated meaningful element; and it means that changes in the other meanings in the field can involve changes in the given element. Meanings can not be identified except in relation to others, and in this way resemble words. The meaning of a word depends, for instance, on those words with which it contrasts, on those which define its place in the language (e.g., those defining 'determinable' dimensions, like colour, shape), on those which define the activity or 'language game' it figures in (describing, invoking, establishing communion), and so on. The relations between meanings in this sense are like those between concepts in a semantic field.

Just as our colour concepts are given their meaning by the field of contrast they set up together, so that the introduction of new concepts will alter the boundaries of others, so the various meanings that a subordinate's demeanour can have for us, as deferential, respectful, cringing, mildly mocking, ironical, insolent, provoking, downright rude, are established by a field of contrast; and as with finer discrimination on our part, or a more sophisticated culture, new possibilities are born, so other terms of this range are altered. And as the meaning of our terms 'red', 'blue', 'green' is fixed by the definition of a field of contrast through the determinable term 'colour', so all these alternative demeanours are only available in a society which has, among other types, hierarchical relations of power and command. And corresponding to the underlying language game of designating coloured objects is the set of social practices which sustain these hierarchical structures and are fulfilled in them.

Meaning in this sense – let us call it experiential meaning – thus is for a subject, of something, in a field. This distinguishes it from linguistic meaning which has a four- and not a three-dimensional structure. Linguistic meaning is for subjects and in a field, but it is the meaning of signifiers and it is about a world of referents. Once we are clear about the likenesses and differences, there should be little doubt that the term 'meaning' is not a misnomer, the product of an illegitimate extension into this context of experience and behaviour.

There is thus a quite legitimate notion of meaning which we use when we speak of the meaning of a situation for an agent. And that this concept has a place is integral to our ordinary consciousness and hence speech about our actions. Our actions are ordinarily characterized by the purpose sought and explained by desires, feelings, emotions. But the language by which we describe our goals, feelings, desires is also a definition of the meaning things have for us. The vocabulary defining meaning – words like 'terrifying', 'attractive' – is linked with that describing feeling – 'fear', 'desire' – and that describing goals – 'safety', 'possession'.

Moreover, our understanding of these terms moves inescapably in a hermeneutical circle. An emotion term like 'shame', for instance, essentially refers us to a certain kind of situation, the 'shameful', or 'humiliating', and a certain mode of response, that of hiding oneself, of covering up, or else 'wiping out' the blot. That is, it is essential to this feeling's being identified as shame that it be related to this situation and give rise to this type of disposition. But this situation in its turn can only be identified in relation to the feelings which it provokes; and the disposition is to a goal which can similarly not be understood without reference to the feelings experienced: the 'hiding' in question is one which will cover up my shame; it is not the same as hiding from an armed pursuer; we can only understand what is meant by 'hiding' here if we understand what kind of feeling and situation is being talked about. We have to be within the circle.

An emotion term like 'shame' can only be explained by reference to other concepts which in turn cannot be understood without reference to shame. To understand these concepts we have to be in on a certain experience, we have to understand a certain language, not just of words, but also a certain language of mutual action and communication, by which we blame, exhort, admire, esteem each other. In the end we are in on this because we grow up in the ambit of certain common meanings. But we can often experience what it is like to be on the outside when we encounter the feeling, action, and experiential meaning language of another civilization. Here there is no translation, no way of explaining in other, more accessible concepts. We can only catch on by getting somehow into their way of life, if only in imagination. Thus if we look at human behaviour as action done out of a background of desire, feeling, emotion, then we are looking at a reality which must be characterized in terms of meaning. But does this mean that it can be the object of a hermeneutical science as this was outlined above?

There are, to remind ourselves, three characteristics that the object of a science of interpretation has: it must have sense or coherence; this must be distinguishable from its expression, and this sense must be for a subject.

Now, in so far as we are talking about behaviour as action, hence in terms of meaning, the category of sense or coherence must apply to it. This is not to say that all behaviour must 'make sense', if we mean by this be rational, avoid contradiction, confusion of purpose, and the like. Plainly a great deal of our action falls short of this goal. But in another sense, even contradictory, irrational action is 'made sense of' when we understand why it was engaged in. We make sense of action when there is a coherence between the actions of the agent and the meaning of his situation for him. We find his action puzzling until we find such a coherence. It may not be bad to repeat that this coherence in no way implies that the action is rational: the meaning of a situation for an agent may be full of confusion and contradiction; but the adequate depiction of this contradiction makes sense of it.

Thus we necessarily have a hermeneutical circle. Our conviction that the account makes sense is contingent on our reading of action and situation. But these readings cannot be explained or justified except by reference to other such readings, and their relation to the whole. If an interlocutor does not understand this kind of reading, or will not accept it as valid, there is nowhere else the argument can go. Ultimately, a good explanation is one which makes sense of the behaviour; but then to appreciate a good explanation, one has to agree on what makes good sense; what makes good sense is a function of one's readings; and these in turn are based on the kind of sense one understands.

But how about the second characteristic, that sense should be distinguishable from its embodiment? This is necessary for a science of interpretation because interpretation lays a claim to make a confused meaning clearer; hence there must be some sense in which the 'same' meaning is expressed, but differently.

This immediately raises a difficulty. In talking of experiential meaning above, I mentioned that we can distinguish between a given element and its meaning, between meaning and substrate. This carried the claim that a given meaning *may* be realized in another substrate. But does this mean that we can *always* embody the same meaning in another situation? Perhaps there are some situations, standing before death, for instance, which have a meaning which cannot be embodied otherwise.

But fortunately this difficult question is irrelevant for our purposes. For here we have a case in which the analogy between text and behaviour implicit in the notion of a hermeneutical science of man only applies with important modifications. The text is replaced in the interpretation by another text, one which is clearer. The text-analogue of behaviour is not replaced by another such text-analogue. When this happens we have revolutionary theatre, or terroristic acts designed to make propaganda of the deed, in which the hidden relations of a society are supposedly shown up in a dramatic confrontation. But this is not scientific understanding, even though it may perhaps be based on such understanding, or claim to be.

But in science the text-analogue is replaced by a text, an account. Which might prompt the question how we can even begin to talk of interpretation here, of expressing the same meaning more clearly, when we have two such utterly different terms of comparison, a text and a tract of behaviour? Is the whole thing not just a bad pun?

This question leads us to open up another aspect of experiential meaning which we abstracted from earlier. Experiential meanings are defined in fields of contrast, as words are in semantic fields.

But what was not mentioned above is that these two kinds of definition are not independent of each other. The range of human desires, feelings, emotions, and hence meanings is bound up with the level and type of culture, which in turn is inseparable from the distinctions and categories marked by the language people speak. The field of meanings in which a given situation can find its place is bound up with the semantic field of the terms characterizing these meanings and the related feelings, desires, predicaments.

But the relationship involved here is not a simple one. There are two simple types of models of relation which could be offered here, but both are inadequate. We could think of the feeling vocabulary as simply describing pre-existing feelings, as marking distinctions which would be there without them. But this is not adequate because we often experience in ourselves or others how achieving, say, a more sophisticated vocabulary of the emotions makes our emotional life, not just our descriptions of it, more sophisticated. Reading a good, powerful novel may give me the picture of an emotion which I had not previously been aware of. But we cannot draw a neat line between an increased ability to identify and an altered ability to feel emotions which this enables.

The other simple inadequate model of the relationship is to jump from the above to the conclusion that thinking makes it so. But this clearly will not do either, since not just any new definition can be forced on us, nor can we force it on ourselves; and some which we do gladly take up can be judged inauthentic, or in bad faith, or just wrong-headed by others. These judgements may be wrong, but they are not in principle illicit. Rather we make an effort to be lucid about ourselves and our feelings, and admire a man who achieves this.

Thus, neither the simple correspondence view is correct, nor the view that thinking makes it so. But both have prima facie warrant. There is such a thing as self-lucidity, which points us to a correspondence view; but the achievement of such lucidity means moral change, that is, it changes the object known. At the same time, error about oneself is not just an absence of correspondence; it is also in some form inauthenticity, bad faith, self-delusion, repression of one's human feelings, or something of the kind; it is a matter of the quality of what is felt just as much as what is known about this, just as self-knowledge is.

If this is so, then we have to think of man as a self-interpreting animal. He is necessarily so, for there is no such thing as the structure of meanings for him independently of his interpretation of them; for one is woven into the other. But then the text of our interpretation is not that heterogeneous from what is interpreted; for what is interpreted is itself an interpretation; a self-interpretation which is embedded in a stream of action. It is an interpretation of experiential meaning which contributes to the constitution of this meaning. Or to put it in another way: that of which we are trying to find the coherence is itself partly constituted by self-interpretation.

Our aim is to replace this confused, incomplete, partly erroneous self-interpretation by a correct one. And in doing this we look not only to the self-interpretation but to the stream of behaviour in which it is set; just as in interpreting a historical document we have to place it in the stream of events which it relates to. But of course the analogy is not exact, for here we are interpreting the interpretation and the stream of behaviour in which it is set together, and not just one or the other.

There is thus no utter heterogeneity of interpretation to what it is about; rather there is a slide in the notion of interpretation. Already to be a living agent is to experience one's situation in terms of certain meanings; and this in a sense can be thought of as a sort of proto-'interpretation'. This is in turn interpreted and shaped by the language in which the agent lives these meanings. This whole is then at a third level interpreted by the explanation we proffer of his actions.

In this way the second condition of a hermeneutical science is met. But this account poses in a new light the question mentioned at the beginning: whether the interpretation can ever express the same meaning as the interpreted. And in this case, there is clearly a way in which the two will not be congruent. For if the explanation is really clearer than the lived interpretation then it will be such that it would alter in some way the behaviour if it came to be internalized by the agent as his self-interpretation. In this way a hermeneutical science which achieves its goal, that is, attains greater clarity than the immediate understanding of agent or observer, must offer us an interpretation which is in this way crucially out of phase with the explicandum.

Thus, human behaviour seen as action of agents who desire and are moved, who have goals and aspirations, necessarily offers a purchase for descriptions in terms of meaning – what I have called 'experiential meaning'. The norm of explanation which it posits is one which 'makes sense' of the behaviour, which shows a coherence of meaning. This 'making sense of' is the proferring of an interpretation; and we have seen that what is interpreted meets the conditions of a science of interpretation: first, that we can speak of its sense or coherence; and second, that this sense can be expressed in another form, so that we can speak of the interpretation as giving clearer expression to what is only implicit in the explicandum. The third condition, that this sense be for a subject, is obviously met in this case, although who this subject is is by no means an unproblematical question, as we shall see later on.

This should be enough to show that there is a good prima facie case to the effect that men and their actions are amenable to explanation of a hermeneutical kind. There is, therefore, some reason to raise the issue and challenge the epistemological orientation which would rule interpretation out of the sciences of man. A great deal more must be said to bring out what is involved in the hermeneutical sciences of man. But before getting on to this, it might help to clarify the issue with a couple of examples drawn from a specific field, that of politics.

II

I

In politics, too, the goal of a verifiable science has led to the concentration on features which can supposedly be identified in abstraction from our understanding or not understanding experiential meaning. These – let us call them brute data identifications – are what supposedly enable us to break out from the hermeneutical circle and found our science four square on a verification procedure which meets the requirements of the empiricist tradition.

But in politics the search for such brute data has not gone to the lengths which it has in psychology, where the object of science has been thought of by many as behaviour *qua* 'colourless movement', or as machine-recognizable properties. The tendency in politics has been to stop with something less basic, but – so it is thought – the identification of which cannot be challenged by the offering of another interpretation or reading of the data concerned. This is what is referred to as 'behaviour' in the rhetoric of political scientists, but it has not the rock bottom quality of its psychological homonym.

Political behaviour includes what we would ordinarily call actions, but ones that are supposedly brute data identifiable. How can this be so? Well, actions are usually described by the purpose or end-state realized. But the purposes of some actions can be specified in what might be thought to be brute data terms; some actions, for instance, have physical end-states, like getting the car in the garage or climbing the mountain. Others have end-states which are closely tied by institutional rules to some unmistakable physical movement; thus, when I raise my hand in the meeting at the appropriate time, I am voting for the motion. The only questions we can raise about the corresponding actions, given such movements or the realization of such end-states, are whether the agent was aware of what he was doing, was acting as against simply emitting reflex behaviour, knew the institutional significance of his movement, and so on. Any worries on this score generally turn out to be pretty artificial in the contexts political scientists are concerned with; and where they do arise they can be checked by relatively simple devices, for example asking the subject: did you mean to vote for the motion?

Hence, it would appear that there are actions which can be identified beyond fear of interpretative dispute; and this is what gives the foundation for the category of 'political behaviour'. There are some acts of obvious political relevance which can be specified thus in physical terms, such as killing, sending tanks into the streets, seizing people and confining them to cells; and there is an immense range of others which can be specified from physical acts by institutional rules, such as voting. These can be the object of a science of politics which can hope to meet the stringent requirements of verification. The latter class particularly has provided matter for study in recent decades – most notably in the case of voting studies.

But of course a science of politics confined to such acts would be much too narrow. For on another level these actions also have meaning for the agents which is not exhausted in the brute data descriptions, and which is often crucial to understanding why they were done. Thus, in voting for the motion I am also saving the honour of my party, or defending the value of free speech, or vindicating public morality, or saving civilization from breakdown. It is in such terms that the agents talk about the motivation of much of their political action, and it is difficult to conceive a science of politics which does not come to grips with it.

Behavioural political science comes to grips with it by taking the meanings involved in action as facts about the agent, his beliefs, his affective reactions, his 'values', as the term is frequently used. For it can be thought verifiable in the brute data sense that men will agree to subscribe or not to a certain form of words (expressing a belief, say); or express a positive or negative reaction to certain events, or symbols; or agree or not with the proposition that some act is right or wrong. We can thus get at meanings as just another form of brute data by the techniques of the opinion survey and content analysis.

An immediate objection springs to mind. If we are trying to deal with the meanings which inform political action, then surely interpretive acumen is unavoidable. Let us say we are trying to understand the goals and values of a certain group, or grasp their vision of the polity; we might try to probe this by a questionnaire asking them whether they assent or not to a number of propositions, which are meant to express different goals, evaluations, beliefs. But how did we design the questionnaire? How did we pick these propositions? Here we relied on our understanding of the goals, values, vision involved. But then this understanding can be challenged, and hence the significance of our results questioned. Perhaps the finding of our study, the compiling of proportions of assent and dissent to these propositions, is irrelevant, is without significance for understanding the agents or the polity concerned. This kind of attack is frequently made by critics of mainstream political science, or for that matter social science in general.

To this the proponents of this mainstream reply with a standard move of logical empiricism: distinguishing the process of discovery from the logic of verification. Of course, it is our understanding of these meanings which enables us to draw up the questionnaire which will test people's attitudes in respect to them. And, of course, interpretive dispute about these meanings is potentially endless; there are no brute data at this level, every affirmation can be challenged by a rival interpretation. But this has nothing to do with verifiable science. What is firmly verified is the set of correlations between, say, the assent to certain propositions and certain behaviour. We discover, for instance, that people who are active politically (defined by participation in a certain set of institutions) are more likely to consent to certain sets of propositions supposedly expressing the values underlying the system.[6] This finding is a firmly verified correlation no matter what one thinks of the reasoning, or simple hunches, that went into designing the research which established it. Political science as a body of knowledge is made up of such correlations; it does not give a truth value to the background reasoning or hunch. A good interpretive nose may be useful in hitting on the right correlations to test, but science is never called on to arbitrate the disputes between interpretations.

. Thus, in addition to those overt acts which can be defined physically or institutionally, the category of political behaviour can include assent or dissent to verbal formulae, or the occurrence or not of verbal formulae in speech, or expressions of approval or rejection of certain events or measures as observed in institutionally defined behaviour (for instance, turning out for a demonstration).

Now there are a number of objections which can be made to this notion of political behaviour; one might question in all sorts of ways how interpretation-free it is in fact. But I would like to question it from another angle. One of the basic characteristics of this kind of social science is that it reconstructs reality in line with certain categorial principles. These allow for an inter-subjective social reality which is made up of brute data, identifiable acts and structures, certain institutions, procedures, actions. It allows for beliefs, affective reactions, evaluations as the psychological

---

[6] See H. McClosky, 'Consensus and ideology in American politics', *American Political Science Review*, 5: 58 (1964), pp. 361–82.

properties of individuals. And it allows for correlations between these two orders or reality: for example, that certain beliefs go along with certain acts, certain values with certain institutions, and so on.

To put it another way, what is objectively (inter-subjectively) real is brute data identifiable. This is what social reality *is*. Social reality described in terms of its meaning for the actors, such that disputes could arise about interpretation which could not be settled by brute data (e.g., are people rioting to get a hearing, or are they rioting to redress humiliation, or out of blind anger, or because they recover a sense of dignity in insurrection?), is given subjective reality, that is, there are certain beliefs, affective reactions, evaluations which individuals make or have about or in relation to social reality. These beliefs or reactions can have an effect on this reality; and the fact that such a belief is held is a fact of objective social reality. But the social reality which is the object of these attitudes, beliefs, reactions can only be made up of brute data. Thus any description of reality in terms of meanings which is open to interpretive question is only allowed into this scientific discourse if it is placed, as it were, in quotes and attributed to individuals as their opinion, belief, attitude. That this opinion, belief, etc. is held is thought of as a brute datum, since it is redefined as the respondent's giving a certain answer to the questionnaire.

This aspect of social reality which concerns its meanings for the agents has been taken up in a number of ways, but recently it has been spoken of in terms of political culture. Now the way this is defined and studied illustrates clearly the categorial principles above. For instance, political culture is referred to by Almond and Powell as the 'psychological dimension of the political system'.[7] Further on they state: 'Political culture is the pattern of individual attitudes and orientations towards politics among the members of a political system. It is the subjective realm which underlies and gives meaning to political actions'.[8] The authors then go on to distinguish three different kinds of orientations, cognitive (knowledge and beliefs), affective (feelings), and evaluative (judgements and opinions).

From the point of view of empiricist epistemology, this set of categorial principles leaves nothing out. Both reality and the meanings it has for actors are coped with. But what it in fact cannot allow for are intersubjective meanings, that is, it cannot allow for the validity of descriptions of

[7] Gabriel A. Almond and G. Bingham Powell, *Comparative Politics: a Developmental Approach* (Boston and Toronto, 1966), p. 23.
[8] *Ibid.*, p. 50.

social reality in terms of meanings, hence not as brute data, which are not in quotation marks and attributed as opinion, attitude, etc. to individual(s). It is this exclusion that I would like to challenge in the name of another set of categorial principles, inspired by a quite other epistemology.

2

We spoke earlier about the brute data identification of acts by means of institutional rules. Thus, putting a cross beside someone's name on a slip of paper and putting this in a box counts in the right context as voting for that person; leaving the room, saying or writing a certain form of words, counts as breaking off the negotiations; writing one's name on a piece of paper counts as signing the petition, and so on. But what is worth looking at is what underlies this set of identifications. These identifications are the application of a language of social life, a language which marks distinctions among different possible social acts, relations, structures. But what underlies this language?

Let us take the example of breaking off negotiations above. The language of our society recognizes states or actions like the following: entering into negotiation, breaking off negotiations, offering to negotiate, negotiating in good (bad) faith, concluding negotiations, making a new offer, and so on. In other more jargon-infested language, the semantic 'space' of this range of social activity is carved up in a certain way, by a certain set of distinctions which our vocabulary marks; and the shape and nature of these distinctions is the nature of our language in this area. These distinctions are applied in our society with more or less formalism in different contexts.

But of course this is not true of every society. Our whole notion of negotiation is bound up for instance with the distinct identity and autonomy of the parties, with the willed nature of their relations; it is a very contractual notion. But other societies have no such conception. It is reported about the traditional Japanese village that the foundation of its social life was a powerful form of consensus, which put a high premium on unanimous decision.[9] Such a consensus would be considered shattered if two clearly articulated parties were to separate out, pursuing opposed aims and attempting either to vote down the opposition or push it into a

---

[9] See Thomas C. Smith, *The Agrarian Origins of Modern Japan* (Stanford, 1959), chap. 5. This type of consensus is also found in other traditional societies. See, for instance, the *desa* system of the Indonesian village.

settlement on the most favourable possible terms for themselves. Discussion there must be, and some kind of adjustment of differences. But our idea of bargaining, with the assumption of distinct autonomous parties in willed relationship, has no place there; nor does a series of distinctions, like entering into and leaving negotiation, or bargaining in good faith (sc. with the genuine intention of seeking agreement).

Now difference between our society and one of the kind just described could not be well expressed if we said we have a vocabulary to describe negotiation which they lack. We might say, for instance, that we have a vocabulary to describe the heavens that they lack, viz., that of Newtonian mechanics; for here we assume that they live under the same heavens as we do, only understand it differently. But it is not true that they have the same kind of bargaining as we do. The word, or whatever word of their language we translate as 'bargaining', must have an entirely different gloss, which is marked by the distinctions their vocabulary allows in contrast to those marked by ours. But this different gloss is not just a difference of vocabulary, but also one of social reality.

But this still may be misleading as a way of putting the difference. For it might imply that there is a social reality which can be discovered in each society and which might exist quite independently of the vocabulary of that society, or indeed of any vocabulary, as the heavens would exist whether men theorized about them or not. And this is not the case; the realities here are practices; and these cannot be identified in abstraction from the language we use to describe them, or invoke them, or carry them out. That the practice of negotiation allows us to distinguish bargaining in good or bad faith, or entering into or breaking off negotiations, presupposes that our acts and situation have a certain description for us, for example, that we are distinct parties entering into willed relations. But they cannot have these descriptions for us unless this is somehow expressed in our vocabulary of this practice; if not in our descriptions of the practices (for we may as yet be unconscious of some of the important distinctions), in the appropriate language for carrying them on. (Thus, the language marking a distinction between public and private acts or contexts may exist even where these terms or their equivalents are not part of this language; for the distinction will be marked by the different language which is appropriate in one context and the other, be it perhaps a difference of style, or dialect, even though the distinction is not designated by specific descriptive expressions.)

The situation we have here is one in which the vocabulary of a given social dimension is grounded in the shape of social practice in this dimension; that is, the vocabulary would not make sense, could not be applied sensibly, where this range of practices did not prevail. And yet this range of practices could not exist without the prevalence of this or some related vocabulary. There is no simple one-way dependence here. We can speak of mutual dependence if we like, but really what this points up is the artificiality of the distinction between social reality and the language of description of that social reality. The language is constitutive of the reality, is essential to its being the kind of reality it is. To separate the two and distinguish them as we quite rightly distinguish the heavens from our theories about them is forever to miss the point.

This type of relation has been recently explored, for instance by John Searle, with his concept of a constitutive rule. As Searle points out,[10] we are normally induced to think of rules as applying to behaviour which could be available to us whether or not the rule existed. Some rules are like this, they are regulative like commandments: do not take the goods of another. But there are other rules, for example, those governing the Queen's move in chess, which are not so separable. If one suspends these rules, or imagines a state in which they have not yet been introduced, then the whole range of behaviour in question, in this case chess playing, would not be. There would still, of course, be the activity of pushing a wooden piece around on a board made of eight squares by eight; but this is not chess any longer. Rules of this kind are constitutive rules. By contrast again, there are other rules of chess, such as that one say 'J'adoube' when one touches a piece without intending to play it, which are clearly regulative.[11]

I am suggesting that this notion of the constitutive be extended beyond the domain of rule-governed behaviour. That is why I suggest the vaguer word 'practice'. Even in an area where there are no clearly defined rules, there are distinctions between different sorts of behaviour such that one sort is considered the appropriate form for one action or context, the other for another action or context; for example doing or saying certain things amounts to breaking off negotiations, doing or saying other things amounts to making a new offer. But just as there are constitutive rules, that is rules such that the behaviour they govern could not exist without them, and which are in this sense inseparable from that behaviour, so I am suggesting that there are constitutive distinctions, constitutive ranges of

---

[10] Searle, *Speech Acts*, pp. 33–42.

[11] See the discussion in Stanley Cavell, *Must We Mean What We Say?* (New York, 1969), pp. 21–31.

language which are similarly inseparable, in that certain practices are not without them.

We can reverse this relationship and say that all the institutions and practices by which we live are constituted by certain distinctions and hence a certain language which is thus essential to them. We can take voting, a practice which is central to large numbers of institutions in a democratic society. What is essential to the practice of voting is that some decision or verdict be delivered (a man elected, a measure passed), through some criterion of preponderance (simple majority, two-thirds majority, or whatever) out of a set of micro-choices (the votes of the citizens, MPs, delegates). If there is not some such significance attached to our behaviour, no amount of marking and counting pieces of paper, raising hands, or walking out into lobbies amounts to voting. From this it follows that the institution of voting must be such that certain distinctions have application: for example, that between someone being elected, or a measure passed, and their failing of election, or passage; that between a valid vote and an invalid one which in turn requires a distinction between a real choice and one which is forced or counterfeited. For no matter how far we move from the Rousseauian notion that each man decide in full autonomy, the very institution of the vote requires that in some sense the enfranchised choose. For there to be voting in a sense recognizably like ours, there must be a distinction in men's self-interpretations between autonomy and forced choice.

This is to say that an activity of marking and counting papers has to bear intentional descriptions which fall within a certain range before we can agree to call it voting, just as the intercourse of two men or teams has to bear descriptions of a certain range before we will call it negotiation. Or in other words, that some practice is voting or negotiation has to do in part with the vocabulary established in a society as appropriate for engaging in it or describing it.

Hence implicit in these practices is a certain vision of the agent and his relation to others and to society. We saw in connection with negotiation in our society that it requires a picture of the parties as in some sense autonomous, and as entering into willed relations. And this picture carries with it certain implicit norms, such as that of good faith mentioned above, or a norm of rationality, that agreement correspond to one's goals as far as attainable, or the norm of continued freedom of action as far as attainable. These practices require that one's actions and relations be seen in the light of this picture and the accompanying norms, good faith, autonomy, and rationality. But men do not see themselves in this way in all societies, nor do they understand these norms in all societies. The experience of autonomy as we know it, the sense of rational action and the satisfactions thereof, are unavailable to them. The meaning of these terms is opaque to them because they have a different structure of experiential meaning open to them.

We can think of the difference between our society and the simplified version of the traditional Japanese village as consisting in this, that the range of meaning open to the members of the two societies is very different. But what we are dealing with here is not subjective meaning which can fit into the categorial grid of behavioural political science, but rather inter-subjective meanings. It is not just that the people in our society all or mostly have a given set of ideas in their heads and subscribe to a given set of goals. The meanings and norms implicit in these practices are not just in the minds of the actors but are out there in the practices themselves, practices which cannot be conceived as a set of individual actions, but which are essentially modes of social relation, of mutual action.

The actors may have all sorts of beliefs and attitudes which may be rightly thought of as their individual beliefs and attitudes, even if others share them; they may subscribe to certain policy goals or certain forms of theory about the polity, or feel resentment at certain things, and so on. They bring these with them into their negotiations, and strive to satisfy them. But what they do not bring into the negotiations is the set of ideas and norms constitutive of negotiation themselves. These must be the common property of the society before there can be any question of anyone entering into negotiation or not. Hence they are not subjective meanings, the property of one or some individuals, but rather inter-subjective meanings, which are constitutive of the social matrix in which individuals find themselves and act.

The inter-subjective meanings which are the background to social action are often treated by political scientists under the heading 'consensus'. By this is meant convergence of beliefs on certain basic matters, or of attitude. But the two are not the same. Whether there is consensus or not, the condition of there being either one or the other is a certain set of common terms of reference. A society in which this was lacking would not be a society in the normal sense of the term, but several. Perhaps some multi-racial or multi-tribal states approach this limit. Some multi-national states are bedevilled by consistent cross-purposes, e.g., my own country, Canada. But consensus as a convergence of beliefs or values is not the opposite of this kind of fundamental diversity. Rather the opposite of diversity is a high degree of inter-subjective meanings. And this can go along with profound cleavage.

Indeed, inter-subjective meanings are a condition of a certain kind of very profound cleavage, such as was visible in the Reformation, or the American Civil War, or splits in left wing parties, where the dispute is at fever pitch just because each side can fully understand the other.

In other words, convergence of belief or attitude or its absence presupposes a common language in which these beliefs can be formulated, and in which these formulations can be opposed. Much of this common language in any society is rooted in its institutions and practices; it is constitutive of these institutions and practices. It is part of the inter-subjective meanings. To put the point another way, apart from the question of how much people's beliefs converge is the question of how much they have a common language of social and political reality in which these beliefs are expressed. This second question cannot be reduced to the first; inter-subjective meaning is not a matter of converging beliefs or values. When we speak of consensus we speak of beliefs and values which could be the property of a single person, or many, or all; but inter-subjective meanings could not be the property of a single person because they are rooted in social practice.

We can perhaps see this if we envisage the situation in which the ideas and norms underlying a practice are the property of single individuals. This is what happens when single individuals from one society interiorize the notions and values of another, for example children in missionary schools. Here we have a totally different situation. We *are* really talking now about subjective beliefs and attitudes. The ideas are abstract, they are mere social 'ideals'. Whereas in the original society, these ideas and norms are rooted in their social relations, and they can formulate opinions and ideals on the basis of them.

We can see this in connection with the example we have been using all along, that of negotiations. The vision of a society based on negotiation is coming in for heavy attack by a growing segment of modern youth, as are the attendant norms of rationality and the definition of autonomy. This is a dramatic failure of 'consensus'. But this cleavage takes place in the ambit of this inter-subjective meaning, the social practice of negotiation as it is lived in our society. The rejection would not have the bitter quality it has if what is rejected were not understood in common, because it is part of a social practice which we find hard to avoid, so pervasive is it in our society. At the same time there is a reaching out for other forms which still have the 'abstract' quality of ideals which are subjective in this sense, that is, not rooted in practice; which is what makes the rebellion look so 'unreal' to outsiders, and so irrational.

3

Inter-subjective meanings, ways of experiencing action in society which
are expressed in the language and descriptions constitutive of institutions
and practices, do not fit into the categorial grid of mainstream political
science. This allows only for an inter-subjective reality which is brute
data identifiable. But social practices and institutions which are partly
constituted by certain ways of talking about them are not so identifiable.
We have to understand the language, the underlying meanings, which
constitute them.

We can allow, once we accept a certain set of institutions or practices as
our starting point and not as objects of further questioning, that we can
easily take as brute data that certain acts are judged to take place or
certain states judged to hold within the semantic field of these practices;
for instance, that someone has voted Liberal, or signed the petition. We
can then go on to correlate certain subjective meanings – beliefs, attitudes, etc. – with this behaviour or its lack. But this means that we give up
trying to define further just what these practices and institutions are,
what the meanings are which they require and hence sustain. For these
meanings do not fit into the grid; they are not subjective beliefs or values,
but are constitutive of social reality. In order to get at them we have to
drop the basic premise that social reality is made up of brute data alone.
For any characterization of the meanings underlying these practices is
open to question by someone offering an alternative interpretation. The
negation of this is what was meant as brute data. We have to admit that
inter-subjective social reality has to be partly defined in terms of meanings; that meanings as subjective are not just in causal interaction with a
social reality made up of brute data, but that as inter-subjective they are
constitutive of this reality.

We have been talking here of inter-subjective meaning. Earlier I was
contrasting the question of inter-subjective meaning with that of consensus as convergence of opinions. But there is another kind of non-subjec-
tive meaning which is also often inadequately discussed under the head of
'consensus'. In a society with a strong web of inter-subjective meanings,
there can be a more or less powerful set of common meanings. By these I
mean notions of what is significant, which are not just shared in the sense
that everyone has them, but are also common in the sense of being in the
common reference world. Thus, almost everyone in our society may share
a susceptibility to a certain kind of feminine beauty, but this may not be a
common meaning. It may be known to no one, except perhaps market
researchers, who play on it in their advertisements. But the survival of a

national identity as francophones is a common meaning of *Québecois*; for it is not just shared, and not just known to be shared, but its being a common aspiration is one of the common reference points of all debate, communication, and all public life in the society.

We can speak of a shared belief, aspiration, etc. when there is convergence between the subjective beliefs, aspirations, of many individuals. But it is part of the meaning of a common aspiration, belief, celebration, etc. that it be not just shared but part of the common reference world. Or to put it another way, its being shared is a collective act, it is a consciousness which is communally sustained, whereas sharing is something we do each on his own, as it were, even if each of us is influenced by the others.

Common meanings are the basis of community. Inter-subjective meaning gives a people a common language to talk about social reality and a common understanding of certain norms, but only with common meanings does this common reference world contain significant common actions, celebrations, and feelings. These are objects in the world that everybody shares. This is what makes community.

Once again, we cannot really understand this phenomenon through the usual definition of consensus as convergence of opinion and value. For what is meant here is something more than convergence. Convergence is what happens when our values are shared. But what is required for common meanings is that this shared value be part of the common world, that this sharing be shared. But we could also say that common meanings are quite other than consensus, for they can subsist with a high degree of cleavage; this is what happens when a common meaning comes to be lived and understood differently by different groups in a society. It remains a common meaning, because there is the reference point which is the common purpose, aspiration, celebration. Such is for example the American Way, or freedom as understood in the USA. But this common meaning is differently articulated by different groups. This is the basis of the bitterest fights in a society, and this we are also seeing in the USA today. Perhaps one might say that a common meaning is very often the cause of the most bitter lack of consensus. It thus must not be confused with convergence of opinion, value, attitude.

Of course, common meanings and inter-subjective meanings are closely interwoven. There must be a powerful net of inter-subjective meanings for there to be common meanings; and the result of powerful common meanings is the development of a greater web of inter-subjective meanings as people live in community.

On the other hand, when common meanings wither, which they can do through the kind of deep dissensus we described earlier, the groups tend to grow apart and develop different languages of social reality, hence to share fewer inter-subjective meanings.

To take our above example again, there has been a powerful common meaning in our civilization around a certain vision of the free society in which bargaining has a central place. This has helped to entrench the social practice of negotiation which makes us participate in this inter-subjective meaning. But there is a severe challenge to this common meaning today, as we have seen. Should those who object to it really succeed in building up an alternative society, there would develop a gap between those who remain in the present type of society and those who had founded the new one.

Common meanings, as well as inter-subjective ones, fall through the net of mainstream social science. They can find no place in its categories. For they are not simply a converging set of subjective reactions, but part of the common world. What the ontology of mainstream social science lacks is the notion of meaning as not simply for an individual subject; of a subject who can be a 'we' as well as an 'I'. The exclusion of this possibility, of the communal, comes once again from the baleful influence of the epistemological tradition for which all knowledge has to be reconstructed from the impressions imprinted on the individual subject. But if we free ourselves from the hold of these prejudices, this seems a wildly implausible view about the development of human consciousness; we are aware of the world through a 'we' before we are through an 'I'. Hence we need the distinction between what is just shared in the sense that each of us has it in our individual worlds, and that which is in the common world. But the very idea of something which is in the common world in contradistinction to what is in all the individual worlds is totally opaque to empiricist epistemology. Hence it finds no place in mainstream social science. What this results in must now be seen.

III

I

Thus, to sum up the last pages: a social science which wishes to fulfil the requirements of the empiricist tradition naturally tries to reconstruct social reality as consisting of brute data alone. These data are the acts of people (behaviour) as identified supposedly beyond interpretation either by physical descriptions or by descriptions clearly defined by institutions and practices; and secondly, they include the subjective reality of individuals' beliefs, attitudes, values, as attested by their responses to certain forms of words, or in some cases their overt non-verbal behaviour.

What this excludes is a consideration of social reality as characterized by inter-subjective and common meanings. It excludes, for instance, an attempt to understand our civilization, in which negotiation plays such a central part both in fact and in justificatory theory, by probing the self-definitions of agent, other and social relatedness which it embodies. Such definitions which deal with the meaning for agents of their own and others' action, and of the social relations in which they stand, do not in any sense record brute data, in the sense that this term is being used in this argument; that is, they are in no sense beyond challenge by those who would quarrel with our interpretations of these meanings.

Thus, I tried to adumbrate above the vision implicit in the practice of negotiation by reference to certain notions of autonomy and rationality. But this reading will undoubtedly be challenged by those who have different fundamental conceptions of man, human motivation, the human condition; or even by those who judge other features of our present predicament to have greater importance. If we wish to avoid these disputes, and have a science grounded in verification as this is understood by the logical empiricists, then we have to avoid this level of study altogether and hope to make do with a correlation of behaviour which is brute data identifiable.

A similar point goes for the distinction between common meanings and shared subjective meanings. We can hope to identify the subjective meanings of individuals if we take these in the sense in which there are adequate criteria for them in people's dissent or assent to verbal formulae or their brute data indentifiable behaviour. But once we allow the distinction between such subjective meanings which are widely shared and genuine common meanings, then we can no longer make do with brute data identification. We are in a domain where our definitions can be challenged by those with another reading.

The profound option of mainstream social scientists for the empiricist conception of knowledge and science makes it inevitable that they should accept the verification model of political science and the categorial principles that this entails. This means in turn that a study of our civilization in terms of its inter-subjective and common meanings is ruled out. Rather this whole level of study is made invisible.

On the mainstream view, therefore, the different practices and institutions of different societies are not seen as related to different clusters of inter-subjective or common meanings; rather, we should be able to differentiate them by different clusters of 'behaviour' and/or subjective meaning. The comparison between societies requires on this view that we elaborate a universal vocabulary of behaviour which will allow us to present the different forms and practices of different societies in the same conceptual web.

Now present-day political science is contemptuous of the older attempt at comparative politics via a comparison of institutions. An influential school of our day has therefore shifted comparison to certain practices, or very general classes of practices, and proposes to compare societies according to the different ways in which these practices are carried on. Such are the 'functions' of the influential 'developmental approach'.[12] But it is epistemologically crucial that such functions be identified independently of those inter-subjective meanings which are different in different societies; for otherwise, they will not be genuinely universal; or will be universal only in the loose and unilluminating sense that the function-name can be given application in every society but with varying, and often widely varying, meaning – the same being 'glossed' very differently by different sets of practices and inter-subjective meanings. The danger that such universality might not hold is not even suspected by mainstream political scientists since they are unaware that there is such a level of description as that which defines inter-subjective meanings, and are convinced that functions and the various structures which perform them can be identified in terms of brute data behaviour.

But the result of ignoring the difference in inter-subjective meanings can be disastrous to a science of comparative politics, viz., that we interpret all other societies in the categories of our own. Ironically, this is what seems to have happened to American political science. Having strongly criticized the old institution-focussed comparative politics for its ethnocentricity (or Western bias), it proposes to understand the politics of all society in terms of such functions, for instance, as 'interest articulation' and 'interest aggregation' whose definition is strongly influenced by the bargaining culture of our civilization, but which is far from being guaranteed appropriateness elsewhere. The not surprising result is a theory of political development which places the Atlantic-type polity at the summit of human political achievement.

Much can be said in this area of comparative politics (interestingly

---

[12] See Almond and Powell, *Comparative Politics*.

explored by Alasdair MacIntyre).[13] But I would like to illustrate the significance of these two rival approaches in connection with another common problem area of politics. This is the question of what is called 'legitimacy'.[14]

2

It is an obvious fact, with which politics has been concerned since at least Plato, that some societies enjoy an easier, more spontaneous cohesion which relies less on the use of force than others. It has been an important question of political theory to understand what underlies this difference. Among others, Aristotle, Machiavelli, Montesquieu, and Tocqueville have dealt with it.

Contemporary mainstream political scientists approach this question with the concept 'legitimacy'. The use of the word here can be easily understood. Those societies which are more spontaneously cohesive can be thought to enjoy a greater sense of legitimacy among their members. But the application of the term has been shifted. 'Legitimacy' is a term in which we discuss the authority of the state or polity, its right to our allegiance. However we conceive of this legitimacy, it can only be attributed to a polity in the light of a number of surrounding conceptions – for example, that it provides men freedom, that it emanates from their will, that it secures them order, the rule of law, or that it is founded on tradition, or commands obedience by its superior qualities. These conceptions are all such that they rely on definitions of what is significant for men in general or in some particular society or circumstances, definitions of paradigmatic meaning which cannot be identifiable as brute data. Even where some of these terms might be given an 'operational definition' in terms of brute data – a term like 'freedom', for instance, can be defined in terms of the absence of legal restriction, *à la* Hobbes – this definition would not carry the full force of the term, and in particular that whereby it could be considered significant for men.

According to the empiricist paradigm, this latter aspect of the meaning of such a term is labelled 'evaluative' and is thought to be utterly heterogeneous from the 'descriptive' aspect. But this analysis is far from firmly established; no more so in fact than the empiricist paradigm of knowledge itself with which it is closely bound up. A challenge to this

---

[13] 'How is a comparative science of politics possible?', in Alasdair McIntyre, *Against the Self-Images of the Age* (London, 1971).

[14] MacIntyre's article also contains an interesting discussion of 'legitimacy' from a different, although I think related, angle.

paradigm in the name of a hermeneutical science is also a challenge to the distinction between 'descriptive' and 'evaluative' and the entire conception of *Wertfrieheit* which goes with it.

In any case, whether because it is 'evaluative' or can only be applied in connection with definitions of meaning, 'legitimate' is not a word which can be used in the description of social reality according to the conceptions of mainstream social science. It can only be used as a description of subjective meaning. What enters into scientific consideration is thus not the legitimacy of a polity but the opinions or feelings of its member individuals concerning its legitimacy. The differences between different societies in their manner of spontaneous cohesion and sense of community are to be understood by correlations between the beliefs and feelings of their members towards them on one hand and the prevalence of certain brute data identifiable indices of stability in them on the other.

Thus Robert Dahl in *Modern Political Analysis*[15] speaks of the different ways in which leaders gain 'compliance' for their policies. The more citizens comply because of 'internal rewards and deprivations', the less leaders need to use 'external rewards and deprivations'. But if citizens believe a government is legitimate, then their conscience will bind them to obey it; they will be internally punished if they disobey; hence government will have to use less external resources, including force.

Less crude is the discussion of Seymour Lipset in *Political Man*.[16] But it is founded on the same basic ideas, viz. that legitimacy defined as subjective meaning is correlated with stability. 'Legitimacy involves the capacity of the system to engender and maintain the belief that the existing political institutions are the most appropriate ones for the society.'[17]

Lipset is engaged in a discussion of the determinants of stability in modern polities. He singles out two important ones in this chapter, effectiveness and legitimacy. 'Effectiveness means actual performance, the extent to which the system satisfies the basic functions of government as most of the population and such powerful groups within it as big business or the armed forces see them.'[18] Thus we have one factor which has to do with objective reality, what the government has actually done; and the other which has to do with subjective beliefs and 'values'. 'While effectiveness is primarily instrumental, legitimacy is evaluative.'[19] Hence

---

[15] Foundation of Modern Political Science Series (Englewood Cliffs, 1963), pp. 31–2.
[16] New York, 1963, chap. 3.
[17] *Ibid.*, p. 64.   [18] *Ibid.*   [19] *Ibid.*

from the beginning the stage is set by a distinction between social reality and what men think and feel about it.

Lipset sees two types of crisis of legitimacy that modern societies have affronted more or less well. One concerns the status of major conservative institutions which may be under threat from the development of modern industrial democracies. The second concerns the degree to which all political groups have access to the political process. Thus, under the first head, some traditional groups, such as landed aristocracy or clericals, have been roughly handled in a society like France, and have remained alienated from the democratic system for decades afterwards; whereas in England the traditional classes were more gently handled, themselves were willing to compromise and have been slowly integrated and transformed into the new order. Under the second head, some societies managed to integrate the working class or bourgeoisie into the political process at an early stage, whereas in others they have been kept out till quite recently, and consequently have developed a deep sense of alienation from the system, have tended to adopt extremist ideologies, and have generally contributed to instability. One of the determinants of a society's performance on these two heads is whether or not it is forced to affront the different conflicts of democratic development all at once or one at a time. Another important determinant of legitimacy is effectiveness.

This approach, which sees stability as partly the result of legitimacy beliefs and these in turn as resulting partly from the way the status, welfare, and access to political life of different groups fare, seems at first blush eminently sensible and well designed to help us understand the history of the last century or two. But this approach has no place for a study of the inter-subjective and common meanings which are constitutive of modern civilization. And we may doubt whether we can understand the cohesion of modern societies or their present crisis if we leave these out of account.

Let us take the winning of the allegiance of the working class to the new industrial regimes in the nineteenth and twentieth century. This is far from being a matter simply or even perhaps most significantly of the speed with which this class was integrated into the political process and the effectiveness of the regime. Rather the consideration of the granting of access to the political process as an independent variable may be misleading.

It is not just that we often find ourselves invited by historians to account for class cohesion in particular countries in terms of other factors, such as the impact of Methodism in early nineteenth century

England (Elie Halévy)[20] or the draw of Germany's newly successful nationalism. These factors could be assimilated to the social scientist's grid by being classed as 'ideologies' or widely held 'value systems' or some other such concatenations of subjective meaning.

But perhaps the most important such 'ideology' in accounting for the cohesion of industrial democratic societies has been that of the society of work, the vision of society as a large-scale enterprise of production in which widely different functions are integrated into interdependence; a vision of society in which economic relations are considered as primary, as it is not only in Marxism (and in a sense not really with Marxism) but above all with the tradition of Classical Utilitarianism. In line with this vision there is a fundamental solidarity between all members of society who labour (to use Arendt's language),[21] for they are all engaged in producing what is indispensable to life and happiness in far-reaching interdependence.

This is the 'ideology' which has frequently presided over the integration of the working class into industrial democracies, at first directed polemically against the 'unproductive' classes, for example in England with the anti-Corn Law League, and later with the campaigns of Joseph Chamberlain ('when Adam delved and Eve span, who was then the gentleman?'), but later as a support for social cohesion and solidarity.

But, of course, the reason for putting 'ideology' in quotes above is that this definition of things, which has been well integrated with the conception of social life as based on negotiation, cannot be understood in the terms of mainstream social science, as beliefs and 'values' held by a large number of individuals. For the great interdependent matrix of labour is not just a set of ideas in people's heads but is an important aspect of the reality which we live in modern society. And at the same time, these ideas are embedded in this matrix in that they are constitutive of it; that is, we would not be able to live in this type of society unless we were imbued with these ideas or some others which could call forth the discipline and voluntary coordination needed to operate this kind of economy. All industrial civilizations have required a huge wrench from the traditional peasant populations on which they have been imposed; for they require an entirely unprecedented level of disciplined sustained, monotonous effort, long hours unpunctuated by any meaningful rhythm, such as that of seasons or festivals. In the end this way of life can only be accepted

[20] *Histoire du peuple anglais au XIXe siècle* (Paris, 1913).
[21] *The Human Condition* (New York, 1959).

when the idea of making a living is endowed with more significance than that of just avoiding starvation; and this it is in the civilization of labour.

Now this civilization of work is only one aspect of modern societies, along with the society based on negotiation and willed relations (in Anglo-Saxon countries), and other common and inter-subjective meanings which have different importance in different countries. My point is that it is certainly not implausible to say that it has some importance in explaining the integration of the working class in modern industrial democratic society. But it can only be called a cluster of inter-subjective meaning. As such it cannot come into the purview of mainstream political science; and an author like Lipset cannot take it into consideration when discussing this very problem.

But, of course, such a massive fact does not escape notice. What happens rather is that it is re-interpreted. And what has generally happened is that the interdependent productive and negotiating society has been recognized by political science, but not as one structure of inter-subjective meaning among others, rather as the inescapable background of social action as such. In this guise it no longer need be an object of study. Rather it retreats to the middle distance, where its general outline takes the role of universal framework, within which (it is hoped) actions and structures will be brute data identifiable, and this for any society at any time. The view is then that the political actions of men in all societies can be understood as variants of the processing of 'demands' which is an important part of our political life. The inability to recognize the specificity of our inter-subjective meanings is thus inseparably linked with the belief in the universality of North Atlantic behaviour types or 'functions' which vitiates so much of contemporary comparative politics.

The notion is that what politics is about perennially is the adjustment of differences, or the production of symbolic and effective 'outputs' on the basis of demand and support 'inputs'. The rise of the inter-subjective meaning of the civilization of work is seen as the increase of correct perception of the political process at the expense of 'ideology'. Thus Almond and Powell introduce the concept of 'political secularization' to describe 'the emergence of a pragmatic, empirical orientation' to politics.[22] A secular political culture is opposed not only to a traditional one, but also to an 'ideological' culture, which is characterized by 'an inflexible image of political life, closed to conflicting information' and 'fails to develop the open, bargaining attitudes associated with full

[22] *Comparative Politics*, p. 58.

secularization'.[23] The clear understanding here is that a secularized culture is one which essentially depends less on illusion, which sees things as
they are, which is not infected with the 'false consciousness' of traditional
or ideological culture (to use a term which is not in the mainstream
vocabulary).

3

This way of looking at the civilization of work, as resulting from the
retreat of illusion before the correct perception of what politics perennially and really is, is thus closely bound up with the epistemological
premises of mainstream political science and its resultant inability to
recognize the historical specificity of this civilization's inter-subjective
meanings. But the weakness of this approach, already visible in the
attempts to explain the rise of this civilization and its relation to others,
becomes even more painful when we try to account for its present malaise,
even crisis.

The strains in contemporary society, the breakdown of civility, the rise
of deep alienation, which is translated into even more destructive action,
tend to shake the basic categories of our social science. It is not just that
such a development was quite unpredicted by this science, which saw in
the rise of affluence the cause rather of a further entrenching of the
bargaining culture, a reduction of irrational cleavage, an increase of
tolerance, in short 'the end of ideology'. For prediction, as we shall see
below, cannot be a goal of social science as it is of natural science. It is
rather that this mainstream science hasn't the categories to explain this
breakdown. It is forced to look on extremism either as a bargaining
gambit of the desperate, deliberately raising the ante in order to force a
hearing. Or, alternatively, it can recognize the novelty of the rebellion by
accepting the hypothesis that heightened demands are being made on the
system owing to a revolution of 'expectations', or else to the eruption of
new desires or aspirations which hitherto had no place in the bargaining
process. But these new desires or aspirations must be in the domain of
individual psychology, that is, they must be such that their arousal and
satisfaction is to be understood in terms of states of individuals rather
than in terms of the inter-subjective meanings in which they live. For these
latter have no place in the categories of the mainstream, which thus
cannot accommodate a genuine historical psychology.

But some of the more extreme protests and acts of rebellion in our

---

[23] *Ibid.*, p. 61.

society cannot be interpreted as bargaining gambits in the name of any demands, old or new. These can only be interpreted within the accepted framework of our social science as a return to ideology, and hence as irrational. Now in the case of some of the more bizarre and bloody forms of protest, there will be little disagreement; they will be judged irrational by all but their protagonists. But within the accepted categories this irrationality can only be understood in terms of individual psychology; it is the public eruption of private pathology; it cannot be understood as a malady of society itself, a malaise which afflicts its constitutive meanings.[24]

No one can claim to begin to have an adequate explanation for these major changes which our civilization is undergoing. But in contrast to the incapacity of a science which remains within the accepted categories, a hermeneutical science of man which has a place for a study of intersubjective meaning can at least begin to explore fruitful avenues. Plainly the discipline which was integral to the civilization of work and bargaining is beginning to fail. The structures of this civilization, interdependent work, bargaining, mutual adjustment of individual ends, are beginning to change their meaning for many, and are beginning to be felt not as normal and best suited to man, but as hateful or empty. And yet we are all caught in these inter-subjective meanings in so far as we live in this society, and in a sense more and more all-pervasively as it progresses. Hence the virulence and tension of the critique of our society which is always in some real sense a self-rejection (in a way that the old socialist opposition never was).

Why has this set of meanings gone sour? Plainly, we have to accept that they are not to be understood at their face value. The free, productive, bargaining culture claimed to be sufficient for man. If it was not, then we have to assume that while it did hold our allegiance, it also had other meanings for us which commanded this allegiance and which have now gone.

---

[24] Thus Lewis Feuer in *The Conflict of Generations* (New York, 1969), attempts to account for the 'misperception of social reality' in the Berkeley student uprising of 1968 in terms of a generational conflict (pp. 466–70), which in turn is rooted in the psychology of adolescence and attaining adulthood. Yet Feuer himself in his first chapter notes the comparative recency of self-defining political generations, a phenomenon which dates from the post-Napoleonic era (p. 33). But an adequate attempt to explain this historical shift, which after all underlay the Berkeley rising and many others, would I believe have to take us beyond the ambit of individual psychology to psycho-history, to a study of the intrication of psychological conflict and inter-subjective meanings. A variant of this form of study has been adumbrated in the work of Erik Erikson.

This is the starting point of a set of hypotheses which attempt to redefine our past in order to make our present and future intelligible. We might think that the productive, bargaining culture offered in the past common meanings (even though there was no place for them in its philosophy), and hence a basis for community, which were essentially linked with its being in the process of building. It linked men who could see themselves as breaking with the past to build a new happiness in America, for instance. But in all essentials that future is built; the notion of a horizon to be attained by future greater production (as against social transformation) verges on the absurd in contemporary America. Suddenly the horizon which was essential to the sense of meaningful purpose has collapsed, which would show that like so many other Enlightenment-based dreams the free, productive, bargaining society can only sustain man as a goal, not as a reality.

Or we can look at this development in terms of identity. A sense of building their future through the civilization of work can sustain men as long as they see themselves as having broken with a millennial past of injustice and hardship in order to create qualitatively different conditions for their children. All the requirements of a humanly acceptable identity can be met by this predicament, a relation to the past (one soars above it but preserves it in folkloric memory), to the social world (the inter-dependent world of free, productive men), to the earth (the raw material which awaits shaping), to the future and one's own death (the everlasting monument in the lives of prosperous children), to the absolute (the absolute values of freedom, integrity, dignity).

But at some point the children will be unable to sustain this forward thrust into the future. This effort has placed them in a private haven of security, within which they are unable to reach and recover touch with the great realities: their parents have only a negated past, lives which have been oriented wholly to the future; the social world is distant and without shape; rather one can only insert oneself into it by taking one's place in the future-oriented productive juggernaut. But this now seems without any sense; the relation to the earth as raw material is therefore experienced as empty and alienating, but the recovery of a valid relation to the earth is the hardest thing once lost; and there is no relation to the absolute where we are caught in the web of meanings which have gone dead for us. Hence past, future, earth, world, and absolute are in some way or another occluded; and what must arise is an identity crisis of frightening proportions.

These two hypotheses are mainly focussed on the crisis in US civilization, and they would perhaps help account for the fact that the USA is in some sense going first through this crisis of all Atlantic nations; not, that is, only because it is the most affluent, but more because it has been more fully based on the civilization of work than European countries who retained something of more traditional common meanings.

But they might also help us to understand why alienation is most severe among groups which have been but marginal in affluent bargaining societies. These have had the greatest strain in living in this civilization while their identity was in some ways antithetical to it. Such are blacks in the USA, and the community of French-speaking Canadians, each in different ways. For many immigrant groups the strain was also great, but they forced themselves to surmount the obstacles, and the new identity is sealed in the blood of the old, as it were.

But for those who would not or could not succeed in thus transforming themselves, but always lived a life of strain on the defensive, the breakdown of the central, powerful identity is the trigger to a deep turnover. It can be thought of as a liberation but at the same time it is deeply unsettling, because the basic parameters of former life are being changed and there are not yet the new images and definitions to live a new fully acceptable identity. In a sense we are in a condition where a new social compact (rather the first social compact) has to be made between these groups and those they live with, and no one knows where to start.

In the last pages, I have presented some hypotheses which may appear very speculative; and they may indeed turn out to be without foundation, even without much interest. But their aim was mainly illustrative. My principal claim is that we can only come to grips with this phenomenon of breakdown by trying to understand more clearly and profoundly the common and inter-subjective meanings of the society in which we have been living. For it is these which no longer hold us, and to understand this change we have to have an adequate grasp of these meanings. But this we cannot do as long as we remain within the ambit of mainstream social science, for it will not recognize inter-subjective meaning, and is forced to look at the central meanings of our society as though they were the inescapable background of all political action. Breakdown is thus inexplicable in political terms; it is an outbreak of irrationality which must ultimately be explained by some form of psychological illness.

Mainstream science may thus venture into the area explored by the above hypotheses, but after its own fashion, by forcing the psychohistorical facts of identity into the grid of an individual psychology, in short, by re-interpreting all meanings as subjective. The result might be a psychological theory of emotional maladjustment, perhaps traced to certain features of family background, analogous to the theories of the authoritarian personality and the California F-scale. But this would no longer be a political or social theory. We would be giving up the attempt to understand the change in social reality at the level of its constitutive inter-subjective meanings.

IV

It can be argued, then, that mainstream social science is kept within certain limits by its categorial principles which are rooted in the traditional epistemology of empiricism; and secondly that these restrictions are a severe handicap and prevent us from coming to grips with important problems of our day which should be the object of political science. We need to go beyond the bounds of a science based on verification to one which would study the inter-subjective and common meanings embedded in social reality.

But this science would be hermeneutical in the sense that has been developed in this paper. It would not be founded on brute data; its most primitive data would be readings of meanings, and its object would have the three properties mentioned above: the meanings are for a subject in a field or fields; they are moreover meanings which are partially constituted by self-definitions, which are in this sense already interpretations, and which can thus be re-expressed or made explicit by a science of politics. In our case, the subject may be a society or community; but the inter-subjective meanings, as we saw, embody a certain self-definition, a vision of the agent and his society, which is that of the society or community.

But then the difficulties which the proponents of the verification model foresee will arise. If we have a science which has no brute data, which relies on readings, then it cannot but move in a hermeneutical circle. A given reading of the inter-subjective meanings of a society, or of given institutions or practices, may seem well founded, because it makes sense of these practices or the development of that society. But the conviction that it does make sense of this history itself is founded on further related readings. Thus, what I said above on the identity crisis which is generated by our society makes sense and holds together only if one accepts this reading of the inter-subjective meanings of our society, and if one accepts this reading of the rebellion against our society by many young people (sc. the reading in terms of identity crisis). These two readings make sense together, so that in a sense the explanation as a whole reposes on the readings, and the readings in their turn are strengthened by the explanation as a whole.

But if these readings seem implausible, or even more, if they are not understood by our interlocutor, there is no verification procedure which we can fall back on. We can only continue to offer interpretations; we are in an interpretative circle.

But the ideal of a science of verification is to find an appeal beyond differences of interpretation. Insight will always be useful in discovery, but should not have to play any part in establishing the truth of its findings. This ideal can be said to have been met by our natural sciences. But a hermeneutic science cannot but rely on insight. It requires that one have the sensibility and understanding necessary to be able to make and comprehend the readings by which we can explain the reality concerned. In physics we might argue that if someone does not accept a true theory, then either he has not been shown enough (brute data) evidence (perhaps not enough is yet available), or he cannot understand and apply some formalized language. But in the sciences of man conceived as hermeneutical, the non-acceptance of a true or illuminating theory may come from neither of these, indeed is unlikely to be due to either of these, but rather from a failure to grasp the meaning field in question, an inability to make and understand readings of this field.

In other words, in a hermeneutical science, a certain measure of insight is indispensable, and this insight cannot be communicated by the gathering of brute data, or initiation in modes of formal reasoning or some combination of these. It is unformalizable. But this is a scandalous result according to the authoritative conception of science in our tradition, which is shared even by many of those who are highly critical of the approach of mainstream psychology, or sociology, or political science. For it means that this is not a study in which anyone can engage, regardless of their level of insight; that some claims of the form: 'if you don't understand, then your intuitions are at fault, are blind or inadequate' will be justified; that some differences will be non-arbitrable by further evidence, but that each side can only make appeal to deeper insight on the part of the other. The superiority of one position over another will thus consist in this, that from the more adequate position one can understand one's own stand and that of one's opponent, but not the other way around. It goes without saying that this argument can only have weight for those in the superior position.

Thus, a hermeneutical science encounters a gap in intuitions, which is the other side, as it were, of the hermeneutical circle. But the situation is graver than this; for this gap is bound up with our divergent options in politics and life.

We speak of a gap when some cannot understand the kind of self-definition which others are proposing as underlying a certain society or set of institutions. Thus some positivistically minded thinkers will find the language of identity-theory quite opaque; and some thinkers will not recognize any theory which does not fit with the categorial presuppositions of empiricism. But self-definitions are not only important to us as scientists who are trying to understand some, perhaps distant, social reality. As men we are self-defining beings, and we are partly what we are in virtue of the self-definitions which we have accepted, however we have come by them. What self-definitions we understand and what ones we do not, is closely linked with the self-definitions which help to constitute what we are. If it is too simple to say that one only understands an 'ideology' which one subscribes to, it is nevertheless hard to deny that we have great difficulty grasping definitions whose terms structure the world in ways which are utterly different from or incompatible with our own.

Hence the gap in intuitions doesn't just divide different theoretical positions, it also tends to divide different fundamental options in life. The practical and the theoretical are inextricably joined here. It may not just be that to understand a certain explanation one has to sharpen one's intuitions, it may be that one has to change one's orientation – if not in adopting another orientation, at least in living one's own in a way which allows for greater comprehension of others. Thus, in the sciences of man in so far as they are hermeneutical there can be a valid response to 'I don't understand' which takes the form, not only 'develop your intuitions', but more radically 'change yourself'. This puts an end to any aspiration to a value-free or 'ideology-free' science of man. A study of the science of man is inseparable from an examination of the options between which men must choose.

This means that we can speak here not only of error, but of illusion. We speak of 'illusion' when we are dealing with something of greater substance than error, error which in a sense builds a counterfeit reality of its own. But errors of interpretation of meaning, which are also self-definitions of those who interpret and hence inform their lives, are more than errors in this sense: they are sustained by certain practices of which they are constitutive. It is not implausible to single out as examples two rampant illusions in our present society. One is that of the proponents of the bargaining society who can recognize nothing but either bargaining gambits or madness in those who rebel against this society. Here the error is sustained by the practices of the bargaining culture, and given a semblance of reality by the refusal to treat any protests on other terms; it hence acquires the more substantive reality of illusion. The second example is provided by much 'revolutionary' activity in our society which in desperate search for an alternative mode of life purports to see its situation in that of an Andean guerilla or Chinese peasants. Lived out, this passes from the stage of laughable error to tragic illusion. One illusion cannot recognize the possibility of human variation, the other cannot see any limits to man's ability to transform itself. Both make a valid science of man impossible.

In face of all this, we might be so scandalized by the prospect of such a hermeneutical science, that we will want to go back to the verification model. Why can we not take our understanding of meaning as part of the logic of discovery, as the logical empiricists suggest for our unformalizable insights, and still found our science on the exactness of our predictions? Our insightful understanding of the inter-subjective meanings of our society will then serve to elaborate fruitful hypotheses, but the proof of these puddings will remain in the degree they enable us to predict.

The answer is that if the epistemological views underlying the science of interpretation are right, such exact prediction is radically impossible, for three reasons of ascending order of fundamentalness.

The first is the well-known 'open system' predicament, one shared by human life and meteorology, that we cannot shield a certain domain of human events, the psychological, economic, political, from external interference; it is impossible to delineate a closed system.

The second, more fundamental, is that if we are to understand men by a science of interpretation, we cannot achieve the degree of fine exactitude of a science based on brute data. The data of natural science admit of measurement to virtually any degree of exactitude. But different interpretations cannot be judged in this way. At the same time different nuances of interpretation may lead to different predictions in some circumstances, and these different outcomes may eventually create widely varying futures. Hence it is more than easy to be wide of the mark.

But the third and most fundamental reason for the impossibility of hard prediction is that man is a self-defining animal. With changes in his self-definition go changes in what man is, such that he has to be understood in different terms. But the conceptual mutations in human history can and frequently do produce conceptual webs which are incommensurable, that is, where the terms cannot be defined in relation to a common stratum of expressions. The entirely different notions of bargaining in our society and in some primitive ones provide an example. Each will be glossed in terms of practices, institutions, ideas in each society which have nothing corresponding to them in the other.

The success of prediction in the natural sciences is bound up with the fact that all states of the system, past and future, can be described in the same range of concepts, as values, say, of the same variables. Hence all future states of the solar system can be characterized, as past ones are, in the language of Newtonian mechanics. This is far from being a sufficient condition of exact prediction, but it is a necessary one in this sense, that only if past and future are brought under the same conceptual net can one understand the states of the latter as some function of the states of the former, and hence predict.

This conceptual unity is vitiated in the sciences of man by the fact of conceptual innovation which in turn alters human reality. The very terms in which the future will have to be characterized if we are to understand it properly are not all available to us at present. Hence we have such radically unpredictable events as the culture of youth today, the Puritan rebellion of the sixteenth and seventeenth centuries, the development of Soviet society, and so on.

Thus it is much easier to understand after the fact than it is to predict. Human science is largely *ex post* understanding. Or often one has the sense of impending change, of some big reorganization, but is powerless to make clear what it will consist in: one lacks the vocabulary. But there is a clear asymmetry here, which there is not (or not supposed to be) in natural science, where events are said to be predicted from the theory with exactly the same ease with which one explains past events and by exactly the same process. In human science this will never be the case.

Of course, we strive *ex post* to understand the changes, and to do this we try to develop a language in which we can situate the incommensurable webs of concepts. We see the rise of Puritanism, for instance, as a shift in man's stance to the sacred; and thus, we have a language in which we can express both stances – the earlier medieval Catholic one and the Puritan rebellion – as 'glosses' on this fundamental term. We thus have a language in which to talk of the transition. But think how we acquired it. This general category of the sacred is acquired not only from our experience of the shift which came in the Reformation, but from the study of human religion in general, including primitive religion, and with the detachment which came with secularization. It would be conceivable, but unthinkable, that a medieval Catholic could have this conception – or for that matter a Puritan. These two protagonists only had a language of condemnation for each other: 'heretic', 'idolator'. The place for such a concept was pre-empted by a certain way of living the sacred. After a big change has happened, and the trauma has been resorbed, it is possible to try to understand it, because one now has available the new language, the transformed meaning world. But hard prediction before just makes one a laughing stock. Really to be able to predict the future would be to have explicited so clearly the human condition that one would already have pre-empted all cultural innovation and transformation. This is hardly in the bounds of the possible.

Sometimes men show amazing prescience: the myth of Faust, for instance, which is treated several times at the beginning of the modern era. There is a kind of prophesy here, a premonition. But what characterizes these bursts of foresight is that they see through a glass darkly, for they see in terms of the old language: Faust sells his soul to the devil. They are in no sense hard predictions. Human science looks backward. It is inescapably historical.

There are thus good grounds both in epistemological arguments and in their greater fruitfulness for opting for hermeneutical sciences of man. But we cannot hide from ourselves how greatly this opinion breaks with certain commonly held notions about our scientific tradition. We cannot measure such sciences against the requirements of a science of verification: we cannot judge them by their predictive capacity. We have to accept that they are founded on intuitions which all do not share, and what is worse that these intuitions are closely bound up with our fundamental options. These sciences cannot be *wertfrei*; they are moral sciences in a more radical sense than the eighteenth century understood. Finally, their successful prosecution requires a high degree of self-knowledge, a freedom from illusion, in the sense of error which is rooted and expressed in one's way of life; for our incapacity to understand is rooted in our own self-definitions, hence in what we are. To say this is not to say anything new: Aristotle makes a similar point in Book I of the *Ethics*. But it is still radically shocking and unassimilable to the mainstream of modern science.

CHAPTER TWO

NEUTRALITY IN POLITICAL SCIENCE

I

I

A few years ago one heard it frequently said that political philosophy was dead, that it had been killed by the growth of science, the growth of positivism, the end of ideology, or some combination of these forces, but that, whatever the cause, it was dead.

It is not my intention to rake over the coals of this old issue once more. I am simply using this as a starting point for a reflection on the relation between political science and political philosophy. For behind the view that political philosophy was dead, behind any view which holds that it *can* die, lies the belief that its fate can be separated from that of political science; for no one would claim that the science of politics is dead, however one might disapprove of this or that manner of carrying it on. It remains a perpetually possible, and indeed important enterprise.

The view was indeed that political science has come of age in freeing itself finally of the incubus of political philosophy. No more would its scope be narrowed and its work prejudiced by some value position which operated as an initial weight holding back the whole enterprise. The belief was that political science had freed itself from philosophy in becoming value-free and in adopting the scientific method. These two moves were felt to be closely connected; indeed, the second contains the first. For scientific method is, if nothing else, a dispassionate study of the facts as they are, without metaphysical presuppositions, and without value biasses.

As Vernon van Dyke puts it:

science and *scientific*, then, are words that relate to only one kind of knowledge, i.e., to knowledge of what is observable, and not to any other kinds of knowledge that may exist. They do not relate to alleged knowledge of the normative –

knowledge of what ought to be. Science concerns what has been, is, or will be, regardless of the 'oughts' of the situation.[1]

Those who could hold that political philosophy was dead, therefore, were those who held to a conception of the social sciences as *wertfrei*; like natural science, political science must dispassionately study the facts. This position received support from the views of the logical empiricists who had, for philosophers, an extraordinarily wide influence among scientists in general, and among the sciences of man in particular. Emboldened by their teaching, some orthodox political scientists tended to claim that the business of normative theory, making recommendations, and evaluating different courses of action could be entirely separated from the study of the facts, from the theoretical attempt to account for them.

Many, of course, had doubts; and these doubts seem to be growing today among political scientists. But they do not touch the thesis of the logical separation between fact and value. They centre rather around the possibility of setting one's values to one side when one undertakes the study of politics. The relation between factual study and normative beliefs is therefore thought of in the same traditional positivist way: that the relationship if any is from value to fact, not from fact to value. Thus, scientific findings are held to be neutral: that is, the facts as we discover them do not help to establish or give support to any set of values; we cannot move from fact to value. It is, however, often admitted that our values can influence our findings. This can be thought of as a vicious interference, as when we approach our work with bias which obscures the truth, or as something anodyne and inevitable, as when our values select for us the area of research on which we wish to embark. Or it can be thought of as a factor whose ill effects can be compensated by a clear consciousness of it: thus many theorists today recommend that one set out one's value position in detail at the beginning of a work so as to set the reader (and perhaps also the writer) on guard.

Value beliefs remain therefore as unfounded on scientific fact for the new generation of more cautious theorists as they were for the thinkers of the hey-day of 'value-freedom'. They arise, as it were, from outside factual study; they spring from deep choices which are independent of the facts. Thus David Easton, who goes on to attempt to show that 'whatever effort is exerted, in undertaking research we cannot shed our values in the

[1] *Political Science* (Stanford and London, 1960), p. 192.

way we remove our coats',[2] nevertheless states his acceptance at the outset
of the 'working assumption' which is 'generally adopted today in the
social sciences', and which 'holds that values can ultimately be reduced to
emotional responses conditioned by the individual's total life-experien-
ces'.[3] Thus there is no question of founding values on scientific findings.
Emotional responses can be explained by life-experience, but not justified
or shown to be appropriate by the facts about society:

> The moral aspect of a proposition ... expresses only the emotional response of an
> individual to a state of real or presumed facts ... Although we can say that the
> aspect of a proposition referring to a fact can be true or false, it is meaningless to
> characterize the value aspect of a proposition in this way.[4]

The import of these words is clear. For, if value positions could be supported or undermined by the findings of science, then they could not
simply be characterized as emotional responses, and we could not say
simply that it was *meaningless* (although it might be misleading) to speak
of them as true or false.

Political philosophy, therefore, as reasoned argument about fundamental political values, can be entirely separated from political science,
even on the mitigated positivist view which is now gaining ground among
political scientists. 'Values' steer, as it were, the process of discovery, but
they do not gain or lose plausibility by it. Thus although values may be
somehow ineradicable from political science, reasoned argument concerning them would seem easily separable (though theorists may differ as
to whether this is wise or not).[5] Indeed, it is hard to see in what such
reasoned argument could consist. The findings of science will be relevant
to our values, of course, in this sense, that they will tell us how to realize
the goals we set ourselves. We can reconstruct political science in the
mould of a 'policy science', like engineering and medicine, which shows
us how to attain our goals. But the goals and values still come from
somewhere else; they are founded on choices whose basis remains
obscure.

The aim of this paper is to call into question this notion of the relation
of factual findings in politics to value positions, and thus the implied
relation between political science and political philosophy. In particular
my aim is to call into question the view that the findings of political
science leave us, as it were, as free as before, that they do not go some way

---

[2] *The Political System* (New York, 1953), p. 225.   [3] *Ibid.*, p. 221.   [4] *Ibid.*
[5] Cf. *ibid.*

to establishing particular sets of values and undermining others. If this view is shown to be mistaken, then we will have to recognize a convergence between science and normative theory in the field of politics.

It is usual for philosophers, when discussing this question, to leave the realms of the sciences of man and launch into a study of 'good', or commending, or emotive meaning, and so on. I propose to follow another course here, and to discuss the question first in connection with the disciplines in terms of which I have raised it, namely political philosophy and political science. When we have some understanding of the relations between these two on the ground, as it were, it will be time to see if these are considered possible in the heavens of philosophy.

2

The thesis that political science is value-neutral has maximum plausibility when we look at some of its detailed findings. That French workers tend to vote Communist may be judged deplorable or encouraging, but it does not itself determine us to accept either of these judgements. It stands as a fact, neutral between them.

If this were all there is to political science, the debate would end here. But it is no more capable than any other science of proceeding by the random collection of facts. At one time it was believed that science was just concerned with the correlation of observable phenomena – the observables concerned being presumed to lie unproblematically before our gaze. But this position, the offshoot of a more primitive empiricism, is abandoned now by almost everyone, even those in the empiricist tradition.

For the number of features which any given range of phenomena may exhibit, and which can thus figure in correlations, is indefinite; and this because the phenomena themselves can be classified in an indefinite number of ways. Any physical object can be classified according to shape, colour, size, function, aesthetic properties, relation to some process, etc.; when we come to realities as complex as political society, the case is no different. But among these features only a limited range will yield correlations which have some explanatory force.

Nor are these necessarily the most obtrusive. The crucial features, laws or correlations concerning which will explain or help to explain phenomena of the range in question, may at a given stage of the science concerned be only vaguely discerned if not frankly unsuspected. The conceptual resources necessary to pick them out may not yet have been elaborated. It is said, for instance, that the modern physical concept of mass was unknown to the ancients, and only slowly and painfully evolved through the searchings of the later Middle Ages. And yet it is an essential variable in the modern science. A number of more obtrusive features may be irrelevant; that is, they may not be such that they can be linked in functions explanatory of the phenomena. Obvious distinctions may be irrelevant, or have an entirely different relevance from that attributed to them, such as the distinction between Aristotle's 'light' and 'heavy' bodies.

Thus when we wish to go beyond certain immediate low-level correlations whose relevance to the political process is fairly evident, such as the one mentioned above; when we want to explain why French workers vote Communist, or why McCarthyism arises in the United States in the late 1940s, or why the level of abstentionism varies from election to election, or why new African regimes are liable to military take-over, the features by reference to which we can explain these results are not immediately in evidence. Not only is there a wider difference of opinion about them, but we are not even sure that we have as yet the conceptual resources necessary to pick them out. We may easily argue that certain more obtrusive features, those pertaining, say, to the institutional structure, are not relevant, while others less obtrusive, say, the character structure prevalent in certain strata of the society, will yield the real explanation. We may, for instance, refuse to account for McCarthyism in terms of the struggle between Executive and Legislature, and look rather to the development of a certain personality structure among certain sections of the American population. Or else we may reject both these explanations and look to the role of a new status group in American society, newly rich but excluded from the Eastern Establishment. Or we may reject this, and see it as a result of the new position of the United States in the world.

The task of theory in political science, one which cannot be foregone if we are to elaborate any explanations worth the name, is to discover what are the kinds of features to which we should look for explanations of this kind. In which of the above dimensions are we to find an explanation for McCarthyism? Or rather, since all of these dimensions obviously have relevance, how are we to relate them in explaining the political phenomena? The task of theory is to delineate the relevant features in the different dimensions and their relation so that we have some idea of what can be the cause of what, of how character affects political process, or social structure affects character, or economic relations affect social structure, or political process affects economic relations, or vice versa; how ideological divisions affect party systems, or history affects ideological divisions, or culture affects history, or party systems affect culture, or vice versa. Before we have made some at least tentative steps in this direction we do not even have an idea where to look for our explanations; we do not know which facts to gather.

It is not surprising, then, that political science should be the field in which a great and growing number of 'theoretical frameworks' compete to answer these questions. Besides the Marxist approach, and the interest-group theory associated with the name of Bentley, we have seen the recent growth of 'structural-functional' approaches under the influence of systems theory; there have been approaches which have attempted to relate the psychological dimension to political behaviour (e.g. Lasswell), different applications of sociological concepts and methods (e.g. Lipset and Almond), applications of game theory (e.g. Downs and Riker), and so on.

These different approaches are frequently rivals, since they offer different accounts of the features crucial for explanation and the causal relations which hold. We can speak of them, along with their analogues in other sciences, as 'conceptual structures' or 'theoretical frameworks', because they claim to delimit the area in which scientific enquiry will be fruitful. A framework does not give us at once all the variables which will be relevant and the laws which will be true, but it tells us what needs to be explained, and roughly by what kinds of factors. For instance, if we accept the principle of inertia, certain ways of conceiving bodies and therefore certain questions are beyond the pale. To pursue them is fruitless, as was the search for what kept the cannon-ball moving in pre-Galilean physics. Similarly an orthodox Marxist approach cannot allow that McCarthyism can be explained in terms of early upbringing and the resultant personality structure.

But we can also see a theoretical framework as setting the crucial dimensions through which the phenomena can vary. For it sets out the essential functional relations by which they can be explained, while at the same time ruling out other functional relations belonging to other, rival frameworks. But the given set of functional relations defines certain dimensions in which the phenomena can vary; a given framework therefore affirms some dimensions of variation and denies others. Thus for a Marxist, capitalist societies do not vary as to who wields power, no matter what the constitution or the party in office; supposed variations in these dimensions, which are central to a great many theories, are sham; the crucial dimension is that concerning class structure.

In the more exact sciences theoretical discovery may be couched in the form of laws and be called principles, such as, e.g., of inertia, or the rectilinear propagation of light. But in the less exact, such as politics, it may consist simply of a general description of the phenomena couched in the crucial concepts. Or it may be implicit in a series of distinctions which a given theory makes (e.g. Aristotle's classification of the types of polity), or in a story of how the phenomena came to be (e.g. the myth of the social contract), or in a general statement of causal relations (e.g. Marx's preface to *A Contribution to the Critique of Political Economy*).

But, however expressed, theoretical discovery can be seen as the delineating of the important dimensions of variation for the range of phenomena concerned.

3

Theoretical discovery of this kind is thus one of the concerns of modern political science, as we have seen. But it also is a traditional concern of what we call political philosophy, that is, normative political theory. It is not hard to see why. Normative theorists of the tradition have also been concerned with delineating crucial dimensions of variation – of course, they were looking for the dimensions which were significant for judging the value of polities and policies rather than for explaining them. But the two types of research were in fact closely interwoven so that in pursuing the first they were also led to pursue the second.

Aristotle, for instance, is credited with a revision of Plato's threefold classification of political society which enhanced its explanatory value. He substituted for the number criterion a class criterion which gives a more revealing classification of the differences, and allows us to account for more: it made clear what was at stake between democracy and oligarchy; it opened up the whole range of explanations based on class composition, including the one for which Aristotle is known in history, the balancing role of the middle class.

But this revision was not unconnected with differences in the normative theory of the two thinkers. Plato attempted to achieve a society devoid of class struggle, either in the perfect harmony of the *Republic*, or in the single-class state of the *Laws*. Aristotle is not above weaving the dream of the ideal state in one section of the *Politics*, but there is little connection between this and the political theory of the rest of the work. This latter is solidly based on the understanding that class differences, and hence divergence of interest and tension, are here to stay. In the light of this theory, Plato's idea in the *Republic* of overcoming class tension by discipline, education, a superior constitution, and so on, is so much pie-in-the-sky (not even very tasty pie, in Aristotle's view, as he makes clear in Book II, but that is for other reasons).

Aristotle's insight in political science is incompatible with Plato's normative theory, at least in the *Republic*, and the *Politics* therefore takes a quite different line (for other reasons as well, of course). The difference on this score might perhaps be expressed in this way: both Plato and Aristotle held that social harmony was of crucial importance as a value. But Plato saw this harmony as achieved in the ending of all class conflict; Aristotle saw it as arising from the domestication of this conflict. But crucial to this dispute is the question of the causal relevance of class tension: is it an eradicable blot on social harmony, in the sense that one can say, for instance, that the violent forms of this conflict are? Or is it ineradicable and ever-present, only varying in its forms? In the first case one of the crucial dimensions of variation of our explanatory theory is that concerning the presence or absence of class conflict. In the second case, this dimension is not even recognized as having a basis in fact. If this is so, then the normative theory collapses, or rather is shifted from the realm of political philosophy to that we call Utopia-building. For the idea of a society without class conflict would be one to which we cannot even approach. Moreover, the attempt to approach it would have all the dangerous consequences attendant on large-scale political changes based on illusory hopes.

Thus Plato's theory of the *Republic*, considered as the thesis that a certain dimension of variation is normatively significant, contains claims concerning the dimensions of variation which are relevant for explanation, for it is only compatible with those frameworks which concede the reality of the normatively crucial dimension. It is incompatible with any view of politics as the striving of different classes, or interest groups, or individuals against one another.

It is clear that this is true of any normative theory, that it is linked with certain explanatory theory or theories, and incompatible with others. Aristotle's dimension whereby different constitutions were seen as expressing and moulding different forms of life disappears in the atomistic conception of Hobbes. Rousseau's crucial dimension of the *Social Contract*, marking a sharp discontinuity between popular sovereignty and states of dependence of one form or another, could not survive the validation of the theories of Mosca, or Michels, or Pareto.

Traditional political philosophy was thus forced to engage in the theoretical function that we have seen to be essential to modern political science; and the more elaborate and comprehensive the normative theory, the more complete and defined the conceptual framework which accompanied it. That is why political science can learn something still from the works of Aristotle, Hobbes, Hegel, Marx, and so on. In the tradition one form of enquiry is virtually inseparable from the other.

II

I

This is not a surprising result. Everyone recognized that political philosophers of the tradition were engaged in elaborating on at least embryonic political science. But, one might say, that is just the trouble; that is why political science was so long in getting started. Its framework was always set in the interests of some normative theory. In order to progress science must be liberated from *parti pris* and be value-neutral. Thus if normative theory requires political science and cannot be carried on without it, the reverse is not the case; political science can and should be separated from the older discipline. Let us examine some modern attempts to elaborate a science of politics to see if this is true.

Let us look first at S. M. Lipset's *Political Man*.[6] In this work Lipset sets out the conditions for modern democracy. He sees societies as existing in two dimensions – conflict and consensus. Both are equally necessary for democracy. They are not mere opposites as a simple-minded view might assume. Conflict here is not seen as a simple divergence of interest, or the existence of objective relations of exploitation, but as the actual working out of these through the struggle for power and over policy.

Surprising as it may sound, a stable democracy requires the manifestation of conflict or cleavage so that there will be struggle over ruling positions, challenges to parties in power, and shifts of parties in office; but without consensus – a political system allowing the peaceful 'play' of power, the adherence of the 'outs' to decisions made by the 'ins', and the recognition by the 'ins' of the rights of the 'outs' – there can be no democracy. The study of the conditions encouraging democracy must therefore focus on the sources of both cleavage and consensus.[7]

And again, 'Cleavage – where it is legitimate – contributes to the integration of societies and organizations'.[8] The absence of such conflict, such as where a given group has taken over, or an all-powerful state can produce unanimity, or at least prevent diversity from expressing itself, is a sign that the society is not a free one. De Tocqueville feared that the

---

[6] New York, 1959.   [7] *Ibid.*, p. 21.   [8] *Ibid.*

power of the state would produce apathy and thus do away even with consensus.[9]

Democracy in a complex society may be defined as a political system which supplies regular constitutional opportunities for changing the governing officials, and a social mechanism which permits the largest possible part of the population to influence major decisions by choosing among contenders for political office.[10]

Such a society requires the organization of group interests to fight for their own goals – provided that this is done in a peaceful way, within the rules of the game, and with the acceptance of the arbiter in the form of elections by universal suffrage. If groups are not organized, they have no real part, their interests are neglected, and they cannot have their share of power; they become alienated from the system.

Now this view can at once be seen to conflict with a Rousseauian view which disapproves of the organization of 'factions', and which sees consensus as arising out of isolated individuals. It also goes against the modern conservative view that to organize people on a class basis gratuitously divides the society. In face of Rousseau, Lipset holds that the absence of close agreement among all concerning the general will is not a sign that something has gone wrong. There are ineradicable basic divergences of interest; they have to be adjusted. If we get to some kind of conflictless state, this can only be because some of the parties have been somehow done down and prevented from competing. For Lipset, absence of conflict is a sure sign that some groups are being excluded from the public thing.

This difference closely parallels the one mentioned above between Plato and Aristotle. Indeed, Lipset points out on several occasions the similarity between his position and that of Aristotle. And it is clear that it is a difference of the same kind, one in which a normative theory is undermined because the reality of its crucial dimension of variation is challenged. A similar point can be made concerning the difference with conservatives who allow for divergence in the state, but resist class parties. Here the belief is that the divergence is gratuitous, that the real differences lie elsewhere, either in narrower or in broader interests, and that these are obfuscated and made more difficult of rational adjustment by class divisions. More, the state can be torn apart if these divisions are played up. Conservatives tend to feel about class in politics as liberals do about race in politics. Once again, Lipset's view would undermine the

[9] *Ibid.*, p. 27.   [10] *Ibid.*, p. 45.

position, for he holds that class differences are at the centre of politics, and cannot be removed except by reducing the number of players, as it were. They are therefore the very stuff of democratic politics, provided they are moderately and peacefully expressed. The struggle between rich and poor is ineradicable; it can take different forms, that is all.

Attempts to break outside of this range are thus irrational and dysfunctional. Irrational, because based on false premises; and dysfunctional, because the goal of conflictlessness or absence of class tension can only be achieved at the expense of features of the system which most will accept as valuable; by oppressing some segment of the population, or by its apathy and lack of organization. That is, of course, the usual fate of theories with a false factual base in politics; as was remarked above, they are not just erroneous, but positively dangerous.

It can be seen that the value consequences of Lipset's theory are fairly widespread even restricting ourselves to the alternatives which it negates or undermines. An examination of some of the factors which tend to strengthen democracy according to the theory will increase this list of rejected alternatives. Lipset holds that economic development is conducive to the health of democracy, in that, inter alia, it narrows gaps in wealth and living standards, tends to create a large middle class, and increases the 'cross-pressures' working to damp down class conflict. For a society cannot function properly as a democracy unless, along with an articulation of class differences, there is some consensus which straddles them. Now Lipset's 'cross-pressures' – typically exercised by religious affiliation, for instance, which cuts across class barriers – are the 'opiates' of a strict Marxist. For they are integrators which prevent the system coming apart at the social seam, and thus prevent the class war from coming to a head. But we are not dealing here simply with two value judgements about the same facts understood in the same way. The crucial difference is that for Lipset the stage beyond the class struggle does not and cannot exist; the abolition of the conflict in unanimity is impossible; his view is: 'the rich ye have always with you'. But in this case the integrating factors cease to be 'opiates', breeding false consciousness and hiding the great revolutionary potentiality. There is nothing there to hide. Lipset's view therefore negates revolutionary Marxism in a direct way – in the same way as it negates the views above – by denying that the crucial dimensions of variation have reality.

But if we examine this last example a little more closely, we can see even wider normative consequences of Lipset's view. For if we rule out the transformation to the classless society, then we are left with the choice between different kinds of class conflict: a violent kind which so divides society that it can only survive under some form of tyranny, or one which can reach accommodations in peace. This choice, set out in these terms, virtually makes itself for us. We may point out that this does not cover the range of possibility, since there are also cases in which the class conflict is latent, owing to the relative absence of one party. But this is the result of underdevelopment, of a lack of education, or knowledge, or initiative on the part of the underprivileged. Moreover, it unfailingly leads to a worsening of their position relative to the privileged. As Lipset says in the statement of his political position which forms the introduction to the Anchor Edition of *Political Man*, 'I believe with Marx that all privileged classes seek to maintain and *enhance* their advantages against the desire of the underprivileged to reduce them.'[11]

Thus, for Lipset, the important dimension of variation for political societies can be seen as L-shaped, as it were. On the one end lie societies where the divisions are articulated but are so deep that they cannot be contained without violence, suppression of liberty, and despotic rule; on the other end lie societies which are peaceful but oligarchic and which are therefore run to secure the good of a minority ruling group. At the angle are the societies whose differences are articulated but which are capable of accommodating them in a peaceful way, and which therefore are characterized by a high degree of individual liberty and political organization.

Faced with this choice, it is hard to opt for anywhere else but the angle. For to do so is either to choose violence and despotism and suppression over peace, rule by consent, and liberty, or to choose a society run more for the benefit of a minority over a society run more for the benefit of all, a society which exploits and/or manipulates over a society which tends to secure the common good as determined by the majority. Only in the angle can we have a society really run for the common good, for at one end is oligarchy based on an unorganized mass, at the other despotism.

Lipset himself makes this option explicit:

A basic premise of this book is that democracy is not only or even primarily a means through which different groups can attain their ends or seek the good society; it is the good society itself in operation. Only the give-and-take of a free society's internal struggles offers some guarantee that the products of the society will not accumulate in the hands of a few power-holders, and that men may develop and bring up their children without fear of persecution.[12]

---

[11] *Political Man* (New York, 1959), p. xxii, emphasis in original.   [12] *Ibid.*, p. 403.

This is a succinct statement of the value position implicit in *Political Man*, but it is wrongly characterized as a 'premise'. The use of this term shows the influence of the theory of value-neutrality, but it is misplaced. It would be less misleading to say 'upshot', for the value position flows out of the analysis of the book. Once we accept Lipset's analysis concerning the fundamental role of class in politics, that it always operates even when division is not overt, and that it can never be surmounted in unanimity, then we have no choice but to accept democracy as he defines it, as a society in which most men are doers, take their fate in their own hands, or have a hand in determining it, and at least reduce the degree to which injustice is done to them, or their interests are unfavourably handled by others, as the good society.

2

But now we have gone far beyond the merely negative consequences noted above for Marxism, conservatism, or Rousseau's general will. We are saying that the crucial dimensions of variation of Lipset's theory not only negate dimensions crucial to other normative theories but support one of their own, which is implicit in the theory itself. But this conclusion, if true, goes against the supposed neutrality of scientific fact. Let us examine it a bit more closely.

We have said above that faced with the choice between a regime based on violence and suppression, and one based on consent, between regimes which serve the interests more or less of all versus regimes which serve the interests only of a minority, the choice is clear. Is this simply a rhetorical flourish, playing on generally accepted values among readers? Or is the connection more solid?

Granted that we wish to apply 'better' and 'worse' to regimes characterized along this dimension, can one conceive of reversing what seemed above to be the only possible judgement? Can one say: yes, a regime based on minority rule with violent suppression of the majority is better than one based on general consensus, where all have a chance to have their interests looked to? Certainly this is not a logically absurd position in itself. But if someone accepted the framework of Lipset and proceeded to make this judgement, surely we would expect him to go on and mention some other considerations which led him to this astounding conclusion. We might expect him to say that only minorities are creative, that violence is necessary to keep men from stagnating, or something of this kind. But supposing he said nothing of the sort? Supposing he just maintained that violence was better than its opposite, not *qua* stimulus to creativity, or essential element in progress, but just *qua* violence; that it was better that only the minority interest be served, not because the minority would be more creative but just because it was a minority? A position of this kind would be unintelligible. We could understand that the man was dedicating himself to the furtherance of such a society, but the use of the words 'good' or 'better' would be totally inappropriate here, for there would be no visible grounds for applying them. The question would remain open whether the man had understood these terms, whether, for example, he had not confused 'good' with 'something which gives me a kick', or 'aesthetically pleasing'.

But, it might be argued, this is not a fair example. Supposing our unorthodox thinker did adduce other grounds for preferring violence and majority rule? Surely, then, he would be permitted to differ from us? Yes, but then it is very dubious whether he could still accept Lipset's framework. Suppose, for instance, that one believed (as Hegel did about war) that violence was morally necessary from time to time for the well-being of the state. This would not be without effect on one's conception of political science; the range of possible regimes would be different from that which Lipset gives us; for peaceful democratic regimes would suffer a process of stagnation which would render them less viable; they would not in fact be able to maintain themselves, and thus the spectrum of possible regimes would be different from the one Lipset presents us with; the most viable regime would be one which was able to ration violence and maintain it at a non-disruptive level without falling over into stagnation and decay.

But why need this change of values bring along with it a change in explanatory framework? We seem to be assuming that the evils of internal peace must be such as to have a political effect, to undermine the viability of the political society. Is this assumption justified? Normally, of course, we would expect someone putting forward a theory of this kind to hold that inner violence is good because it contributes to the dynamism, or creativity of people, or progress of the society, or something of the kind which would make peaceful societies less viable. But supposing he chose some other benefits of violence which had nothing to do with the survival or health of political society? Let us say that he held that violence was good for art, that only in societies rent by internal violence could great literature, music, painting be produced? The position, for instance, of Harry Lime in *The Third Man?*

This certainly is a possible case. But let us examine it more closely. Our hypothetical objector has totally forsaken the ground of politics, and is making his judgement on extraneous (here aesthetic) grounds. He cannot deny that, setting these grounds aside, the normal order of preference is valid. He is saying in effect that, although it is better abstracting from aesthetic considerations that society be peaceful, nevertheless this must be over-ridden in the interests of art.

This distinction is important. We must distinguish between two kinds of objection to a given valuation. It may be that the valuation is accepted, but that its verdict for our actual choices is over-ridden, as it were, by other more important valuations. Thus we may think that freedom of speech is always a good, while reluctantly conceding that it must be curtailed in an emergency because of the great risks it would entail here. We are in this case self-consciously curtailing a good. The other kind of objection is the one which undermines the valuation itself, seeks to deprive the putative good of its status. This is what Lipset does, for instance, to spiritual followers of Rousseau in showing that their harmony can only be the silence of minority rule.[13] In one case we are conceding that the thing in question does really have the properties which its proponents attribute to it (e.g. that free speech does contribute to justice, progress, human development, or whatever), but we are adding that it also has other properties which force us to proceed against it (e.g. it is potentially disruptive) temporarily or permanently. In the other case, we are denying the condition in question the very properties by which it is judged good (e.g. that the legislation of the society without cleavage emanates from the free conscious will of all its citizens). Let us call these two objections respectively over-riding and undermining.

Now what is being claimed here is that an objection which undermines the values which seem to arise out of a given framework must alter the framework; that in this sense the framework is inextricably connected to a certain set of values; and that if we can reverse the valuation without touching the framework, then we are dealing with an over-riding.

To go back to the example above: in order to undermine the judgement against violence we would have to show that it does not have the property claimed for it. Now obviously violence has the property of killing and maiming which goes some way towards putting it in the list of undesirables, one might think irrevocably; so that it could only be over-ridden. But here we are not dealing with a judgement about violence *per se*, but rather with one concerning the alternative of peace and violence; and the judgement rests on the ground that violence has properties which peace has not,

---

[13] Of course, Rousseau's general will may remain a value in the hypothetical world he casts for it, but that concerns Utopia building, not political philosophy.

that the evils obviously attributed to violence are effectively avoided by peace. But if one can show that peace leads to stagnation, and thus to breakdown (and hence eventual chaos or violence) or foreign conquest, then the supposed gap between the two narrows. On the contrary, one is presented with a new alternative, that between more or less controlled violence and the destructive uncontrolled kind associated with internal breakdown or foreign conquest. What the undermining job has done is to destroy the alternative on which the original judgement was based, and thus deprive the previously preferred alternative of its differential property for which it was valued.

But any undermining of this kind is bound to alter the explanatory framework of which the original alternative was an essential part. If we cannot maintain a peaceful polity, then the gamut of possibilities is very different, and Lipset is guilty of neglecting a whole host of factors, to do with the gamut tension-stagnation.

To take the other example, let our objector make a case for rule by the minority. Let him claim that only the minority are creative, that if they are not given preference, then they will not produce, and then everyone will suffer. Thus the supposed difference between rule for the minority and that for all, viz. that the ordinary bloke gets something out of the second that he does not out of the first, is set aside; rather the opposite turns out to be the case. The value is undermined. But so is the political framework altered, for now we have an elitist thesis about the importance of minority rule; another variable has entered the picture which was not present in the previous framework and which cuts across it, in so far as the previous framework presented the possibility of good progressive societies run for all.

Let us hold, however, that violence or elite rule is good for painting, and we have an over-ruling; for it remains the case that it would be better to have no violence and everybody getting a square deal, but alas—

Thus the framework does secrete a certain value position, albeit one that can be over-ridden. In general we can see this arising in the following way: the framework gives us as it were the geography of the range of phenomena in question, it tells us how they can vary, what are the major dimensions of variation. But since we are dealing with matters which are of great importance to human beings, a given map will have, as it were, its own built-in value-slope. That is to say, a given dimension of variation will usually determine for itself how we are to judge of good and bad, because of its relation to obvious human wants and needs.

Now this may seem a somewhat startling result, since it is well known that there are wide differences over what human needs, desires, and purposes are. Not that there is not a wide area of agreement over basic things like life; but this clearly breaks down when one tries to extend the list. There can thus be great disagreement over the putative human need for self-expression or for autonomous development, both of which can and do play important parts in debates and conflicts over political theory.

Does this mean, therefore, that we can reject the previous result and imagine a state of affairs where we could accept the framework of explanation of a given theory, and yet refuse the value judgements it secretes, because we took a different view of the schedule of human needs?[14] Or, to put it another way, does this mean that the step between accepting a framework of explanation and accepting a certain notion of the political good is mediated by a premise concerning human needs, which may be widely enough held to go unnoticed, but which nevertheless can be challenged, thus breaking the connection?

The answer is no. For the connection between a given framework of explanation and a certain notion of the schedule of needs, wants, and purposes which seems to mediate the inference to value theory is not fortuitous. If one adopted a quite different view of human need, one would upset the framework. Thus to pursue another example from Lipset, stable democracies are judged better than stable oligarchies, since the latter can only exist where the majority is so uneducated and tradition-bound or narrowed that it has not yet learned to demand its rights. But suppose we tried to upset this judgement by holding that under-development is good for men, that they are happier when they are led by some unquestioned norms, do not have to think for themselves, and so on? One would then be reversing the value judgement. But at the same time one would be changing the framework. For we are introducing a notion of anomie here, and we cannot suppose this factor to exist without having some important effect on the working of political society. If anomie is the result of the development of education and the breakdown of tradition, then it will affect the stability of the societies which promote this kind of development. They will be subject to constant danger of being undermined as their citizens, suffering from anomie, look for havens of

---

[14] This could involve either an undermining or an over-riding of the value judgement. For we can deny something, a condition or outcome, the property by which it is judged good not only by denying it a property by which it fulfils certain human needs, wants, or purposes, but also by denying that these needs, wants, or purposes exist. And we can over-ride the judgement that it is good by pointing to other needs, wants, or purposes that it frustrates.

certainty. If men are made unhappy by democracy, then undoubtedly it is not as good as its protagonists make out, but it is not so viable either.

The view above that we could accept the framework of explanation and reject the value conclusion by positing a different schedule of needs cannot be sustained. For a given framework is linked to a given conception of the schedule of human needs, wants, and purposes, such that, if the schedule turns out to have been mistaken in some significant way, the framework itself cannot be maintained. This is for the fairly obvious reason that human needs, wants, and purposes have an important bearing on the way people act, and that therefore one has to have a notion of the schedule which is not too wildly inaccurate if one is to establish the framework for any science of human behaviour, that of politics not excepted. A conception of human needs thus enters into a given political theory, and cannot be considered something extraneous which we later add to the framework to yield a set of value judgements.

This is not to say that there cannot be needs or purposes which we might add to those implicit in any framework, and which would not alter the framework since their effect on political events might be marginal. But this would at most give us the ground of an over-ruling, not for an undermining. In order to undermine the valuation we would have to show that the putative need fulfilled was not a need, or that what looked like fulfilling a need, or a want, or a human purpose was really not so, or really did the opposite. Now even an over-ruling might destroy the framework, if a new need were introduced which was important enough motivationally to dictate quite different behaviour. But certainly an undermining, which implies that one has misidentified the schedule of needs, would do so.

3

It would appear from the above example that the adoption of a framework of explanation carries with it the adoption of the 'value-slope' implicit in it, although the valuations can be over-ruled by considerations of an extra-political kind. But it might be objected that the study of one example is not a wide enough base for such a far-reaching conclusion. The example might even be thought to be peculiarly inappropriate because of Lipset's closeness to the tradition of political philosophy, and particularly his esteem for Aristotle.

If we wish, however, to extend the range of examples, we can see immediately that Lipset's theory is not exceptional. There is, for instance, a whole range of theories in which the connection between factual base and valuation is built in, as it were, to the conceptual structure. Such is the case of many theories which make use of the notion of function. To fulfil a function is to meet a requirement of some kind, and when the term is used in social theory, the requirement concerned is generally connected with human needs, wants, and purposes. The requirement or end concerned may be the maintenance of the political system which is seen as essential to man, or the securing of some of the benefits which political systems are in a position to attain for men – stability, security, peace, fulfilment of some wants, and so on. Since politics is largely made up of human purposeful activity, a characterization of political societies in terms of function is not implausible. But in so far as we characterize societies in terms of their fulfilling in different ways and to different degrees the same set of functions, the crucial dimension of variation for explanatory purposes is also a normatively significant one. Those societies which fulfil the functions more completely are *pro tanto* better.

We can take as an example the 'structural-functional' theory of Gabriel Almond as outlined in his *Politics of the Developing Areas*.[15] Among the functions Almond outlines that all polities must fulfil is that of 'interest articulation'. It is an essential part of the process by which the demands, interests, and claims of members of a society can be brought to bear on government and produce some result. Almond sees four main types of structures as involved in interest articulation.[16] Of three of these (institutional, non-associational, and anomic interest groups), he says that a prominent role for them in interest articulation tends to indicate poor 'boundary maintenance', between society and polity. Only the fourth (associational interest groups) can carry the main burden of interest articulation in such a way as to maintain a smooth-running system 'by virtue of the regulatory role of associational interest groups in processing raw claims or interest articulations occurring elsewhere in the society and the political system, and directing them in an orderly way and in aggregable form through the party system, legislature, and bureaucracy'.[17]

The view here is of a flow of raw demands which have to be processed by the system before satisfaction can be meted out. If the processing is inefficient, then the satisfaction will be less, the system will increase frustration, uncertainty, and often as a consequence instability. In this context boundary maintenance between society and polity is important for clarity and efficiency. Speaking of the functions of articulation and aggregation together, Almond says:

[15] Princeton, 1963.   [16] *Ibid.*, p. 33.   [17] *Ibid.*, pp. 35–6.

Thus, to attain a maximum flow of inputs of raw claims from the society, a low level of processing into a common language of claims is required which is performed by associated interest groups. To assimilate and transform these interests into a relatively small number of alternatives of policy and personnel, a middle range of processing is necessary. If these two functions are performed in substantial part before the authoritative governmental structures are reached, then the output functions of rule-making and rule application are facilitated, and the political and governmental processes become calculable and responsible. The outputs may be related to and controlled by the inputs, and thus circulation becomes relatively free by virtue of good boundary maintenance or division of labour.[18]

Thus in characterizing different institutions by the way they articulate or aggregate interests, Almond is also evaluating them. For obviously a society with the above characteristics is preferable to one without; where, that is, there is less free circulation, where 'outputs' correspond less to 'inputs' (what people want, claim, or demand), where government is less responsible, and so on. The characterization of the system in terms of function contains the criteria of 'eufunction' and 'dysfunction', as they are sometimes called. The dimension of variation leaves only one answer to the question, 'Which is better?', because of the clear relation in which it stands to men's wants and needs.

Theories of this kind include not only those which make explicit use of 'function', but also other derivatives of systems theory and frameworks which build on the analogy with organisms. This might be thought to include, for instance, David Easton and Karl Deutsch.[19] For the requirements by which we will judge the performance of different political systems are explicit in the theory.

But what about theories which set out explicitly to separate fact from evaluations, to 'state conditions' without in any way 'justifying preferences'? What about a theory of the 'behavioural' type, like that of Harold Lasswell?

4

Harold Lasswell is clearly a believer in the neutrality of scientific findings. Lasswell is openly committed to certain values, notably those of the democratic society as he defines it, a society 'in which human dignity is

---

[18] *Ibid.*, p. 39.
[19] Easton, *A Framework for Political Analysis* (Englewood Cliffs, NJ, 1965) and *A Systems Analysis of Political Life* (New York, 1965), and Deutsch, *The Nerves of Government* (Glencoe, Ill., 1963).

realized in theory and fact'.[20] He believes that scientific findings can be brought to bear on the realization of these goals. A science so oriented is what he calls a 'policy science'. But this does not affect the neutrality of the findings: a policy science simply determines a certain grouping and selection of findings which help us to encompass the goal we have set. It follows that if there are policy sciences of democracy, there can also be a 'policy science of tyranny'.[21]

In Lasswell's 'configurative analysis', then, both fact and valuation enter; but they remain entirely separable. The following passage from the introduction of *Power and Society* makes the point unambiguously:

The present conception conforms ... to the philosophical tradition in which politics and ethics have always been closely associated. But it deviates from the tradition in giving full recognition to the existence of two distinct components in political theory – empirical propositions of political science and the value judgments of political doctrine. Only statements of the first kind are formulated in the present work.[22]

Yet the implied separation between factual analysis and evaluation is belied by the text itself. In the sections dealing with different types of polity,[23] the authors introduce a number of dimensions of variation of political society. Polities vary (1) as to the allocation of power (between autocracy, oligarchy, republic), (2) as to the scope of power (society either undergoes greater regimentation or liberalization), (3) as to the concentration or dispersion of power (taking in questions concerning the separation of powers, or federalism), (4) as to the degree to which a rule is equalitarian (the degree of equality in power potential), (5) the degree to which it is libertarian or authoritarian, (6) the degree to which it is impartial, (7) and the degree to which it is juridical or tyrannical. Democracy is defined as a rule which is libertarian, juridical, and impartial.

It is not surprising to find one's sympathies growing towards democracy as one ploughs through this list of definitions. For they leave us little choice. Dimension (5) clearly determines our preference. Liberty is defined not just in terms of an absence of coercion, but of genuine responsibility to self. 'A rule is libertarian where initiative, individuality and choice are widespread; authoritarian, if obedience, conformity and coercion are characteristic.'[24] Quoting Spinoza with approval, Lasswell and

---

[20] 'The democratic character', in *Political Writings* (Glencoe, Ill., 1951), p. 473.

[21] *Ibid.*, p. 471n.

[22] *Power and Society* (New Haven, Conn., 1952), p. xiii.

[23] *Ibid.*, chap. 9, sections 3 and 4.

[24] *Ibid.*, p. 228.

Kaplan come down in favour of a notion of liberty as the capacity to 'live by ... free reason'. 'On this conception, there is liberty in a state only where each individual has sufficient self-respect to respect others.'[25]

Thus it is clear that liberty is preferable to its opposite. Many thinkers of the orthodox school, while agreeing with this verdict, might attribute it simply to careless wording on the author's part, to a temporary relaxation of that perpetual vigil which must be maintained against creeping value bias. It is important to point out therefore that the value force here is more than a question of wording. It lies in the type of alternative which is presented to us: on the one hand, a man can be manipulated by others, obeying a law and standards set up by others which he cannot judge; on the other hand, he is developed to the point where he can judge for himself, exercise reason, and apply his own standards; he comes to respect himself and is more capable of respecting others. If this is really the alternative before us, how can we fail to judge freedom better (whether or not we believe there are over-riding considerations)?

Dimension (6) also determines our choice. 'Impartiality' is said to 'correspond in certain ways to the concepts of "justice" in the classical tradition',[26] and an impartial rule is called a 'commonwealth', 'enhancing the value position of all members of the society impartially, rather than that of some restricted class'.[27] Now if the choice is simply between a regime which works for the common good and a regime which works for the good of some smaller group, there is no doubt which is better in the absence of any over-riding considerations.

Similarly dimension (7) is value-determinate. 'Juridical' is opposed to 'tyrannical' and is defined as a state of affairs where 'decisions are made in accord with specified rules ... rather than arbitrarily',[28] or where a 'decision is challenged by an appraisal of it in terms of ... conditions, which must be met by rulers as well as ruled'. Since the alternative presented here is *arbitrary* decision, and one which cannot be checked by any due process, there is no question which is preferable. If we had wanted to present a justification of rule outside law (such as Plato did), we would never accept the adjective 'arbitrary' in our description of the alternative to 'juridical'.

As far as the other dimensions are concerned, the authors relate them to these three key ones, so that they too cannot be seen as neutral, although their value relevance is derivative. Thus voluntarization is better for liberty than regimentation, and the dispersion of power can be seen as

---

[25] *Ibid.*, p. 229.   [26] *Ibid.*, p. 231.   [27] *Ibid.*   [28] *Ibid.*, p. 232.

conducive to juridicalness. In short, we come out with a full-dress justification of democracy, and this in a work which claims neutrality. The work, we are told in the introduction, 'contains no elaborations of political doctrine, of what the state and society *ought* to be'.[29] Even during the very exposition of the section on democracy, there are ritual disclaimers: for instance, when the term 'justice' is mentioned, a parenthesis is inserted: 'the present term, however, is to be understood altogether in a descriptive, non-normative sense';[30] and at the end of the chapter: 'the formulations throughout are descriptive rather than normatively ambiguous'.[31]

But neutral they are not, as we have seen: we cannot accept these descriptions and fail to agree that democracy is a better form of government than its opposite (a 'tyrannical', 'exploitative', 'authoritarian' rule: you can take your choice). Only the hold of the neutrality myth can hide this truth from the authors.

Of course these sections do not represent adequately Lasswell's total work. Indeed, one of the problems in discussing Lasswell is that he has espoused a bewildering variety of conceptual frameworks of explanation. This is evident from a perusal of *Power and Society* alone, quite apart from his numerous other works. These may all cohere in some unified system, but if this is the case, it is far from obvious. Yet the link between factual analysis and evaluation reappears in each of the different approaches. There is not space to cover them all; one further example will have to suffice here.

In the later psychiatrically oriented works, such as *Power and Personality*, 'The democratic character',[32] the goal explicitly set for policy science is democracy. But the implication that this is a goal chosen independently of what is discovered to be true about politics is belied all along the line. For the alternative to a society where people have a 'self-system' which suits the democratic character is one in which various pathologies, often of a dangerous kind, are rampant. The problem of democracy is to create, among other things, a self-system which is 'multi-valued, rather than single-valued, and ... disposed to share rather than to hoard or to monopolize'.[33] One might have some quarrel with this: perhaps single-minded people are an asset to society. But after seeing the alternative to multi-valuedness as set out in the 'Democratic character',[34]

---

[29] *Ibid.*, p. xi.   [30] *Ibid.*, p. 231.   [31] *Ibid.*, p. 239.   [32] *Political Writings.*
[33] *Ibid.*, pp. 497–8.   [34] *Ibid.*, pp. 497–502.

one can understand why Lasswell holds this view. Lasswell lays out for us a series of what he describes frankly at one point as 'character deformations'.[35] In talking about the *homo politicus* who concentrates on the pursuit of power, he remarks 'The psychiatrist feels at home in the study of ardent seekers after power in the arena of politics because the physician recognizes the extreme egocentricity and sly ruthlessness of some of the paranoid patients with whom he has come in contact in the clinic.'[36]

The point here is not that Lasswell introduces valuation illegitimately by the use of subtly weighted language, or unnecessarily pejorative terms. Perhaps politicians do tend to approximate to unbalanced personalities seeking to make up deprivation by any means. The point is that, if this is true, then some important judgements follow about political psychiatry. And these are not, as it were, suspended on some independent value-judgement, but arise from the facts themselves. There *could* be a policy science of tyranny, but then there could also be a medical science aimed at producing disease (as when nations do research into bacteriological warfare). But we could not say that the second was more worthy of pursuit than the first, unless we advanced some very powerful over-riding reasons (which is what proponents of bacteriological warfare try – unsuccessfully – to do). The science of health, however, needs no such special justification.

III

I

The thesis we have been defending, however plausible it may appear in the context of a discussion of the different theories of political science, is unacceptable to an important school of philosophy today. Throughout the foregoing analysis, philosophers will have felt uneasy. For this conclusion tells against the well-entrenched doctrine according to which questions of value are independent of questions of fact; the view which holds that before any set of facts we are free to adopt an indefinite number of value positions. According to the view defended here, on the other hand, a given framework of explanation in political science tends to support an associated value position, secretes its own norms for the assessment of polities and policies.

It is of course this philosophical belief which, because of its immense influence among scientists in general and political scientists as well, has

---

[35] *Ibid.*, p. 500. [36] *Ibid.*, p. 498.

contributed to the cult of neutrality in political science, and the belief that genuine science gives no guidance as to right and wrong. It is time, therefore, to come to grips with this philosophical view.

There are two points about the use of 'good' which are overlooked or negated by the standard 'non-naturalist' view: (1) to apply 'good' may or may not be to commend, but it is always to claim that there are reasons for commending whatever it is applied to, (2) to say of something that it fulfils human needs, wants, or purposes always constitutes a prima facie reason for calling it 'good', that is, for applying the term in the absence of over-riding considerations.[37]

Now the non-naturalist view, as expressed, for instance, by Hare or Stevenson, denies both these propositions. Its starting point is the casting of moral argument in deductive form – all the arguments against the so-called 'naturalistic fallacy' have turned on the validity of deductive inference. The ordinary man may think that he is moving from a factual consideration about something to a judgement that it is good or bad, but in fact one cannot deduce a statement concerning the goodness or badness of something from a statement attributing some descriptive property to it. Thus the ordinary man's argument is really an enthymeme: he is assuming some major premise: when he moves from 'X will make men happy' to 'X is good', he is operating with the suppressed premise 'What makes men happy is good', for only by adding this can one derive the conclusion by valid inference.

To put the point in another way: the ordinary man sees 'X will make men happy' as the reason for his favourable verdict on it. But on the non-naturalist view, it is a reason only because he accepts the suppressed major premise. For one could, logically, reject this premise, and then the conclusion would not follow at all. Hence, that something is a reason for judging X good depends on what values the man who judges holds. Of course, one can find reasons for holding these values; that is, facts from which we could derive the major premise, but only by adopting a higher major which would allow us to derive our first major as a valid conclusion. Ultimately, we have to decide beyond all reasons, as it were, what our values are. For at each stage where we adduce a reason, we have already to have accepted some value (enshrined in a major premise) in virtue of which this reason is

[37] We might also speak of 'interests' here, but this can be seen as included in 'wants' and 'needs'. Interest may deviate from want, but can only be explicated in terms of such concepts as 'satisfaction', 'happiness', 'unhappiness', etc., the criteria for whose application are ultimately to be found in what we want.

valid. But then our ultimate major premises stand without reasons; they are the fruit of a pure choice.

Proposition (1) above, then, is immediately denied by non-naturalism. For in the highest major premises 'good' is applied to commend without the claim that there are reasons for this commendation. And (2) also is rejected, for nothing can claim always to constitute a reason for calling something good. Whether it does or not depends on the decisions a man has made about his values, and it is not logically impossible that he should decide to consider human needs, wants, and purposes irrelevant to judgements about good and bad. A reason is always a reason-for-somebody, and has this status because of the values he has accepted.

The question at issue, then, is first, whether 'good' can be used where there are no reasons, either evident or which can be cited for its application.[38] Consider the following case:[39] There are two segregationists who disapprove of miscegenation. The first claims that mixing races will produce general unhappiness, a decline in the intellectual capacity and moral standards of the race, the abolition of a creative tension, and so on. The second, however, refuses to assent to any of these beliefs; the race will not deteriorate, men may even be happier; in any case they will be just as intelligent, moral, etc. But, he insists, miscegenation is bad. When challenged to produce some substitute reason for this judgement, he simply replies: 'I have no reasons; everyone is entitled, indeed has to accept some higher major premise and stop the search for reasons somewhere. I have chosen to stop here, rather than seeking grounds in such fashionable quarters as human happiness, moral stature, etc.' Or supposing he looked at us in puzzlement and said: 'Reasons? why do you ask for reasons? Miscegenation is just bad.'

Now no one would question that the first segregationist was making the judgement 'miscegenation is bad'. But in the case of the second, a difficulty arises. This can be seen as soon as we ask the question: how can we tell whether the man is really making a judgement about the badness of miscegenation and not just, say, giving vent to a strongly felt repulsion, or a neurotic phobia against sexual relations between people of different races? Now it is essential to the notions 'good' and 'bad' as we use them in judgements that there be a distinction of this kind between these judgements and

---

[38] In what follows I am indebted to the arguments of Mrs P. Foot, e.g. to her 'When is a principle a moral principle?', *Aristotelian Society, Supplementary Vol. xxviii* (1954), and her 'Moral Arguments', *Mind*, ASSV lxvii (1958), although I do not know whether she would agree with the conclusions I draw from them.

[39] Borrowed with changes from Hare's *Freedom and Reason* (Oxford, 1963).

expressions of horror, delight, liking, disliking, and so on. It is essential that we be able, e.g. to correct a speaker by saying : 'What you want to say would be better put as "miscegenation horrifies me", or "miscegenation makes me go all creepy inside".' Because it is an essential part of the grammar of 'good' and 'bad' that they claim more than is claimed by expressions of delight, horror, etc. For we set aside someone's judgement that X is good when we say: 'All you are saying is that you *like* X.' To which the man can hotly reply: 'I do not like X any more than you do, but I recognize that it is good.'

There must therefore be criteria of distinction between these two cases if 'good' and 'bad' are to have the grammar that they have. But if we allow that our second segregationist is making the judgement 'miscegenation is bad', then no such distinction can be made. A judgement that I like something does not need grounds. That is, the absence of grounds does not undermine the claim 'I like X' (though other things, e.g. in my behaviour, may undermine it). But unless we adduce reasons for it (and moreover reasons of a certain kind as we shall see below) we cannot show that our claim that X is good says more than 'I like X.' Thus a man can only defend himself against the charge that all he is saying is that he likes X by giving his grounds. If there are no grounds, then judgement becomes indistinguishable from expression; which means that there are no more judgements of good and bad, since the distinction is essential to them, as we have seen.

Those who believe in the fact–value dichotomy have naturally tried to avoid this conclusion; they have tried to distinguish the two cases by fastening on the use made of judgements of good and bad in commending, prescribing, expressing approval, and so on. Thus, no matter what a man's grounds, if any, we could know that he was making a judgement of good and bad by the fact that he was commending, prescribing, or committing himself to pursue the thing in question, or something of the kind. But this begs the question, for we can raise the query: what constitutes commending, or prescribing, or committing myself, or expressing approval, or whatever? How does one tell whether a man is doing one of these things as against just giving vent to his feelings?

If we can say that we can tell by what the man accepts as following from his stand – whether he accepts that he should strive to realize the thing in question – then the same problem breaks out afresh: how do we distinguish his accepting the proposition that he should seek the end and his just being hell-bent on seeking this end? Presumably, both our segregationists would agree that they should fight miscegenation, but this would still leave us just as puzzled and uncertain about the position of the second. Perhaps we can tell by whether they are willing to universalize their prescription? But here again we have no touchstone, for both segregationists would assent that everyone should seek racial purity, but the question would remain open whether this had a different meaning in the two cases. Perhaps the second one just means that he cannot stand interracial mating, whether done by himself or by anyone else. Similarly, a compulsive may keep his hands scrupulously clean and feel disgust at the uncleanliness of others, even plead with them to follow his example; but we still want to distinguish his case from one who had judged that cleanliness was good.

Can we fall back on behavioural criteria, meaning by 'behaviour' what a man does in contrast to how he thinks about what he does? But there is no rea. n why a man with a neurotic phobia against X should not do all the things which the man who judges X is bad does, i.e. avoiding X himself, trying to stop others from doing it, and so on.

Thus the non-naturalists would leave us with no criteria except what the man was willing to say. But then we would have no way of knowing whether the words were correctly applied or not, which is to say that they would have no meaning. All that we achieve by trying to mark the distinction by what follows from the judgement is that the same question which we raised about 'X is bad' as against 'X makes me shudder' can be raised about the complex 'X is bad, I/you should not do X' as against the complex 'X makes me shudder, please I/you do not do X.' We simply appeal from what the man is willing to say on the first question to what he is willing to say on the second. The distinction can only be properly drawn if we look to the reasons for the judgement, and this is why a judgement without reasons cannot be allowed, for it can no longer be distinguished from an expression of feeling.[40]

---

[40] We may use behaviour, of course, to judge which of the two constructions to put on a man's words, but the two are not distinguished by behavioural criteria alone, but also by what a man thinks and feels. It is possible, of course, to challenge a man's even sincere belief that he is judging of good and bad, and to disvalue it on the grounds that one holds it to be based largely on irrational prejudice or unavowed ambitions or fears. Thus our first segregationist may be judged as not too different from our second. For there is some evidence that segregationist ideas can at least partly be assimilated to neurotic phobias in their psychological roots. But this is just why many people look on the judgements of segregationists as self-deception and unconscious sham. 'Really', they are just expressions of horror. But this respects the logic of 'good' as we have outlined it: for it concludes that if the rational base is mere show, then the judgement is mere show. Segregationists, for their part, rarely are of the second type, and pay homage to the logic of 'good' by casting about for all sorts of specious reasons of the correct form.

2

This analysis may sound plausible for 'miscegenation is bad', but how about 'anything conducive to human happiness is good'? What can we say here, if asked to give grounds for this affirmation? The answer is that we can say nothing, but also we need say nothing. For that something conduces to human happiness is already an adequate ground for judging it good – adequate, that is, in the absence of countervailing considerations. We come, then to the second point at issue, the claim that to say of something that it fulfils human needs, wants or purposes always constitutes a prima facie reason for calling it 'good'.

For in fact it is not just necessary that there be grounds for the affirmation if we are to take it at its face value as an attribution of good or bad, they must also be grounds of a certain kind. They must be grounds which relate in some intelligible way to what men need, desire, or seek after. This may become clearer if we look at another example. Suppose a man says: 'To make medical care available to more people is good'; suppose, then, that another man wishes to deny this. We could, of course, imagine reasons for this: world population will grow too fast, there are other more urgent claims on scarce resources, the goal can only be obtained by objectionable social policies, such as socialized medicine, and so on. The espousal of any of these would make the opposition to the above judgement intelligible, even if not acceptable, and make it clear that it was *this* judgement that was being denied, and not just, say, an emotional reaction which was being countered with another. If, however, our objector said nothing, and claimed to have nothing to say, his position would be unintelligible, as we have seen; or else we would construe his words as expressing some feeling of distaste or horror or sadness at the thought.

But supposing he was willing to give grounds for his position, but none of the above or their like, saying instead, for instance, 'There would be too many doctors', or 'Too many people would be dressed in white'? We would remain in doubt as to how to take his opposition, for we would be led to ask of his opposition to the increase of doctors, say, whether he was making a judgement concerning good and bad or simply expressing a dislike. And we would decide this question by looking at grounds he adduced for *this* position. And if he claimed to have nothing to say, his position would be unintelligible in exactly the same way as if he had decided to remain silent at the outset and leave his original statement unsupported. 'What is this?' we would say, 'You are against an increase in medical services, because it would increase the number of doctors? But are you just expressing the feelings of dislike that doctors evoke in you or are you really trying to tell us that the increase is bad?' In the absence of any defence on his part, we would take the first interpretation.

It is clear that the problem would remain unsolved, if our opponent grounded his opposition to doctors on the fact that they generally wore dark suits, or washed their hands frequently. We might at this point suspect him of having us on. So that the length or elaboration of the reasoning has nothing to do with the question one way or another.

What would make his position intelligible, and intelligible as a judgement of good and bad, would be his telling some story about the evil influence doctors exercise on society, or the sinister plot they were hatching to take over and exploit the rest of mankind, or something of the kind. For this would relate the increase of doctors in an intelligible way to the interests, needs, or purposes of men. In the absence of such a relation, we remain in the dark, and are tempted to assume the worst.

What is meant by 'intelligibility' here is that we can understand the judgement as a use of 'good' and 'bad'. It is now widely agreed that a word gets its meaning from its place in the skein of discourse; we can give its meaning, for instance, by making clear its relations to other words. But this is not to say that we can give the meaning in a set of logical relations of equivalence, entailment, and so on, that an earlier positivism saw as the content of philosophical endeavour. For the relation to other terms may pass through a certain context. Thus, there is a relation between 'good' and commending, expressing approval, and so on. But this is not to say that we can construe 'X is good', for instance, as *meaning* 'I commend X.'[41] Rather, we can say that 'good' can be used for commending, that to apply the word involves being ready to commend in certain circumstances, for if you are not then you are shown to have been unserious in your application of it, and so on.[42]

The relation between 'good' and commending, expressing approval, persuading, and so on, has been stressed by non-naturalist theorists of ethics (though not always adequately understood, because of the narrow concentration on logical relations), but the term has another set of relations, to the grounds of its predication, as we have tried to show. These two aspects correspond respectively to what has often been called the

---

[41] Cf. John Searle's 'Meaning and speech acts', *Philosophical Review*, 71 (1962) 423–32.

[42] Thus, if I say, 'This is a good car', and then my friend comes along and says, 'Help me choose a car', I have to eat my words if I am not willing to commend the car to him, *unless* I can adduce some other countervailing factor such as price, my friend's proclivity to dangerous driving, or whatever. But this complex relationship cannot be expressed in an equivalence, e.g. 'This is a good car' entails 'If you are choosing a car, take this.'

evaluative, emotive, or prescriptive meaning on one hand (depending on the theory) and the 'descriptive' meanings on the other. For half a century an immense barrage of dialectical artillery has been trained on the so-called 'naturalistic fallacy' in an effort to prize 'good' loose from any set range of descriptive meanings. But this immense effort has been beside the point, for it has concentrated on the non-existence of logical relations between descriptive predicates and evaluative terms. But the fact that one cannot find equivalences, make valid deductive argument, and so on, may show nothing about the relation between a given concept and others.

Just as with the 'evaluative' meaning above, so with the 'descriptive' meaning: 'good' does not *mean* 'conducive to the fulfilment of human wants, needs, or purposes'; but its use is unintelligible outside of any relationship to wants, needs, and purposes, as we saw above. For if we abstract from this relation, then we cannot tell whether a man is using 'good' to make a judgement, or simply express some feeling; and it is an essential part of the meaning of the term that such a distinction can be made. The 'descriptive'[43] aspects of 'good's' meaning can rather be shown in this way: 'good' is used in evaluating, commending, persuading, and so on by a race of beings who are such that through their needs, desires, and so on, they are not indifferent to the various outcomes of the world-process. A race of inactive, godless angels, as really disinterested spectators, would have no use for it, could not make use of it, except in the context of cultural anthropology, just as human anthropologists use 'mana'. It is because 'good' has this use, and can only have meaning because there is this role to fill in human life, that it becomes unintelligible when abstracted from this role. Because its having a use arises from the fact that we are not indifferent, its use cannot be understood where we cannot see what there is to be not-indifferent about, as in the strange 'grounds' quoted by our imaginary opponent above. Moreover, its role is such that it is supposed to be predicated on general grounds, and not just according to the likes and dislikes or feelings of individuals. This distinction is essential since (among other things) the race concerned spends a great deal of effort achieving and maintaining consensus within larger or smaller groups, without which it would not survive. But where we cannot

---

[43] The terms 'descriptive meaning' and 'evaluative meaning' can be seen to be seriously misleading, as is evident from the discussion. For they carry the implication that the meaning is 'contained' in the word, and can be 'unpacked' in statements of logical equivalence. There is rather a descriptive aspect and an evaluative aspect of its role or use, which are, moreover, connected, for we cannot see whether a use of the term carries the evaluation force of 'good' unless we can also see whether it enters into the skein of relations which constitute the descriptive dimension of its meaning.

see what the grounds could be, we are tempted to go on treating the use of 'good' as an expression of partiality, only of the more trivial, individual kind.

We can thus see why, for instance, 'anything conducive to human happiness is good' does not need any further grounds to be adduced on its behalf. In human happiness, which by definition men desire, we have an adequate ground. This does not mean that all argument is foreclosed. We can try to show that men degenerate in .various ways if they seek only happiness, and that certain things which also make men unhappy are necessary for their development. Or we can try to show that there is a higher and a lower happiness, that most men seek under this title only pleasure, and that this turns them away from genuine fulfilment; and so on. But unless we can bring up some countervailing consideration, we cannot deny a thesis of this kind. The fact that we can always bring up such countervailing considerations means that we can never say that 'good' *means* 'conducive to human happiness', as Moore saw. But that something is conducive to human happiness, or in general to the fulfil-ment of human needs, wants, and purposes, is a prima facie reason for calling it good, which stands unless countered.

Thus the non-neutrality of the theoretical findings of political science need not surprise us. In setting out a given framework, a theorist is also setting out the gamut of possible polities and policies. But a *political* framework cannot fail to contain some, even implicit, conception of human needs, wants, and purposes. The context of this conception will determine the value-slope of the gamut, unless we can introduce countervailing considerations. If these countervailing factors are motiva-tionally marginal enough not to have too much relevance to political behaviour, then we can speak of the original valuation as being only over-ridden. For that part of the gamut of possibilities which we origin-ally valued still has the property we attributed to it and thus remains valuable for us in one aspect, even if we have to give it low marks in another. For instance, we still will believe that having a peaceful polity is good, even if it results in bad art. But if the countervailing factor is significant for political behaviour, then it will lead us to revise our framework and hence our views about the gamut of possible polities and policies; this in turn will lead to new valuations. The basis of the old values will be undermined. Thus, if we believe that an absence of violence will lead to stagnation and foreign conquest or breakdown, then we change the gamut of possibility: the choice no longer lies between peace and violence, but between, say, controlled violence and greater uncontrolled violence. Peace ceases to figure on the register: it is not a good we can attain.

Of course, the countervailing factor may not revise our gamut of choices so dramatically. It may simply show that the values of our originally preferred regime cannot be integrally fulfilled or that they will be under threat from a previously unsuspected quarter, or that they will be attended with dangers or disadvantages or disvalues not previously taken into account, so that we have to make a choice as in the peace-versus-good-art case above. Thus not all alterations of the framework will undermine the original values. But we can see that the converse does hold, and all undermining will involve a change in the framework. For if we leave the original framework standing, then the values of its preferred regime will remain as fully realizable goods, even if they are attended with certain evils which force on us a difficult choice, such as that between peace and good art, or progress and psychic harmony, or whatever.

In this sense we can say that a given explanatory framework secretes a notion of good, and a set of valuations, which cannot be done away with – though they can be over-ridden – unless we do away with the framework. Of course because the values can be over-ridden, we can only say that the framework tends to support them, not that it establishes their validity. But this is enough to show that the neutrality of the findings of political science is not what it was thought to be. For establishing a given framework restricts the range of value positions which can be defensibly adopted. For in the light of the framework certain goods can be accepted as such without further argument, whereas other rival ones cannot be adopted without adducing over-riding considerations. The framework can be said to distribute the onus of argument in a certain way. It is thus not neutral.

The only way to avoid this while doing political science would be to stick to the narrow-gauge discoveries which, just because they are, taken alone, compatible with a great number of political frameworks, can bathe in an atmosphere of value neutrality. That Catholics in Detroit tend to vote Democrat can consort with almost anyone's conceptual scheme, and thus with almost anyone's set of political values. But to the extent that political science cannot dispense with theory, with the search for a framework, to that extent it cannot stop developing normative theory.

Nor need this have the vicious results usually attributed to it. There is nothing to stop us making the greatest attempts to avoid bias and achieve objectivity. Of course, it is hard, almost impossible, and precisely because our values are also at stake. But it helps, rather than hinders, the cause to be aware of this.

CHAPTER THREE

SOCIAL THEORY AS PRACTICE

In this chapter and the next, I want to argue that we could gain a great deal by examining our theorizing about social matters as a *practice*. My claim is that the activities of searching for, creating, espousing and rejecting theories are too little understood, and that they are far from being unproblematic, as we often assume in our concern to focus on the *content* of our theories.

Moreover, I want to maintain that gaining clarity about the practice of theorizing will help us to understand more about the scope and validity of our theories. Being more reflectively clear about what we do in our theoretical activity will help us to answer questions which we cannot even properly pose as long as we remain convinced that social theory is a straightforward matter of designing hypotheses and comparing them to the facts.[1]

In particular, I hope to throw light on two important questions in what follows. The first concerns how we validate social theories. The second starts from the answer to the first and asks what is involved in offering a theoretical account of societies very different from our own.

I

What makes the whole matter appear unproblematical to us is the hold of what I want to call the natural science model, the widespread view that the natural sciences can provide us with paradigms for the methods and procedures of social science. We *think* we understand the activity of exploring nature. Here, too, we are certainly over-complacent. But we tell ourselves a tolerably clear story of what goes on in natural science, and the very success of our research seems to indicate that we have here the

---

[1] I realize that there are important points of convergence between the views I'm defending here and the thesis of Pierre Bourdieu in his very interesting book, *Outline of a Theory of Practice* (Cambridge, 1977), but he has a somewhat different starting point and works within a different tradition.

norm for science in general. The prestige of this norm then stops further enquiry.

But this is in fact disastrous. I want to try to show this first by examining the relation of theory to practice, that is, of the practice of theorizing to the other practices which theory guides. Let us look first at the model the natural sciences offer of this relation.

Let us take the example of physical theory. This gives us, among other things, a picture of underlying mechanisms or processes which explain the causal properties and powers of the things we are familiar with. We know that the kettle will heat up in contact with the fire; the kinetic theory will tell us what underlies this heat transmission, so that we understand it as consisting more fundamentally in a transfer of kinetic energy. But in some cases, the picture of the underlying reality turns out to be surprising, or strange, or paradoxical, in the light of our ordinary common-sense understanding of things. We have to adopt quite a radically revised view about the nature of things to explain what goes on.

But part of what is involved in having a better theory is being able more effectively to cope with the world. We are able to intervene successfully to effect our purposes in a way that we were not before. Just as our common-sense pre-understanding was in part a knowing how to cope with the things around us, so the explanatory theory which partly replaces and extends it must give us some of what we need to cope better. Theory relates to practice in an obvious way. We apply our knowledge of the underlying mechanisms in order to manipulate more effectively the features of our environment.

There is a constant temptation to take natural science theory as a model for social theory: that is, to see theory as offering an account of underlying processes and mechanisms of society, and as providing the basis of a more effective planning of social life. But for all the superficial analogies, social theory can never really occupy this role. It is part of a significantly different activity.

There is, of course, an analogy. Social theory is also concerned with finding a more satisfactory fundamental description of what is happening. The basic question of all social theory is in a sense: what is really going on? We have to ask this question because our common-sense descriptions of what is happening are inadequate, or sometimes even illusory. They fail to give us an explanatory grip on our situation, or to help us act effectively. And the answers offered by theory can be surprising, strange, even shocking to common-sense.

But the big disanalogy with natural science lies in the nature of the common-sense understanding that theory challenges, replaces or extends. There is always a pre-theoretical understanding of what is going on among the members of a society, which is formulated in the descriptions of self and other which are involved in the institutions and practices of that society. A society is among other things a set of institutions and practices, and these cannot exist and be carried on without certain self-understandings.

Take the practice of deciding things by majority vote. It carries with it certain standards, of valid and invalid voting, and valid and invalid results, without which it would not be the practice that it is. For instance, it is understood that each participant makes an independent decision. If one can dictate to the others how they vote, we all understand that *this* practice is not being properly carried out. The point of it is to concatenate a social decision out of individual decisions. So only certain kinds of interaction are legitimate. This norm of individual independence is, one might say, constitutive of the practice.

But then those who carry on this practice must, in general and for the most part, be aware of this norm and of its application to their own action. As they vote, they will generally be capable of describing what is going on in terms like these: 'this is a valid vote', or 'there is something dubious about that', or 'that's foul play'. These descriptions may of course be mistaken; but the point is that awareness of this kind is an essential condition for a population's engaging in this practice. If no one involved had any sense of how their behaviour checked out on this dimension, then they would not be engaged in *voting*. They would have to be carrying on some other activity which involved marking papers, some game that we do not yet understand.

In this way, we say that the practices which make up a society require certain self-descriptions on the part of the participants. These self-descriptions can be called constitutive. And the understanding formulated in these can be called pre-theoretical, not in the sense that it is necessarily uninfluenced by theory, but in that it does not rely on theory. There may be no systematic formulation of the norms, and the conception of man and society which underlies them. The understanding is implicit in our ability to apply the appropriate descriptions to particular situations and actions.

In a sense, we could say that social theory arises when we try to formulate explicitly what we are doing, describe the activity which is central to a practice, and articulate the norms which are essential to it. We could imagine a society where people decided things by majority vote, and had a lively sense of what was fair and foul, but had not yet worked out explicitly the norm of individual independence and its rationale in the context of the practice. In one clear sense, their doing so would amount to a step into theory.

But in fact the framing of theory rarely consists simply of making some continuing practice explicit. The stronger motive for making and adopting theories is the sense that our implicit understanding is in some way crucially inadequate or even wrong. Theories do not just make our constitutive self-understandings explicit, but extend, or criticize or even challenge them. It is in this sense that theory makes a claim to tell us what is really going on, to show us the real, hitherto unidentified course of events.

We can distinguish some of the forms this kind of claim can take: it may be that we see what is really going on only when we situate what we are doing in a causal matrix which we had not seen or understood. Marx's theory provides a classic example of this kind of claim: the proletarian is engaged in making contracts with independent owners of capital to exchange his labour power for wages. What he fails to see is that the process in which he so engages by contract is building the entrepreneur as owner of capital, and entrenching his own status as an agent without other recourse than selling his labour for subsistence. What looks like an activity between independent agents is actually part of a process which attributes to these agents their relative positions and status.

In this case, the constitutive self-understanding which is upset is that which belongs to the activity of making and fulfilling contracts between independent agents. On one level, this self-understanding is not wrong; and it is certainly constitutive of a capitalist society in Marx's view. That is, workers have to understand themselves as free labourers in order to be proletarians. But when we see it in the broader matrix, its significance is in an important way reversed. What seemed a set of independent actions are now seen as determined and forced. What seemed like one's making the best of a bad job now is seen as a yoke imposed on one.

But the Marxist theory also upsets the political self-understanding described above, that of decision by majority vote in 'bourgeois' society. For in fact the matrix of the capitalist economy severely restricts the choices open. Options which reduce profitability threaten everyone with economic decline, and potential mass unemployment. These severe limits will in general mean that the very options which are offered to voters will be pre-shrunk, as it were, to be compatible with the continued unhampered operation of the capitalist economy. So once again, what looks like a collective decision freely compounded out of the autonomous individual choices is in fact structurally determined. Or so the story goes according to this theory.

This is one kind of claim, which alters or even overturns our ordinary everyday understanding, on the grounds that our action takes place in an unperceived causal context, and that this gives it a quite different nature. But there are also theories which challenge ordinary self-understanding and claim that our actions have a significance we do not recognize. But this is not in virtue of an unperceived causal context, but because of what one could call a moral context to which we are allegedly blind.

Plato's picture of the decay of the polis in the Republic provides a well-known example of this: what seems like the competition of equals for place and fame is in fact a fatal abandonment of moral order, engendering a chaos which cannot but deepen until it must be brought to an end in tyranny. The inner connection between democracy and tyranny is hidden from the participating citizen, because he cannot understand his action against the background of the true order of things. He just stumbles from one to the other.

In our day, there are a number of theories of this kind abroad. We can think on one hand of Freudian-influenced theories, which portray the real motivations of political actors, and the real sources of political power and prestige quite differently from the rational, instrumental, utilitarian forms of justification that we usually provide for our choices and allegiances. Or think on the other side of the picture often presented by opponents of the culture of growth: we blind ourselves to the importance to us of a harmony with nature and community in order the more effectively to sacrifice these to economic progress. Indeed, some of the most influential of these theories critical of growth find their roots in Plato. We have only to think of the late E. F. Schumacher.

Critical theories of this kind often propound some conception of false consciousness. That is, they see the blindness in question as not just ignorance, but in some sense motivated, even wilful. This is not to say that theories which portray our action as taking place in a broader causal context cannot also invoke false consciousness. Marxism is a case in point. They must do so to the extent that the causal context is one that ought normally to be evident, so that its non-perception is something we have to explain. But this need for a special explanation of non-perception becomes the more obvious when what we allegedly fail to appreciate is the moral or human significance of our action.

There is a particular kind of theory which is sometimes invoked to challenge our everyday understanding that I would like to single out here, because it will be important in the later discussion. Theories of this kind refer to what I will call shared goods. By 'shared good', I mean something different and stronger than mere convergent good, where people may have a common interest in something. A good is shared when part of what makes it a good is precisely that it is shared, that is, sought after and cherished in common. Thus the inhabitants of a river valley have a common interest in preventing floods. This is to say that each one has an interest in the same flood prevention, and this is so irrespective of whether they have some common understanding of it, or indeed, whether they form a community at all. By contrast, shared goods are essentially of a community; their common appreciation is constitutive of them.

The well-known example is the one central to the tradition of civic humanism, the citizen republic. This takes its character from its law; so that the citizen's action takes on a crucial significance by its relation to the laws: whether it tends to preserve them, or undermine them, to defend them from external attack, or to weaken them before enemies, and so on. But the good here is essentially shared. The laws are significant not *qua* mine, but *qua* ours; what gives them their importance for me is not that they are a rule *I* have adopted. The culture in which this could confer importance is a quite different one, a culture of individual responsibility, perhaps even incompatible with that of the republic. Rather the laws are important because they are *ours*. And this cannot simply mean, of course, that our private rules converge on them; their being ours is a matter of our recognizing them as such together, in public space. In other words, that the significance is shared is a crucial part of what is significant here. Public space is a crucial category for republics, as Rousseau saw.

Some theorists in our tradition have taken shared goods seriously. They include, I believe, Aristotle, Machiavelli, Montesquieu, Rousseau, de Tocqueville; in our day, Arendt and Habermas, to mention just two. A rather diverse lot. But a central notion they share is that having important meanings in common puts us on a different footing with each other, and allows us to operate as a society in a radically different way. The thinkers of the civic humanist tradition were interested in how men could become capable of acting together in a spontaneously self-disciplining way, the secret of the strength of republics. Machiavelli, indeed, saw this as the secret of strength in the most direct and crude military terms. But the general insight shared by all thinkers of this cast is that our way of acting together is qualitatively different when we act out of shared significance. This is the basis of what Hannah Arendt called 'power', attempting to redefine the term in the process.

This can be the basis for a challenge to our everyday understanding, where this takes on an atomist cast, as it frequently does in contemporary Western society. People often tend to construe the political process, for instance, as constituted by actions for purely individual goals. The only common goods recognized are convergent. Society is understood as the interaction of individual agents. This self-understanding is challenged by theories of shared goods, with the claim that our actions also take place in a context of shared ends, which our everyday conception does not acknowledge. What we do may strengthen or undermine our shared goods, but this significance of our action escapes us. So that we can, for instance, be in process of destroying our republican political community blindly. The destructive import of our action is lost on us. Of course, this kind of theory can appear paradoxical, since it seems to be supposing that some goods which are shared are not fully perceived. But I hope to show later on how this paradox can be resolved, and that a theory of this kind must be taken quite seriously.

In any case, we have seen several ways in which theory can claim to tell us what is really going on in society, challenging and upsetting our normal self-descriptions, either through identifying an unperceived causal context of our action, or by showing that it has a significance that we fail to appreciate. And I suppose, in order to make this list a trifle less incomplete, I should add that theories are not necessarily as challenging to our self-understanding as the ones I have mentioned here. They can have the function just of clarifying or codifying the significance which is already implicit in our self-descriptions, as I indicated earlier. For instance, some elaborate theory of the order of being, and the related hierarchy of social functions, may fit perfectly into the practices of a stratified society. It may simply codify, or give explicit expression, to the habits of precedence and deference already in being.

And the theories of the causal context can play the same unchallenging role. Since the eighteenth century, our culture is saturated with theories of the economy, which show the train of transactions effecting the production and distribution of goods as following laws. These purport to make us aware of regularities in the social process of which we would otherwise be ignorant. But this knowledge may just complement our self-understanding, not overthrow it. Not all theories of political economy are revolutionary. This was Marx's complaint.

Relative to the 'democratic' picture of ourselves above as deciding matters through majority vote, certain theories of the economy are not at all upsetting. They present us, for instance, with a picture of 'consumer sovereignty', matching in parallel our political image of voter sovereignty. These theories of the economy promise to show us how to design policies which are more effective, which intervene with greater awareness and hence success in the underlying processes of the economy. To do this, as with any application of technology, we have to respect the scientific laws governing this domain. But this is not seen as making a sham of choice, as in the Marxist picture.

II

These theories challenging or not, all claim, to tell us what is really going on. This was the analogy with natural science. But the disanalogy emerges when we see what introducing social theory brings about. The case is different here, because the common-sense view which theory upsets or extends plays a crucial, constitutive role in our practices. This will frequently mean that the alteration in our understanding which theory brings about can alter these practices; so that, unlike with natural science, the theory is not about an independent object, but one that is partly constituted by self-understanding.

Thus a challenging theory can quite undermine a practice, by showing that its essential distinctions are bogus, or have a quite different meaning. What on the 'democratic' picture looks like unconstrained choice is presented as unyielding domination by Marxist theory. But that means that one of the constitutive norms of the practice of majority decision is shown as in principle unfulfillable. The practice is shown to be a sham, a charade. It cannot remain unaffected. People will treat this practice and the connected institutions (e.g., legislatures) very differently if they become convinced of the challenging theory. But this is not a matter of some psychological effect of further information. The disruptive consequences of the theory flow from the nature of the practice, in that one of its constitutive props has been knocked away. This is because the practice requires certain descriptions to make sense, and it is these that the theory undermines.

Theory can also have the radically opposite effect. An interpretation of our predicament can give added point to our practices, or show them to be even more significant than we had thought. This is, for example, the effect of a theory of the chain of being in an hierarchical society. Relative to our 'democratic' picture, some theory which showed that important economic or other issues are up for grabs, and await our determination, would have the same heightening effect.

But a theory can do more than undermine or strengthen practices. It can shape or alter our way of carrying them out by offering an interpretation of the constitutive norms. Let us start again from our picture of 'democratic' decision by majority rule, the picture which is implicit in our practices of elections and voting. There are a number of ways of understanding this process. We can see this by contrasting two of them.

On one hand, we have an atomist model, which sees society as a locus of collaboration and rivalry between independent agents with their individual goals. Different social arrangements and different dispositions of society's resources affect the plans of members differently. So there is naturally struggle and competition over policy and position. 'Democratic' decision-making allows people equal input and weight in determining how things are disposed, or tolerably near to this. This view might be made more sophisticated, so that we see the political system as open to 'inputs' in the form of 'demands' and 'supports', and as producing as output an 'authoritative allocation of values', in which case we could develop quite a complex intellectual grip to describe/explain the political process.[2]

Quite different from that would be a republican model, issuing from one of the theories of shared goods mentioned above. From this standpoint the atomist theory is ignoring one of the most crucial dimensions of social life, viz., the degree to which the society constitutes a political community, that is, the kind and degree of shared ends. A society in which all goals are really those of individuals, as they are portrayed in the atomist scheme, would be an extreme case, and a degenerate one. It would be a society so fragmented that it was capable of very little common action, and was constantly on the point of stasis or stalemate.

A society strong in its capacity for common action would be one with important shared goods. But to the extent that this was so, the process of common decision would have to be understood differently. It could not just be a matter of how and whose individual demands are fed through to the process of decision, but would also have to be understood at least partly as the process of formulating a common understanding of what was required by the shared goals and values. These are, of course, the two

---

[2] David Easton, *The Political System* (New York, 1953), and *A Systems Analysis of Political Life* (New York, 1965).

models of decision that are invoked in the first two books of the *Social Contract*. Rousseau's aim is to show how one can move from the first to the second; so that we no longer ask ourselves severally, what is in our individual interest (our particular will), but rather what is the proper content of the general will. The proper mode of social choice is where the policy selected is agreed upon under the right intentional description. It is vital that it be adopted as the right form of a common purpose, and not as the point of convergence of individual aims. The latter gives us merely *la volonté de tous*, whereas a true community is ruled by its *volonté générale*.

Rousseau thus presents in very schematic sketch the notion of a certain form of social decision, which for all those thinkers who fall in the civic humanist tradition is seen as normative. Societies fail to have true unity, cohesion, strength to the extent that their decisions emerge from the will of all as against the general will. The immense gap between the atomist and general will theories is thus clear. What the second sees as a defining feature of the degenerate case is understood by the first as a structural feature of all societies. Which is just another way of saying that what is for the second the crucial dimension of variation among societies is quite unrecognized by the first.

But it ought to be clear that the general acceptance of either of these models will have an important effect on the practices of social decision. These practices may be established in certain institutions, which may be the same from society to society, or in the same society over time. But within this similarity, the way of operating these institutions will obviously be very different according to whether one or the other model is dominant, that is, has become the accepted interpretation. Where the atomist model is dominant, decision-making of the general will form will be severely hampered, suppressed and confused. Where on the contrary some self-understanding of common meanings is dominant, the scope for will-of-all decisions will be circumscribed within the bounds of explicit common goals.

Indeed, there might be no quarrel with this point about the effect of these theories. The problem might be seeing why their effect is not greater; why, for instance, the dominance of atomist theories does not put paid to general will decisions altogether. The answer lies in the fact that a theory is the making explicit of a society's life, that is, a set of institutions and practices. It may shape these practices, but it does not replace them. So even though some feature may find no place in the reigning theory, it may still be a constitutive part of a living practice.

The notion of the general will can be seen as a way of formulating the constitutive norm of decision-making for communities with shared goods. Even if this norm remains unformulated and unrecognized, it may still be that the community retains certain shared goods. These will still be central to certain of its practices, for example, to the kinds of arguments that are acceptable/unacceptable in public debate, even if there is no theoretical formulation of why this is so. Shared goods may be reflected in the norms strongly held to govern public life, or in the ceremonial surrounding the state, even where they have dropped out of the accounts of politics that citizens give to themselves and others.

Of course, these goods will be considerably restricted, and much less vigorous in public life than where they are explicitly acknowledged. And they will certainly be in danger of eclipse. But they may nevertheless still be operative. Theory can never be the simple determinant of practice. I want to claim later that something like this gap between theory and practice is true of our society.

This is the striking disanalogy between natural science and political theories. The latter can undermine, strengthen or shape the practice that they bear on. And that is because (a) they are theories about practices, which (b) are partly constituted by certain self-understandings. To the extent that (c) theories transform this self-understanding, they undercut, bolster or transform the constitutive features of practices. We could put this another way by saying that political theories are not about independent objects in the way that theories are in natural science. There the relation of knowledge to practice is that one applies what one knows about causal powers to particular cases, but the truths about such causal powers that one banks on are thought to remain unchanged. That is the point of saying that theory here is about an independent object. In politics, on the other hand, accepting a theory can itself transform what that theory bears on.

Put a third way, we can say that while natural science theory also transforms practice, the practice it transforms is not what the theory is about. It is in this sense external to the theory. We think of it as an 'application' of the theory. But in politics, the practice is the object of theory. Theory in this domain transforms its own object.

This raises different problems about validation in political theory. We cannot think of this according to a simple correspondence model, where a theory is true to the extent that it correctly characterizes an independent object. But it is also totally wrong to abandon the notion of validation altogether, as though in this area thinking makes it so. The fact that

theory can transform its object does not make it the case that just anything goes, as we shall see below. Rather we have to understand how
certain kinds of changes wrought by theory are validating, and others
show it to be mistaken.

But before trying to show how this is so, I have to acknowledge that a
powerful current in our culture resists strongly the idea of political theory
as transforming its object. Partly because of the very puzzlement about
validation just mentioned, and partly for other reasons, the temptation
has been strong to assimilate political theory to the natural science model.
This would then aspire like physics to yield knowledge about the unchanging conditions and regularities of political life. This knowledge could be
applied to effect our ends more fully should we find occasion and
justification.

Of course, it is difficult to present theories which claim to identify the
true significance of our actions in this light. And so the attempt is usually
made with theories of the causal context. The various theories of the
political economy have tended to be of this form: certain consequences
attend our actions regardless of the intentions with which they are carried
out. So no alteration in our self-understanding will alter *these*
regularities. Our only way of changing the course of things is by *using*
these regularities to our own ends. In short, practice must apply the truths
of theory. We have here exactly the relation of natural science.

We have been brought generally to consider economics as a science of
this kind. People believe, for instance, that monetarism is true or false as a
proposition about how certain economic transactions concatenate with
others. If true, it could thus be the basis of a policy which would bring
about its effects in a given economy regardless of the intentions and
self-understanding of the agents in that economy. The policy would be
merely technical, in the sense that it would work entirely without altering
the way people conceive their predicament or understand the alternatives
open to them. For the economic laws the policy banks on allegedly
operate quite irrespective of such changes.

Perhaps there is some justification for this as far as economics is concerned. There are certain regularities which attend our economic
behaviour, and which change only very slowly. But it would be absurd to
make this the model for social theory in general and political theory in
particular.

First, there are cultural conditions of our behaving according to these
regularities. Economics can hope to predict and sometimes control
behaviour to the extent that it can because we can be confident that in

some department of their lives people will behave according to rather tightly calculable considerations of instrumental rationality. But it took a whole vast development of civilization before the culture developed in which people do so behave, in which it became a cultural possibility to act like this; and in which the discipline involved in so acting became widespread enough for this behaviour to be generalized. And it took the development of a host of institutions, money, banks, international markets, and so on, before behaviour of this form could assume the scale it has. Economics can aspire to the status of a science, and sometimes appear to approach it, because there has developed a culture in which a certain form of rationality is a (if not the) dominant value. And even now, it fails often because this rationality cannot be a precise enough guide. What is the rational response to galloping inflation? Economics is uncertain where we ordinary agents are perplexed.

Second, we could not hope to have a theory of this kind, so resistant to our self-understanding (relatively resistant, as we have seen), outside of the economic sphere. The regularities are there, and resistant, to the extent that behaviour responds to narrow, circumscribed considerations. Economic behaviour can be predictable as some game behaviour can be; because the goals sought and the criteria for their attainment are closely circumscribed in a given domain. But for that very reason, a theory of this kind could never help explain our motivated action in general.

Various attempts to explain political behaviour with an economic-model theory always end up either laughable, or begging the major question, or both. They beg the question to the extent that they reconstruct political behaviour according to some narrowly defined conception of rationality. But in doing this, they achieve not accuracy of description of political behaviour in general, but rather they offer one way of conceiving what it is to act politically, and therefore one way of shaping this action. Rather than being theories of how things always operate, they actually end up strengthening one way of acting over others. For instance, in the light of our distinction above between atomist and general will constructions of democratic decision-making, they help to entrench the atomist party. Setting out with the ambition of being natural science-type theories of an independent reality, they actually end up functioning as transforming theories, as political theories normally do, but unconsciously and *malgré elles*. They thus beg the interesting question: 'Is this the right transforming theory?' because they cannot raise it; they do not see that it has to be raised.

If, on the other hand, they try to avoid this partisanship by becoming rather vague and general in their application, allowing just about any behaviour to count somehow as rational, then they become laughable. Theories of this kind generally hover between these two extremes. An excellent example is the conversion theory of politics mentioned above in connection with the name of David Easton.

What emerges from this is that the model of theory as of an independent object, or as bearing an object resistant to our self-understanding, has at best only partial application in the sciences of man. It can apply only in certain rather specialized domains, where behaviour is rather rigid, either because largely controlled by physiological factors, or because a culture has developed in which what is done in a given department is controlled by a narrow range of considerations, as in games or (to some degree) economic life. But this could never be the general model for social science, and certainly not that for a science of politics.

III

Which brings us back to the question of validation. What is it for a theory to be right? We cannot just reply that it is right when it corresponds to the facts it is about. Because, to oversimplify slightly, political theories are about our practices (as well as the institutions and relations in which these practices are carried on), and their rise and adoption can alter these practices. They are not about a domain of fact independent of, or resistant to, the development of theory.

Put tersely, our social theories can be validated, because they can be tested in practice. If theory can transform practice, then it can be tested in the quality of the practice it informs. What makes a theory right is that it brings practice out in the clear; that its adoption makes possible what is in some sense a more effective practice.

But this notion of validating theories through practice may seem even more bizarre and suspect than the idea that theories may not be verified by the facts. What we need in order to make it less strange is to come to a better understanding of the uses of theory.

Our reflections on natural science familiarize us with the idea that theories describe and explain the phenomena of some domain, and help us to predict them. But it should be clear from the above discussion that this cannot be all that social theory does for us. I argued above that social theory can affect practice, just because it can alter our self-descriptions, and our self-descriptions can be constitutive of our practices. One of the things social theory does, I suggested, is make explicit the self-understandings which constitute our social life.

But then it is clear that our formulations can serve more than descriptive purposes. We may be led to formulate some self-understanding in order to rescue a practice, to make it possible to continue it, to put it on a securer basis, or perhaps to reform it, or purify it. The point, one might say, of the formulation here is just to provide the constitutive understanding necessary for the continuing, or reformed, or purified practice.

This of course is true first of all of many of our pre-theoretical formulations in myth and ritual. A founding myth, or our public ceremonial, expresses in public space our common ends, or shared goods, without which we would be incapable of acting together in the way our institutions call for. For example, we are capable of fighting together in war, or sharing power in some particular way, only because we have a common understanding, to which some public expression is indispensable, and these formulations are its public expressions.

But with certain advances in culture, there may arise the need for theoretical formulations, that is, we feel the need to submit our discourse of self-understanding to the special disciplines of objectivity, rigour, and respect for truth which are constitutive of the activity we know as theorizing. This may be the case as much with our common understandings as with the individual attempts at orientation, by which we try to define our place in society and/or history.

There is no doubt that modern culture makes this demand. Ours is a very theoretical civilization. We see this both in the fact that certain understandings formulated in modern theories have become incorporated in the common understandings by which political society operates in the West, and also in that, however oversimplified and vulgarized these theories may become in attaining general currency, an important part of their prestige and credibility reposes on their being believed to be correct theories, truly validated as knowledge, as this is understood in a scientific age.

For instance, I would claim that atomist theories of the polity, and even more obtrusively, corresponding theories of the economy, have entered into the common understanding of modern Western democracies, perhaps in a debased and garbled and oversimplified form, but with the prestige of theoretical truth behind them. These views are indeed not without rivals in the general understanding; it is not simply atomist. But part of the challenge to them comes from rival theories propounded by minorities, for instance Marxism. This too may be thought vulgarized and oversimplified, but essential to its appeal is the prestige of Science, to which it lays claim.

Ours is an inescapably theoretical civilization. Some of the reasons for this are not too hard to identify. One of the basic underlying conditions, of course, is the prestige of science in our way of life. But on top of this, the rise and prominence of political economy has been of great importance.

We are all convinced that there are mechanisms of social interaction which are not clear on the surface, regularities which have to be identified through study and research. Even people who are not at all uneasy about the implicit understanding of the society's institutions, and are not tempted at all to think that this understanding is somehow illusory, nevertheless accept that there is more to social interaction than can meet the eye. There are laws of society which have to be laid bare in a theory.

But people also turn to political theory because they feel the need to get clearer what society's practices involve. These practices seem problematic because they are already the locus of strife and trouble and uncertainty, and have been since their inception. I am thinking in particular of the central political practices of modern Western democracies: elections, decisions by majority vote, adversary negotiations, the claiming and according of rights, and the like. These practices have grown in our civilization in a context of strife, replacing sometimes violently earlier practices which were incompatible with them. And they are practices which by their nature leave scope for struggle between different conceptions, policies, ambitions. Moreover, their introduction was justified by polemical theories which challenged the dominant views of the pre-modern era. Hence by their nature and history these practices constantly push us to find and redefine their theoretical basis.

And so our society is a very theory-prone one. A great deal of our political life is related to theories. The political struggle is often seen as between rival theories, the programmes of governments are justified by theories, and so on. There never has been an age so theory-drenched as ours.

In this situation, while political agents may turn to theories as guides, or as rhetorical devices of struggle, many others turn to them in order to orient themselves. People reach for theories in order to make sense of a political universe which is full of conflict and rival interpretations, and which moreover everyone agrees is partly opaque. When in addition, people's purposes are frustrated in unexpected ways, for example when they are beset with intractable stagflation, or anomic violence, or economic decline, the sense of bewilderment is all the greater; and the only cure for bewilderment seems to be correct theory.

Theory thus has an important use to define common understandings, and hence to sustain or reform political practices, as well as serving on an individual level to help people orient themselves. Let me coin the term 'self-defining' for these uses of theory, in contrast to the explanatory ones that we usually focus on.

Then two points emerge from the above discussion: this self-definition is essentially also a definition of norms, goods, or values; and there are in each case practices of which it is the essential enabling condition.

This is pretty obvious with theories which formulate common understandings. A theory of the self-governing republic gives us a certain notion of our shared good, which as we saw is constitutive of certain practices. But its principal rival, the atomist theory, which gives us an instrumental picture of political society, involves no less of a definition of the political good.[3] This is seen quite differently, and reposes principally in the efficiency of the political system in satisfying our demands, as well as in the responsiveness of political institutions to the demands of different categories of people, and thus in the distributive justice of demand-satisfaction. Some of the central features of modern society, such as the trend towards rationality and bureaucratization in government, are essentially linked to this instrumentalist understanding.

But the same points can be made about individuals' attempts at orientation. In fact, people seek orientation in their political world not just to have a cognitively tidy universe, but for much more powerful reasons. In some cases, it will be because they need the political realm to be a locus of important significance. Either they want political structures to reflect their central values, or they require that political leaders be paradigms of these values, or they seek a form of political action which will be truly significant, or they require the political system to be the guardian of the right order of things; be it in one way or another, they are reluctant to look on political structures simply as instruments which are without value in themselves – albeit an influential strand of modern political theory tends in just this direction.

Others desire to feel in control. They want to objectify the social world by science, so as to have the confidence that they can cope with it, manipulate it given the right conditions. This is, of course, one of the strong motives for natural science modelled theories. Still others seek to establish

---

[3] See chapter 2 above.

a sense of their own worth by espousing theories which show themselves to be clearly separate from, perhaps even in combat with, the evil, muddle, ambiguity, or failure they see around them. This is especially evident in theories which justify terrorist violence. But then the very satisfactions of becoming oriented, in one or more of these ways, may give one a sense of having achieved more clairvoyant practice which is quite specious. This can generate very powerful mechanisms of self-delusion. And these orientations are the basis of certain practices, just because they define our relation to the good, to what is really or potentially of value in political life.

In any case, it is clear that theories do much more than explain social life; they also define the understandings that underpin different forms of social practice, and they help to orient us in the social world. And obviously the most satisfying theories are those that do both at once: they offer the individual an orientation which he shares with his compatriots, and which is reflected in their common institutions.

But we might be tempted to reply that all this, while true, has nothing to do with our question, how do we validate theory? Sure, there are all sorts of self-defining uses of theory, but these have nothing to do with its truth. Naturally, granted what is at stake, human beings will always be tempted to espouse theories that give them a sense of moral orientation, and perhaps even more theories which support the practices they find advantageous. So that those who are doing well in capitalist society, and to whom governments are responsive, will easily warm to an atomist, instrumentalist theory, while those who are pushed to desperation as victims of systematic deprivation may well be attracted to theories of extreme conflict, and accept some justification of terrorism.

In short, the self-defining uses of theory are simply ideological in the pejorative sense. One can scientifically explain why certain theories serve the self-definition of certain people, but that they do so says nothing of itself for their truth. Of their truth, we can only judge by seeing how they describe and explain. In the end, all our objections to validating by correspondence with the facts must be swept aside. If we are talking scientifically, that is what it comes down to. So runs the reply.

Social theories would be in this respect exactly like theories in the natural sciences. If someone told us that he accepted a theory in physics or chemistry because it gave him a satisfactory moral orientation to his world, or supported the right political practices, we should judge him irrational or corrupt. These are motives of the crimes against science, such as the suppression of Galileo, or the propagation of Lysenko's theories in the Soviet Union. These considerations cannot be allowed as relevant to truth.

My central claim is that this reply, and the parallel it invokes, is deeply mistaken. Of course, nothing could be more common than the interested and 'ideological' use of social theory. How could it be otherwise when so much is at stake? But this is not the same thing as saying that there is no such thing as the objective validation of a theory in its self-defining use. The fact that we have an overwhelming temptation to fudge in this domain in the service of our material and psychological interests does not at all mean that there is no truth of the matter here, and that the self-defining uses of theory are nothing but the reflection of these interests.

My thesis can perhaps best be expressed here in two related propositions:

1. There is such a thing as validating a social theory in its self-defining use, as well as establishing it as explanation/description.
2. Validating a theory as self-definition is in an important sense primary, because understanding what is involved in such validation will frequently be essential to confirming a theory, even as an adequate description/explanation.

Theories as self-definitions cannot just be seen as reflections of interest, because they make a certain kind of claim. They claim to offer a perspicuous account of the good or norm which is the point of a certain practice. Rousseau's republican theory of the general will offers a certain conception of the shared good informing the practices of republican self-rule. The atomist theories define conceptions of rationality and efficacy. If I accept an orientation towards my political society as rightfully the guardian of the correct order of value, then I define a certain notion of guardianship, which I see as the point of certain laws, ceremonies, structures.

Now this is the kind of claim that can be right or wrong, and that in principle at least, we can validate or disconfirm. It is something we can test in practice. This is so, because since theories enable practices to take a certain shape, a theory which badly misidentifies the goods we can seek in a certain domain will ground a practice which will fail to realize these goods. The practices informed by wrong theories will be in an important way self-defeating.

And this is, I would argue, the essence of the claim made by opponents of a given theory in real political debate. Thus people who are sceptical of a Rousseauian view hold that his conception of the shared good in the general will is too simplistic and unitary. Precisely for this reason they see the practice it grounds as self-defeating, because it fails to achieve a generally acknowledged freedom, but on the contrary degenerates into despotism. This is rightly thought of as self-defeating, because freedom was the point of the practice. On the other side, opponents of atomist views argue that a truly atomist polity would be utterly devoid of civic spirit; it would therefore require a maximum of bureaucratic surveillance and enforcement to function. It would thus defeat the ends of freedom, justice and demand-satisfaction.

These examples are, I believe, representative of real debate between living theories. It is rare that one sees two utterly independent goods, whose definition is not in dispute, but which define rival policy goals, at the centre of a major political debate. As one looks at the Soviet system from the outside, a Westerner may feel that it would make more sense if they defended their society on the grounds that it minimizes disorder, while we prefer ours for its freedom and democracy. But in fact, this is not what the debate is about between the two systems. It concerns the nature of freedom and democracy, whose definition is in dispute.

Between two quite independent rival goods, the practice criterion could not select. But between two rival conceptions of the goods we can seek in societies of a certain kind, practice can allow us to arbitrate in principle. Of course, when something big is at stake, both sides will have every motive to lie, and fudge, and suppress the truth and confuse the issues. But this is not to say that the issue cannot be arbitrated by reason.

On the contrary, it can; and we can now perhaps see better how. First, it should be clearer why the disputes are not like those between rival causal hypotheses, where one affirms and another denies a hypothetical: if p happens, then q will befall. This latter kind of dispute supposes that we agree on the descriptions 'p' and 'q'. But it is the basic terms of politics which are in question when theories clash. The contestants will probably disagree over certain hypotheticals in the course of the argument (e.g., whether pursuing certain objectives will lead to bureaucratization, or will undermine stability). But what is at stake is not a set of hypothetical propositions, for example, of the kind: if we carry out the practices as the theory prescribes, the good will ensue. Because we are dealing with an ordinary hypothetical here, where the condition described in the protasis is independent of that described in the apodosis. Rather the good sought under the description offered by the theory is constitutive of the practice we seek to realize. What is at stake is more like rival maps of the terrain. One might say, the terrain of possible practices is being mapped in contour, and this purports to give the shape and slope of the heights of value.

The proof of a map is how well you can get around using it. And this is the test of theories considered as self-definitions. In this they are closely analogous to the pre-theoretical understandings we have of things. When I overcome some confusion I may be in about the disposition of my limbs, or the way I am moving my body, or the lie of the land, and have a more perspicuous view of things, this shows its superiority in enabling me to act more effectively. I know I have a better grasp of things when I am able to overcome the muddle, confusion, and cross purposes which affected my activity hitherto.

Analogously, I want to argue that to have a better theoretical self-definition is to understand better what we are doing; and this means that our action can be somewhat freer of the stumbling, self-defeating character which previously afflicted it. Our action becomes less haphazard and contradictory, less prone to produce what we did not want at all.

In sum, I want to say that, because theories which are about practices are self-definitions, and hence alter the practices, the proof of the validity of a theory can come in the changed quality of the practice it enables. Let me introduce terms of art for this shift of quality, and say that good theory enables practice to become less stumbling and more clairvoyant.

We should note that attaining clairvoyant practice is not the same thing as being more successful in our practices. It may be that there is something deeply muddled and contradictory in our original activity, as for instance Marxism would claim about the practices of 'bourgeois' democracy. In which case, theoretical clarity is not going to enable us better to determine our own fate within the context of bourgeois institutions. Rather what the theory will have revealed is that this enterprise is vain; it is vitiated at the very base. But practice can be more clairvoyant here because we can abandon this self-defeating enterprise, and turn to another goal which makes sense, that is, revolution. Of course, if we bring this off, we shall have been more successful overall; but not in the practices we originally set out to understand, which we have on the contrary abandoned. And just getting the right theory does not ensure that we can bring off the revolutionary change. We may just be stymied. Still, if the theory is right we would be capable of more clairvoyant practice, which in this case would just consist in our abandoning the muddled, self-stultifying effort to determine our fate freely within the structures of the capitalist economy.

My second thesis is that for some theories understanding what is involved in validating the self-defining use will be essential to their confirmation.

This can be the case in two ways. First, there can be cases in which the historical evidence is insufficient, in the sense that certain possibilities have not been tried. Or in any case, this is what one side in the argument can often claim. This always arises in debates about radical social theories, for example of egalitarian participatory democracy, or anarchism. Their opponents ask us to look at the historical record: when have these theories ever been successfully applied? Their protagonists reply that the conditions have never been right; the real test case is yet to come.

To the extent that the protagonists are right, then the validation we are waiting for is of the theory in its self-defining use. We are awaiting a case in which our social life can be shaped by it, and it can show its value in practice.

But of course the hotly contested question in this kind of debate will bear on just this, how incomplete is the historical record? To what degree can past experiences be deemed valid predictors of new possible experiments? Does the virtual absence of anarchist societies from the historical record show this form to be impossible? Does the fact that the experience of mass democracies up to now exemplifies to a large degree the elite competition model show more participatory forms to be impossible?

How do you decide this kind of question? Presumably the answer turns on how you interpret the historical record. But this is relevant precisely as a record of *stumbling or clairvoyant practice*. The conservative claim is just that the failure of previous attempts amounts to a case of the self-defeat that attends a practice informed by a wrong theory. The radical answer will always be that the failure springs from other sources, external factors, lack of propitious economic, or educational, or military conditions, and so on.

The argument about a general will theory mentioned above is a case in point. For its opponents, the disaster which has attended various attempts to supersede 'bourgeois' representative democracy is sufficient proof of the error of this theory. But its defenders will argue that it has only been tried in the most unfavourable economic, cultural or military conditions; where it ought never to be attempted; and that the obstinate refusal of those responsible for these attempts to acknowledge the unpropitiousness of the conditions has turned their theory itself into a travesty of the original idea. It is in these terms that the debate is frequently engaged between conservatives and socialists about the lessons to be drawn from the Soviet experience. For the former, this experience is a crucial negative test; for the latter, it is a grotesque caricature of socialism.

I do not want to try to show who is right here. My point is rather that one cannot make and argue for a reading of this kind unless one understands what it is for a wrong theory to render a practice self-defeating, or a more correct theory to make it relatively unimpeded. In other words, you have to understand what it is to validate a theory as self-definition in order to glean from the historical record some defensible view of the theory's future prospects.

This kind of validation of a theory against the historical record is thus quite different from what is normally understood as the verification of a theory by comparison with an independent domain of objects. Here the confirmation has to take account of the way in which theory shapes practice. To test the theory in practice means here not to see how well the theory describes the practices as a range of independent entities; but rather to judge how practices fare when informed by the theory.

My claim is then that testing theories in practice plays an essential part in validating social theories. In the immediately preceding discussion, I have been talking about reading history to settle disputes about theories as self-definitions. But the same theories serve both for self-definition and for explanation. To give good grounds for a theory in an argument about either is to give good grounds for it *tout court*.

For in fact disputes about self-definition are inextricably bound up with questions of explanation, and vice versa. The argument whether the inhumanities of the Soviet system are to be put to the account of socialist theory, or rather attributed to other factors, is also an argument about how various developments of Soviet history are to be explained. And the reverse: any explanatory hypotheses about Soviet history have inescapable relevance to the question, what lessons are to be drawn about the theories which ought to inform our future practice.

A little reflection will show why this must be so. What makes it the case that there is such a thing as the self-defining use of theory, and that it can be validated in practice, viz., the fact that human beings frame self-understandings which shape their activity, this same basic feature has to be taken into account wherever it is relevant when we are trying to explain human action in history. In other words, where and to the extent that social action has been informed by self-understanding, this will have to figure in any valid explanatory account, together with an assessment of the way and degree to which this understanding facilitated or impeded the action.

It follows that explanatory theories have to be concerned with the same basic inter-weaving of theory and practice which we examine when we test self-definitions. Explanation also involves inescapably an appraisal of how theory has shaped practice, and of whether or how this has been self-defeating. Thus whether we examine the record for purposes of explanation of self-definition, we have to ask largely over-lapping questions. The same core of judgements will be central to both enquiries.

And that is why I have spoken above of theories which have explanatory or self-definitional *uses*. This is to take the core of judgements at the heart of both enquiries and identify it with the theory. But even if we think of the two enquiries as issuing in distinct theories, the close connection emerges in the fact that adopting a given self-definitional theory has strong consequences for the explanatory theories one can consistently adopt, and vice versa. The two orders of questions are logically linked via their common core. You cannot establish something in relation to one debate without deciding a great deal about the other.

Thus the activity that I am calling testing theories in practice is indispensable to the validation of our social theories. It is not just that we may sometimes be called on to test theories as self-definitions in our own practice. What is of much more general relevance, we have to make use of our understanding of what it is to test in practice when we examine the historical record; and this whether our interest in the disputed theories is explanation or self-definition.

And this is what distinguishes social from natural science, where testing theories in practice plays no role at all. Of course, the contrast is not complete. Some social theories can be at least partly tested on a simple verification model. Certain economic theories, like monetarism, are of this kind. One might think that monetarism can be refuted if controlling the money supply does not succeed in slowing inflation while leaving growth unimpeded.

But economic theories of this sort are the exception rather than the rule in social science. Most theories are not of the kind that can simply be *applied* in practice; they affect practice only in shaping or informing it. And for these, simple verification against an independent domain is impossible.

And even these seemingly clear cases of verifiable theory may turn out to be muddy. Suppose the defenders of monetarism try to save it from the discredit of its failure as a policy by arguing that extraneous cultural or political factors – managerial practices, trade union rigidities – prevented its beneficent effects from ensuing. Won't we have to follow the argument back into the domain where theories as self-definitions shape our practice?

As a matter of fact, the entire debate about inflation in the last decade can be seen as an illustration of this shift. Economists started off with an unshaken faith in their science as the source of verifiable explanations. Inflation was explained by factors that could be manipulated, that is, by factors which could be adjusted without any change in people's self-definitions: the level of demand, levels of taxation, size of government deficit, growth of money supply. At the beginning of the 1980s, we are more ready to ask ourselves whether inflation isn't largely fuelled by our political relations, in other words, in part by the self-definitions implicit in our dominant practices. From the point of view of our discussion here, this reappraisal means a shift from reliance on theories which still fit the natural science models to theories which are self-consciously about practices.

What I have been arguing in the preceding discussion is that theories about practices are validated in a way special to them. And this way can only be understood, if we see more clearly what we are doing when we create, espouse, propound social theories. In this way, I am trying to redeem my opening claim, that we need to see social theory as practice in order to understand what its validation amounts to.

In the next chapter I will turn to another issue which I think is also illuminated by this understanding.

CHAPTER FOUR

UNDERSTANDING AND ETHNOCENTRICITY

I

The main thesis of the last chapter has been that we ought to turn to look at what we *do* when we theorize; that when we do we see that theories serve more than descriptive and explanatory purposes, they also serve to *define* ourselves; and that such self-definition *shapes* practice. But if all this is true, I argued, then the use of theory as self-definition also has to be borne in mind when we come to explain, when we practise, social science.

For even though theory may be serving us, the social scientists, simply as an instrument of explanation, the agents whose behaviour we are trying to explain will be using (the same or another) theory, or proto-theory, to define themselves. So that whether we are trying to validate a theory as self-definition, or establish it as an explanation, we have to be alive to the way that understanding shapes practice, disrupts or facilitates it.

But this raises a number of questions about the relation between the scientist's explanatory theory and the self-definitions of his subjects. Suppose they offer very different, even incompatible, views of the world and of the subjects' action? Does the scientist have the last word? Can he set the world-view of his subjects aside as erroneous? But to condemn this world-view does he not have to stand outside it, and is this external stance compatible with understanding their self-definitions?

We come here to one of the main issues of the debate around *verstehende* social science. And this had to arise. Because in fact my thesis amounts to an alternative statement of the main proposition of interpretive social science, that an adequate account of human action must make the agents more understandable. On this view, it cannot be a sufficient objective of social theory that it just predict, or allow us to derive, the actual pattern of social or historical events, and the regularities which occur in it, described in whatever language admits of unambiguous verification. A satisfactory explanation must also make sense of the agents.

This is not to say, of course, that it must show their action as making sense. For it very often does not. Frequently they are confused, malinformed, contradictory in their goals and actions. But in identifying the contradictions, confusions, etc., *we* make sense of what they did. And this means that we come to see how as *agents* – i.e., beings who act, have purposes, desires – they came to do what they did, and to bring about what befell.

Now my argument has been converging onto a similar conclusion. For my contention has been that social theory has to take subjects as agents of self-definition, whose practice is shaped by their understanding. And this is just an alternative way of stating the thesis that we have to give an account of them as agents, and that we cannot do this unless we understand them, that is, grasp their self-understanding. The opposing ideal of a verifiable, predictive science, on the model of the natural sciences, is, I have argued, a chimaera.

I hope that the above discussion may help us to set aside two common misapprehensions about interpretive social science. The first is that what it demands of us is empathy with our subjects. But this is to miss the point. Empathy may certainly be useful in coming to have the understanding we seek; but it is not what understanding consists in. Science is a form of discourse, and what we want is an account which sets out the significance of action and situation. What we are crucially looking for, therefore, is the right language in which we can make this clear. I will say more on this shortly.

The second misapprehension is the one evoked by my questions above. It is to the effect that understanding the agent involves adopting his point of view; or, to speak in terms of language, describing and accounting for what he does in his own terms, or those of his society and time. This is the thesis which has been associated (rightly or wrongly) with the name of Peter Winch.[1] Taken strictly, it would seem to make social science rather unilluminating, and in some circumstances next to impossible. It would make it unilluminating, since in many cases actors are confused, misinformed, have contradictory purposes, and their language may reflect this. Simply recovering their self-description may cast no light at all on what was going on. Indeed, the starting point of our scientific effort may be that we find something perplexing in their action as they understood it. And in the limit case where we are dealing with a so-called 'primitive' society,

---

[1] See his *The Idea of a Social Science* (London, 1958) and 'Understanding a primitive society', *American Philosophical Quarterly*, 1 (1964), pp. 307–24.

that is one which is pre-scientific, which has not yet produced a discourse of reflective theory, a scientific account in their terms would be quite impossible.

But this kind of demand has nothing to do with interpretive social science as I have been expounding it here. On the contrary, in the normal case what is demanded of a theoretical account is that it make the agent's doings clearer than they were to him. And this may easily involve challenging what he sees/saw as the normal language of self-description. We saw a case in the previous chapter with the Marxist theory claiming to reveal the language of free contract as a sham. But the need to challenge the agent's self-descriptions does not take away in the least from the requirement that we understand him as an agent. Understanding someone cannot simply mean adopting his point of view, for otherwise a good account could never be the basis of more clairvoyant practice.

There is, however, an important truth which underlies this confusion. And that is that making sense of agents does require that we *understand* their self-descriptions. We may, indeed often must, take account of their confusion, malinformation, illusion; but we make sense of them if we grasp *both* how they see things *and* what is wrong, lacunary, contradictory in this. Interpretive social science cannot by-pass the agent's self-understanding.

We might distinguish the two theses in this way: interpretive social science requires that we master the agent's self-description in order to identify our *explananda*; but it by no means requires that we couch our *explanantia* in the same language. On the contrary it generally demands that we go beyond it. The false assimilation of interpretive science with adopting the agent's point of view does place exactly this crippling restriction on the explanantia. But if, on the other hand, we attempt to by-pass his self-descriptions even in picking out our explananda, we have put paid to any attempt to make sense of him.

Now there is a strong temptation to by-pass these self-descriptions, which is felt particularly by those who accept natural sciences as the model for social science. We can easily see why this is so, if we examine what is involved here.

The kind of understanding we are looking for is what we could call 'human understanding'. It is the kind we invoke when we say things like: 'I find him incomprehensible', or 'At last I understand what makes her tick', or 'Now we understand each other'. And as I said above, having this is not just a matter of feeling empathy. Because what we are talking about here is discursive understanding. We can sometimes, of course, just be 'on the same wave-length' with someone, have a kind of unformulated pre-understanding of him, but this is not the kind of thing we need for a theoretical account.

Getting the kind of human understanding of someone which we can formulate involves coming to be able to apply what I want to call (following Elizabeth Anscombe) the 'desirability characterizations' which define his world. I come to understand someone when I understand his emotions, his aspirations, what he finds admirable and contemptible in himself and others, what he yearns for, what he loathes, and so on. Being able to formulate this understanding is being able to apply correctly the desirability characterizations which he applies in the way he applies them. For instance, if he admires sophisticated people, then understanding him requires that I be able to apply this concept 'sophisticated' in the sense it has for him.

Perhaps that way of putting it is a bit too quick, because some of what he feels, desires, etc., will be unformulated by himself; whereas to figure in my account, it has to be formulated. So, in slightly more complex terms, my claim amounts to this: that the explicit formulation of what I understand when I understand you requires my grasping the desirability characterizations that you yourself clairvoyantly use, or else those which you would use if you had arrived at a more reflective formulation of your loves, hates, aspirations, admirabilia, etc. These are the self-descriptions (in a somewhat extended use of this term) which I want to claim are crucial for social science, for grasping those applied by the agent is essential to identifying our explananda.

Now thereby hangs a problem for science. Take, for example, the desirability characterizations we attach to actions to make ourselves more understandable, such as 'just', 'charitable', 'generous'; and those we apply to ways of life, such as 'integrated', 'fulfilled', 'dedicated', 'free from illusion'; and also negative ones, like 'fragmented', 'false', 'hollow', 'shallow', etc.; all of these pose two problems as candidates for scientific discourse as this is usually conceived.

First, they cannot be intersubjectively validated in an unproblematic way. Whether a way of life is truly integrated or free from illusion is a matter of potentially endless interpretive dispute. Moreover, we tend to believe that there are or may be certain moral pre-conditions, certain pre-conditions of character, for the successful discernment of these properties. We do not expect callow youth to have as good an eye for the life free from illusion as those who have grown wiser with age (a class which is not, of course, co-extensional with those who have aged). When it comes to understanding what a life of fine sensibility is, some people are distressingly philistine. And so on. Using this kind of concept, one cannot hope for replicable findings on the part of any scientifically competent observer. Or put another way, 'scientific competence' for terms of this kind would have to include certain developments of character and sensibility which themselves are only recognizable as such from the standpoint of those who have acquired them.

Closely connected with this vulnerability to interpretive challenge is a second feature: these terms are inextricably evaluative; and what is more, they are what one could call strongly evaluative. I want to speak of strong evaluation when the goods putatively identified are not seen as consti-tuted as good by the fact that we desire them, but rather are seen as normative for desire. That is, they are seen as goods which we ought to desire, even if we do not, goods such that we show ourselves up as inferior or bad by our not desiring them. Now along with unambiguous applica-tion, it is usually thought that the terms of a scientific discourse should offer a value-free account. And thus in this respect, too, the desirability characterizations whereby we understand people seem inappropriate for a science of society.

Thirdly, and for some thinkers decisively, the use of desirability descriptions seems to endanger the aspiration to a universal science of society. For those descriptions are culturally specific. The values of one culture are frequently not replicable in another; we can find nothing exactly corresponding to them. To describe people in their terms is to describe each culture in different terms, and terms which are incommen-surable, that is, which have no exact translation in other languages.

But then this brings us up against the issue which Winch's writings have raised. Suppose we are trying to give an account of a society very different from our own, say a primitive society. The society has (what we call) religious and magical practices. To understand them in the strong sense discussed above would require that we come to grasp how they use the key words in which they praise and blame, describe what they yearn for or seek, what they abhor and fear, and so on. Understanding their religious practices would require that we come to understand what they see them-selves as doing when they are carrying out the ritual we have provisionally identified as a 'sacrifice', what they seek after in the state we may pro-visionally identify as 'blessedness' or 'union with the spirits'. (Our pro-visional identifications, of course, just place their actions/states in rela-tion to our religious tradition, or ones familiar to us. If we stick with these, we may fall into the most distorted ethnocentric readings.) We have no way of knowing that we have managed to penetrate this world in this way short of finding that we are able to use their key words in the same way they do, and that means that we grasp their desirability characterizations.

But because applying any desirability characterizations has the three difficulties mentioned above, it is naturally tempting to try to finesse this understanding. We can see this temptation at work in many of the theories adopted in social science. For instance, a case like the one we are examining here might tempt us to finesse understanding with a functionalist theory. We come at the society in question with some general thesis about religion, that religious practices perform certain functions in society, for example, that they contribute to social integration. On the strength of this principle, we can perhaps dispense with an understanding of what the priest or medicine man is doing in the terms of his own society. One identification we have of this ritual activity is that it is part of a process which contributes to social integration. This may allow us to explain what is going on, for instance, why rituals happen when they do, at the times of year they do, or more frequently in periods of stress, and so on. We may perhaps thus hope to dispense altogether with an understanding of ritual action in the agents' own terms.

This will seem the more plausible if we argue that the significance of a great many actions of people in any society escape their full consciousness or understanding. We cannot expect that the members of the tribe will have a clear grasp of the socially integrative nature of their religion as we do. Their understanding of this is, on the contrary, almost bound to be distorted, fragmentary, 'ideological'. Why should we pay any special attention to it, once we are on to a more satisfactory account of what is going on, which we now have, thanks to our functional theory? This course seems all the more evidently superior, since our theory is in a language of science, whereas the discourse of the tribe's self-understanding manifestly is not.

Now the interpretation thesis, which I want to defend, holds that the attempt to finesse understanding in this way is futile. It can only lead to sterility. I hope that, if I cannot prove, I can at least illustrate this thesis if we examine a bit further this example of a functional account of religious practices. I hope it will be clear, however, that the argument is meant to apply to any attempt to finesse understanding through a putatively 'scientific' identification of the action of the subjects under study, whether this be on the individual or the social level.

Consider the problem of validating a functional theory. Here a great many of the criticisms made of functionalism, even by other mainstream social scientists, can be shown, I think, to demonstrate rather the indispensability of understanding. Take the question of knowing how much you have explained. Even if a functional theory could get over the challenge of showing how it could be positively established, that is, of what can be said to make us believe it – and this is no small issue, because brute induction will not be decisive in this kind of case – the question can arise of how much we have explained. Let us say there is some truth in the claim that religions generally contribute to social integration; and that we can establish this. The question still arises of the significance of this finding. How much can we explain of the actual shape of the religious practice in this society by this functional theory?

It could be, for instance, that although religions are generally integrative, a very large number of possible religious practices could have done the job equally well in this society. In this case, our functional theory would do nothing to explain the kind of religion we see here, why there is this kind of ritual, that form of hierarchy, that type of fervour, those modes of blessedness, and so on. In short, most of what we want to explain in a given society may lie outside the scope of the explanation; which may at the limit sink to the marginal significance of the background observation that disruptive religions tend to destroy the societies in which they take root, and hence flourishing religion tends not to be disruptive.

Even though we may show our theory to be true, in some sense, we may be challenged to show that it is significant. Does it explain something substantive about the religious forms of the society, or is it rather in the nature of a banal observation about the poor long-term prospects of disruptive religions?

The only way to meet this challenge is to take up the attempt to show how the detail of the religious form – the kind of ritual, the form hierarchy, etc. – can be explained by the functional theory. We have a closely analogous case if we take historical materialism, which is very much like a functional theory – and indeed, is a functional theory, if we agree with G. A. Cohen's interpretation.[2] Historical materialism claims to be able to explain the evolution of the 'superstructure' of society, for example the political and religious forms, in terms of the evolution of the 'base', that is the relations of production. Sceptics of historical materialism have doubts precisely about the scope of what is to be explained by the relations of production. Can we really account for political and religious change in these terms?

---

[2] *Karl Marx's Theory of History* (Oxford, 1978).

Marxists are thus challenged to explain precisely the detail of political and religious development: can one explain the rise of Protestantism, the differential spread of Lutheran and Calvinist theologies? And so on.

The challenge to explain details is essential to the validation of this kind of theory. But it is a challenge which cannot be met, except by acquiring an adequate understanding (in our strong sense) of the actions, theologies, ideals, and so on, which we are trying to explain. There is no way to finesse the requirement of understanding. Our Marxist or other historian convinces us he has explained the detail when he can give a convincing interpretation of it in his canonical terms. But to give a convincing interpretation, one has to show that one has understood what the agent is doing, feeling here. His action/feeling/aspirations/outlook in his terms constitutes our explanandum.

In the end, there is no way to finesse understanding if we are to give a convincing account of the explanatory significance of our theory. I hope it will be evident that this applies not only to functionalist theories, but to any attempt to identify what agents are doing in 'scientific' language, be it that of holistic functionalism, or of individual utility-maximization, or whatever.

II

What I have been trying to show is that although there is a strong temptation to by-pass agents' self-descriptions arising from the strong pull of the natural science model, any attempt to do this is stultifying, and leads to an account which cannot be adequately validated.

The view which I am defending here, which I can call the interpretive view, or the *verstehen* view, or the thesis that social theories are about practices, has to be marked off from two other conceptions. One is the original enemy, the natural science model, which I have been arguing against all along. And the other is a false ally, the view that misconstrues interpretation as adopting the agent's point of view. Let me call this 'the incorrigibility thesis', just to give it a name, because in requiring that we explain each culture or society in its own terms, it rules out an account which shows them up as wrong, confused or deluded. Each culture on this view is incorrigible.

The interpretive view, I want to argue, avoids the two equal and opposite mistakes: on one hand, of ignoring self-descriptions altogether, and attempting to operate in some neutral 'scientific' language; on the other hand, of taking these descriptions with ultimate seriousness, so that they become incorrigible. Social theory in general, and political theory especially, is very much in the business of correcting common-sense understanding. It is of very little use unless it goes beyond, unless it frequently challenges and negates what we think we are doing, saying, feeling, aiming at. But its criterion of success is that it makes us as agents more comprehensible, that it makes sense of what we feel, do, aim at. And this it cannot do without getting clear on what we think about our action and feeling. That is, after all, what offers the puzzle which theory tries to resolve. And so there is no way of showing that some theory has actually explained *us* and *our* action until it can be shown to make sense of what we did under *our* description (where this emphatically does *not* mean, let me repeat, showing how what we did made sense). For otherwise, we may have an interesting, speculative rational reconstruction (like the functional theory above), but no way of showing that it actually *explains* anything.

But it might still be thought that I have been too quick with the incorrigibility thesis. It does not just come from a confusion of explananda and explanantia. There is also a serious moral point. Social science aspires not just to understand a single society, but to be universal. In principle, social scientists strive to understand not just their own society and culture but foreign ones. Indeed, the discipline of anthropology is concerned with virtually nothing else.

In this context, to insist blithely that social science has the task of correcting our common-sense understanding – a demand which may sound properly radical when it comes to understanding our own culture – may be to encourage dangerous illusions when it comes to understanding other cultures. One of the striking faults of transcultural and comparative social science has been its tendency to ethnocentrism. At the outset, it was European students who interpreted other societies in terms derived from European culture, very often at the cost of extreme distortion, and frequently also in an unflattering light. Now students from other cultures are also engaged, but the difficulties and dangers are still present. Some have been even tempted to despair of any cross-cultural understanding.

In this situation, it might be argued, to speak of social science as correcting everyday understanding is to invite scientists of a dominant culture to 'correct' the self-understandings of the less dominant ones by substituting their own. What is really going on then becomes simply what *we* can recognize in our own terms; and their self-descriptions are wrong to the extent that they deviate from ours. Transcultural study becomes a field for the exercise of ethnocentric prejudice.

No one can doubt that this has happened. We have only to think of theories like that of Sir James Frazer, which portrayed primitive magic as a kind of early and largely mistaken technology, to see how distorted our perspective can be.

It is in face of this tendency that the incorrigibility thesis seems to have a lot going for it. For it seems guaranteed against ethnocentricity. Indeed, one could easily come to believe that it is the only real safe-guard against it. We understand each culture in its own terms, and we never can fall into the error of misunderstanding one according to the categories of another. This seems to be the message that emerges from Peter Winch's very persuasive 'Understanding a primitive society'.[3]

From this point of view, the interpretive thesis may seem especially vulnerable. At least the natural science model can make a claim for neutrality, by looking for a scientific language which is outside all cultures, and thus can hope to be non-culture-relative. But the *verstehen* view, while not allowing for such neutral languages, nevertheless sets us the task of challenging and going beyond other people's self-understanding. But if not in their terms, how else can we understand them but in our own? Aren't we unavoidably committed to ethnocentricity?

No, I want to argue, we are not. The error in this view is to hold that the language of a cross-cultural theory has to be either theirs or ours. If this were so, then any attempt at understanding across cultures would be faced with an impossible dilemma: either accept incorrigibility, or be arrogantly ethnocentric. But as a matter of fact, while challenging their language of self-understanding, we may also be challenging ours. Indeed, what I want to argue is that there are times where we cannot question the one properly without also questioning the other.

In fact, it will almost always be the case that the adequate language in which we can understand another society is not our language of understanding, or theirs, but rather what one could call a language of perspicuous contrast. This would be a language in which we could formulate both their way of life and ours as alternative possibilities in relation to some human constants at work in both. It would be a language in which the possible human variations would be so formulated that both our form of life and theirs could be perspicuously described as alternative such variations. Such a language of contrast might show their language of understanding to be distorted or inadequate in some respects, or it might show ours to be so (in which case, we might find that understanding them

[3] *American Philosophical Quarterly*, 1 (1964), pp. 307–24.

leads to an alteration of our self-understanding, and hence our form of life – a far from unknown process in history); or it might show both to be so.

This notion of a language of perspicuous contrast is obviously very close to Gadamer's conception of the 'fusion of horizons' and owes a great deal to it. An excellent example of an illuminating theory in comparative politics which uses such a language (or languages) is Montesquieu's. The contrast with despotism was, of course, not an unqualified success, because it was not based on a real understanding of the alien (Turkish or Persian) society. But Montesquieu's contrast between monarchy and republic brought about a great deal of understanding of modern society precisely by placing it relative to (at least the traditional image of) republican society in a language of perspicuous contrast.

This conception of contrast clearly avoids the pitfalls of the incorrigibility thesis. Our account does not have to be in the language of understanding of the agents' society, but rather in the language of contrast. And the agents' language clearly is not taken as incorrigible. At the same time, we are not committed to an ethnocentric course. This much has been learned from the arguments of Winch and others, that the other society may be incomprehensible in our terms; that is, in terms of our self-understanding.

And our conception is also superior to the natural science model. For it can accept the validity of the *verstehen* thesis. In fact, allegedly neutral scientific languages, by claiming to avoid understanding, always end up being unwittingly ethnocentric. The supposedly neutral terms in which other people's actions are identified: the functions of functional theory, or the maximization-descriptions of various consequentialist accounts of individual action, all reflect the stress on instrumental reason in our civilization since the seventeenth century. To see them everywhere is really to distort the action, beliefs, and so on of alien societies in an ethnocentric way. A good example is the theory of development dominant until recently in American political science. This was based on the notion that certain functions were being performed by all political systems, only in different ways by different structures. But these functions, for example interest-aggregation and articulation, are only clearly identifiable in advanced industrial society, where the political process is played out through the articulation of individual and group interests. This identification of functions pre-supposes a degree of individuation which is not present everywhere. The importance of understanding another people's language of self-understanding is precisely that it can protect us against this kind of ethnocentric projection.

We can see how the three approaches – the natural science model, the incorrigibility thesis and the interpretative view – relate if we take a well-discussed example. This is the question of how to account for the exotic practices of primitive societies; for instance their magic. This is the issue taken up by Winch in his 'Understanding a primitive society'.[4]

Very crudely put, there are two families of position on this issue. The traditional view of earlier Western anthropology, going back to Frazer, is to see magic as a kind of proto-science/technology, an attempt by primitive people to master their environment, to do what we do better by modern science and technology. This view naturally gave grounds for criticizing the factual beliefs seen as implicit in the magical practices, for instance the belief in magical powers and spirits.

This theory is naturally congenial to proponents of a 'neutral' scientific language. It allows us a way of identifying what these people are doing, at least what general category their actions fit in, transculturally. At least to get this far, we do not need to grasp their self-understanding in all its peculiarity.

In contrast to this, the rival view is influenced by the incorrigibility thesis or by other similar doctrines. It holds that identifying these practices as a proto-technology is an ethnocentric howler. Rather we have to understand what is going on here as a quite different practice, which may have no corresponding activity in our society. The various rituals of magic are thought to have a 'symbolic' or 'expressive' function, rather than being intended to get things done in the world.[5] The tribe dances to recover its sense of the important meanings it lives by in face of the challenge of drought, rather than seeing the dance as a mechanism to bring on rain – the way we see seeding clouds, for instance.

We can see that this view puts the magical practices beyond the strictures of our modern science and technology. The tribe is not making a factual error about what causes precipitation, they are doing something quite different which cannot be judged in these terms; indeed, should not be judged at all, since this is just their form of life, the way that they face the human constants of birth, death, marriage, drought, plenty, etc. There may be nothing quite corresponding to it in our society. We have to understand it in its own terms; and it is the height of ethnocentric gaucherie to judge it in terms of one of our practices which are all quite

---

[4] *Ibid.*

[5] See J. H. M. Beattie, 'On understanding ritual', in Bryan Wilson (ed.), *Rationality* (Oxford, 1970).

incommensurable with it. To come to grips with it we need understanding.

Now the view I am defending here would disagree with both these approaches. Perhaps somewhat paradoxically, it would accuse both of them of sharing an ethnocentric assumption: that the tribe's practice must be *either* proto-science/technology *or* the integration of meaning through symbolism. For it is a signal feature of our civilization that we have separated these two, and sorted them out. Even our pre-modern forebears of four centuries ago might have found this a little difficult to understand. If we examine the dominant pre-seventeenth-century worldviews, such as the conceptions of the correspondences that were so important in the High Renaissance, it is clear that what we would consider two quite independent goals – understanding what reality is like, and putting ourselves in tune with it – were not separated, nor separable. For us, these are goals which we pursue respectively through science, and (for some of us perhaps) poetry, or music, or flights into the wilderness, or whatever.

But if your conception of man as rational animal is of a being who can understand the rational order of things, and if (following Plato) we hold that understanding this order is necessarily loving it, hence being in tune with it, then it is not so clear how understanding the world and getting in tune with it can be separated. For the terms in which we get in tune with it, and lay bare the significance of things, must be those in which we present it as rational order. And since it is rational order, these will be the most perspicuous terms of understanding. On the other side, to step beyond the conceptual limits of attunement to the world, to cease to see it as a rational order, to adopt, say, a Democritan perspective on it, must be to step beyond the conceptual limits of perspicuous understanding.

I am reminding us of this bit of our past only to illustrate what it can be like not to have sorted out two goals which we now consider quite distinct and incombinable. We do this because the seventeenth-century revolution in science involved, inter alia, sorting these out and rigorously separating them. This has been the basis for our spectacular progress in natural science of the last three centuries.

So the hypothesis I put forward is that the way to understand the magical practices of some primitive societies might be to see them not through the disjunction, either proto-technology or expressive activity, but rather as partaking of a mode of activity in which this kind of clear separation and segregation is not yet made. Now identifying these two possibilities – respectively, the fusion and the segregation of the cognitive or manipulative on one hand, and the symbolic or integrative on the other

– amounts to finding a language of perspicuous contrast. It is a language which enables us to give an account of the procedures of both societies in terms of the same cluster of possibilities.

Unlike the neutralist account, it does not involve projecting our own gamut of activities on to the agents of the other society. It allows for the fact that their range of activities may be crucially different from ours, that they may have activities which have no correspondent in ours; which in fact they turn out to do. But unlike the incorrigibility view, it does not just accept that their particular activities will be incommensurable with ours, and must somehow be understood on their own terms or not at all. On the contrary, it searches for a language of perspicuous contrast in which we can understand their practices in relation to ours.

This means that their self-understanding is not incorrigible. We avoid criticizing them on irrelevant grounds. We do not see them as just making a set of scientific/technological errors. But we can criticize them. For the separation perspective has *in certain respects* shown its undoubted superiority over the fusion perspective. It is infinitely superior for the understanding of the natural world. Our immense technological success is proof of this. It may be that we are inferior to the primitives in other respects, for example our integration with our world, as some contemporaries would hold. But this is something which the language of contrast should help us to assess more clear-headedly. It certainly contributes to our understanding, whatever the verdict, because we can see how the modern scientific perspective is an historic achievement and not the perennial human mode of thought.

This example was meant to show how the interpretive approach, far from leading to ethnocentrism, ought properly understood to bring about the exact opposite, because it will frequently be the case that we cannot understand another society until we have understood ourselves better as well. This will be so wherever the language of perspicuous contrast which is adequate to the case also forces us to redescribe what we are doing. In the above example, it forces us to see the separation of knowledge of and attunement with the cosmos as something we have brought about, one possibility among others, and not as the inescapable framework of all thought. We are always in danger of seeing our ways of acting and thinking as the only conceivable ones. That is exactly what ethnocentricity consists in. Understanding other societies ought to wrench us out of this; it ought to alter our self-understanding. It is the merit of the interpretive view that it explains how this comes about, when it does.

As a matter of fact, in the world encounter of cultures over the last four centuries, there has been a great deal of alteration in self-understanding through meeting with others. Only it has been very unevenly distributed. It was the societies who were less powerful who felt the full force of the constraint to alter their traditional terms of understanding. The dominant culture, the European, was for a while afforded the luxury of ethnocentricity. Power can allow itself illusions.

But as the world moves towards a new equilibriu⌐ of power, a new kind of mutual understanding ought also to be possible unless the different parties are again tempted to flee from it into the convenient illusions of scientific or religious infallibility. In so far as a new mutual understanding involves a new self-understanding – and this can be disturbing – the temptations to flee may be all too pressing.

III

I have tried to present a view here of social and political theories as theories about practice. In this they are to be sharply contrasted with the theories which have developed in the natural sciences. The temptation to assimilate the two is very strong in our civilization, partly because of the signal success of the natural sciences, partly because they seem to promise a degree of technological control over things which we often long for in society.

But to yield to this temptation is to fall into a distorted conception of what we are doing in social science. And this has a cost. We generate not only bogus explanations and specious knowledge, but we also encourage ourselves to look for technological solutions to our deepest social problems, which are frequently aggravated by our misguided attempts to manipulate their parameters.

I have tried to argue that learning to situate our social theorizing among our *practices* can free us from these misconceptions. It can enable us to understand better what it is to validate a theory. We can see how explaining another involves understanding him. And at the same time, it can give us some insight into the complex relations that bind explanation and self-definition, and the understanding of self and other.

In this paper, I have tried to get to the root of the intellectual and moral malaise which we feel in theorizing about very different societies. If explanation demands understanding, then how can we ever be confident that we have explained what goes on in another society? But more, if the account is to make sense to us, how can it avoid being critical? And what gives us this right to declare that others are wrong about themselves? The moral malaise in particular makes us want to flee into a supposedly neutral social science, or into a debilitating relativism.

My contention has been that there is no cause to lose our nerve. Understanding is inseparable from criticism, but this in turn is inseparable from self-criticism. Seeing this, of course, may give us an even stronger motive to panic and take refuge in a bogus objectivity, but it ought to discredit decisively the justifying grounds for this move.

This brings to the fore another facet of the interweaving of explanation and self-definition which has been implicit in much of the above discussion. What I have been trying to sketch above is the way in which understanding another society can make us challenge our self-definitions. It can force us to this, because we cannot get an adequate explanatory account of them until we understand their self-definitions, and these may be different enough from ours to force us to extend our language of human possibilities.

But what this also shows is the way in which explanatory sciences of society are logically and historically dependent on our self-definitions. They are logically dependent, because a valid account, I have argued, must take the subject as an agent. But this points also to an historical dependence: within any given culture, the languages of social science are developed out of and nourished by the languages of self-definition which have grown within it. The idea of a science which could ignore culture and history, which could simply by-pass the historically developed languages of political and social self-understanding, has been one of the great recurring illusions of modern Western civilization.

Supposedly independent and culture-transcendant theories of politics turn out to be heavily dependent on certain parochial Western forms of political culture. For instance, a conception of the political system as responding to the demands generated by individuals or partial groups within society is obviously heavily dependent for whatever plausibility it may possess on the individualist practices of modern Western politics, within which government institutions figure mainly as instruments. If we did not have an institutional and political life in which negotiation and brokerage between individual and group interests played such a large and legitimately accepted role, there would not even be a surface case for explaining our political life by these theories.

But the fact that our practices are of this kind is itself dependent on the self-definitions of an individualist kind which have grown in our civilization; and these in turn have been fed by the atomist-instrumentalist theories which bulk so large in modern thought. So that contemporary political science has a large unacknowledged, and hence also undischarged, debt to modern political theory.

The self-definitions, in other words, give the explanatory theory some fit. Which is far from saying that the fit is perfect. On the contrary, the vice of these individualist theories is that they ignore important other sides of Western political reality, those that are bound up with the practices of self-rule, and our self-understanding as citizen republics. It can be argued that these are as fundamental and integral to our reality as the practices captured in atomist-instrumentalist theories. And these, of course, have been explored and further defined in other traditions of political theory, for example the tradition of civic humanism, or from a revolutionary perspective, Marxist or anarchist theory. The practice of Western society today is partly shaped by the definitions these theories have provided. And they have correspondingly offered the bases of critical political science.

Thus the supposedly culture-free political science, which models its independence of history on the paradigm of natural science, is in fact deeply rooted in Western culture. What is worse, its roots are in one of the warring tendencies in Western political culture. So that it is not only unaware of its origins, but also deeply and unconsciously partisan. It weighs in on behalf of atomist and instrumentalist politics against the rival orientations to community and citizen self-rule.

But when one comes to comparative politics, the distortion is even greater. The supposedly culture-free model is applied to societies in which nothing closely analogous to the atomist-instrumentalist politics of the West exists, and the result is both unilluminating and tendentious. That is, nothing very much is explained in the politics of these non-Western societies, while the theory insinuates the norm of instrumentalist good function as the unquestionable telos of development. The confused model of value-free, culture-transcendent science hides from its practitioners both their ethnocentrism and their norm-setting. In fact they are unconsciously setting for non-Western society a goal which no Western society would consent to for a minute. Because in fact, in Western politics, instrumentalist politics has been tempered and counter-balanced and controlled by the politics of citizen participation. Indeed, the fact that this equilibrium is now under threat is, I believe, the source of a major crisis in Western society.

But the influence of inappropriate, Western and pseudo-universal models over the social science of some non-Western Countries — exemplified, I would argue, by the impact of American behaviouralism on

Indian political science – is due to more than historic relations of unequal political power. If we take this impact as an example, it is closely bound up, I should want to claim, with a failure to appreciate that an illuminating political science of Indian society would have to be based on Indian self-definitions.

But this failure itself is due to the relative absence in traditional Indian thought of self-definitions of *politics*, by which I mean something like: the practices by which people contribute, cooperatively or in struggle, to shape the way power and authority are exercised in their lives. As Ashis Nandy has argued,[6] there is a traditional Indian reflection on statecraft, focussed on non-moral and non-responsible uses of power; and there are conceptions of the proper order of things, even with a specific place for political power, if we follow Louis Dumont.[7] But politics as a realm of activity with its own intrinsic norms, its own specific good or fulfilments, had no place in this tradition.

This is not surprising. This notion of politics, it could be argued, was invented in the West, more specifically, by the Greeks. And this was itself no accident, in that the Greeks had developed practices of participation in power that few other peoples had. Traditional India, one could say, did not need the concept of a practice it did not possess.

But politics exist in contemporary India. There are practices by which people contribute to shape the incidence of power, whatever inequalities and exclusions may mar the democratic process. Contemporary India thus does need a concept of this kind. But if I am right, this is one thing that cannot be provided ready-made from outside. An appropriate concept – or concepts – of politics in India will only arise through an articulation of the self-definitions of people engaged in the practices of politics in India. That is, after all, how the few notions of politics which offer us any insight at all arose in the West. It is, I believe, the only path by which such concepts can arise. And it follows from what I argued above that this would not just be of relevance to India. A more appropriate political science for this society would transform comparative politics. It would put the challenge of developing an adequate theoretical language in which very different practices of politics, Indian and Western, could be compared in an illuminating way. To achieve such a language would in turn transform the understanding each of our societies has of itself. The international community of scholars has potentially a great deal to gain from work in India.

---

[6] See his 'The making and unmaking of political cultures in India', in Ashis Nandy, *At the Edge of Psychology* (New Delhi, 1980).

[7] See *Homo hierarchicus* (Paris, 1966).

CHAPTER FIVE

RATIONALITY

What do we mean by rationality? We often tend to reach for a characterization in formal terms. Rationality can be seen as logical consistency, for instance. We can call someone irrational who affirms both p and not-p. By extension, someone who acts flagrantly in violation of his own interests, or of his own avowed objectives, can be considered irrational.

This can be seen as a possible extension of the case of logical inconsistency, because we are imputing to this agent end E, and we throw in the principle: who wills the end wills the means. And then we see him acting to prevent means M from happening, acting as it were on the maxim: let me prevent M. Once you spell it out, this makes a formal inconsistency.

Can we then understand the irrationality in terms of the notion of inconsistency? It might appear so for the following reason: the mere fact of having E as an end and acting to prevent M is not sufficient to convict the agent of irrationality. He might not realize that the correct description of his end was 'E'; he might not know that M was the indispensable means; he might not know that what he was now doing was incompatible with M. In short, he has to know, in some sense, that he is frustrating his own goals, before we are ready to call him irrational. Of course, the knowledge we attribute to him may be of a rather special kind. He may be unable or unwilling to acknowledge the contradiction; but in this case, our imputation of irrationality depends on our attributing unconscious knowledge to him.

Thus logical inconsistency may seem the core of our concept of irrationality, because we think of the person who acts irrationally as having the wherewithal to formulate the maxims of his action and objectives which are in contradiction with each other.

Possibly inconsistency is enough to explain the accusations of irrationality that we bandy around in our civilization. But our concept of rationality is richer. And this we can see when we consider the issue: are there standards of rationality which are valid across cultures? Can we claim that, for instance, peoples of pre-scientific culture who believe, let us say, in witchcraft or magic are less rational than we are? Or at least that their beliefs are less rational?

This is the question discussed by Peter Winch in his celebrated article 'Understanding a primitive society'.[1] He takes as the basis of his discussion Evans-Pritchard's study of witchcraft among the Azande, and he vigorously rebuts the suggestion that we can condemn Azande beliefs about witchcraft and oracles as irrational.

One might think that this imputation was pretty hard to rebut when Evans-Pritchard seems to catch Azande in what looks like a flagrant contradiction. Post-mortem examination of a suspect's intestines can reveal or fail to reveal 'witchcraft substance', and hence show conclusively that he was/was not a witch. Now this belief, together with beliefs about the inheritance of witchcraft, ought to make the test sufficient to show that all members of the suspect's clan were/were not witches. A very few post-mortem results scattered among the clans ought to settle the question for everyone for all time. But the Azande apparently do not draw this conclusion. They go on treating the question as an open one, whether X or Y is a witch. Are they irrational?

Winch argues against this conclusion. The above just shows that the Azande are engaged in a quite different language game: 'Zande notions of witchcraft do not constitute a theoretical system in terms of which Azande try to gain a quasi-scientific understanding of the world.'[2] So it is a misunderstanding to try to press Zande thought to a contradiction here.

I cannot help feeling that this answer is insufficient as it stands. Even if the Azande are not interested in building a theoretical understanding of the world, it surely matters to them if their whole system for imputing witch status lands them in a contradiction. Their whole practice seems to imply that there is very much a fact of the matter whether X is a witch, and it is this which would seem to be threatened if the criteria were to yield contradictory results.

But in fact the Azande were probably quite justified on their own terms in brushing off Evans-Pritchard's objections. If one wanted to derive a theoretical defence from what is implicit in their judgements and practice, it might not be hard to do so. One might say something of the kind: witch power is mysterious; it doesn't operate according to the exceptionless laws that you Europeans take as the basis of what you call science. But only if you assume this does the contradiction arise.

But of course, no such answer was forthcoming. And here we come to what is perhaps the crucial difference for our question between Zande society and ours: we have this activity of theoretical under-standing which seems to have no counterpart among them.

What is theoretical understanding? The term goes back, of course, to the Greek expression which we translate as 'contemplation' (*theōria*). And however far the modern usage has strayed from the original, there is a continuity. This consists in the fact that a theoretical understand-ing aims at a disengaged perspective. We are not trying to understand things merely as they impinge on us, or are relevant to the purposes we are pursuing, but rather grasp them as they are, outside the immediate perspective of our goals and desires and activities. This is not to say that a theory may not have a big pay-off in practical or productive terms; nor even that the motivation for engaging in theoretical enquiry may not be this expected pay-off. But it remains the case that the understanding itself is framed in terms of a broader perspective, and it gives us a picture of reality which is not simply valid in the context of our goals. The paradox of modern scientific practice is the discovery that such detached understanding has a much higher eventual pay-off.

The original idea of 'contemplation' carried the sense of this disen-gaged perspective; and although there has been a battle in our civiliz-ation as to what this entailed, and most notably a sharp discontinuity in the scientific revolution of the seventeenth century, about which more below, we are still recognizably the heirs of those who coined this Greek term. This kind of activity implies two connected things: that we come to distinguish this disengaged perspective from our ordi-nary stances of engagement, and that one values it as offering a higher – or in some sense superior – view of reality. We do not find these things in every culture, and this makes for an immense difference in the things we think and say.

Now theoretical understanding is related to rationality, since the beginning of our intellectual culture. The Greek word we translate as 'reason' is of course *logos*, which has a large range of related meanings, including 'word', 'speech', 'account' as well as 'reason'. Reason is taken by both Plato and Aristotle as a condition of really knowing something.

For Plato in the *Republic*, to have real knowledge of something (*epistēmē*) is to be able to 'give an account' of it (*logon didōnai*). This seems to involve being able to *say* clearly what the matter in question is. Rational understanding is linked to articulation.

This offers a possible interpretation of 'rational' which we might see as very important in our tradition: we have a rational grasp of something when we can *articulate* it, that means, distinguish and lay out the different features of the matter in perspicuous order. This is involved when we try to formulate things in language, which is why the Greek philosophical vocabulary marks this inner connection between speech and reason, even though at the time not very much was made of language itself as an object of philosophical enquiry.

But if this is so, then theory and rationality are connected. The best articulation of something is what lays it out in the most perspicuous order. But for those matters amenable to theoretical understanding, the most perspicuous order will be that from the disengaged perspective. This offers a broader, more comprehensive grasp on things. Thus one might say: the demands of rationality are to go for theoretical understanding where this is possible.

We have to add this last rider, because not everything may be amenable to theory. For instance, Aristotle thought that moral matters were not, in which he saw himself as disagreeing with Plato. But it may be possible to be more or less rational in these matters as well, as indeed Aristotle believed we could be. There may be a kind of perspicuous articulation which cannot be theoretical, for example because disengagement does not make sense here as a demand, but attaining which constitutes being rational.

But the connection between rational and theoretical is none the less close, if theoretical understanding is the most rational kind in its field, even if it is not the whole of rationality.

I think that we who live in a theoretical culture tend to find some view of this kind plausible. And so we are tempted to judge other, atheoretical cultures as *ipso facto* less rational. This is quite a distinct question from finding them contradictory or inconsistent.

Indeed, the above understanding of rationality can show how consistency can be a key criterion, without exhausting the force of the term. To strive for rationality is to be engaged in articulation, in finding the appropriate formulations. But it is a standard intrinsic to the activity of formulating that the formulations be consistent. Nothing is clearly articulated with contradictory formulations (unless one wants to claim that being is itself subject to contradiction, a view which has well-known defenders). So consistency is plainly a necessary condition of rationality.

But within the context of our theoretical culture, there are more than these formal criteria of rationality. Someone who flagrantly violates the canons of theoretical discourse (or what are understood to be such), while claiming to talk about things and describe how things are, seems also to be sinning against rationality. Of course, if the agent concerned is a member of our culture, we can interpret this as contradictory behaviour. For we assume that one among us who opens his mouth to describe understands his own activity as falling under the appropriate canons; to violate them is to frustrate his own ends.

But the judgement of irrationality, or at least of lesser rationality, does not depend on contradiction. For we are tempted to judge as less rational members of atheoretical cultures who plainly do not accept our canons – or at least may not, for it may not be at first sight as plain as all that what canons they do accept.

This brings us back to the Azande. We cannot jump to the conclusion that they are irrational on the grounds that we have caught them in a contradiction which they persist in disregarding; but this is not because they are playing some language game in which contradiction does not matter. There may be such, but I find it hard to see how witchcraft imputation could be one. Rather it is plausible that the apparent contradictions could be ironed out if the peculiar nature of witches and witchcraft were to be given theoretical description. We already have a hint of this in the Azande sense that it all adds up somehow, which must underlie their unconcern when Evans-Pritchard points to the seeming contradictions. But of course, they are quite uninterested in working this out for Evans-Pritchard or anyone else, as might the members of some theoretical culture – the kind of thing that some of our cleverest ancestors did who went along with the witch craze of early modern Europe. (And some of the intellectual techniques are already in evidence in Zande in attempts to explain inconsistent poison oracle results.)

But their very disinterest creates an imputation of lesser rationality in our minds. From our point of view, we feel like saying of them that they are not interested in how things really are, outside how things function for them in their world of social practices. They are not interested in justifying what they say and believe from this broader perspective; from which perspective, were they to adopt it, we believe that some of their central tenets would collapse (and perhaps even from inner contradiction in some cases).

This is the imputation which Winch rejects, on the grounds, if I can put it my way, that it is wrong to judge an atheoretical culture by the standards of a theoretical one. And wrong in the sense of being a mistake, though there is undoubtedly some arrogance involved here as well. The activities engaged in are different, and it would be wrong to assess them in the same way.

Others have argued that this thesis of incommensurable activities is wrong-headed, and that the problem of rationality cannot be side-stepped in this way. This is the issue I would like to take up. Thus Winch in the article quoted above goes on to take Alasdair MacIntyre to task for claiming to be able to apply standards of rationality cross-culturally. This would allow us to judge in certain cases that the practices of another culture were deficient in rationality relative to the analogous ones in our culture; and the practices of witchcraft would be a paradigm target for this kind of judgement.

Winch argues against this that standards of rationality may differ from culture to culture; and that we have to beware of applying our standards for a foreign practice where they may be entirely inappropriate. What lies behind the difference in standards of rationality is the difference in activities. Something quite different is probably afoot in a primitive society's practice of magic. There has been a tendency among modern Western thinkers to understand magic as a kind of proto-technology, an early attempt to get control over nature by less effective means than scientifically informed technique. The primitive practice naturally suffers from the comparison, and can even be made to look irrational in its resistance to refutation by the standards of modern science.

Sir James Frazer offers the classical formulation of a view of this kind. And although his Victorian confidence in his categories now seems to us flat-footedly ethnocentric, it is not entirely clear that we manage to avoid more sophisticated variants of the same basic error. So Winch seems to argue here: 'MacIntyre criticizes, justly, Sir James Frazer for having imposed the image of his own culture on more primitive ones; but that is exactly what MacIntyre himself is doing here.'[3]

We should consider more seriously the possibility that we have quite failed to understand what the point of the activity is. Zande magic may not be just 'a (misguided) technique for producing consumer goods'.[4] Rather the rites may constitute a 'form of expression' through which the possibilities and dangers inherent in life 'may be contemplated and reflected on – and perhaps also thereby transformed and deepened'. The rites 'express an attitude to contingencies', while at the same time 'they are also fundamental to social relations'.

[3] *Ibid.*, p. 319.   [4] *Ibid.*, p. 321.

The judgement of lesser rationality seems to be based on a misunderstanding. It is not just itself mistaken; it is based on an approach which will never allow us to achieve an adequate account of the foreign society studied. The very nature of human action requires that we understand it, at least initially, in its own terms; that means that we understand the descriptions that it bears for the agents. It is only because we have failed to do that that we can fall into the fatal error of assimilating foreign practices to our own familiar ones.

Now I am attracted by this Winchian argument, but I think there is something still inadequate about it as it stands. Somehow the contrast does not quite come off. It may sound convincing that the Azande are among other things 'expressing an attitude to contingencies' in their magical rites. But can we say that they are doing this *as against* trying to control certain of these contingencies? It would seem not. And Winch himself makes this point: the rites have a relation to consumption; they are undertaken to make the crops grow free of the hazards that threaten them. Winch's thesis is that they *also* have this other dimension which he stresses.

That is why the position Winch criticizes always will have a certain plausibility. We can all too easily find analogies between primitive magical practices and some of our own, because they *do* overlap. Thus a lot of what Robin Horton says in his 'African traditional thought and Western science'[5] concerning the analogies between African religious thinking and Western scientific theory is very convincing: both bring unity out of diversity, place things in a wider causal context, and so on.

But this is beside the point which is really at issue. Only if the claim were that primitive religion and magic comprised a set of activities clearly distinct from and contrasted to those involved in modern science would the very useful and illuminating points of the kind made by Horton constitute a valid objection. Sometimes people who inveigh against ethnocentric interpretations sound as though they are making a claim of this kind. For instance, J. Beattie ('On understanding ritual')[6] distinguishes practical from symbolic or expressive activity, and argues that we ought to understand ritual mainly as concerned with the second.

But to make this kind of clear contrast is, paradoxically, to be insufficiently radical in our critique of ethnocentricity. For it describes the difference between the two societies in terms of a contrast between activities that makes sense to us in virtue of our form of life, but would be

---

[5] In R. Wilson (ed.), *Rationality* (Oxford, 1970), pp. 131–71.
[6] In Wilson, *Rationality*, pp. 240–68.

unintelligible to the people whose form of life we are trying to understand. It is a feature of our civilization that we have developed a practice of scientific research and its technological application from which the symbolic and expressive dimensions have been to a great extent purged. The seventeenth-century revolution in scientific thought rejected previously dominant scientific languages in which what one can call an expressive dimension had an important part. This was the case, for instance, with the language of 'correspondences', in which elements in different domains of being could be thought to correspond to each other in virtue of embodying the same principle.

We have an example of this kind of thinking in a passage like the following, which is an early-seventeenth-century 'refutation' of Galileo's discovery of the moons of Jupiter:

There are seven windows given to animals in the domicile of the head, through which the air is admitted to the tabernacle of the body, to enlighten, to warm and to nourish it. What are these parts of the microcosmos: Two nostrils, two eyes, two ears and a mouth. So in the heavens, as in a macrocosmos, there are two favourable stars, two unpropitious, two luminaries, and Mercury undecided and indifferent. From this and from many other similarities in nature, such as the seven metals, etc., which it were tedious to enumerate, we gather that the number of planets is necessarily seven.[7]

The argument seems ludicrous to us today, and we are likely to remember the scene in Berthold Brecht's *Galileo*, where the Paduan philosophers refuse to look through his telescope, preferring to show by argument from Aristotle that the moons could not be there. What could be more irrational from our point of view?

But of course the argument would make sense if we could be confident that the world order was actually put together in such a way as to embody the same set of principles in its different domains: just as when we enter an airline washroom and see 'No Smoking', 'Ne pas fumer', and some inscription in Japanese, we feel entitled to suppose that any account of how those letter marks got there would have to incorporate some reference to the speech act of instructing users to refrain from smoking.

But why should people feel confident of this? I think we can understand this if we reach back into the past of our own civilization, to which after all this kind of reasoning belongs, and note the quite different boundaries that were then drawn between activities: why must the universe exhibit some meaningful order, in terms of which the contours of the parts could be

⁷ S. Warhaft (ed.), *Francis Bacon: A Selection of his Works* (Toronto, 1965), p. 17.

explained? I think this becomes understandable if we see understanding the universe and coming into attunement with it as inseparable activities.

To see what this might involve, let us look at one of the interpretations of Plato which was extremely influential in the development of the mode of thought which underlies the above passage. Presented over-simply, we could say that it gives us a view of man as a rational animal; and rationality as the capacity to grasp the order of being. To say that man is a rational animal is to say that this is his telos, the goal he implicitly is directed towards by nature. To achieve it is to attain happiness and well-being. Not to have attained it, or worse, not even to be endeavouring to do so, is to be in misery and confusion. There must be confusion, because properly understood our nature can only turn us towards our proper goal. To know it is to love it; consequently, to have anything else as a goal is to have imperfect knowledge of our own nature, and hence of the order of things of which it is a part.

But then there is a close connection between understanding the order of things and being in attunement with it. We do not understand the order of things without understanding our place in it, because we are part of this order. And we cannot understand the order and our place in it without loving it, without seeing its goodness, which is what I want to call being in attunement with it. Not being in attunement with it is a sufficient condition of not understanding it, for anyone who genuinely understands must love it; and not understanding it is incompatible with being in attunement with it, since this presupposes understanding.

For anyone with this outlook there is a strong temptation to believe in a meaningful order, or at any rate an order of things such that it could be loved, seen to be good, an order with which we could be attuned. If this were not the case, then there could not be a kind of understanding inseparable from attunement; and this seems to threaten the close connection between understanding the world and the wisdom of self-knowledge and self-reconciliation. Those who see the world-order purely in terms of accident and chance are not thereby led to love it more or to be happier with themselves; and this means they must be wrong, if knowledge and wisdom are closely linked.

I am not here trying to reconstruct an *argument* of an influential premodern tradition of thought, let alone of Plato's. I am just trying to point to a close connection between a certain view of the universe as meaningful order and a conception of the close link between understanding and attunement, or knowledge and wisdom. These stand in a relation of mutual support. And if one stands inside an *epistēmē*, to use Foucault's term, which links them together, it becomes not at all strained or unnatural to argue along the lines of the above passage.

I may seem to have wandered a bit far in discussing a controversy three centuries old, but all this relates closely to the main issue. For first it allows us to see how the breaking of the connection between understanding and attunement was an essential part of the modern revolution in science.[8] The conception of the universe as meaningful order, as a possible object of attunement, was seen as a projection, a comforting illusion which stood in the way of scientific knowledge. Science could only be carried on by a kind of ascesis, where we discipline ourselves to register the way things are without regard to the meanings they might have for us.

And this discipline has become central to the norms and practice of modern science. Our civilization is full of admonitions to avoid the facile path of projecting on to the world the order of things which we find satisfying or meaningful or flattering, with criticism for those who follow this, and much self-congratulation on the part of those who believe they do not. We are given early and often the edifying stories of Darwin or Freud, who had the courage to face truths allegedly shattering to our comforting images of cosmic hierarchy and our place in it, and they are sometimes placed in a Trinity with Copernicus (or Galileo) for this reason.

So it comes quite naturally to us to distinguish sharply between scientific study of reality and its accompanying technological spin-off, on one hand, and symbolic activity in which we try to come to terms with the world on the other. This kind of contrast is one that has developed out of our form of life. But exactly for this reason, it is probably going to be unhelpful in understanding people who are very different from us. It certainly would not help to say, for instance, that ritual practices in some primitive society were to be understood simply as symbolic, that is, as being exclusively directed at attunement and not at all at practical control; or that the body of religious beliefs was merely expressive of certain attitudes to the contingencies of life, and not also concerned with giving

---

[8] This is in important ways an oversimplification. It can be argued that one of the motives of the rejection of the conception of the universe as meaningful order was theological. This can be seen to some extent in Bacon's language – his talk of 'Idols' for instance – or with Mersenne. As was already evident earlier with nominalist thinkers in the later Middle Ages, some saw a conception of the universe as self-justifying order as incompatible with the sovereignty and transcendence of the creator. To see reality 'without superstition or imposture, error or confusion', in Bacon's phrase (*Novum Organum*, I. CXXIX), was to help to put oneself back in tune with *God*. But this meant dissolving the identity between scientific understanding of the world and wisdom.

an account of how things are. To this kind of position (if anyone really holds it), arguments like those of Horton are a sufficient answer.

But it is still insufficiently helpful to say something to the effect that ritual practices somehow combine the practical and the symbolic. This may not be flatly untrue, but it is putting the point in ethnocentric language. Somebody might try to combine the two in our civilization, and we could describe his attempt in these terms because we distinguish them clearly. But the point about quite different societies is that the question at least arises whether this distinction has any sense for them.

Here is where the example of the earlier phase of our civilization may help. Within the bounds of that *epistēmē* understanding and attunement cannot be separated. You cannot know the order of things without loving it, nor the other way around. The very attempt to identify separate activities here, two different goals, would have to be based on a confusion. The difference between the two phases is not that they have made different selections or combinations out of the same catalogue of activities, but that their very catalogues are different and, what is more, incommensurable.

I use this latter term to point to the fact that the activities are not just different but incompatible in principle. Two activities are incompatible in practice when as a matter of fact you could not carry on both at the same time. This is a case for football and chess, for instance. The impossibility is merely *de facto*. We could imagine some incredibly athletic genius who could be figuring out how to put his opponent in check at the same time as he feints to get around the defence man and shoots for the goal. But when we come to soccer and rugby football, we have two activities which are incompatible in principle. For the rules which partly define these games prescribe actions in contradiction to each other. Picking up the ball and running with it is against the rules of soccer.

Something like this kind of relation holds between pre- and post-Galilean science. Giving an account in terms of the correspondences just is not a valid move for modern science. Nothing has been accomplished which can be recognized as an explanation. Presented as an account of how things are, it is a 'foul', a violation of the canons of science. But plainly it was meant to be taken as just such an account. Galileo's opponents above were arguing that the moons of Jupiter could not exist on the basis of the order of things of which they would have to be a part. This would only make sense if the order explained how things are as they are. Because the order of things expressed by the correspondences is explanatory, we conclude that the number of planets *must* be seven. It is because we know what underlies and explains what is, that we know what is.

Now the difficult thing about the relation of ritual magic in primitive societies to some of the practices of our society is that it is clearly not identical with any of our practices, nor is it simply different, as other of their practices – their games, for instance – might be. Rather they are incommensurable. They are different, yet they somehow occupy the same space.

If we focus just on the second aspect, at the expense of the first, we will see the primitive practice as the same as one of ours; and then we will be tempted to judge it as inferior, perhaps irrational. And so to avoid ethnocentric arrogance, we may be tempted to seize on the first aspect and forget the second. But then we have just as false a picture, for example practitioners of magic as engaged in an exercise of pure symbolic expression, rather as we do when we sing the national anthem. And *au fond*, we will probably still be guilty of ethnocentricity, since we will be projecting on to them one of the things *we* do, which *we* have distinguished from science or technology: this kind of pure symbolic activity, which is not meant to *effect* anything, is a quintessentially modern thing.

The real challenge is to see the incommensurability, to come to understand how their range of possible activities, that is, the way in which they identify and distinguish activities, differs from ours. As Winch says, 'we do not initially have a category that looks at all like the Zande category of magic';[9] but this is not because their magic is concerned with ends quite foreign to our society, but rather because the ends defined in it cut across ours in disconcerting ways. Really overcoming ethnocentricity is being able to understand two incommensurable classifications.

What does this mean for our main issue, whether we can make judgements of rationality cross-culturally? Winch's argument seemed to be that such judgements were likely to be very dubious, because standards of rationality can differ greatly. And they differ because the activities concerned are different. But when we look at the key cases that interest us, like primitive magic, we find that the activities are not simply different, but rather that they are incommensurable. And this seems to be Winch's view too, because he is far from subscribing to the simple view that primitive magic is some purely expressive activity. If it were, we would already have a category for it, for *we* have lots of purely expressive rituals: singing anthems, striking the flag, etc.

But realizing this threatens to undermine Winch's conclusion. For incommensurable activities are rivals; their constitutive rules prescribe in

[9] Winch, 'Understanding a primitive society', p. 319.

contradiction to each other. Only where two activities are simply different is there no question of judging one to be an inferior version of the other, and perhaps in some cases inferior in rationality. That is what is tempting to the anti-imperialist liberal conscience, wary of ethnocentrism, in a view which assimilates magic to pure symbolic activity. It takes the heat off; we no longer have to judge whose way of life is superior. Or if any judgements are to be made, pre-technological societies seem to come off better because their symbolic activity is so much richer than ours.

But incommensurable ways of life seem to raise the question insistently of who is right. It is hard to avoid this, since anyone seriously practising magic in our society would be considered to have lost his grip on reality, and if he continued impervious to counter-arguments, he would be thought less than fully rational. How do you keep this judgement from extending to the whole way of life in which magic fits?

One answer might be to argue that even though incommensurable, the activities still have their distinct internal criteria of success; that therefore each is bound to come off best by its own standards; and hence that one cannot make any non-ethnocentric judgements of relative superiority.

If I can be permitted to revert once more to my example comparing two phases of our theoretical culture, in order to cast light on comparisons between theoretical and atheoretical cultures, we can see what this would mean. The science of the High Renaissance which Galileo and others pulverized was concerned both with explaining how things are and with wisdom. The Renaissance sage had a different ideal from the modern scientific researcher's. From our point of view within this culture, we may want to argue that our science is clearly superior. We point to the tremendous technological spin-off it has generated in order to silence many doubters.

But a defender of relativism might retort that this begs the question. We are the ones who value technological control; so to us our way is clearly superior. But the sage did not value this, but rather wisdom. And this seems to be a quality we are rather short of, and very often seem shortest of in precisely those societies where technological control is at its greatest. So we still do not seem to have a reason why a Renaissance sage, should one still exist, ought to listen to us. He would still be scoring higher by *his* criteria, even as we are by ours. Each would be invulnerable to others.

Now, as a matter of fact, this argument seems historically inaccurate, since many of the figures of High Renaissance sciences, like Giordano Bruno, for instance, or John Dee, seemed to have very far-reaching ambitions of technological achievement, of which producing gold out of baser metals is merely the most notorious. It is true that these achievements were also seen as having a spiritual dimension quite lacking in our modern goal of technological control, but that is just the standard difference between the two outlooks.

But this objection might seem of no great significance in principle, since there certainly were earlier phases of Western history in which the ideal of the sage had no close connections with that of the magus, or wonder-worker. The in-principle point about the impossibility of non-ethnocentric judgements of superiority would go through even though it might break down adventitiously in this case.

But the point in fact bites deeper. It is not just an accident that there are no more Renaissance magi among us. There is an inner connection between understanding the world and achieving technological control which rightly commands everyone's attention, and doesn't just justify our practices in our own eyes.

I realize I am running up against a widely held contemporary view. For instance, Mary Hesse in her 'Theory and value in the social sciences'[10] speaks of prediction and control as 'pragmatic' criteria – as though we could have chosen to assess our sciences by other ones! But I do not see how this could be. To make a really convincing rebuttal is probably beyond my powers in any circumstances, and certainly it is in the space I have here. But let me say a few things in defence of my view.

Our ordinary, pre-scientific understanding of the world around us is inseparable from an ability to make our way around in it, and deal with the things in it. That is why so much of our pre-scientific language identifies the objects surrounding us by their standard functions and uses in our lives. This goes, for instance, for our words for most of our artefacts, and for many of the distinctions we mark among natural objects – for instance, between the edible and the non-edible, and so on.

In these circumstances, it is difficult to understand how an increase in scientific knowledge beyond pre-scientific common sense could fail to offer potential recipes for more effective practice. Once we see what properties lie behind and explain edibility, how can we fail to notice that the distinction applies also in ways we had not suspected? Once we understand the principles underlying our ability to lift heavy objects in certain stances and not in others, viz., those of leverage, how can we fail to see that we can also apply them to lift objects with other objects? And so on. The basic point is that given the kind of beings we are, embodied and active in the world, and

---

[10] In C. Hookway and P. Pettit (eds), *Action and Interpretation* (Cambridge, 1979), p. 2.

given the way that scientific knowledge extends and supersedes our ordinary understanding of things, it is impossible to see how it could fail to yield further and more far-reaching recipes for action.

But further and more far-reaching recipes for action, when applied, are what we call increased technological control. And this means that the protagonist of modern science has an argument which the Renaissance magus must listen to. One can almost put it in the form of a *modus tollens:* there is not scientific advance without increased technological applicability; but in your case, we see no increased technological application; so you are making no advance. This is of course not a fully conclusive argument, among other reasons because we had to shift from 'applicability' to 'application' in moving from the first premise to the second. The opponent could retort that he was not concerned about these applications, unlike our degenerate consumer society, but that the recipes were being generated none the less. (Once again, I repeat that this unconcern was not in fact true of the magus, but this does not affect the argument.) But assuming that this loophole could be plugged, or at least the opponent placed under challenge to show what these recipes were, we have a prima facie convincing argument in favour of the superiority of modern science.

Of course, the argument could break out at another level, around in just what superiority had been proved. Certainly not in the way of life as a whole. Perhaps, after all, it is better all things considered to live as a Renaissance magus. But surely one could say that modern science represents a superior understanding of the universe, or if you like, the physical universe. Let us suppose even that the retort comes back, say from a Platonist, that the physical universe is hardly an important thing to understand, so why make all this fuss? We do not consider people who have collected a great deal of insignificant knowledge as being scientific tyros; for instance a man who knew how many flies there were in Oxfordshire. Surely we could then reply that Platonic reasons for finding this kind of knowledge without significance are themselves belied by the success of our science. The realm of the material was meant to be that of the flux; the stable reality which can be grasped in truly universal propositions was supposed to lie beyond. But the very technological success of a science of the material based on general laws shows this view to be in serious need of revision.

In short, there is a definite respect in which modern science is superior to its Renaissance predecessor; and this is evident not in spite of but because of their incommensurability. The issue can be seen in this way. One view ties understanding nature to wisdom and attunement, the other dissociates them. In this they have incompatible norms. This is what makes the incommensurability. But precisely because they are not simply different, but are in principle incompatible, we can assess one as superior to the other. One can see, in this case, that the science which dissociates understanding and attunement achieves greater understanding at least of physical nature. And the interlocutor is forced to recognize that something has been achieved here which at least creates a presumption against him and in favour of the new science.

This is not to say that there is some common criterion by which one is proved inferior to the other, if that implies some criterion already accepted by both sides. The whole dimension of technological pay-off may have been profoundly depreciated and considered irrelevant, as it was in the Platonist tradition. But once a spectacular degree of technological control is achieved, it commands attention and demands explanation. The superiority of modern science is that it has a very simple explanation for this: that it has greatly advanced our understanding of the material world. It is not clear what traditional Platonism could say about this phenomenon, or where it could go for an explanation.

What we have here is not an antecedently accepted common criterion, but a facet of our activity – here the connection between scientific advance and technological pay-off – which remains implicit or unrecognized in earlier views, but which cannot be ignored once realized in practice. The very existence of the technological advance forces the issue. In this way, one set of practices can pose a challenge for an incommensurable interlocutor, not indeed in the language of this interlocutor, but in terms which the interlocutor cannot ignore. And out of this can arise valid transcultural judgements of superiority.

Of course, I must repeat, there is no such thing as a single argument proving *global* superiority. The dissociation of understanding of nature and attunement to the world has been very good for the former. Arguably it has been disastrous for the latter goal. Perhaps the critics are right who hold that we have been made progressively more estranged from ourselves and our world in technological civilization. Maybe this could even be shown as convincingly as the scientific superiority of moderns.[11]

But even if it were, it would not refute this scientific superiority. It would just mean that we now had two transcultural judgements of superiority;

---

[11] And certainly the natural science model dissociating understanding and attunement has wreaked havoc in its successive misapplications in the sciences of man in the last few centuries. But this again says nothing about its validity as an approach to inanimate nature.

only unfortunately they would fall on different sides. We should be in a cruel dilemma when it came to choosing the proper human form of life. This may be really our predicament. Or it might be that we are superior in both respects. Or some third alternative might be the case. But wherever the final global verdict falls, it does not invalidate but rather depends on such transcultural judgements.

What does this mean for transcultural judgements of rationality between theoretical and atheoretical societies? It means, it seems to me, that such judgements can be made. They can arise precisely where there are incommensurabilities, such as between the set of beliefs underlying primitive magic, for instance, and modern science.

Both offer articulations, they lay out different features of the world and human action in some perspicuous order. In that, they are both involved in the kind of activity which I have argued is central to rationality. But one culture can surely lay claim to a higher, or fuller, or more effective rationality, if it is in a position to achieve a more perspicuous order than another.

It seems to me that a claim of this kind can be made by theoretical cultures against atheoretical ones. If one protests and asks why the theoretical order is more perspicuous transculturally, granted the admitted difference between the aims of the activities compared, and granted that the two cultures identify and distinguish the activities differently, the answer is that at least in some respects theoretical cultures score successes which command the attention of atheoretical ones, and in fact invariably have done so when they met. A case in point is the immense technological successes of one particular theoretical culture, our modern scientific one.

Of course, this particular superiority commands attention in a quite non-theoretical way as well. We are reminded of the ditty about nineteenth-century British colonial forces in Africa: 'Whatever happens We have got The Gatling gun, And they have not.' But as I have argued above, technological superiority also commands attention for good intellectual reasons. And it is not only through Gatling guns that theoretical cultures have impressed others in time with their superiority, and hence become diffused. They were spreading well before the explosion of modern technology.

Once again, it may be that considerations which we in theoretical cultures can no longer appreciate so overweigh the balance in favour of the pre-theoretical ones as to make them offer the overall superior form of life. But even if this were so, it would not invalidate the transcultural comparisons we do make; and in particular the claim to a higher rationality. It would just overweigh these judgements with other more important ones which told in the other direction.

What does this argument make of Winch's plurality of standards of rationality? In a sense, I entirely agree that we must speak of a plurality of standards. The discourse in which matters are articulated in different societies can be very different; as we can see in the Azande disinterest in explaining away the paradox Evans-Pritchard put to them in witchcraft diagnosis. The standards are different, because they belong to incommensurable activities. But where I want to disagree with Winch is in claiming that plurality does not rule out judgements of superiority. I think the kind of plurality we have here, between the incommensurable, precisely opens the door to such judgements.

But does this mean that I have to say Azande are irrational? This seems a foolish as well as an arrogant thing to say. And so it is, because we naturally make the difference between someone who is in violation of the basic standards governing articulation in his own culture, and people of another culture where the standards are different, even if inferior. The terms 'irrational' we reserve for the first kind of case. That is why I argued in the first section that inconsistency lies at the basis of most of the accusations of irrationality which we trade in our society.

But the concept of rationality is richer than this. Rationality involves more than avoiding inconsistency. What more is involved comes out in the different judgements we make when we compare incommensurable cultures and activities. These judgements take us beyond merely formal criteria of rationality, and point us toward the human activities of articulation which give the value of rationality its sense.

CHAPTER SIX

FOUCAULT ON FREEDOM AND TRUTH

Foucault disconcerts. In a number of ways, perhaps. But the way I want to examine is this: certain of Foucault's most interesting historical analyses, while they are highly original, seem to lie along already familiar lines of critical thought. That is, they seem to offer an insight into what has happened, and into what we have become, which at the same time offers a critique, and hence some notion of a good unrealized or repressed in history, which we therefore understand better how to rescue.

But Foucault himself repudiates this suggestion. He dashes the hope, if we had one, that there is some good we can *affirm*, as a result of the understanding these analyses give us. And by the same token, he seems to raise a question whether there is such a thing as a way out. This is rather paradoxical, because Foucault's analyses seem to bring *evils* to light; and yet he wants to distance himself from the suggestion which would seem inescapably to follow, that the negation or overcoming of these evils promotes a good.

More specifically, Foucault's analyses, as we shall see in greater detail, turn a great deal on power/domination, and on disguise/illusion. He lays bare a modern system of power, which is both more all-penetrating and much more insidious than previous forms. Its strength lies partly in the fact that it is not seen as power, but as science, or fulfilment, even 'liberation'. Foucault's work is thus partly an unmasking.

You would think that implicit in all this was the notion of two goods which need rescuing, and which the analyses help to rescue: freedom and truth; two goods which would be deeply linked granted the fact that the negation of one (domination) makes essential use of the negation of the other (disguise). We would be back on familiar terrain, with an old Enlightenment-inspired combination. But Foucault seems to repudiate both. The idea of a liberating truth is a profound illusion. There is no truth which can be espoused, defended, rescued *against* systems of power. On the contrary, each such system defines its own variant of truth. And there is no escape from power into freedom, for such systems of power are co-extensive with human society. We can only step from one to another.

Or at least, this is what Foucault *seems* to be saying in passages like the following:

contrary to a myth whose history and functions would repay further study, truth isn't the reward of free spirits, . . . nor the privilege of those who have succeeded in liberating themselves. Truth is a thing of this world: it is produced only by virtue of multiple forms of constraint. And it induces regular effects of power. Each society has its own régime of truth, its 'general politics' of truth: that is, the type of discourse which it accepts and makes function as true . . .[1]

Is there confusion/contradiction here, or a genuinely original position? The answer I want to offer cannot be put in a single phrase, but roughly, I think that there is some of both. However, the nature of the combination is not easy to understand.

I

I would like to examine this issue in connection with some of the analyses of Foucault's recent historical works, *Surveiller et punir* and *Histoire de la sexualité*.[2] For the sake of my discussion, I want to isolate three lines of analysis, each of which suggests, or is historically connected with, a certain line of critique, but where in each case Foucault repudiates the latter. But I have ordered these analyses so that the argument arising from them moves towards more radical repudiations. That is, at first sight, analysis 2 will seem to offer a reason for repudiating the good suggested by analysis 1; and 3 will seem to offer a reason for rejecting the good implicit in 2; only to be in turn rejected. Or so it would seem.

1

The first that I want to take up is the contrast drawn in *Surveiller et punir* between modes of punishment in the classical age and today. The book opens with a riveting description of the execution of a parricide in seventeenth-century France. The modern is appalled, horrified. We seem to be more in the world of our contemporary fanatical perpetrators of massacre, the Pol Pots, the Idi Amins, rather than in that of the orderly process of law in a civilized, well-established regime. Obviously something very

---

[1] *Power/Knowledge* (New York, 1980), p. 131.
[2] *Surveiller et punir* (Paris, 1975); *Histoire de la sexualité* (Paris, 1976), vol. 1.

big has changed in our whole understanding of ourselves, of crime and punishment.

Bringing us up against this evidence of radical historical discontinuity is what Foucault does superlatively well. For our eyes, the details of the execution of Damiens bespeak gratuitous cruelty, sadism. Foucault shows that they had another reason then. The punishment can be seen as a kind of 'liturgy' ('la liturgie des supplices').[3] Human beings are seen as set in a cosmic order, constituted by a hierarchy of beings which is also a hierarchy of goods. They stand also in a political order, which is related to and in a sense endorsed by the cosmic one. This kind of order is hard to explain in modern terms, because it is not simply an order of things, but an order of meanings. Or to put it in other terms, the order of things which we see around us is thought to reflect or embody an order of Ideas. You can explain the coherence things have in terms of a certain kind of making sense.

Certain kinds of crime – parricide is a good example – are offences against this order, as well as against the political order. They do not just represent damage done to the interests of certain other individuals, or even of the ensemble of individuals making up the society. They represent a violation of the order, tearing things out of their place, as it were. And so punishment is not just a matter of making reparation for damage inflicted, or of removing a dangerous criminal, or of deterring others. The order must be set right. In the language of the time, the criminal must make *amenda honorable*.

So the punishments have a meaning. I find Foucault convincing on this. The violence done to the order is restored by being visited on the wrong-doer. Moreover this restoral is made the more effective by his participation in the (to us) grisly scenario, in particular his avowal. As Foucault puts it, one of the goals was to 'instaurer le supplice comme moment de vérité'.[4] Moreover, since the order violated includes the political order – royal power in this case – and this order is public, not in the modern Benthamian sense of touching the general interest, but in the older sense of a power which essentially manifests itself in public space, the restoral has to be enacted in public space. What to us is the additional barbarity of making a spectacle of all these gruesome goings-on was an essential part of what was being *effected* in the punishments of that age.

L'atrocité qui hante le supplice joue donc un double rôle: principe de la communication du crime avec la peine, elle est d'autre part l'exaspération du châtiment par

---

[3] *Surveiller et punir*, p. 53.   [4] *Ibid.*, p. 47.

rapport au crime. Elle assure d'un même coup l'éclat de la vérité et celui du pouvoir; elle est le rituel de l'enquête qui s'achève et la cérémonie où triomphe le souverain.[5]

It is clear that one of the things which makes us so different from the people of that epoch is that the whole background notion of order has disappeared for us. This has been connected to, is in a sense the obverse side of, the development of the modern identity, the sense we have of ourselves as free, self-defining subjects, whose understanding of their own essence or of their paradigm purposes is drawn from 'within', and no longer from a supposed cosmic order in which they are set. But this is not the whole story; it is not just that we have lost their background rationale. It is also that a new notion of the good has arisen. This is defined by what has often been called modern 'humanitarianism'. We have acquired, since the eighteenth century, a concern for the preservation of life, for the fulfilling of human need, and above all for the relief of suffering, which gives us an utterly different set of priorities from our forbears. It is this, and not just our loss of their background, which makes them seem to us so barbaric.

What lies behind this modern humanitarianism? This is a big and deep story. No one can claim to understand it fully. But I have to go into it a little, because his interpretation of it is central to Foucault's position. I think one of the important factors which underlies it is the modern sense of the significance of what I want to call 'ordinary life'. I use this as a term of art for that ensemble of activities which are concerned with the sustaining of life, with its continuation and reproduction: the activities of producing and consuming, or marriage, love and the family. While in the traditional ethics which came to us from the ancients, this had merely infra-structural significance (it was the first term in Aristotle's duo of ends: 'life and the good life' (*zên kai euzên*); a career (*bios*) concerned with it alone put us on a level with animals and slaves), in modern times, it becomes the prime locus of significance.

In traditional ethics, ordinary life is overshadowed by what are identified as higher activities – contemplation, for some, the citizen life, for others. And in medieval Catholicism something like this overshadowing of ordinary lay life occurs relative to the dedicated life of priestly or monastic celibacy. It was particularly the Protestant Reformation, with its demand for personal commitment, its refusal of the notion

[5] *Ibid.*, pp 59–60.

of first- and second-class Christians (unless it be the distinction between saved and damned), its refusal of any location of the sacred in human space, time or rite, and its insistence on the Biblical notion that life was hallowed, which brought about the reversal. This reversal continues through the various secularized philosophies. It underlies the Baconian insistence on utility, and partly in this way feeds into the mainstream humanism of the Enlightenment. It has obviously levelling, anti-aristocratic potential.

But more than this, it has come, I would claim, to inform the entirety of modern culture. Think for instance of the growth of the new understanding of the companionate marriage in the seventeenth and eighteenth centuries, the growing sense of the importance of *emotional* fulfilment in marriage – indeed, the whole modern sense that one's *feelings* are a key to the good life. This is now defined as involving certain emotional experiences. If I can use the term 'the good life' as an absolutely general, ethic-neutral term for whatever is considered good-/holy/of ultimate value on any given view, then I would want to say that the Reformation theologies, with their new stress on the calling, made ordinary life the significant locus of the issues which distinguish the good life. *Euzên* now occurs within *zên*. And modern culture has continued this.

This, I believe, is an important part of the background to modern humanitarianism. Because with the ethics of ordinary life arises the notion that serving life (and with later, more subjectivist variants, avoiding suffering) is a paradigm goal in itself, while at the same time the supposed higher ends which previously trumped life – aristocratic honour, the sustaining of cosmic order, eventually even religious orthodoxy itself – are progressively discredited.

This perspective would make one envisage the change in philosophies of punishment since the seventeenth century as a gain; perhaps in other respects also a loss, but at least in this one respect as a gain. In other words, it seems to contain a critique of the older view as based on a mystification, in the name of which human beings were sacrificed, and terrible suffering was inflicted. At least that has been the Enlightenment-inspired reaction.

But Foucault doesn't take that stance at all. Ultimately, as is well-known, he wants to take a stance of neutrality. Here are just two systems of power, classical and modern. But at first blush, there seems to be a *value* reason for refusing the Enlightenment valuation. This lies in a reading of modern humanitarianism as the reflection of a new system of domination, directed towards the maintenance and increase of 'bio-mass'. This is the second analysis, which I would like to look at briefly.

2

The picture is drawn, in both *Surveiller et punir* and volume 1 of *Histoire de la sexualité*, of a constellation combining modern humanitarianism, the new social sciences, and the new disciplines which develop in armies, schools, and hospitals in the eighteenth century, all seen as the formation of new modes of domination. In an immensely rich series of analyses, Foucault draws the portrait of a new form of power coming to be. Where the old power depended on the idea of public space, and of a public authority which essentially manifested itself in this space, which over-awed us with its majesty, and relegated the subjects to a less visible status, the new power operates by universal surveillance. It does away with the notion of public space; power no longer appears, it is hidden, but the lives of all the subjects are now under scrutiny. This is the beginning of a world we are familiar with, in which computerized data banks are at the disposal of authorities, whose key agencies are not clearly identifiable, and whose *modus operandi* is often partly secret.[6]

The image or emblem of this new society for Foucault is Bentham's Panopticon, where a single central vantage point permits the surveillance of a host of prisoners, each of whom is isolated from all the rest, and incapable of seeing his watcher. In a striking image, he contrasts ancient to modern society through the emblematic structure of temple and pan-opticon. The ancients strove to make a few things visible to the many; we try to make many things visible to the few. 'Nous sommes bien moins grecs que nous ne le croyons.'[7]

The new philosophy of punishment is thus seen as inspired not by humanitarianism but by the need to control. Or rather, humanitarianism itself seems to be understood as a kind of stratagem of the new growing mode of control.[8] The new forms of knowledge serve this end. People are

---

[6] Cf. the ancient idea of tyranny as power *hiding* itself, as in the myth of Gyges.

[7] *Surveiller et punir*, p. 219.

[8] Thus in explaining the unplanned rise of this new form, Foucault says: 'Take the example of philanthropy in the early nineteenth century: people appear who make it their business to involve themselves in other people's lives, health, nutrition, housing: then, out of this confused set of functions there emerge certain personages, institutions, forms of know-ledge: public hygiene, inspectors, social workers, psychologists' (*Power/Knowledge*, p. 62). Foucault is precisely *not* claiming that there was a plot laid by anyone. The explana-tory model of history here seems to be that certain things arise for a whole host of possible reasons, and then get taken up and used by the emerging constellation. But what is clear is that the dominating thrust of the constellation which uses them is not humanitarian benificence but control. I will discuss this understanding of historical change below.

measured, classed, examined in various ways, and thus made the better subject to a control which tends to normalization. In particular, Foucault speaks of the medical examination, and the various kinds of inspection which arose on its model, as a key instrument in this. The examination, he says, is at once 'le déploiement de la force et l'établissement de la vérité'.

Far from explaining the rise of this new technology of control in terms of the modern identity of man as an individual, Foucault wants to explain the modern notion of individuality as one of its products. This new technology brings about the modern individual as an objective of control. The being who is thus examined, measured, categorized, made the target of policies of normalization, is the one whom we have come to define as the modern individual.[9]

There is another way of contrasting modern power with the classical. Foucault touches on it in *Surveiller et punir* but sets it out more explicitly in later work.[10] The classical understanding of power turned on the notions of sovereignty and law. Much of early modern thought was taken up with definitions of sovereignty and legitimacy. In part these intellectual efforts were deployed in the service of the new centralized royal governments, which built up towards their apogee in the 'absolute' monarchies of the seventeenth century. In part they were concerned with the opposite movement, a definition of the limits of rightful sovereignty, and hence the rights of resistance of the subject. At the limit, this line of thought issues in the post-Rousseauian definitions of legitimate sovereignty as essentially founded on self-rule.

But in either case, these theories present an image of power as turning on the fact that some give commands and others obey. They address this question in terms of law or right. Foucault's thesis is that, while we have not ceased talking and thinking in terms of this model, we actually live in relations of power which are quite different, and which cannot be properly described in its terms. What is wielded through the modern technologies of control is something quite different, in that (a) it is not concerned with law but with normalization. That is, it is above all concerned with bringing about a certain result, defined as health or good function, whereas relative to any such goal, law is always concerned with what Nozick calls 'side-constraints'. In fact, what has happened is a kind of infiltration of the process of law itself by this quite alien species of control. Criminals are

---

[9] Cf. *Power/Knowledge*, p. 98.   [10] E.g. in *ibid.*, chap. 5.

more and more treated as 'cases' to be 'rehabilitated' and brought back to normal.[11]

This change goes along with two others. First, (b) where the old law/power was concerned with prohibitions, with instructions requiring that we in some way restrict our behaviour to conform to them, the new kind of power is *productive*. It brings about a new kind of subject and new kinds of desire and behaviour which belong to him. It is concerned to form us as modern individuals.[12] Second, (c) this power is not wielded by a *subject*. It is essential to the old model that power presupposes a location of the source of command. Even if no longer in the hands of the king, it will now be located in a sovereign assembly, or perhaps in the people who have the right to elect it. In any case, the orders start from somewhere. But the new kind of power is not wielded by specific people against others, at least not in this way. It is rather a complex form of organization in which we are all involved.[13]

We still live in the theory of the old power, understood in terms of sovereignty/obedience. But the reality we have is the new one, which must be understood in terms of domination/subjugation.[14] In political theory, we still 'need to cut off the king's head'.[15]

Now this second analysis may remind us of another important theme of critical political theory, indeed, a central theme of Critical Theory (in capitals), that of the link between the domination of nature and the domination of man. This is set out in perhaps its clearest form, and in one of its most influential formulations, in Schiller's *Letters on the Aesthetic Education of Man* (1975).[16] But it was taken up and continued in a variety of ways, and emerges as an explicit theme in the writings of the Frankfurt School.

The basic notion is a critique of mainstream enlightenment humanism with its exaltation of instrumental reason and an instrumental stance towards nature, both within and without us. To objectify our own nature and to try to bring it under the control of reason is to divide what should be a living unity. It introduces a master within, in Schiller's language, a relation of domination internal to the person. The proper stance of reason to nature is that of articulator. In expression – in Schiller's formulation, in beauty – nature and reason come to reconciliation.

The relation of domination within man, which is part of a stance of

[11] *Surveiller et punir*, p. 224. Cf. 'society of normalization', *Power/Knowledge*, p. 107.
[12] Cf. the references to Marcuse and *Power/Knowledge*, pp. 59, 120.
[13] *Power/Knowledge*, p. 140 points out the close link between (b) and (c).
[14] *Ibid.*, p. 96.   [15] *Ibid.*, p. 121.   [16] Esp. letter 6.

domination towards nature in general, cannot help engendering a domination of man by man. What goes on within must also end up happening between men. Schiller's account of this connection is via the breakdown of a true consensual community among atomic individuals which necessitates a regime of enforced conformity to law. But Foucault seems to offer to the Schillerian perspective another connection (supplementing, not replacing the first). The objectifying and domination of inner nature comes about in fact not just through a change of attitude but through training in an interiorization of certain disciplines. The disciplines of organized bodily movement, of the employment of time, of ordered dispositions of living/working space; these are the paths by which objectification really takes place, becomes more than a philosopher's dream, or the achievement of a small elite of spiritual explorers, and takes on the dimensions of a mass phenomenon.

But the disciplines which build this new way of being are social; they are the disciplines of the barracks, the hospital, the school, the factory. By their very nature they lend themselves to the control of some by others. In these contexts, the inculcation of habits of self-discipline is often the imposition of discipline by some on others. These are the loci where forms of domination become entrenched through being interiorized.

Seen in this way, Foucault offers the Frankfurt school an account of the inner connection between the domination of nature and the domination of man which is rather more detailed and more convincing than what they came up with themselves. It is the measure of the great richness of his work that this 'gift' is not at all part of his intentions. On the contrary, Foucault will have nothing to do with this Romantic-derived view of the oppression of nature and our 'liberation' from it.

Once again, this seems ultimately to be a matter of his Nietzschean refusal of the notion of truth as having any meaning outside a given order of power. But once again, there looks to be a more immediate, value-related reason. This comes out in the third analysis, which is the subject of the *Histoire de la sexualité*.

3

Central to the Romantic notion of liberation is the notion that the nature within us must come to expression. The wrong stance of reason is that of objectification, and the application of instrumental reason: the right stance is that which brings to authentic expression what we have within us. In accordance with the whole modern rehabilitation of ordinary life, of which the Romantic movement is heir, one of the crucial aspects of this inner nature which must be articulated is our nature as sexual beings. There is a truth of this; an authentic way for each of us to love. This is distorted by custom, or the demands of power external to us; in more modern variants, it is distorted by the demands of the capitalist work-ethic, or the disciplines of a bureaucratic society. In any case, whatever the distorting agent, it needs to be liberated, and coming to true expression is both a means and a fruit of this liberation.

Foucault aims to dismantle this whole conception, and show it to be thorough-going illusion. The idea that we have a sexual nature, and that we can get at it by speech, by avowal – perhaps with the help of experts – Foucault sees as an idea with deep roots in Christian civilization. It links together earlier practices of confession, through counter-reformation practices of self-scrutiny (and also reformed ones, naturally; but Foucault tends to be more familiar with French Catholic sources) to Freudian psychoanalysis, the 'talking cure'. We live in 'une société singulièrement avouante'.[17] But this idea is not the statement of a deep, culture-independent truth about us. It is rather one of these 'truths' which are produced by a certain regime of power. And in fact, it is a product of the same regime of power through the technology of control that we have just been examining.

Foucault's idea seems to be that the notion that we have a sexual nature is itself a product of those modes of knowledge designed to make us objects of control. Our acceptance that we have such a nature makes us an object of such control. For now we have to find it, and set our lives to rights by it. And finding it requires the 'help' of experts, requires that we put ourselves in their care, be they the priests of old or the psychoanalysts or social workers of today. And part of putting ourselves in their hands is our avowal, the requirement that we go on trying to *say* what we are like, what our experience is, how things are with us.

This whole idea turns out to be a stratagem of power. It helps the cause of control partly in that it presents us as enigmas who need external help to resolve ourselves; and partly in that it has created the very idea of sex. Not, of course, the desire, the instinct, but the understanding of sexuality as the locus of a crucial fulfilment for ourselves as human beings. This self-understanding in terms of an enigmatic nature requiring expression has made us into modern sexual beings, where a key element of the good life is some kind of sexual *fulfilment*. The question of the meaning of our life is bound up with the authentic nature of our sexual longing. 'La

[17] *Histoire de la sexualité*, p. 79.

question de ce que nous sommes, une certaine pente nous a conduits, en quelques siècles, à la poser au sexe. Et, non pas tellement au sexe-nature (élément du système du vivant, objet pour une biologie), mais au sexe-histoire, ou sexe-signification, au sexe-discours.'[18]

And this makes us objects of control in all sorts of ways which we barely understand. The important thing to grasp is that we are not controlled on the old model, through certain prohibitions being laid on us. We may think we are gaining some freedom when we throw off sexual prohibitions, but in fact we are dominated by certain images of what it is to be a full, healthy, fulfilled sexual being. And these images are in fact very powerful instruments of control. We may think of the contemporary wave of sexual permissiveness as a kind of 'revolt of the sexual body'. But

What is the response on the side of power? An economic (and perhaps also ideological) exploitation of eroticisation, from sun-tan products to pornographic films. Responding precisely to the revolt of the body, we find a new mode of investment which presents itself no longer in the form of control by repression but that of control by stimulation. 'Get undressed – but be slim, be good-looking, tanned!'[19]

The ruse is diabolic. The whole idea that we are generally too sexually repressed, and need above all liberation; that we need to be able to talk more freely, that we need to throw off tabus and enjoy our sexual nature: this is not just another of those illusions which makes us see power always in terms of prohibitions. In fact the self experience whereby we have a sexual nature which is held down or confined by rules and tabus is itself a creation of the new kind of power/control. In going for liberation, we see ourselves as escaping a power understood on the old model. But in fact we live under a power of the new kind, and this we are not escaping; far from it, we are playing its game, we are assuming the shape it has moulded for us. It keeps us tied to the whole 'dispositif de sexualité'.[20]

The very idea of modern sexuality thus develops as part of technologies of control. It is at the hinge where two axes of such development join.[21]

---

[18] *Ibid.*, p. 102.   [19] *Power/Knowledge*, p. 57.

[20] Cf. the reference to Wilhelm Reich in *Histoire de la sexualité*, p. 173. This analysis obviously has parallels to Marcuse's about 'repressive de-sublimation', and this just underlines the point above about the possible utility of Foucault's analysis for critical theory. But the crucial difference remains, that Critical Theory stays within the notion of liberation through true expression, while Foucault denounces this. Hence the critique of Marcuse (*Power/Knowledge*, p. 59) for thinking of power still purely in terms of repression.

[21] *Histoire de la sexualité*, p. 191.

On one hand, it is related to the disciplines of the body; on the other, to the regulation of populations. It serves the preservation and extension of life as the 'bio-mass', which is the over-riding direction of much modern policy.

II

Let me try to sum up the discussion of the three analyses of Foucault. I have been trying through them to get to the point where we can see the break in Foucault's thought, the point which disconcerts, where he adopts a Nietzschean-derived stance of neutrality between the different historical system of power, and thus seems to neutralize the evaluations which arise out of his analyses. In analysis 1, he opposes the classical liturgical idea of punishment to the modern 'humanitarian' one. And refuses to value the second over the first. But this refusal is over-determined, in a sense. It doesn't seem to depend only on the bottom-line Nietzschean stance of neutrality, but also on his concrete reading of this 'humanitarianism', which is seen as a growing system of control.

And so we have analysis 2, which seems to give us an *evaluational* reason for refusing the evaluation which issues from analysis 1. But the evaluation on which this depends would be something akin to the Schillerian/Critical Theory notion that modern discipline has repressed our own natures and constituted systems of domination of man by man, and this evaluation is also repudiated. Once again, though, we seem to have an over-determined judgement. It is not a pure case of Nietzschean neutrality. For there is another reason to refuse this whole Romantic-inspired notion of liberation from the domination of nature within and without. And that is that the ideology of expressive liberation, particularly in connection with sexual life, is itself just a strategy of power. This is analysis 3.

And so we come to the bottom line. What about the evaluation which seems to flow from 3? This would offer us some idea of a liberation, but not via the correct or authentic expression of our natures. It would be a liberation from the whole ideology of such expression, and hence from the mechanisms of control which use this ideology. It would be a liberation which was helped by our unmasking falsehood; a liberation aided by the truth.

In short, it would be something which had certain parallels to the Romantic-originating notion. We would achieve a liberation from a system of control which operates in us largely through masks, disguises and false pretences. It operates by inducing in us a certain self-understanding, an identity. We can help to throw it off partly by unmasking this identity and the manner of its implantation, and thus cease to be accomplices in its control and shaping of ourselves.

This would be a notion of liberation through the truth, parallel to the Romantic-derived one, but different in that it would see the very notion of ourselves as having a true identity to express as part of the *dispositif* of control, rather than as what defines our liberation.

Now the official Nietzschean stance of Foucault would refuse this value-position as well. And here, at last, we would be at the pure case, where the refusal was not over-determined, but depended purely on the Nietzschean stance. But can he do it? Does he really do it? What does it mean to do it? These are the central questions which arise about Foucault's repudiation of the goods which seem implicit in his analyses. And this is the right place to pose these questions, where no extraneous considerations, no other possible value-positions muddy the waters.

Does he really do it? Even this is not so clear. There are moments where some notion of liberation seems to peek through. It is true (?) that he repudiates the notion of liberation through the truth: 'La vérité n'est pas libre, ni l'erreur serve.'[22] But later there is the hint of a possible *point d'appui* for at least a relative freeing: 'Contre le dispositif de la sexualité, le point d'appui de la contre-attaque ne doit pas être le sexe-désir, mais les corps et les plaisirs.'[23] What exactly this could mean I want to discuss later. But here, I just want to point to the implication that once one has rejected the false idea of a liberation through the truth of one's natural sexual desires (*le sexe-désir*), there remains something else it can be founded on. In this connection, we might also mention the passages where Foucault talks about the need for a kind of revolutionary practice which did not just reproduce the forms of control which exist in the structures against which they are rebelling.[24]

But the question I would like to explore here is: can he do it? By that I mean: what can be coherently said in this domain? Just how much sense does a Nietzschean position make?

Before I do this, I want just to mention another line of critique that one could take up against Foucault, but that I do not want to pursue here. Foucault's analyses are terribly one-sided. Their strength is their

---

[22] *Ibid.*, p. 81.   [23] *Ibid.*, p. 208.   [24] *Power/Knowledge*, pp. 60, 61.

insightfulness and originality, in bringing usually neglected aspects to light. The weakness is that the other aspects seem denied altogether. We can see this with the three analyses above.

I already mentioned with analysis 1 how Foucault reads the rise of humanitarianism exclusively in terms of the new technologies of control. The development of the new ethics of life is given no independent significance. This seems to me quite absurdly one-sided.

In the second analysis, the rise of the new forms of discipline is seen exclusively in its relation to domination. Once again, I think there is a mine of valuable historical insights here. Foucault has filled in, as I mentioned above, some of the background which Critical Theory always supposed, but did not adequately work out. But Foucault has missed the ambivalence of these new disciplines. The point is, they have not only served to feed a system of control. They have also taken the form of genuine self-disciplines which have made possible new kinds of collective action characterized by more egalitarian forms of participation. This is not a new discovery. It is a truism of the civic humanist tradition of political theory that free participatory institutions require some commonly accepted self-disciplines. The free citizen has the *vertu* to give willingly the contribution which otherwise the despot would coerce from him, perhaps in some other form. Without this, free institutions cannot exist. There is a tremendous difference between societies which find their cohesion through such common disciplines grounded on a public identity, and which thus permit of and call for the participatory action of equals, on one hand, and the multiplicity of kinds of society which require chains of command based on unquestionable authority on the other.

Aside from the moral differences, there are also differences in efficacy, which Machiavelli examined, particularly military. Modern history has been shaped by striking examples of the citizen military, from the New Model Army to the Israeli Defence Forces. This is really too big a phenomenon to ignore.

The point is that collective disciplines can function in both ways, as structures of domination, and as bases for equal collective action. And they can also slide over time from one to the other. It can be argued that some of the disciplines which helped to found the societies based on contract and responsible government in earlier times, which represented a great leap forward in egalitarian politics, are now serving bureaucratic modes of irresponsible power which are sapping our democracy. I think that there is a lot in this. And undoubtedly the feeling that something like this is happening adds plausibility to Foucault's analysis, at first blush.

But on reflection, we can see that Foucault's notion of modern power incapacitates us from understanding this process.

That is because we cannot understand modern bureaucratization unless we see how collective disciplines can function both for and against despotic control. The threatened degeneracy of modern mass democracies is a *slide* from one of these directions to the other. We will never see what is going on if we think of the disciplines as having their exclusive historical and social significance in forms of domination.

Foucault's attraction is partly that of a *terrible simplificateur*. His espousal of the reversal of Clausewitz's aphorism, which makes us see politics as war carried on by other means,[25] can open insights in certain situations. But to make this one's basic axiom for the examination of modern power as such leaves out too much. Foucault's opposition between the old model of power, based on sovereignty/obedience, and the new one based on domination/subjugation leaves out everything in Western history which has been animated by civic humanism or analogous movements.[26] And that means a massive amount of what is specific to our civilization. Without this in one's conceptual armoury, Western history and societies become incomprehensible, as they are for that reason to so many Russians (like Solzhenitsyn).

In the third analysis, Foucault is certainly on to something in the claim that sexual desire has been given exceptional importance in Western civilization, and that in the very attempts to control it, neutralize it and go beyond it. He is certainly right to point to the Christian roots of this. Again, we can appreciate the force of the point that we have somehow been led to place a tremendous weight of significance on our sexual lives and fulfilment in this culture, more than these can bear. But then to understand this simply in terms of technologies of control (I am not sure whether Foucault really does this; I await eagerly the second volume of *Histoire de la sexualité* to find out) leaves out its roots in the theologies/ethics of ordinary life, in the Christian concern for the quality of the will, which Foucault himself rightly sees as basic to this.[27] And to reduce the whole Western, post-Romantic business of trying to save

---

[25] *Ibid.*, p. 90; see also *Histoire de la sexualité*, p. 123.

[26] The sovereignty model is *meant* to cope with the rebellion against despotic power and the rise of representative institutions. But in fact, it can only illuminate its Lockean aspect. The civic humanist aspect precisely cannot be put in terms of who is giving orders to whom. The concept of sovereignty cannot be integrated without strain in this form of thought.

[27] *London Review of Books* (21 May–3 June 1981), p. 5.

oneself to an artefact of such a technology of control approaches absurdity. That the aspiration to express one's true nature can *become* a mechanism of control is indeed true, and Foucault can offer insights on this. But just as in the case of bureaucratization above, you incapacitate yourself to understand this *becoming* if you conceive it from the beginning as essentially *being* control.

III

But I am less interested in hammering this line of critique than in seeing what can be coherently said in this area. I think Foucault's position is ultimately incoherent, but that this escapes detection because the points where it falls into contradiction are misidentified as new and deeper formulations of what many would recognize as valuable insights. I would like to explore this under three heads.

I

First, the idea of power without a subject. There are a number of interesting ideas here, of which two are especially important for this discussion. (i) Foucault is setting aside the old model, where power is a matter of one person (group) exercising sovereign control over another; where some give orders and others obey, where some impose their wills on the others. This is usually conceived as a relation alongside the others – social, economic, familial, sexual, etc. – that people stand in with each other; conditioned by and conditioning the others, but distinct from them. On the contrary, the power Foucault is interested in is internal to, intrinsic to these other relations. One could say that it is constitutive of them, that built in to the very understanding of the common activity, or goods sought, or whatever forms the substance of the micro-relation, are forms of domination.[28] Thus the doctor–patient relation is defined by a supposed common goal, constituted by a stance of helper on the part of the professional, and a recognition of need on the part of the patient. But this coming together in a common goal is inseparable from a relation of power, founded on the presumption that one *knows*, and that the other has an overwhelming interest in taking advice. The relation of force is integral to the common goal as defined.

This is a relation of power, but it cannot be conceived on the Hobbesian model. It is rare that a doctor can/wants to wreak his arbitrary and

---

[28] *Histoire de la sexualité*, pp. 123–4.

unrestrained will on his patient. Both parties are constrained in a sense by the common understanding, the common activity. But within this, there is a domination on the part of the doctor.

This helps us to understand another difference from the Hobbesian model: frequently, in this kind of situation, the dominated cooperate in their subordination. They often come to interiorize the norms of the common activity; they go willingly. They are utterly unaware of a relation of domination. Foucault's example is the ideology of sexual liberation, where we play along unwittingly with a technology of control, even as we are 'letting it all hang out'.

And we can see from this, also, how this kind of relationship can permit reversals. There is not necessarily a continuing identity of dominators and dominated over time. There was for instance an ensemble of father, mother, educator and doctor constituted in the nineteenth century around the control of the child's sexuality. The original relation puts the doctor on top, offering 'advice' to parents, who are in turn controlling their children. But later, the relation of psychiatrist to child is the basis on which the adult's sexuality is called into question.[29]

(ii) But Foucault is also putting forward another thesis under this head, one about the relations of micro- to macro-contexts of power. It is not entirely clear what this thesis is, because it is stated somewhat differently in different places. But the baldest statement is perhaps this: 'que le pouvoir vient d'en bas'.[30] This seems to mean that we cannot hope to explain the local 'rapports de force' in terms of some global relation of dominators and dominated. This is not to say that there may not be identifiable classes or groups of those who are 'on top', or 'on the bottom' at any given time. But we have to explain this division in terms of the combinations, alignments, mutual effects, oppositions, side-effects, etc, which the micro-contexts of domination produce on each other and with each other. Or perhaps better, we have to allow for a circular relation, in which the grand alignments, which become concretized in, say, political or military institutions, both result from and have repercussions on the micro 'rapports de forces'.[31]

The grand strategies of the macro-contexts – state, ruling class, or whatever – form the context in which the micro-relations come to be, modify or reproduce themselves, while reciprocally these provide the soil and point of anchorage for the grand strategies. Thus, more than saying that power comes from the bottom, we should say that there is endless relation of reciprocal conditioning between global and micro-contexts.

[29] *Ibid.*, p. 131.   [30] *Ibid.*, p. 124.   [31] *Ibid.*, pp. 131–2.

Foucault's target in this thesis is plainly Marxism, even as he rejects the Hobbesian model with the other. It is a mistake to take the relations of opposition at one level as explanatorily *basic*. That is what Marxism does. It is the global class struggle and its exigencies which are used to explain the way people square off in the micro-contexts, of family, factory, professional association, and so on. There is a widely accepted view that we ought to explain, for example, the incarceration of the mad in the sixteenth century, or the repressive interest in infantile sexuality in the nineteenth century, in terms of the requirements of the rising bourgeois economy. Foucault rejects this. Rather the relation was that these contexts of domination developed in their own fashion, and were then taken up and used by the macro-context of domination. They 'came to be colonized and maintained by the global mechanisms and the entire state system,' in which the bourgeoisie was hegemonic.[32]

So far, so clear. Indeed, we might be tempted to say: so far, so true. But now there is a third thesis under this head which Foucault also seems to be propounding. Perhaps this is a good statement of it: 'que les relations de pouvoir sont à la fois intentionnelles et non subjectives'.[33] What Foucault seems to be affirming here is that, aside from the particular conscious purpose which agents pursue in their given context, there is disconcernible a strategic logic of the context itself, but this cannot be attributed to anyone as their plan, as their conscious purpose. As he puts it in *Power/Knowledge*, talking of the kind of history he writes, 'the coherence of such a history does not derive from the revelation of a project, but from the logic of opposing strategies'.[34]

Strategies without projects; this would be a good formula to describe Foucault's historiography. Besides the strategies of individuals, which *are* their projects, there is a strategy of the context. The whole constitution and maintenance of the modern system of control and domination is an example. Foucault speaks of its growth and self-maintenance in strategic terms. He speaks of power using certain stratagems, or certain points of purchase. Thus in describing the reversals which occur as power and the resistance to it each take up each other's instruments, he gives this example:

Power, after investing itself in the body, finds itself exposed to a counter-attack in that same body. Do you recall the panic of the institutions of the social body, the doctors and politicians, at the idea of non-legalized cohabitation (*l'union libre*) or

[32] *Power/Knowledge*, p. 99–101.   [33] *Histoire de la sexualité*, p. 124.
[34] *Power/Knowledge*, p. 61.

free abortion? But the impression that power weakens and vacillates here is in fact mistaken; power can retreat here, re-organize its forces, invest itself elsewhere ... and so the battle continues.[35]

This notion of global strategies is essential to Foucault's reverse Clausewitzian thesis that we are engaged in perpetual war. This is not just the banality that there is much strife and rivalry among individuals. It is the thesis that there is a continuing struggle traversing the context in which we are all caught up. The use of the term 'strategy' in Foucault recovers its full original etymological force.

It is this third thesis which makes no sense, in Foucault's version. I stress this last phrase, because it would be quite wrong to say that no thesis of this kind makes sense. On the contrary, we can think of good examples where it makes sense to attribute a 'purposefulness without purpose' to history, or at least a logic to events without design. Let us look at some examples, in order to see what is required by this kind of explanation. (a) We can recognize a certain purposefulness in people's action where their motivation and goals are unacknowledged or perhaps unacknowledgeable. An example would be the (I think profound) Dostoyevskian analysis of modern political terrorism in terms of projected self-hatred and the response to a sense of emptiness. These purposes are not only unacknowledged, they *could not* be acknowledged without undermining the whole enterprise, which depends crucially on the notion that one is acting out of purely political-strategic considerations. But they might explain certain systematic features of terrorism better than the overly avowed goals.

(b) Then there are theories of unintended but systematic consequences, such as 'invisible hand' theories, that is, theories where the situation is so constituted that individual decisions are bound to concatenate in a certain systematic way. The best known example is the (malign) invisible hand account of capitalism by Marx. The structure of a capitalist economy is that individual decisions have to concatenate towards an ever-greater polarization, immiseration of the masses, concentration of capital, falling rate of profit and so on.

(c) There are unintended consequences theories which touch on the results of collective action, and not just the combination of individual actions. As an example, we can perhaps see a certain pattern in Leninist politics whereby the possibilities of devolution and a move towards participation are more and more restricted. This is a consequence unintended

[35] *Ibid.*, p. 56.

by Leninist parties at the outset, but it could perhaps be shown that it follows ineluctably from their model of mass mobilization, which systematically ends up destroying the bases for devolved power. The tragedy would be that a movement aimed at liberation and radical democratization should end up destroying these more effectively than predecessor regimes.

I am citing these types and examples to illustrate my main point, which is that purposefulness without purpose requires a certain kind of explanation to be intelligible. The undesigned systematicity has to be related to the purposeful action of agents in a way that we can understand. This is a requirement which the above kinds of explanation try to fulfil. The reason for this requirement is that the text of history, which we are trying to explain, is made up of purposeful human action. Where there are patterns in this action which are not on purpose, we have to explain why action done under one description on purpose also bears this other, undesigned description. We have to show how the two descriptions relate. A strategic pattern cannot just be left hanging, unrelated to our conscious ends and projects.

It is a mistake to think that the only intelligible relation between a pattern and our conscious purposes is the direct one where the pattern is consciously willed. This is a hang-up which did come down to us from classical Cartesian-empiricist views of the mind. Foucault is right to ridicule it: 'ne cherchons pas l'état-major qui préside à sa rationalité' (sc. du pouvoir).[36] But this must not be confused with the explanatory requirement outlined above. It is certainly not the case that all patterns *issue* from conscious action, but all patterns have to be made *intelligible* in relation to conscious action.

Now Foucault not only does not meet this requirement; it is difficult to see how he could without abandoning some or other part of his declared position. We could explain the constitution of the growing system of technologies of control, if we could understand it (on model (a)) as meeting the (largely unacknowledged) purposes of some group. But this Foucault could not do without going back on his thesis (ii), that there is no priority here of explanation in terms of the interest of some dominant class. The system has to arise out of the micro-contexts in which people act and react. It would be even worse for his case if the 'group' whose interest of purposes was the motor of change was co-terminous with society at large, or at least widely distributed within it; for then the

---

[36] *Histoire de la sexualité*, p. 125.

changes would be thought of as largely self-wrought, and a problem might arise about interpreting these as relations of *domination*. The same difficulty with thesis (ii) rules out explanations on model (c), in terms of the unintended consequences of collective action (which might itself be motivated by partly unacknowledged purposes).

In order to stick by (ii) in this case, we would need some account on model (b), where micro-reactions concatenate in this systematic way. I don't say something like this cannot be found, but I am at a loss to say even where one should start looking for it. And Foucault doesn't even feel the need to start looking.

This is not to say that there is a difficulty with Foucault's thesis (ii) in principle. On the contrary, there are obviously lots of aspects of social life in which this reciprocal play of micro-practice and global structures, each producing (largely unintended) consequences for the other, is the right explanatory model. The problem arises only when one combines this with Foucault's very strong claims to systematicity, in the idea that there are pervasive *strategies* afoot which condition the battle in each micro-context, that 'power' can 'retreat' or 're-organize its forces'. These can only be combined via some account of how actions concatenate systematically some model of type (b). But Foucault doesn't even try. He leaves us with a strange kind of Schopenhauerian will, ungrounded in human action.[37]

One of the most important reasons why Foucault doesn't feel a need to offer an account here is the confusion which has afflicted the republic of letters during these last decades about the supposed 'death of subjectivity'. This had its epicentre in Paris. Foucault took part in it.[38] Hacking[39] praises Foucault for having stepped beyond the old conception of subjectivity, which required all purposefulness in history to have a purposer.

The confusion lies in not seeing that there not only can be but *must* be something between total subjectivism, on the one hand, holding that there are no undesigned patterns in history, and the strange Schopenhauerianism-without-the-will in which Foucault leaves us. Much play is

---

[37] Hacking, *New York Review of Books* (14 May 1981), has already pointed out the Schopenhauerian overtones of the title of volume 1 of *Histoire de la sexualité, La Volonté de savoir*. But even Schopenhauer would not do as a theoretical background for Foucault, for that would give an account in our 'nature'. He has to be more evasive than this.

[38] This set of doctrines is sometimes called 'structuralist', or 'post-structuralist', but the aspiration to overcome subjectivity goes well beyond people who hold some structuralist model or other. Foucault is a case in point.

[39] *New York Review of Books*, p. 35.

made of the discovery (which structuralists did a lot to put in vogue) that any act requires a background language of practices and institutions to make sense; and that while there will be a particular goal sought in the act, those features of it which pertain to the structural background will not be objects of individual purpose. That my declarations in this paper are all made with uninflected words has nothing to do with what I have decided, and everything to do with the fact that the medium of my thought is English (and I didn't really choose *that* either).

No one can deny that this is an invaluable point to have in mind in studies of power. The utter sterility of the view popular a while ago in American political science, that one could analyse power in terms of A's ability to make B do something he otherwise would not, or some such thing, illustrates this. The approach is sterile, just because acts of power are so heterogeneous; they absolutely do not admit of being described in such a homogeneous medium of culturally neutral makings and doings. The power of the audience over the star craving approval is utterly incommensurable with the power of the general, which is incommensurable with the power of the elected minister, and that in turn with the power of the guru, and so on. Power can only be understood within a context; and this is the obverse of the point that the contexts can only in turn be understood in relation to the kind of power which constitutes them (Foucault's thesis).

But all this does not mean that there is no such thing as explaining the rise and fall of these contexts in history. On the contrary, this is one of the major tasks of historiography. And that is the issue we were talking about in connection with Foucault's system of modern technologies of control. How does it arise? *Of course*, you don't explain it by some big bad man/class *designing* it (who ever suggested anything so absurd?), but you do need to explain it nevertheless, that is relate this systematicity to the purposeful human action in which it arose and which it has come to shape. You cannot evade *this* question by talking of the priority of structure over element, of language over speech act. What we want to know is why a language *arises*.

Indeed, for purposes of such diachronic explanation, we can question whether we ought to speak of a priority of language over act. There is a circular relation. Structures of action or languages are only maintained by being renewed constantly in action/speech. And it is in action/speech that they also fail to be maintained, that they are altered. This is a crashing truism, but the fog emanating from Paris in recent decades makes it necessary to clutch it as a beacon in the darkness. To give an absolute priority to the structure makes *exactly as little sense* as the equal and opposite error of subjectivism, which gave absolute priority to the action, as a kind of total beginning.

This helps explain why Foucault feels he can be evasive on this issue; but not why he feels the need to be. Here we touch the question of his motivations, which I would like to adjourn till later (if I dare take it up at all). Meanwhile, I turn to the second head under which there is incoherence.

2

'Power' without 'freedom' or 'truth': can there really be an analysis which uses the notion of power, and which leaves no place for freedom, or truth? I have already raised the question whether Foucault *really* does away with freedom (section II above). But this uncertainty of utterance is just the symptom, I believe, of a deeper problem. The Nietzschean programme on this level does not make sense.

This is because of the very nature of a notion like 'power', or 'domination'. True, they do not require that we have one agent who is imposing his will on another. There are all sorts of ways in which power can be inscribed in a situation in which both dominators and dominated are caught up. The first may see himself largely as the agent of the demands of the larger context: the second may see the demands on him as emanating from the nature of things. Nevertheless, the notion of power or domination requires some notion of constraint imposed on someone by a process in some way related to human agency. Otherwise the term loses all meaning.

'Power' in the way Foucault sees it, closely linked to 'domination', does not require a clearly demarcated perpetrator, but it requires a victim. It cannot be a 'victimless crime', so to speak. Perhaps the victims also exercise it, also victimize others. But power needs targets.[40] Something must be being imposed on someone, if there is to be domination. Perhaps that person is also helping to impose it on himself, but then there must be an element of fraud, illusion, false pretences involved in this. Otherwise, it is not clear that the imposition is in any sense an exercise of *domination*.[41]

But now something is only an *imposition* on me against a background

---

[40] *Power/Knowledge*, p. 98: '[Individuals] are not only its [sc. power's] inept or consenting target: they are also the elements of its articulation.' But this means that they *are* targets.

[41] I indicated above how heedless Foucault is of this boundary, in which the self-disciplines of freedom are distinguished from the disciplines of domination. This all turns on whether and how they are *imposed*.

of desires, interests, purposes, that I have. It is only an imposition if it makes some dent in these, if it frustrates them, prevents them from fulfilment, or perhaps even from formulation. If some external situation or agency wreaks some change in me which in no way lies athwart some such desire/purpose/aspiration/interest, then there is no call to speak of an exercise of power/domination. Take the phenomenon of imprinting. In human life, it also exists after a fashion. We generally come to like the foods which have assuaged our hunger, those we are fed as children in our culture. Is this an index of the 'domination' of our culture over us? The word would lose all useful profile, would have no more distinctiveness, if we let it roam this wide.

Moreover, the desire/purposes, etc., have to be of some significance. The trivial is not relevant here. If something makes it impossible for me to act on the slight preference that I have for striped over unstriped tooth-paste, this is not a serious exercise of power. Shaping my life by 'imposition' in this respect would not figure in an analysis of power.

This is recognized by Foucault in his thesis that there is no power without 'resistances'.[42] Indeed, Foucault is sometimes dramatically aware of the force and savagery of the imposition. Take this passage, about knowledge, but illustrating its close connection to power:

its development [sc. of knowledge] is not tied to the constitution and affirmation of a free subject: rather it creates a progressive enslavement to its instinctive violence. Where religion once demanded the sacrifice of bodies, knowledge now calls for experimentation on ourselves,[43] calls us to the sacrifice of the subject of knowledge.

But this means that 'power' belongs in a semantic field from which 'truth' and 'freedom' cannot be excluded. Because it is linked with the notion of the imposition on our significant desires/purposes, it cannot be separated from the notion of some relative lifting of this restraint, from an unimpeded fulfilment of these desires/purposes. But this is just what is involved in a notion of freedom. There may, indeed, be all sorts of reasons why in certain situations certain impositions just cannot be lifted. There are empirical obstacles, and some very deep-lying ones in man's historical situation. But that is not Foucault's point. He wants to discredit as some-how based on a misunderstanding the very idea of liberation from power. But I am arguing that power, in his sense, *does not make sense* without at

[42] *Histoire de la sexualité*, pp. 125–7; *Power/Knowledge*, p. 142.
[43] M. Foucault, *Language, Counter-Memory, Practice* (Oxford, 1977), p. 163; quoted in an unpublished paper by Mark Philp.

least the idea of liberation. It may then be shown that the specific liberation, defined in a given context as the negation of the power wielded therein, is not realizable for this or that reason. But that is another, quite different issue, into which Foucault doesn't even enter.

The Foucaultian thesis involves combining the fact that any set of institutions and practices form the background to our action within them, and are in that sense unremovable while we engage in that kind of action, with the point that different forms of power are indeed constituted by different complexes of practice, to form the illegitimate conclusion that there can be no question of liberation from the power implicit in a given set of practices. Not only is there the possibility of frequently moving from one set of practices to another; but even within a given set, the level and kind of imposition can vary. Foucault implicitly discounts both these possibilities, the first because of the fundamentally Nietzschean thesis which is basic to his work: the move from one context to another cannot be seen as a liberation because there is no common measure between the impositions of the one and those of the other. I want to address this in the next discussion (section 3 below). And he discounts the second, because of his over-simple and global notion of the modern system of control and domination, which I have already touched on above.

So 'power' requires 'liberty'. But it also requires 'truth' — if we want to allow, as Foucault does, that we can collaborate in our own subjugation. Indeed, that is a crucial feature of the modern system of control, that it gets us to agree and concur in the name of truth, or liberation or our own nature. If we want to allow this, then 'truth' is an essential notion. Because the imposition proceeds here by foisting illusion on us. It proceeds by disguises and masks. It proceeds thus by falsehood.

C'est à la condition de masquer une part importante de lui-même que le pouvoir est tolérable. Sa réussite est en proportion de ce qu'il parvient à cacher de ses mécanismes. Le pouvoir serait-il accepté s'il était entièrement cynique? Le secret n'est pas pour lui de l'ordre de l'abus: il est indispensable à son fonctionnement.[44]

Mask, falsehood makes no sense without a corresponding notion of truth. The truth here is subversive of power: it is on the side of the lifting of impositions, of what we have just called liberation. The Foucaultian notion of power not only requires for its sense the correlative notions of truth and liberation, but even the standard link between them, which

---

[44] *Histoire de la sexualité*, p. 113.

makes truth the condition of liberation. To speak of power, and to want to deny a place to 'liberation' and 'truth', as well as the link between them, is to to speak coherently. That is, indeed, the reason why Foucault seems to be contradicting himself in the passages I quoted above (section II). He doesn't just slip into these formulations, which seem to allow for the possibility of a liberation, and indeed, one founded on a puncturing of illusions, a defence founded on 'les corps, les plaisirs, les savoirs, dans leur multiplicité et leur possibilité de résistance'.[45] He is *driven* into them by the contradictory position he has adopted.[46]

3

In the end, the final basis of Foucault's refusal of 'truth' and 'liberation' seems to be a Nietzschean one. This is not all of Nietzsche; there is more, and not all of it compatible with this part. But at least in the *Fröhliche Wissenschaft* we have a doctrine which Foucault seems to have made his own; there is no order of human life, or way we are, or human nature, that one can appeal to in order to judge or evaluate between ways of life. There are only different orders imposed by men on primal chaos, following their will to power. Foucault espouses both the relativistic thesis from this view, that one cannot judge between forms of life/thought/valuation, and also the notion that these different forms involve the imposition of power. The idea of 'régimes of truth',[47] and of their close intrication with systems of dominance, is profoundly Nietzschean. In this relationship Foucault sees truth as subordinated to power. Let me quote that passage again more fully:

Each society has its régime of truth, its 'general politics' of truth; that is, the types of discourse which it accepts and makes function as true; the mechanisms and instances which enable one to distinguish true and false statements, the means by which each is sanctioned; the techniques and procedures accorded value in the acquisition of truth; the status of those who are charged with saying what counts as true.[48]

---

[45] *Ibid.*, p. 208.

[46] Of course, there is a question whether Foucault isn't trying to have it both ways with his notion of a resistance founded on 'les corps et les plaisirs', on something quite in-articulate, not on an *understanding* of ourselves, or an *articulation* of our desires/pur-poses. But does this make sense? Can we 'faire valoir contre les prises du pouvoir les corps et les plaisirs ...' (*ibid.*) without articulating them for ourselves, and affirming the truth of that articulation against the specious claims of the system of control? I don't see how. Foucault seems to be talking here out of both sides of his mouth.

[47] *Power/Knowledge*, p. 131.   [48] *Ibid.*

If this is so (true?) in general, it is even more emphatically so in our society:

There can be no possible exercise of power without a certain economy of discourses of truth which operates through and on the basis of this association. We are subjected to the production of truth through power and we cannot exercise power except through the production of truth. This is the case for every society, but I believe that in ours the relationship between power, right and truth is organized in a highly specific fashion ... I would say that we are forced to produce the truth of power that our society demands, of which it has need, in order to function: we *must* speak the truth; we are constrained or condemned to confess to or discover the truth. Power never ceases its interrogation, its inquisition, its registration of truth; it institutionalizes, professionalizes and rewards its pursuit. In the last analysis, we must produce truth as we must produce wealth ...[49]

This regime-relativity of truth means that we cannot raise the banner of truth against our own regime. There can be no such thing as a truth independent of its regime, unless it be that of another. So that liberation in the name of 'truth' could only be the substitution of another system of power for this one, as indeed the modern course of history has substituted the techniques of control for the royal sovereignty which dominated the seventeenth century

This position is easy enough to state baldly, but difficult – or impossible – actually to integrate into the logic of one's analytical discourse, as I have just been trying to show in section 2 above. The 'truth' manufactured by power also turns out to be its 'masks' or disguises and hence untruth. The idea of a manufactured or imposed 'truth' inescapably slips the word into inverted commas, and opens the space of a truth-outside-quotes, the kind of truth, for instance, which the sentences unmasking power manifest, or which the sentences expounding the general theory of regime relativity themselves manifest (a paradox).

There has to be a place for revolt/resistance aided by unmasking in a position like Foucault's, and he allows for it. But the general relativity thesis will not allow for liberation through a transformation of power relations. Because of relativity, transformation from one regime to another cannot be a *gain* in truth or freedom, because each is redefined in the new context. They are incomparable. And because of the Nietzschean notion of truth imposed by a regime of power, Foucault cannot envisage liberating transformations *within* a regime. The regime is entirely identified with its imposed truth. Unmasking can only destabilize it; we

[49] *Ibid.*, p. 93.

cannot bring about a new, stable, freer, less mendacious form of it by this route. Foucault's Nietzschean theory can only be the basis of utterly monolithic analyses; which is what we saw above in his failure to recognize the ambivalence of modern disciplines, which are the bases both of domination and self-rule.

And so, for him, unmasking can only be the basis for a kind of local resistance within the regime. In chapter 5 of *Power/Knowledge*, he speaks of rehabilitating subjugated and local knowledges against the established dominant truth. He uses the expression 'insurrection of subjugated knowledges'.[50] The term bespeaks his basic idea: there is no question of a new form, just of a kind of resistance movement, a set of destabilizing actions, always local specific, within the dominant form. One of Foucault's historical paradigms seems to be the popular riots and uprisings which occurred in the former regimes at some of the execution scenes. Plebeian resistance is a kind of model.

No doubt it would be mistaken to conceive the plebs as the permanent ground of history, the final objective of all subjections, the ever smouldering centre of all revolts. The plebs is no doubt not a real sociological entity. But there is indeed always something in the social body, in classes, groups and individuals themselves which in some sense escapes relations of power, something which is by no means a more or less docile or reactive primal matter, but rather a centrifugal movement, an inverse energy, a discharge. There is certainly no such thing as 'the' plebs; rather there is, as it were, a certain plebian quality or aspect. There is plebs in bodies, in souls, in individuals, in the proletariat, in the bourgeoisie, but everywhere in a diversity of forms and extensions, of energies and irreducibilities. This measure of plebs is not so much what stands outside relations of power as their limit, their underside, their counter-stroke, that which responds to every advance of power by a movement of disengagement.[51]

We can see at least some of the motivation for this espousal of local insurrections. Foucault is deeply suspicious of 'global, totalitarian theories'[52] which claim to offer the overall solution to our ills. The target, as it must be in the world Foucault inhabits, is of course principally

---

[50] *Ibid.*, p. 81.

[51] *Ibid.*, pp. 137–8. This idea of political resistance without a positive new vision is parallel to the notion of resistance to the dominant sexuality based on the essentially unarticulated 'bodies and pleasures'. In both cases, the question very much arises whether Foucault can have it both ways. Is there a plebeian resistance which does not at least *point* to an alternative model, even if it may for some reasons be unrealizable in practice? Or if there is, if we can find really mindless insurrections in history, do they really offer us models for our political action?

[52] *Ibid.*, p. 80.

Marxism. And one can have a great deal of sympathy for this reaction, in face of the destruction wrought by such global revolutionary schemes. There is a great deal to be said on the Left for a politics which stays close to the local, to lived experience, to the aspirations which groups spontaneously adopt. But this by itself does not determine one to adopt the Nietzschean model of truth, with its relativism and its monolithic analyses. Just because some claims to truth are unacceptable, we do not need to blow the whole conception to pieces.

Something else drives Foucault to Nietzscheanism. I think it will come out if I try to grapple with the central issue around this position. What does this combination of relativism between forms and monolithism of forms leave out? It leaves out – or better, it blocks out – the possibility of a change of life-form which can be understood as a move towards a greater acceptance of truth – and hence also, in certain conditions, a move towards greater freedom. But in order to conceive a change in these terms we have to see the two forms as commensurable; the form before and the form after the change cannot be seen as incommensurable universes. How can this come about?

Biographically, we see examples all the time. After a long period of stress and confusion, I come to see that I really love A, or I really don't want to take that job. I now see retrospectively that the image of myself as quite free and uncommitted had a merely superficial hold on me. It did not correspond to a profound aspiration. It just stood in the way of my recognizing the depths of my commitment to A. Or, the picture of a career which that job instantiated, which seemed before so powerful, so non-gainsayable, turns out to be a model which my entourage was pressing on me, but which I cannot really endorse.

What makes these biographical changes of outlook/life possible, which seem to be steps towards the truth? Our sense of ourselves, of our *identity*, of what we are. I see this change as a discovery of what I am, of what really matters to me. And that is why I do not see this as a kind of character change, what a lobotomy might produce, for instance. Rather I see it as a step towards truth (or perhaps better put, it is a step out of error), and even in certain conditions as a kind of liberation.

Is there nothing comparable in politics/history? There is. There are changes which turn on, which are justified by, what we have become as a society, a civilization. The American revolutionaries called on their compatriots to rise in the name of the liberties which defined their way of life (ironically as Englishmen). This kind of claim is always contested (there were Tories, there were Loyalists, as is well known where I come from). But is it by its nature unacceptable? Is it always sham? Foucault would have us believe so.

But it seems clear to me that there is a reality here. We have become certain things in Western civilization. Our humanitarianism, our notions of freedom – both personal independence and collective self-rule – have helped to define a political identity we share; and one which is deeply rooted in our more basic, seemingly infra-political understandings: of what it is to be an individual, of the person as a being with 'inner' depths – all the features which seem to us to be rock-bottom, almost biological properties of human beings, so long as we refrain from looking outside and experiencing the shock of encountering other cultures. Of course, these elements of identity are contested; they are not neatly and definitely articulated once and for all, but the subject of perpetual revisionist strife. And worse, they are not all easily compatible – the freedom of independence is hard to combine with that of self-rule, as we constantly experience – and so we fight among ourselves in the name of incompatible weightings. But they all count for us. None of them can be simply repudiated in the political struggle. We struggle over interpretation and weightings, but we cannot shrug them off. They *define* humanity, politics, for us.

This means that we can look at the kind of change Foucault described, from seventeenth-century punishments to our own, in a way which renders them partly commensurable. It is not for nothing that we are the descendants and heirs of the people who so tortured Damiens. The makings of our present stress on the significance of life were already there, in that Christian civilization. One of the important features of their world, which made them act so differently, was their sense of belonging to a cosmic order in which the polity was set. But *this* difference cannot be seen purely in a relativist light. One of the reasons why we can no longer believe in this kind of order is the advance in our civilization of a scientific understanding of the natural world, which we have every reason to believe represents a significant gain of truth. Some dimensions at least of the 'disenchantment' which helps share modern culture represent an advance in the truth. To the extent that this change is operative, we can understand our difference from them as a change that denizens of Western Christendom have undergone under the impact of a stronger dose of truth.

Of course, this is not *all*. We can also discern losses. Indeed, Foucault ought perhaps best to be interpreted as having documented some of these losses. The growth of modern control has involved in some respects a dehumanization, an inability to understand and respond to some key features of the human context, those which are suppressed in a stance of thoroughgoing instrumental reason. That is why there is such a malaise in our civilization: so much groaning and travailling to recover what is lost, all the way from the Romantic period down to the most recent battles over ecology. But the point is that the sense both of gain and of loss depends on comparability, on our understanding of our identity, of what we now realize more fully, or are betraying and mutilating.

Gains and losses do not tell the whole story. There are also elements of incomparability. The reality of history is mixed and messy. The problem is that Foucault tidies it up too much, makes it into a series of hermetically sealed, monolithic truth-regimes, a picture which is as far from reality as the blandest Whig perspective of smoothly broadening freedom. Monolithism and relativism are two sides of the same coin. One is as necessary as the other to create this total incomparability across the changes of history.

Foucault's monolithic relativism only seems plausible if one takes the outsider's perspective, the view from Sirius; or perhaps imagines oneself a soul in Plato's myth of Er. Do I want to be born a Sung dynasty Chinese, or a subject of Hammurabi of Babylon, or a twentieth-century American? Without a prior identity, I couldn't begin to choose. They incarnate incommensurable goods (at least prior to some deep comparative study, and conceivably even after this). But this is not my/our situation. We have already *become* something. Questions of truth and freedom can arise for us in the transformations we undergo or project. In short, we have a *history*. We live in time not just self-enclosed in the present, but essentially related to a past which has helped define our identity, and a future which puts it again in question.

And indeed, in his major works, like *Les Mots et les choses* and *Surveiller et punir*, Foucault *sounds* as though he believed that, as an historian, he could stand nowhere, identifying with none of the *epistemai* or structures of power whose coming and going he impartially surveys. But there are signs that this is not his last word. It would appear that Foucault is going to elaborate in forthcoming publications his own conception of a good life.

From certain indications,[53] this would seem to be based, as one would expect, on a rejection of the whole idea that we have a deep self or nature which we have to decipher. Foucault thinks that Christianity introduced

---

[53] See the new chapters in the second edition of Hubert Dreyfus and Paul Rabinow, *Michel Foucault: Beyond Structuralism and Hermeneutics* (Chicago, 1983).

this false turn into Western culture. Where the ancient 'care of the self' was concerned with self-making and self-mastery, Christian spirituality was preoccupied rather with purity and self-renunciation. 'From that moment on the self was no longer something to be made but something to be renounced and deciphered.'[54]

Foucault's project seems to be to return to these ancient sources, not in order to revive them — even if this were possible, he believes there is lots to criticize in ancient culture on other grounds — but as the point of departure for a different line of development. This would bring us to a conception of the good life as a kind of self-making, related in this way to the ancient 'aesthetic of existence'[55] that one would make one's own life a work of art. '. . . the principal work of art one has to take care of, the main area to which one has to apply aesthetic values is oneself, one's life, one's existence.'[56]

It is understandable how Foucault, from the standpoint of an ethic of this kind, should want to distance himself from the banners of 'freedom' and 'truth', since these have been the key terms in the view he is repudiating, that we ought to bring to light our true nature or deep self. And the affinity with Nietzsche in the stress on self-making is very understandable also. But this in no way lessens the paradox involved in the attempt to avoid these terms altogether. Indeed, in offering us a new way of re-appropriating our history, and in rescuing us from the supposed illusion that the issues of the deep self are somehow inescapable, what is Foucault laying open for us, if not a truth which frees us for self-making?

Perhaps Foucault was moving, before his sudden and premature death, to free his position from this paradox, seemingly linked with the impossible attempt to stand nowhere. Perhaps we can see the last work[57] as a step towards and acknowledgement of his own sources, an identification of the moments when these sources were lost or obscured (the rise of Christian spirituality), and a definition of what we have to undo to rescue what needs saving. At that point, the really interesting debate can begin, on the issues which count, which Foucault's mode of expression up to now has obscured.

There are two such issues, which it is worth tabling for future discussions. (1) Can we really step outside the identity we have developed in Western civilization to such a degree that we can repudiate all that comes to us from the Christian understanding of the will? Can we toss aside the whole tradition of Augustinian inwardness? (2) Granted we really can set this aside, is the resulting 'aesthetic of existence' all that admirable? These

---

[54] *Ibid.*, p. 248.   [55] *Ibid.*, p. 251.   [56] *Ibid.*, p. 245.

[57] *Histoire de la sexualité* (Paris, 1984), vol. 2, *L'Usage des plaisirs*, and vol. 3, *Le Souci de soi.*

questions are hard to separate, and even harder to answer. But they are among the most fundamental raised by the admirable work of Michel Foucault.

PART II

POLITICAL PHILOSOPHY

CHAPTER SEVEN

ATOMISM

I would like to examine the issue of political atomism, or at least to try to clarify what this issue is. I want to say what I think atomist doctrines consist in, and to examine how the issue can be joined around them – this is, how they might be proved or disproved, or at least cogently argued for or against, and what in turn they may be used to prove.

The term 'atomism' is used loosely to characterize the doctrines of social contract theory which arose in the seventeenth century and also successor doctrines which may not have made use of the notion of social contract but which inherited a vision of society as in some sense constituted by individuals for the fulfilment of ends which were primarily individual. Certain forms of utilitarianism are successor doctrines in this sense. The term is also applied to contemporary doctrines which hark back to social contract theory, or which try to defend in some sense the priority of the individual and his rights over society, or which present a purely instrumental view of society.

Of course, any term loosely used in political discourse can be defined in a host of ways. And perhaps one should even leave out of philosophical discourse altogether those terms which tend to be branded as epithets of condemnation in the battle between different views. One might well argue that 'atomism' is one such, because it seems to be used almost exclusively by its enemies. Even extreme individualists like Nozick don't seem to warm to this term, but tend to prefer others, like 'individualism'.

Perhaps I am dealing with the wrong term. But there is a central issue in political theory which is eminently worth getting at under some description. And perhaps the best way of getting at it is this: what I am calling atomist doctrines underlie the seventeenth-century revolution in the terms of normative discourse, which we associated with the names of Hobbes and Locke.

These writers, and others who presented social contract views, have left us a legacy of political thinking in which the notion of rights plays a central part in the justification of political structures and action. The central doctrine of this tradition is an affirmation of what we could call the primacy of rights.

Theories which assert the primacy of rights are those which take as the fundamental, or at least a fundamental, principle of their political theory the ascription of certain rights to individuals and which deny the same status to a principle of belonging or obligation, that is a principle which states our obligation as men to belong to or sustain society, or a society of a certain type, or to obey authority or an authority of a certain type. Primacy-of-right theories in other words accept a principle ascribing rights to men as binding unconditionally,[1] binding, that is, on men as such. But they do not accept as similarly unconditional a principle of belonging or obligation. Rather our obligation to belong to or sustain a society, or to obey its authorities, is seen as derivative, as laid on us conditionally, through our consent, or through its being to our advantage. The obligation to belong is derived in certain conditions from the more fundamental principle which ascribes rights.[2]

The paradigm of primacy-of-right theories is plainly that of Locke. But there are contemporary theories of this kind, one of the best known in recent years being that of Robert Nozick.[3] Nozick too makes the assertion of rights to individuals fundamental and then proceeds to discuss whether and in what conditions we can legitimately demand obedience to a state.

Primacy-of-right theories have been one of the formative influences on

---

[1] The words 'conditional/unconditional' may mislead, because there are certain theories of belonging, to use this term for them, which hold that our obligation to obey, or to belong to a particular society, may in certain circumstances be inoperative. For instance, medieval theories which justified tyrannicide still portrayed man as a social animal and were thus theories of belonging in the sense used here. But they allowed that in certain circumstances our obligation to obey that authority by which our society cohered was abrogated, and that when the ruler was a tyrant he might be killed. In this sense we could say that the obligation to obey was 'conditional'. But this is not the same as a theory of the primacy of right. For in theories of belonging it is clear that men *qua* men have an obligation to belong to and sustain society. There may be a restriction on what kind of society would fulfil the underlying goal, and from this a licence to break with perverted forms; but the obligation to belong itself was fundamental and unconditional; it held 'by nature'. In primacy-of-right theories the notion is that simply by nature we are under no obligation to belong whatever; we have first to contract such an obligation.

[2] This may not be true of all doctrines which found a political theory on an affirmation of natural right. For the new doctrine of human rights which Professor Macpherson envisages in, for example, *Democratic Theory: Essays in Retrieval* (Oxford, 1973), p. 236, and which would free itself of 'the postulate of the inherent and permanent contentiousness of men', would seem to involve an affirmation of individual rights which presuppose society, rather than merely setting the boundary conditions of its possible legitimacy.

[3] *Anarchy, State and Utopia* (Boston, 1974).

modern political consciousness. Thus arguments like that of Nozick have
at least a surface plausibility for our contemporaries and sometimes considerably more. At the very least, opponents are brought up short, and
have to ponder how to meet the claims of an argument, which reaches
conclusions about political obedience which lie far outside the common
sense of our society; and this because the starting point in individual
rights has an undeniable prima facie force for us.

This is striking because it would not always have been so. In an earlier
phase of Western civilization, of course, not to speak of other civilizations, these arguments would have seemed wildly eccentric and
implausible. The very idea of starting an argument whose foundation was
the rights of the individual would have been strange and puzzling – about
as puzzling as if I were to start with the premise that the Queen rules by
divine right. You might not dismiss what I said out of hand, but you
would expect that I should at least have the sense to start with some less
contentious premise and argue up to divine right, not take it as my
starting point.

Why do we even begin to find it reasonable to start a political theory
with an assertion of individual rights and to give these primacy? I want to
argue that the answer to this question lies in the hold on us of what I have
called atomism. Atomism represents a view about human nature and the
human condition which (among other things) makes a doctrine of the
primacy of rights plausible; or to put it negatively, it is a view in the
absence of which this doctrine is suspect to the point of being virtually
untenable.

How can we formulate this view? Perhaps the best way is to borrow the
terms of the opposed thesis – the view that man is a social animal. One of
the most influential formulations of this view is Aristotle's. He puts the
point in terms of the notion of self-sufficiency (*autarkeia*). Man is a social
animal, indeed a political animal, because he is not self-sufficient alone,
and in an important sense is not self-sufficient outside a polis. Borrowing
this term then we could say that atomism affirms the self-sufficiency of
man alone or, if you prefer, of the individual.

That the primacy-of-rights doctrine needs a background of this kind
may appear evident to some; but it needs to be argued because it is
vigorously denied by others. And generally proponents of the doctrine are
among the most vigorous deniers. They will not generally admit that the
assertion of rights is dependent on any particular view about the nature of
man, especially one as difficult to formulate and make clear as this. And to
make their political theory dependent on a thesis formulated in just this

way seems to be adding insult to injury. For if atomism means that man is self-sufficient alone, then surely it is a very questionable thesis.

What then does it mean to say that men are self-sufficient alone? That they would survive outside of society? Clearly, lots of men would not. And the best and luckiest would survive only in the most austere sense that they would not succumb. It would not be living as we know it. Surely proponents of the primacy of rights do not have to deny these brute facts. Just because one would fail a survival course and not live for a week if dropped north of Great Slave Lake with only a hatchet and a box of (waterproof) matches, does one have to stop writing books arguing for the minimal state on the basis of the inviolable rights of the individual?

Under the impact of this rhetorical question, one might be tempted to conclude that the whole effort to find a background for the arguments which start from rights is misguided. They do not seem to have anything to do with any beliefs. If we take the widely held view that normative questions are autonomous and not to be adjudicated by factual considerations, then why shouldn't a normative position in which rights are the ultimate standard be combinable with any set of factual beliefs about what men can and cannot do, and what society does or does not do for them?

From this point of view it would be a matter of uninteresting historical accident that the great classical theorists of atomism also held to some strange views about the historicity of a state of nature in which men lived without society. Indeed, one could argue that even they were not committed to the self-sufficiency of man as we defined the issue in the above paragraph. It was not only Hobbes who saw man's life in the state of nature as nasty, brutish, and short. All social contract theorists stressed the great and irresistible advantages that men gained from entering society. And in the case of Locke, one could claim that even his state of nature was not one of self-sufficiency in the sense of our survivor north of Great Slave Lake; rather it was clearly a condition of exchange and fairly developed and widespread social relations, in which only political authority was lacking.

Perhaps then we should not look for a background at all, and the whole enterprise of this paper is misguided. Readers who are convinced by this argument should, of course, stop here. But I am convinced that there is a lot more to be said.

To begin with, what is at stake is not self-sufficiency in the Great Slave Lake sense, but rather something else. What has been argued in the different theories of the social nature of man is not just that men cannot physically survive alone, but much more that they only develop their characteristically

human capacities in society. The claim is that living in society is a necessary condition of the development of rationality, in some sense of this
property, or of becoming a moral agent in the full sense of the term, or of
becoming a fully responsible, autonomous being. These variations and
other similar ones represent the different forms in which a thesis about
man as a social animal have been or could be couched. What they have in
common is the view that outside society, or in some variants outside
certain kinds of society, our distinctively human capacities could not
develop. From the standpoint of this thesis, too, it is irrelevant whether an
organism born from a human womb would go on living in the wilderness;
what is important is that this organism could not realize its specifically
human potential.

But, one might argue, all this too is irrelevant to the individual-rights
argument. Such argument is as independent of any thesis about the conditions of development of human potential, whatever this is, as it is of the
conditions of survival in the wilderness. The argument simply affirms that
justification of political authority ought to start from a foundation of
individual rights. The proof of this independence is usually taken to be
this: that plainly we do not deny rights to beings born of woman who lack
the fully developed human potential, for instance infants. And if one
objects that these are on the way to develop to full humanity, the reply is
that we accord rights to lunatics, people in a coma, people who are
irreversibly senile, and so on. Plainly, in our ordinary attribution of
rights, we accord them to human beings as such, quite regardless of
whether they have developed such potential or not. And so why should
any thesis about the conditions for developing such potential be relevant
to arguments about such rights?

The answer is that the question is not closed by the reflection that we
attribute rights to idiots. It can nevertheless be the case that our conception of the human specific potential is an essential part of the background
of our ascription of rights. Why, for instance, do we ascribe them to
human beings, and not to animals, trees, rocks, and mountains? Someone
might reply that some people do want to ascribe them to animals. Nozick
himself is among their number, in fact. But an examination of this position will help make the case I want to plead.

Why ascribe rights to animals? Or if this sounds too bizarre, why claim
that it is wrong to kill or inflict pain on animals? The answer commonly
given is that they are sentient beings. But this concept of sentience is not as
simple as it looks, as those who have argued this position readily acknowledge. We cannot take it to mean simply 'capable of feeling pain', and

argue from that common factor that we ought not to inflict pain on any sentient being; because in fact we want to claim more: we would not agree, if there were some utterly painless way of killing, say by a laser-ray, that vegetarians ought to drop their objections to killing cattle for food, let alone that it would be licit to kill people for the convenience of others or for the demands of progress (though in the human case, the argument would be complicated by the anxiety about being a potential victim of the laser-ray).

'Sentience' here has to mean something more; it has to mean something like 'capable of enjoying life and one's various capacities', where 'enjoying' has something like its old-fashioned or legal sense, as in 'enjoying the use of one's limbs', rather than its narrower colloquial sense of having a good time. Sentience in this sense involves some kind of self-awareness of self-feeling; and the intuition underlying a prohibition on killing animals is that this capacity ought to be respected wherever it exists and that one ought not to snuff it out or seriously impair it in beings who have it.

The point that emerges from this reflection is that attributing rights to animals is bound up with discerning in them a capacity which we sense we must respect, in the sense of 'respect' used in the previous paragraph, that is, that it is something which we ought to foster and which we are forbidden to impair. Nor is the relation simply this, that the content of the rights we accord (e.g., to life or to the unimpaired use of limbs) restricts them to these beings, since others (e.g., rocks and mountains) could not exercise these rights. For that a given being has capacity C is not a sufficient condition of our according it a right to C. The sand on certain beaches tends to form in dunes, but no one would claim that in levelling it out for the tourists we are violating any rights.

Rather the intuition, if we want to call it such or whatever we want to say lies behind the conviction that certain beings have rights to A, B, or C, is that these beings exhibit a capacity which commands respect, which capacity helps determine the shape of the rights, or what the rights are rights to. Once we accept that beings with this capacity command respect, then indeed, it is sufficient that we identify A as possessing this capacity to make A a bearer of rights. And it is clearly always a necessary condition as well of bearing those rights, if only because what the rights are to will be defined in relation to the capacity. But the mere possession of the capacity will have no normative consequences at all for us if we do not share the conviction that this capacity commands respect.

I apologize to the non-partisan for this long excursus into the rights of animals. But perhaps it will help us to make clear the point about the rights of man, that they too are ascribed in virtue of a capacity which also helps to determine their shape. Even the strongest defenders of animal rights will agree that men have different rights – for example, the right to free choice of their religious or metaphysical convictions, to will their property, and so on. And it is not a sufficient explanation of this difference that animals cannot do these things; most animals cannot scratch themselves in the small of their backs, but this does not induce us to inscribe this capacity in the UN Charter. Rather, the intuition that men have the right to life, to freedom, to the unmolested profession of their own convictions, to the exercise of their moral or religious beliefs, is but another facet of the intuition that the life-form characterized by these specifically human capacities commands our respect.[4]

Beings with these capacities command our respect, because these capacities are of special significance for us; they have a special moral status. And from this we can see why the schedule of rights is what it is: life, of course, is protected, because these beings are life-forms, and so are integrity of limb and freedom protected from molestation for the same reason. But the schedule also includes protection for those activities which realize the specifically human capacities; and hence we have a right to our own convictions, the practice of our religion, and so on.

In other words, our conception of the specifically human is not at all irrelevant to our ascription of rights to people. On the contrary, there would be something incoherent and incomprehensible in a position which claimed to ascribe rights to men but which disclaimed any conviction about the special moral status of any human capacities whatever and which denied that they had any value or worth.[5]

---

[4] I do not pretend to have given a satisfactory formulation here to what it is in human beings which commands our respect. That is far from an easy task. Cf. the interesting discussion in *ibid.*, chap. 3, pp. 48–51, and also the discussion preceding. But while a satisfactory general formulation eludes us, we can readily agree on some of the specifically human capacities, and this is enough to state my argument.

[5] There is indeed a position which is approached by utilitarians which makes sentience the ground of right (or rather its weak utilitarian analogue, the status of a being whose desires and interests are to be weighed in moral calculations) and thus would in its extreme form deny any special consideration to humans as against other animals. But this is linked to the conviction that sentience commands our respect, that it enjoys this special moral status. And indeed, in a position of this kind the incoherence will break out elsewhere, in the schedule of human rights which will be difficult to square with the reduction of human beings and animals to the same level. How to justify the assertion of the right to one's own moral or religious convictions? Perhaps with drugs of a certain kind people could be made very happy, even euphoric, while they were induced to profess almost anything to please whomever they were with. We would still feel that injecting them with these drugs was a

But, an opponent might object, what if we do admit that in asserting a right we affirm that a certain form of life or certain capacities command our respect? What are we allowing over and above the conviction that these capacities are the basis of right? What else does this commit us to? For surely, the normative consequences in either case are the same, viz., that we should refrain from violating the rights of any beings with these capacities.

But in fact the normative consequences are broader, and this is what the second formula brings out. To say that certain capacities command respect or have worth in our eyes is to say that we acknowledge a commitment to further and foster them. We do not just acknowledge people's (and/or animals') right to them, and hence the negative injunction that we ought not to invade or impair the exercise of these capacities in others. We also affirm that it is good that such capacities be developed, that under certain circumstances we ought to help and foster their development, and that we ought to realize them in ourselves.

It is true, of course, that the scope of this affirmation of worth will not be very great in the limiting case where we take sentience as the basis of right, because sentience is a capacity which, broadly speaking, either exists or does not in a given being; it is not a potential which needs to be developed and which can be realized to greater or lesser degree. Even here, however, the affirmation of worth still says something more than the assertion of right; it says, for instance, that other things being equal it is good to bring sentient beings into the world.

In the case where we are dealing with the full schedule of human rights, the scope of the affirmation of worth becomes significantly greater. To affirm the worth of the human capacity to form moral and religious convictions goes far beyond the assertion of the right to one's convictions. It also says that I ought to become the kind of agent who is capable of authentic conviction, that I ought to be true to my own convictions and not live a lie or a self-delusion out of fear or for favour, that I ought in certain circumstances to help foster this capacity in others, that I ought to bring up my own children to have it, that I ought not to inhibit it in others by influencing them towards a facile and shallow complaisance, and so on. This is because we are dealing with a characteristically human

---

violation of their rights. See an analogous point by Nozick – 'the experience machine' in *ibid.*, pp. 42–5. But this right to one's own convictions cannot be squared with the notion that sentience alone is the basis of right. And this difficulty of extreme utilitarianism shows how the affirmation of rights is bound up with the conviction that certain capacities are of special worth.

capacity which can be aborted or distorted or underdeveloped or inhibited or, alternatively, can be properly realized or even realized to an exemplary degree.

The claim I am trying to make could be summed up in this way. (1) To ascribe the natural (not just legal) right of X to agent A is to affirm that A commands our respect, such that we are morally bound not to interfere with A's doing or enjoying of X. This means that to ascribe the right is far more than simply to issue the injunction: don't interfere with A's doing or enjoying X. The injunction can be issued, to self or others, without grounds, should we so choose. But to affirm the right is to say that a creature such as A lays a moral claim on us not to interfere. It thus also asserts something about A: A is such that this injunction is somehow inescapable.

(2) We may probe further and try to define what it is about A which makes the injunction inescapable. We can call this, whatever it is, A's essential property or properties, E. Then it is E (in our case, the essentially human capacities) which defines not only who are the bearers of rights but what they have rights to. A has a natural right to X, if doing or enjoying X is essentially part of manifesting E (e.g., if E is being a rational life-form, then A's have a natural right to life and also to the unimpeded development of rationality); or if X is a causally necessary condition of manifesting E (e.g., the ownership of property, which has been widely believed to be a necessary safe-guard of life or freedom, or a living wage).

(3) The assertion of a natural right, while it lays on us the injunction to respect A in his doing or enjoying of X, cannot but have other moral consequences as well. For if A is such that this injunction is inescapable and he is such in virtue of E, then E is of great moral worth and ought to be fostered and developed in a host of appropriate ways, and not just not interfered with.

Hence asserting a right is more than issuing an injunction. It has an essential conceptual background, in some notion of the moral worth of certain properties or capacities, without which it would not make sense. Thus, for example, our position would be incomprehensible and incoherent, if we ascribed rights to human beings in respect of the specifically human capacities (such as the right to one's own convictions or to the free choice of one's life-style or profession) while at the same time denying that these capacities ought to be developed, or if we thought it a matter of indifference whether they were realized or stifled in ourselves or others.

From this we can see that the answer to our question of a few pages ago (why do we ascribe these rights to men and not to animals, rocks, or trees?) is quite straightforward. It is because men and women are the beings who exhibit certain capacities which are worthy of respect. The fact that we ascribe rights to idiots, people in a coma, bad men who have irretrievably turned their back on the proper development of these capacities, and so on, does not show that the capacities are irrelevant. It shows only that we have a powerful sense that the status of being a creature defined by its potential for these capacities cannot be lost. This sense has been given a rational account in certain ways, such as for instance by the belief in an immortal soul. But it is interestingly enough shared even by those who have rejected all such traditional rationales. We sense that in the incurable psychotic there runs a current of human life, where the definition of 'human' may be uncertain but relates to the specifically human capacities; we sense that he has feelings that only a human being, a language-using animal can have, that his dreams and fantasies are those which only a human can have. Pushed however deep, and however distorted, his humanity cannot be eradicated.

If we look at another extreme case, that of persons in a terminal but long-lasting coma, it would seem that the sense that many have that the life-support machines should be disconnected is based partly on the feeling that the patients themselves, should they *per impossibile* be able to choose, would not want to continue, precisely because the range of human life has been shrunk here to zero.

How does the notion then arise that we can assert rights outside of a context of affirming the worth of certain capacities? The answer to this question will take us deep into the issue central to modern thought of the nature of the subject. We can give but a partial account here. There clearly are a wide number of different conceptions of the characteristically human capacities and thus differences too in what are recognized as rights. I will come back to this in another connection later.

But what is relevant for our purposes here is that there are some views of the properly human which give absolutely central importance to the freedom to choose one's own mode of life. Those who hold this ultra-liberal view are chary about allowing that the assertion of right involves any affirmation about realizing certain potentialities; for they fear that the affirming of any obligations will offer a pretext for the restriction of freedom. To say that we have a right to be free to choose our life-form must be to say that any choice is equally compatible with this principle of freedom and that no choices can be judged morally better or worse by this principle – although, of course, we might want to discriminate between them on the basis of other principles.

Thus if I have a right to do what I want with my property, then any disposition I choose is equally justifiable from the point of view of this principle: I may be judged uncharitable if I hoard it to myself and won't help those in need, or uncreative if I bury it in the ground and don't engage in interesting enterprises with it. But these latter criticisms arise from our accepting other moral standards, quite independent from the view that we have a right to do what we want with our own.

But this independence from a moral obligation of self-realization cannot be made good all around. All choices are equally valid; but they must be *choices*. The view that makes freedom of choice this absolute is one that exalts choice as a human capacity. It carries with it the demand that we become beings capable of choice, that we rise to the level of self-consciousness and autonomy where we can exercise choice, that we not remain enmired through fear, sloth, ignorance, or superstition in some code imposed by tradition, society, or fate which tells us how we should dispose of what belongs to us. Ultra-liberalism can only appear unconnected with any affirmation of worth and hence obligation of self-fulfilment, where people have come to accept the utterly facile moral psychology of traditional empiricism, according to which human agents possess the full capacity of choice as a given rather than as a potential which has to be developed.

If all this is valid, then the doctrine of the primacy of rights is not as independent as its proponents want to claim from considerations about human nature and the human social condition. For the doctrine could be undermined by arguments which succeeded in showing that men were not self-sufficient in the sense of the above argument – that is, that they could not develop their characteristically human potentialities outside of society or outside of certain kinds of society. The doctrine would in this sense be dependent on an atomist thesis, which affirms this kind of self-sufficiency.

The connection I want to establish here can be made following the earlier discussion of the background of rights. If we cannot ascribe natural rights without affirming the worth of certain human capacities, and if this affirmation has other normative consequences (i.e., that we should foster and nurture these capacities in ourselves and others), then any proof that these capacities can only develop in society or in a society of a certain kind is a proof that we ought to belong to or sustain society or this kind of society. But then, provided a social (i.e., an anti-atomist) thesis of the right kind can be true, an assertion of the primacy of rights is impossible; for to assert the rights in question is to affirm the capacities, and granted the social thesis is true concerning these capacities, this commits us to an obligation to belong. This will be as fundamental as the assertion of rights, because it will be inseparable from it. So that it would be incoherent to try to assert the rights, while denying the obligation or giving it the status of optional extra which we may or may not contract; this assertion is what the primacy doctrine makes.

The normative incoherence becomes evident if we see what it would be to assert the primacy of rights in the face of such a social thesis. Let us accept, for the sake of this argument, the view that men cannot develop the fullness of moral autonomy – that is, the capacity to form independent moral convictions – outside a political culture sustained by institutions of political participation and guarantees of personal independence. In fact, I do not think this thesis is true as it stands, although I do believe that a much more complicated view, formed from this one by adding a number of significant reservations, is tenable. But for the sake of simplicity let us accept this thesis in order to see the logic of the arguments.

Now if we assert the right to one's own independent moral convictions, we cannot in the face of this social thesis go on to assert the primacy of rights, that is, claim that we are not under obligation 'by nature' to belong to and sustain a society of the relevant type. We could not, for instance, unreservedly assert our right in the face of, or at the expense of, such a society; in the event of conflict we should have to acknowledge that we were legitimately pulled both ways. For in undermining such a society we should be making the activity defended by the right assertion impossible of realization. But if we are justified in asserting the right, we cannot be justified in our undermining; for the same considerations which justify the first condemn the second.

In whatever way the conflict might arise it poses a moral dilemma for us. It may be that we have already been formed in this culture and that the demise of this mode of society will not deprive us of this capacity. But in asserting our rights to the point of destroying the society, we should be depriving all those who follow after us of the exercise of the same capacity. To believe that there is a right to independent moral convictions must be to believe that the exercise of the relevant capacity is a human good. But then it cannot be right, if no over-riding considerations intervene, to act so as to make this good less available to others, even though in so doing I could not be said to be depriving them of their rights.

The incoherence of asserting primacy of rights is even clearer if we imagine another way in which the conflict could arise: that, in destroying the society, I would be undermining my own future ability to realize this capacity. For then in defending my right, I should be condemning myself to what I should have to acknowledge as a truncated mode of life, in virtue of the same considerations that make me affirm the right. And this would be a paradoxical thing to defend as an affirmation of my rights – in the same way as it would be paradoxical for me to offer to defend you against those who menace your freedom by hiding you in my deep freeze. I would have to have misunderstood what freedom is all about; and similarly in the above case, I should have lost my grasp of what affirming a right is.

We could put the point in another way. The affirmation of certain rights involves us in affirming the worth of certain capacities and thus in accepting certain standards by which a life may be judged full or truncated. We cannot then sensibly claim the morality of a truncated form of life for people on the ground of defending their rights. Would I be respecting your right to life if I agreed to leave you alive in a hospital bed, in an irreversible coma, hooked up to life-support machines? Or suppose I offered to use my new machine to erase totally your personality and memories and give you quite different ones? These questions are inescapably rhetorical. We cannot take them seriously as genuine questions because of the whole set of intuitions which surround our affirmation of the right to life. We assert this right because human life has a certain worth; but exactly wherein it has worth is negated by the appalling conditions I am offering you. That is why the offer is a sick joke, the lines of the mad scientist in a B movie.

It is the mad scientist's question, and not the question whether the person in the coma still enjoys rights, which should be decisive for the issue of whether asserting rights involves affirming the worth of certain capacities. For the latter question just probes the conditions of a right being valid; whereas the former shows us what it is to respect a right and hence what is really being asserted in a rights claim. It enables us to see what else we are committed to in asserting a right.

How would it do for the scientist to say, 'Well, I have respected his right to *life*, it is other rights (free movement, exercise of his profession, etc.) which I have violated'? For the separation in this context is absurd. True, we do sometimes enumerate these and other rights. But the right to life could never have been understood as excluding all these activities, as a right just to biological non-death in a coma. It is incomprehensible how anyone could assert a right to life meaning just this. 'Who calls that living?' would be the standard reaction. We could understand such an exiguous definition of life in the context of forensic medicine, for instance, but not in the affirmation of a right to life. And this is because the right-assertion is also an affirmation of worth, and this would be incomprehensible on behalf of this shadow of life.

If these arguments are valid, then the terms of the arguments are very different from what they are seen to be by most believers in the primacy of rights. Nozick, for instance, seems to feel that he can start from our intuitions that people have certain rights to dispose, say, of what they own so long as they harm no one else in doing so; and that we can build up (or fail to build up) a case for legitimate allegiance to certain forms of society and/or authority from this basis, by showing how they do not violate the rights. But he does not recognize that asserting rights itself involves acknowledging an obligation to belong. If the above considerations are valid, one cannot just baldly start with such an assertion of primacy. We would have to show that the relevant potentially mediating social theses are not valid; or, in other terms, we would have to defend a thesis of social atomism, that men are self-sufficient outside of society. We would have to establish the validity of arguing from the primacy of right.

But we can still try to resist this conclusion, in two ways. We can resist it first of all in asserting a certain schedule of rights. Suppose I make the basic right I assert that to life, on the grounds of sentience. This I understand in the broad sense that includes also other animals. Now sentience, as was said above, is not a capacity which can be realized or remain undeveloped; living things have it, and in dying they fail to have it; and there is an end to it. This is not to say that there are not conditions of severe impairment which constitute an infringement on sentient life, short of death. And clearly a right to life based on sentience would rule out accepting the mad scientist's offer just as much as any other conception of this right. But sentient life, while it can be impaired, is not a potential which we must develop and frequently fail to develop, as is the capacity to be a morally autonomous agent, or the capacity for self-determining freedom, or the capacity for the full realization of our talents.

But if we are not dealing with a capacity which can be underdeveloped in this sense, then there is no room for a thesis about the conditions of its development, whether social or otherwise. No social thesis is relevant. We are sentient beings whatever the social organization (or lack of it) of our existence; and if our basic right is to life, and the grounds of this right concern sentience (being capable of self-feeling, of desire and its satisfaction/frustration, of experiencing pain and pleasure), then surely we are beings of this kind in any society or none. In this regard we are surely self-sufficient.

I am not sure that even this is true – that is, that we really are self-sufficient even in regard to sentience. But it certainly is widely thought likely that we are. And therefore it is not surprising that the turn to theories of the primacy of rights goes along with an accentuation of the right to life which stresses life as sentience. For Hobbes our attachment to life is our desire to go on being agents of desire. The connection is not hard to understand. Social theories require a conception of the properly human life which is such that we are not assured it by simply being alive, but it must be developed and it can fail to be developed; on this basis they can argue that society or a certain form of society is the essential condition of this development. But Hobbesian nominalism involves rejecting utterly all such talk of forms or qualities of life which are properly human. Man is a being with desires, all of them on the same level. 'Whatsoever is the object of any man's desire ... that is it which he for his part calleth good.'[6] At one stroke there is no further room for a social thesis; and at the same time the right to life is interpreted in terms of desire. To be alive now in the meaning of the act is to be an agent of desires.

So we can escape the whole argument about self-sufficiency, it would seem, by making our schedule of rights sparse enough. Primacy-of-rights talk tends to go with a tough-mindedness which dismisses discussion of the properly human life-form as empty and metaphysical. From within its philosophical position, it is impregnable; but this does not mean that it is not still open to objection.

For the impregnability is purchased at a high price. To affirm a right for man merely *qua* desiring being, or a being feeling pleasure and pain, is to restrict his rights to those of life, desire-fulfilment, and freedom and pain. Other widely claimed rights, like freedom, enter only as means to these basic ones. If one is a monster of (at least attempted) consistency, like Hobbes, then one will be willing to stick to this exiguous conception of rights regardless of the consequences. But even then the question will arise of what on this view is the value of human as against animal life; and of whether it really is not a violation of people's rights if we transform them, unknown to themselves, into child-like lotus-eaters, say, by injecting them with some drug.

In fact, most of those who want to affirm the primacy of rights are more interested in asserting the right of freedom, and moreover, in a sense

---

[6] *Leviathan*, I, chap. 6.

which can only be attributed to humans, freedom to choose life plans, to dispose of possessions, to form one's own convictions and within reason act on them, and so on. But then we are dealing with capacities which do not simply belong to us in virtue of being alive – capacities which at least in some cases can fail to be properly developed; thus, the question of the proper conditions for their development arises.

We might query whether this is so with one of the freedoms mentioned above – that to dispose of one's own possessions. This is the right to property which has figured prominently with the right to life in the schedules put forward by defenders of primacy. Surely this right, while not something we can attribute to an animal, does not presuppose a capacity which could fail to be developed, at least for normal adults! We all are capable of possessing things, of knowing what we possess, and of deciding what we want to do with these possessions. This right does not seem to presuppose a capacity needing development, as does the right to profess independent convictions, for instance.

But those who assert this right almost always are affirming a capacity which we can fail to develop. And this becomes evident when we probe the reason for asserting this right. The standard answer, which comes to us from Locke, is that we need the right to property as an essential underpinning of life. But this is patently not true. Men have survived very well in communal societies all the way from paleolithic hunting clans through the Inca empire to contemporary China. And if one protests that the issue is not under what conditions one would not starve to death, but rather under what conditions one is independent enough of society not to be at its mercy for one's life, then the answer is that, if the whole point is being secure in my life, then I would be at less risk of death from agents of my own society in the contemporary Chinese commune than I would be in contemporary Chile. The property regime is hardly the only relevant variable.

But the real point is this: supposing a proponent of the right to property were to admit that the above was true – that the right to property does not as such secure life – would he change his mind? And the answer is, in the vast majority of cases, no. For what is at stake for him is not just life, but life in freedom. My life is safe in a Chinese commune, he might agree, but that is so only for so long as I keep quiet and do not profess heterodox opinions; otherwise the risks are very great. Private property is seen as essential, because it is thought to be an essential part of a life of genuine independence. But realizing a life of this form involves developing the capacity to act and choose in a genuinely independent way. And here the issue of whether a relevant social thesis is not valid can arise.

Hence this way of resisting the necessity of arguing for self-sufficiency (by scaling down one's schedules of rights to mere sentience or desire) is hardly likely to appeal to most proponents of primacy – once they understand the price they pay. For it involves sacrificing the central good of freedom, which it is their principal motive to safe-guard.

There remains another way of avoiding the issue. A proponent of primacy could admit that the question arises of the conditions for the development of the relevant capacities; he could even agree that a human being entirely alone could not possibly develop them (this is pretty hard to contest: wolf-boys are not candidates for properly human freedoms), and yet argue that society in the relevant sense was not necessary.

Certainly humans need others in order to develop as full human beings, he would agree. We must all be nurtured by others as children. We can only flourish as adults in relationship with friends, mates, children, and so on. But all this has nothing to do with any obligations to belong to political society. The argument about the state of nature should never have been taken as applying to human beings alone in the wilderness. This is a Rousseauian gloss, but is clearly not the conception of the state of nature with Locke, for instance. Rather it is clear that men must live in families (however families are constituted); that they need families even to grow up human; and that they continue to need them to express an important part of their humanity.

But what obligations to belong does this put on them? It gives us obligations in regard to our parents. But these are obligations of gratitude, and are of a different kind; for when we are ready to discharge these obligations our parents are no longer essential conditions of our human development. The corresponding obligations are to our children, to give them what we have been given; and for the rest we owe a debt to those with whom we are linked in marriage, friendship, association, and the like. But all this is perfectly acceptable to a proponent of the primacy of rights. For all obligations to other adults are freely taken on in contracting marriage, friendships, and the like; there is no natural obligation to belong. The only involuntary associations are those between generations: our obligations to our parents and those to our children (if we can think of these as involuntary associations, since no one picks his children in the process of natural generation). But these are obligations to specific people and do not necessarily involve continuing associations; and they are neither of them cases where the obligation arises in the way it does in the social thesis, viz., that we must maintain the association as a condition of our continued development.

Hence we can accommodate whatever is valid in the social thesis without any danger to the primacy of rights. Family obligations and obligations of friendship can be kept separate from any obligations to belong.

I do not think that this argument will hold. But I cannot really undertake to refute it here, not just on the usual cowardly grounds of lack of space, but because we enter here precisely on the central issue of the human condition which divides atomism from social theories. And this issue concerning as it does the human condition cannot be settled in a knockdown argument. My aim in this paper was just to show that it is an issue, and therefore has to be addressed by proponents of primacy. For this purpose I would like to lay out some considerations to which I subscribe, but of which I can do more than sketch an outline in these pages.

The kind of freedom valued by the protagonists of the primacy of rights, and indeed by many others of us as well, is a freedom by which men are capable of conceiving alternatives and arriving at a definition of what they really want, as well as discerning what commands their adherence or their allegiance. This kind of freedom is unavailable to one whose sympathies and horizons are so narrow that he can conceive only one way of life, for whom indeed the very notion of a way of life which is *his* as against everyone's has no sense. Nor is it available to one who is riveted by fear of the unknown to one familiar life-form, or who has been so formed in suspicion and hate of outsiders that he can never put himself in their place. Moreover, this capacity to conceive alternatives must not only be available for the less important choices of one's life. The greatest bigot or the narrowest xenophobe can ponder whether to have Dover sole or Wiener schnitzel for dinner. What is truly important is that one be able to exercise autonomy in the basic issues of life, in one's most important commitments.

Now, it is very dubious whether the developed capacity for this kind of autonomy can arise simply within the family. Of course, men may learn, and perhaps in part must learn, this from those close to them. But my question is whether this kind of capacity can develop within the compass of a single family. Surely it is something which only develops within an entire civilization. Think of the developments of art, philosophy, theology, science, of the evolving practices of politics and social organization, which have contributed to the historic birth of this aspiration to freedom, to making this ideal of autonomy a comprehensible goal men can aim at – something which is in their universe of potential aspiration (and it is not yet so for all men, and may never be).

But this civilization was not only necessary for the genesis of freedom. How could successive generations discover what it is to be an autonomous agent, to have one's own way of feeling, of acting, of expression, which cannot be simply derived from authoritative models? This is an identity, a way of understanding themselves, which men are not born with. They have to acquire it. And they do not in every society; nor do they all successfully come to terms with it in ours. But how can they acquire it unless it is implicit in at least some of their common practices, in the ways that they recognize and treat each other in their common life (for instance, in the acknowledgement of certain rights), or in the manner in which they deliberate with or address each other, or engage in economic exchange, or in some mode of public recognition of individuality and the worth of autonomy?

Thus we live in a world in which there is such a thing as public debate about moral and political questions and other basic issues. We constantly forget how remarkable that is, how it did not have to be so, and may one day no longer be so. What would happen to our capacity to be free agents if this debate should die away, or if the more specialized debate among intellectuals who attempt to define and clarify the alternatives facing us should also cease, or if the attempts to bring the culture of the past to life again as well as the drives to cultural innovation were to fall off? What would there be left to choose between? And if the atrophy went beyond a certain point, could we speak of choice at all? How long would we go on understanding what autonomous choice was? Again, what would happen if our legal culture were not constantly sustained by a contact with our traditions of the rule of law and a confrontation with our contemporary moral institutions? Would we have as sure a grasp of what the rule of law and the defence of rights required?

In other words, the free individual or autonomous moral agent can only achieve and maintain his identity in a certain type of culture, some of whose facets and activities I have briefly referred to. But these and others of the same significance do not come into existence spontaneously each successive instant. They are carried on in institutions and associations which require stability and continuity and frequently also support from society as a whole – almost always the moral support of being commonly recognized as important, but frequently also considerable material support. These bearers of our culture include museums, symphony orchestras, universities, laboratories, political parties, law courts, representative assemblies, newspapers, publishing houses, television stations, and so on. And I have to mention also the mundane elements of infrastructure without which we could not carry on these higher activities: buildings, railroads, sewage plants, power grids, and so on. Thus requirement of a living and varied culture is also the requirement of a complex and integrated society, which is willing and able to support all these institutions.[7]

I am arguing that the free individual of the West is only what he is by virtue of the whole society and civilization which brought him to be and which nourishes him; that our families can only form us up to this capacity and these aspirations because they are set in this civilization; and that a family alone outside of this context – the real old patriarchal family – was a quite different animal which never tended these horizons. And I want to claim finally that all this creates a significant obligation to belong for whoever would affirm the value of this freedom; this includes all those who want to assert rights either to this freedom or for its sake.

One could answer this by saying that the role of my civilization in forming me is a thing of the past; that, once adult, I have the capacity to be an autonomous being; and that I have no further obligation arising out of the exigencies of my development to sustain this civilization. I doubt whether this is in fact true; I doubt whether we could maintain our sense of ourselves as autonomous beings or whether even only a heroic few of us would succeed in doing so, if this liberal civilization of ours were to be thoroughly destroyed. I hope never to have to make the experiment. But even if we could, the considerations advanced a few pages back would be sufficient here: future generations will need this civilization to reach these aspirations; and if we affirm their worth, we have an obligation to make them available to others. This obligation is only increased if we ourselves have benefited from this civilization and have been enabled to become free agents ourselves.

But then the proponent of primacy could answer by questioning what all this has to do with political authority, with the obligation to belong to

---

[7] This is what makes so paradoxical the position of someone like Robert Nozick. He presents (*Anarchy, State and Utopia*, particularly chap. 10) the model of an ideal society where within the framework of the minimal state individuals form or join only those associations which they desire and which will admit them. There is no requirement laid down concerning the over-all pattern that will result from this. But can we really do without this? The aim of Nozick's utopian framework is to enable people to give expression to their real diversity. But what if the essential cultural activities which makes a great diversity conceivable to people begin to falter? Or are we somehow guaranteed against this? Nozick does not discuss this; it is as though the conditions of a creative, diversifying freedom were given by nature. In this respect the standard utopian literature, which as Nozick says is concerned with the character of the ideal community and not just with a framework for any community, is more realistic. For it faces the question of what kind of community we need in order to be free men, and then goes on to assume that this is given non-coercively.

a polity or to abide by the rules of a political society. Certainly, we could accept that we are only what we are in virtue of living in a civilization and hence in a large society, since a family or clan could not sustain this. But this does not mean that we must accept allegiance to a polity.

To this there are two responses. First, there is something persuasive about this objection in that it seems to hold out the alternative of an anarchist civilization – one where we have all the benefits of wide association and none of the pains of politics. And indeed, some libertarians come close to espousing an anarchist position and express sympathy for anarchism, as does Nozick. Now it is perfectly true that there is nothing in principle which excludes anarchism in the reflection that we owe our identity as free men to our civilization. But the point is that the commitment we recognize in affirming the worth of this freedom is a commitment to this civilization whatever are the conditions of its survival. If these can be assured in conditions of anarchy, that is very fortunate. But if they can only be assured under some form of representative government to which we all would have to give allegiance, then this is the society we ought to try to create and sustain and belong to. For this is by hypothesis the condition of what we have identified as a crucial human good, by the very fact of affirming this right. (I have, of course, taken as evident that this civilization could not be assured by some tyrannical form of government, because the civilization I am talking about is that which is the essential milieu for free agency.)

The crucial point here is this: since the free individual can only maintain his identity within a society/culture of a certain kind, he has to be concerned about the shape of this society/culture as a whole. He cannot, following the libertarian anarchist model that Nozick sketched,[8] be concerned purely with his individual choices and the associations formed from such choices to the neglect of the matrix in which such choices can be open or closed, rich or meagre. It is important to him that certain activities and institutions flourish in society. It is even of importance to him what the moral tone of the whole society is – shocking as it may be to libertarians to raise this issue – because freedom and individual diversity can only flourish in a society where there is a general recognition of their worth. They are threatened by the spread of bigotry, but also by other conceptions of life – for example, those which look on originality, innovation, and diversity as luxuries which society can ill afford given the need for efficiency, productivity, or growth, or those which in a host of other ways depreciate freedom.

---

[8] *Ibid.*, chap. 10.

Now, it is possible that a society and culture propitious for freedom might arise from the spontaneous association of anarchist communes. But it seems much more likely from the historical record that we need rather some species of political society. And if this is so then we must acknowledge an obligation to belong to this kind of society in affirming freedom. But there is more. If realizing our freedom partly depends on the society and culture in which we live, then we exercise a fuller freedom if we can help determine the shape of this society and culture. And this we can only do through instruments of common decision. This means that the political institutions in which we live may themselves be a crucial part of what is necessary to realize our identity as free beings.

This is the second answer to the last objection. In fact, men's deliberating together about what will be binding on all of them is an essential part of the exercise of freedom. It is only in this way that they can come to grips with certain basic issues in a way which will actually have an effect in their lives. Those issues, which can only be effectively decided by society as a whole and which often set the boundary and framework for our lives, can indeed be discussed freely by politically irresponsible individuals wherever they have licence to do so. But they can only be truly *deliberated* about politically. A society in which such deliberation was public and involved everyone would realize a freedom not available anywhere else or in any other mode.

Thus, always granted that an anarchist society is not an available option, it is hard to see how one can affirm the worth of freedom in this sense of the exercise of autonomous deliberation and at the same time recognize no obligation to bring about and sustain a political order of this kind.

The argument has gone far enough to show how difficult it is to conclude here. This is because we are on a terrain in which our conception of freedom touches on the issue of the nature of the human subject, and the degree and manner in which this subject is a social one. To open this up is to open the issue of atomism, which is all I hoped to do in this paper. I wanted to show that there is an issue in the 'self-sufficiency' or not of man outside political society and that this issue cannot be side-stepped by those who argue from natural rights. This issue, as we can see, leads us very deep, and perhaps we can see some of the motivation of those who have waited to side-step it. It seems much easier and clearer to remain on the level of our intuitions about rights.

For we can now see more clearly what the issue about atomism is, and how uncommonly difficult it is. It concerns self-sufficiency, but not in the sense of the ability to survive north of Great Slave Lake. That is a question whether we can fulfil certain causal conditions for our continued existence. But the alleged social conditions for the full development of our human capacities are not causal in the same sense. They open another set of issues altogether: whether the condition for the full development of our capacities is not that we achieve a certain identity, which requires a certain conception of ourselves; and more fundamentally whether this identity is ever something we can attain on our own, or whether the crucial modes of self-understanding are not always created and sustained by the common expression and recognition they receive in the life of the society.

Thus the thesis just sketched about the social conditions of freedom is based on the notion, first, that developed freedom requires a certain understanding of self, one in which the aspirations to autonomy and self-direction become conceivable; and second, that this self-understanding is not something we can sustain on our own, but that our identity is always partly defined in conversation with others or through the common understanding which underlies the practices of our society. The thesis is that the identity of the autonomous, self-determining individual requires a social matrix, one for instance which through a series of practices recognizes the right to autonomous decision and which calls for the individual having a voice in deliberation about public action.

The issue between the atomists and their opponents therefore goes deep; it touches the nature of freedom, and beyond this what it is to be a human subject; what is human identity, and how it is defined and sustained. It is not surprising therefore that the two sides talk past each other. For atomists the talk about identity and its conditions in social practice seems impossibly abstruse and speculative. They would rather found themselves on the clear and distinct intuition which we all share (all of us in this society, that is) about human rights.

For non-atomists, however, this very confidence in their starting point is a kind of blindness, a delusion of self-sufficiency which prevents them from seeing that the free individual, the bearer of rights, can only assume this identity thanks to his relationship to a developed liberal civilization; that there is an absurdity in placing this subject in a state of nature where he could never attain this identity and hence never create by contract a society which respects it. Rather, the free individual who affirms himself as such *already* has an obligation to complete, restore, or sustain the society within which this identity is possible.

It is clear that we can only join this issue by opening up questions about the nature of man. But it is also clear that the two sides are not on the same footing in relationship to these questions. Atomists are more comfortable standing with the intuitions of common sense about the rights of individuals and are not at all keen to open these wider issues. And in this they derive support in those philosophical traditions which come to us from the seventeenth century and which started with the postulation of an extensionless subject, epistemologically a *tabula rasa* and politically a presuppositionless bearer of rights. It is not an accident that these epistemological and political doctrines are often found in the writings of the same founding figures.

But if this starting point no longer appears to us self-evident, then we have to open up questions about the nature of the subject and the conditions of human agency. Among these is the issue about atomism. This is important for any theory of rights, but also for a great deal else besides. For the issue about atomism also underlies many of our discussions about obligation and the nature of freedom, as can already be sensed from the above. That is why it is useful to put it again on our agenda.

CHAPTER EIGHT

WHAT'S WRONG WITH NEGATIVE LIBERTY

This is an attempt to resolve one of the issues that separate 'positive' and 'negative' theories of freedom, as these have been distinguished in Isaiah Berlin's seminal essay, 'Two concepts of liberty'.[1] Although one can discuss almost endlessly the detailed formulation of the distinction, I believe it is undeniable that there are two such families of conceptions of political freedom abroad in our civilization.

Thus there clearly are theories, widely canvassed in liberal society, which want to define freedom exclusively in terms of the independence of the individual from interference by others, be these governments, corporations or private persons; and equally clearly these theories are challenged by those who believe that freedom resides at least in part in collective control over the common life. We unproblematically recognize theories descended from Rousseau and Marx as fitting in this category.

There is quite a gamut of views in each category. And this is worth bearing in mind, because it is too easy in the course of polemic to fix on the extreme, almost caricatural variants of each family. When people attack positive theories of freedom, they generally have some Left totalitarian theory in mind, according to which freedom resides exclusively in exercising collective control over one's destiny in a classless society, the kind of theory which underlies, for instance, official communism. This view, in its caricaturally extreme form, refuses to recognize the freedoms guaranteed in other societies as genuine. The destruction of 'bourgeois freedoms' is no real loss of freedom, and coercion can be justified in the name of freedom if it is needed to bring into existence the classless society in which alone men are properly free. Men can, in short, be forced to be free.

Even as applied to official communism, this portrait is a little extreme, although it undoubtedly expresses the inner logic of this kind of theory. But it is an absurd caricature if applied to the whole family of positive conceptions. This includes all those views of modern political life which

---

[1] *Four Essays on Liberty* (London, 1969), pp. 118–72.

owe something to the ancient republican tradition, according to which men's ruling themselves is seen as an activity valuable in itself, and not only for instrumental reasons. It includes in its scope thinkers like Tocqueville, and even arguably the J. S. Mill of *On Representative Government*. It has no necessary connection with the view that freedom consists *purely and simply* in the collective control over the common life, or that there is no freedom worth the name outside a context of collective control. And it does not therefore generate necessarily a doctrine that men can be forced to be free.

On the other side, there is a corresponding caricatural version of negative freedom which tends to come to the fore. This is the tough-minded version, going back to Hobbes, or in another way to Bentham, which sees freedom simply as the absence of external physical or legal obstacles. This view will have no truck with other less immediately obvious obstacles to freedom, for instance, lack of awareness, or false consciousness, or repression, or other inner factors of this kind. It holds firmly to the view that to speak of such inner factors as relevant to the issue about freedom, to speak for instance of someone's being less free because of false consciousness, is to abuse words. The only clear meaning which can be given to freedom is that of the absence of external obstacles.

I call this view caricatural as a representative portrait of the negative view, because it rules out of court one of the most powerful motives behind the modern defence of freedom as individual independence, viz., the post-Romantic idea that each person's form of self-realization is original to him/her, and can therefore only be worked out independently. This is one of the reasons for the defence of individual liberty by among others J. S. Mill (this time in his *On Liberty*). But if we think of freedom as including something like the freedom of self-fulfilment, or self-realization according to our own pattern, then we plainly have something which can fail for inner reasons as well as because of external obstacles. We can fail to achieve our own self-realization through inner fears, or false consciousness, as well as because of external coercion. Thus the modern notion of negative freedom which gives weight to the securing of each person's right to realize him/herself in his/her own way cannot make do with the Hobbes/Bentham notion of freedom. The moral psychology of these authors is too simple, or perhaps we should say too crude, for its purposes.

Now there is a strange asymmetry here. The extreme caricatural views tend to come to the fore in the polemic, as I mentioned above. But whereas the extreme 'forced-to-be-free' view is one which the opponents of positive liberty try to pin on them, as one would expect in the heat of argument, the proponents of negative liberty themselves often seem anxious to espouse their extreme, Hobbesian view. Thus even Isaiah Berlin, in his eloquent exposition of the two concepts of liberty, seems to quote Bentham[2] approvingly and Hobbes[3] as well. Why is this?

To see this we have to examine more closely what is at stake between the two views. The negative theories, as we saw, want to define freedom in terms of individual independence from others; the positive also want to identify freedom with collective self-government. But behind this lie some deeper differences of doctrines.

Isaiah Berlin points out that negative theories are concerned with the area in which the subject should be left without interference, whereas the positive doctrines are concerned with who or what controls. I should like to put the point behind this in a slightly different way. Doctrines of positive freedom are concerned with a view of freedom which involves essentially the exercising of control over one's life. On this view, one is free only to the extent that one has effectively determined oneself and the shape of one's life. The concept of freedom here is an exercise-concept.

By contrast, negative theories can rely simply on an opportunity-concept, where being free is a matter of what we can do, of what it is open to us to do, whether or not we do anything to exercise these options. This certainly is the case of the crude, original Hobbesian concept. Freedom consists just in there being no obstacle. It is a sufficient condition of one's being free that nothing stand in the way.

But we have to say that negative theories *can* rely on an opportunity-concept, rather than that they necessarily do so rely, for we have to allow for that part of the gamut of negative theories mentioned above which incorporates some notion of self-realization. Plainly this kind of view cannot rely simply on an opportunity-concept. We cannot say that someone is free, on a self-realization view, if he is totally unrealized, if for instance he is totally unaware of his potential, if fulfilling it has never even arisen as a question for him, or if he is paralysed by the fear of breaking with some norm which he has internalized but which does not authentically reflect him. Within this conceptual scheme, some degree of exercise is necessary for a man to be thought free. Or if we want to think of the internal bars to freedom as obstacles on all fours with the external ones, then being in a position to exercise freedom, having the opportunity, involves removing the internal barriers; and this is not possible without having to some extent realized myself. So that with the freedom

---

[2] *Four Essays on Liberty*, p. 148, note 1.   [3] *Ibid.*, p. 164.

of self-realization, having the opportunity to be free requires that I already be exercising freedom. A pure opportunity-concept is impossible here.

But if negative theories can be grounded on either an opportunity- or an exercise-concept, the same is not true of positive theories. The view that freedom involves at least partially collective self-rule is essentially grounded on an exercise-concept. For this view (at least partly) identifies freedom with self-direction, that is, the actual exercise of directing control over one's life.

But this already gives us a hint towards illuminating the above paradox, that while the extreme variant of positive freedom is usually pinned on its protagonists by their opponents, negative theorists seem prone to embrace the crudest versions of their theory themselves. For if an opportunity-concept is not combinable with a positive theory, but either it or its alternative can suit a negative theory, then one way of ruling out positive theories in principle is by firmly espousing an opportunity-concept. One cuts off the positive theories by the root, as it were, even though one may also pay a price in the atrophy of a wide range of negative theories as well. At least by taking one's stand firmly on the crude side of the negative range, where only opportunity concepts are recognized, one leaves no place for a positive theory to grow.

Taking one's stand here has the advantage that one is holding the line around a very simple and basic issue of principle, and one where the negative view seems to have some backing in common sense. The basic intuition here is that freedom is a matter of being able to do something or other, of not having obstacles in one's way, rather than being a capacity that we have to realize. It naturally seems more prudent to fight the Totalitarian Menace at this last-ditch position, digging in behind the natural frontier of this simple issue, rather than engaging the enemy on the open terrain of exercise-concepts, where one will have to fight to discriminate the good from the bad among such concepts; fight, for instance, for a view of individual self-realization against various notions of collective self-realization, of a nation, or a class. It seems easier and safer to cut all the nonsense off at the start by declaring all self-realization views to be metaphysical hog-wash. Freedom should just be tough-mindedly defined as the absence of external obstacles.

Of course, there are independent reasons for wanting to define freedom tough-mindedly. In particular there is the immense influence of the anti-metaphysical, materialist, natural-science-oriented temper of thought in our civilization. Something of this spirit at its inception induced Hobbes to take the line that he did, and the same spirit goes marching on today. Indeed, it is because of the prevalence of this spirit that the line is so easy to defend, forensically speaking, in our society.

Nevertheless, I think that one of the strongest motives for defending the crude Hobbes–Bentham concept, that freedom is the absence of external obstacles, physical or legal, is the strategic one above. For most of those who take this line thereby abandon many of their own intuitions, sharing as they do with the rest of us in a post-Romantic civilization which puts great value on self-realization, and values freedom largely because of this. It is fear of the Totalitarian Menace, I would argue, which has led them to abandon this terrain to the enemy.

I want to argue that this not only robs their eventual forensic victory of much of its value, since they become incapable of defending liberalism in the form we in fact value it, but I want to make the stronger claim that this Maginot Line mentality actually ensures defeat, as is often the case with Maginot Line mentalities. The Hobbes–Bentham view, I want to argue, is indefensible as a view of freedom.

To see this, let us examine the line more closely, and the temptation to stand on it. The advantage of the view that freedom is the absence of external obstacles is its simplicity. It allows us to say that freedom is being able to do what you want, where what you want is unproblematically understood as what the agent can identify as his desires. By contrast an exercise-concept of freedom requires that we discriminate among motivations. If we are free in the exercise of certain capacities, then we are not free, or less free, when these capacities are in some way unfulfilled or blocked. But the obstacles can be internal as well as external. And this must be so, for the capacities relevant to freedom must involve some self-awareness, self-understanding, moral discrimination and self-control, otherwise their exercise could not amount to freedom in the sense of self-direction; and this being so, we can fail to be free because these internal conditions are not realized. But where this happens, where, for example, we are quite self-deceived, or utterly fail to discriminate properly the ends we seek, or have lost self-control, we can quite easily be doing what we want in the sense of what we can identify as our wants, without being free; indeed, we can be further entrenching our unfreedom.

Once one adopts a self-realization view, or indeed any exercise-concept of freedom, then being able to do what one wants can no longer be accepted as a sufficient condition of being free. For this view puts certain conditions on one's motivation. You are not free if you are motivated, through fear, inauthentically internalized standards, or false consciousness, to thwart your self-realization. This is sometimes put by saying that for a self-realization view, you have to be able to do what you really want, or to follow your real will, or to fulfil the desires of your own true self. But these formulae, particularly the last, may mislead, by making us think that exercise-concepts of freedom are tied to some particular metaphysic, in particular that of a higher and lower self. We shall see below that this is far from being the case, and that there is a much wider range of bases for discriminating authentic desires.

In any case, the point for our discussion here is that for an exercise-concept of freedom, being free cannot just be a question of doing what you want in the unproblematic sense. It must also be that what you want does not run against the grain of your basic purposes, or your self-realization. Or to put the issue in another way, which converges on the same point, the subject himself cannot be the final authority on the question whether he is free; for he cannot be the final authority on the question whether his desires are authentic, whether they do or do not frustrate his purposes.

To put the issue in this second way is to make more palpable the temptation for defenders of the negative view to hold their Maginot Line. For once we admit that the agent himself is not the final authority on his own freedom, do we not open the way to totalitarian manipulation? Do we not legitimate others, supposedly wiser about his purposes than himself, redirecting his feet on the right path, perhaps even by force, and all this in the name of freedom?

The answer is that of course we don't. Not by this concession alone. For there may also be good reasons for holding that others are not likely to be in a better position to understand his real purposes. This indeed plausibly follows from the post-Romantic view above that each person has his own original form of realization. Some others, who know us intimately, and who surpass us in wisdom, are undoubtedly in a position to advise us, but no official body can possess a doctrine or a technique whereby they could know how to put us on the rails, because such a doctrine or technique cannot in principle exist if human beings really differ in their self-realization.

Or again, we may hold a self-realization view of freedom, and hence believe that there are certain conditions on my motivation necessary to my being free, but also believe that there are other necessary conditions which rule out my being forcibly led towards some definition of my self-realization by external authority. Indeed, in these last two paragraphs I have given a portrait of what I think is a very widely held view in liberal society, a view which values self-realization, and accepts that it can fail for internal reasons, but which believes that no valid guidance can be provided in principle by social authority, because of human diversity and originality, and holds that the attempt to impose such guidance will destroy other necessary conditions of freedom.

It is however true that totalitarian theories of positive freedom do build on a conception which involves discriminating between motivations. Indeed, one can represent the path from the negative to the positive conceptions of freedom as consisting of two steps: the first moves us from a notion of freedom as doing what one wants to a notion which discriminates motivations and equates freedom with doing what we really want, or obeying our real will, or truly directing our lives. The second step introduces some doctrine purporting to show that we cannot do what we really want, or follow our real will, outside of a society of a certain canonical form, incorporating true self-government. It follows that we can only be free in such a society, and that being free *is* governing ourselves collectively according to this canonical form.

We might see an example of this second step in Rousseau's view that only a social contract society in which all give themselves totally to the whole preserves us from other-dependence and ensures that we obey only ourselves; or in Marx's doctrine of man as a species-being who realizes his potential in a mode of social production, and who must thus take control of this mode collectively.

Faced with this two-step process, it seems safer and easier to stop it at the first step, to insist firmly that freedom is just a matter of the absence of external obstacles, that it therefore involves no discrimination of motivation and permits in principle no second-guessing of the subject by any one else. This is the essence of the Maginot Line strategy. It is very tempting. But I want to claim that it is wrong. I want to argue that we cannot defend a view of freedom which does not involve at least some qualitative discrimination as to motive, that is which does not put some restrictions on motivation among the necessary conditions of freedom, and hence which could rule out second-guessing in principle.

There are some considerations one can put forward straight off to show that the pure Hobbesian concept will not work, that there are some discriminations among motivations which are essential to the concept of freedom as we use it. Even where we think of freedom as the absence of external obstacles, it is not the absence of such obstacles *simpliciter*. For we make discriminations between obstacles as representing more or less serious infringements of freedom. And we do this, because we deploy the concept against a background understanding that certain goals and activities are more significant than others.

Thus we could say that my freedom is restricted if the local authority puts up a new traffic light at an intersection close to my home; so that where previously I could cross as I liked, consistently with avoiding collision with other cars, now I have to wait until the light is green. In a philosophical argument, we might call this a restriction of freedom, but not in a serious political debate. The reason is that it is too trivial, the activity and purposes inhibited here are not really significant. It is not just a matter of our having made a trade-off, and considered that a small loss of liberty was worth fewer traffic accidents, or less danger for the children; we are reluctant to speak here of a loss of liberty at all; what we feel we are trading off is convenience against safety.

By contrast a law which forbids me from worshipping according to the form I believe in is a serious blow to liberty; even a law which tried to restrict this to certain times (as the traffic light restricts my crossing of the intersection to certain times) would be seen as a serious restriction. Why this difference between the two cases? Because we have a background understanding, too obvious to spell out, of some activities and goals as highly significant for human beings and others as less so. One's religious belief is recognized, even by atheists, as supremely important, because it is that by which the believer defines himself as a moral being. By contrast my rhythm of movement through the city traffic is trivial. We do not want to speak of these two in the same breath. We do not even readily admit that liberty is at stake in the traffic light case. For *de minimis non curat libertas*.

But this recourse to significance takes us beyond a Hobbesian scheme. Freedom is no longer just the absence of external obstacle *tout court*, but the absence of external obstacle to significant action, to what is important to man. There are discriminations to be made; some restrictions are more serious than others, some are utterly trivial. About many, there is of course controversy. But what the judgement turns on is some sense of what is significant for human life. Restricting the expression of people's religious and ethical convictions is more signficant than restricting their movement around uninhabited parts of the country; and both are more significant than the trivia of traffic control.

But the Hobbesian scheme has no place for the notion of significance. It will allow only for purely quantitative judgements. On the toughest-minded version of his conception, where Hobbes seems to be about to define liberty in terms of the absence of physical obstacles, one is presented with the vertiginous prospect of human freedom being measurable in the same way as the degrees of freedom of some physical object, say a lever. Later we see that this will not do, because we have to take account of legal obstacles to my action. But in any case, such a quantitative conception of freedom is a non-starter.

Consider the following diabolical defence of Albania as a free country. We recognize that religion has been abolished in Albania, whereas it hasn't been in Britain. But on the other hand there are probably far fewer traffic lights per head in Tirana than in London. (I haven't checked for myself, but this is a very plausible assumption.) Suppose an apologist for Albanian socialism were nevertheless to claim that this country was freer than Britain, because the number of acts restricted was far smaller. After all, only a minority of Londoners practise some religion in public places, but all have to negotiate their way through traffic. Those who do practise a religion generally do so on one day of the week, while they are held up at traffic lights every day. In sheer quantitative terms, the number of acts restricted by traffic lights must be greater than that restricted by a ban on public religious practice. So if Britain is considered a free society, why not Albania?

Thus the application even of our negative notion of freedom requires a background conception of what is significant, according to which some restrictions are seen to be without relevance for freedom altogether, and others are judged as being of greater and lesser importance. So some discrimination among motivations seems essential to our concept of freedom. A minute's reflection shows why this must be so. Freedom is important to us because we are purposive beings. But then there must be distinctions in the significance of different kinds of freedom based on the distinction in the significance of different purposes.

But of course, this still does not involve the kind of discrimination mentioned above, the kind which would allow us to say that someone who was doing what he wanted (in the unproblematic sense) was not really free, the kind of discrimination which allows us to put conditions on people's motivations necessary to their being free, and hence to second-guess them. All we have shown is that we make discriminations between more or less significant freedoms, based on discriminations among the purposes people have.

This creates some embarrassment for the crude negative theory, but it can cope with it by simply adding a recognition that we make judgements of significance. Its central claim that freedom just is the absence of external obstacles seems untouched, as also its view of freedom as an opportunity-concept. It is just that we now have to admit that not all opportunities are equal.

But there is more trouble in store for the crude view when we examine further what these qualitative discriminations are based on. What lies behind our judging certain purposes/feelings as more significant than others? One might think that there was room here again for another quantitative theory; that the more significant purposes are those we want more. But this account is either vacuous or false.

It is true but vacuous if we take wanting more just to mean being more significant. It is false as soon as we try to give wanting more an independent criterion, such as, for instance, the urgency or force of a desire, or the prevalence of one desire over another, because it is a matter of the most banal experience that the purposes we know to be more significant are not always those which we desire with the greatest urgency to encompass, nor the ones that actually always win out in cases of conflict of desires.

When we reflect on this kind of significance, we come up against what I have called elsewhere the fact of strong evaluation, the fact that we human subjects are not only subjects of first-order desires, but of second-order desires, desires about desires. We experience our desires and purposes as qualitatively discriminated, as higher or lower, noble or base, integrated or fragmented, significant or trivial, good and bad. This means that we experience some of our desires and goals as intrinsically more significant than others: some passing comfort is less important than the fulfilment of our life-time vocation, our *amour propre* less important than a love relationship; while we experience some others as bad, not just comparatively but absolutely: we desire not to be moved by spite, or some childish desire to impress at all costs. And these judgements of significance are quite independent of the strength of the respective desires: the craving for comfort may be overwhelming at this moment, we may be obsessed with our *amour propre*, but the judgement of significance stands.

But then the question arises whether this fact of strong evaluation doesn't have other consequences for our notion of freedom, than just that it permits us to rank freedoms in importance. Is freedom not at stake when we find ourselves carried away by a less significant goal to over-ride a highly significant one? Or when we are led to act out of a motive we consider bad or despicable?

The answer is that we sometimes do speak in this way. Suppose I have some irrational fear, which is preventing me from doing something I very much want to do. Say the fear of public speaking is preventing me from taking up a career that I should find very fulfilling, and that I should be quite good at, if I could just get over this 'hang-up'. It is clear that we experience this fear as an obstacle, and that we feel we are less than we would be if we could overcome it.

Or again, consider the case where I am very attached to comfort. To go on short rations, and to miss my creature comforts for a time, makes me very depressed. I find myself making a big thing of this. Because of this reaction I cannot do certain things that I should like very much to do, such as going on an expedition over the Andes, or a canoe trip in the Yukon. Once again, it is quite understandable if I experience this attachment as an obstacle, and feel that I should be freer without it.

Or I could find that my spiteful feelings and reactions which I almost cannot inhibit are undermining a relationship which is terribly important to me. At times, I feel as though I am almost assisting as a helpless witness at my own destructive behaviour, as I lash out again with my unbridled tongue at her. I long to be able not to feel this spite. As long as I feel it, even control is not an option, because it just builds up inside until it either bursts out, or else the feeling somehow communicates itself, and queers things between us. I long to be free of this feeling.

These are quite understandable cases, where we can speak of freedom or its absence without strain. What I have called strong evaluation is essentially involved here. For these are not just cases of conflict, even cases of painful conflict. If the conflict is between two desires with which I have no trouble identifying, there can be no talk of lesser freedom, no matter how painful or fateful. Thus if what is breaking up my relationship is my finding fulfilment in a job which, say, takes me away from home a lot, I have indeed a terrible conflict, but I would have no temptation to speak of myself as less free.

Even seeing a great difference in the significance of the two terms doesn't seem to be a sufficient condition of my wanting to speak of freedom and its absence. Thus my marriage may be breaking up because I like going to the pub and playing cards on Saturday nights with the boys. I may feel quite unequivocally that my marriage is much more important than the release and comradeship of the Saturday night bash. But nevertheless I would not want to talk of my being freer if I could slough off this desire.

The difference seems to be that in this case, unlike the ones above, I still identify with the less important desire, I still see it as expressive of myself, so that I could not lose it without altering who I am, losing something of my personality. Whereas my irrational fear, my being quite distressed by discomfort, my spite – these are all things which I can easily see myself losing without any loss whatsoever to what I am. This is why I can see them as obstacles to my purposes, and hence to my freedom, even though they are in a sense unquestionably desires and feelings of mine.

Before exploring further what is involved in this, let us go back and keep score. It would seem that these cases make a bigger breach in the crude negative theory. For they seem to be cases in which the obstacles to freedom are internal; and if this is so, then freedom cannot simply be interpreted as the absence of *external* obstacles; and the fact that I am doing what I want, in the sense of following my strongest desire, is not sufficient to establish that I am free. On the contrary, we have to make discriminations among motivations, and accept that acting out of some motivations, for example irrational fear or spite, or this too great need for comfort, is not freedom, is even a negation of freedom.

But although the crude negative theory cannot be sustained in the face of these examples, perhaps something which springs from the same concerns can be reconstructed. For although we have to admit that there are internal, motivational, necessary conditions for freedom, we can perhaps still avoid any legitimation of what I called above the second-guessing of the subject. If our negative theory allows for strong evaluation, allows that some goals are really important to us, and that other desires are seen as not fully ours, then can it not retain the thesis that freedom is being able to do what I want, that is, what I can identify myself as wanting, where this means not just what I identify as my strongest desire, but what I identify as my true, authentic desire or purpose? The subject would still be the final arbiter of his being free/unfree, as indeed he is clearly capable of discerning this in the examples above, where I relied precisely on the subject's own experience of constraint, of motives with which he cannot identify. We should have sloughed off the untenable Hobbesian reductive-materialist metaphysics, according to which only external obstacles count, as though action were just movement, and there could be no internal, motivational obstacles to our deeper purposes. But we would be retaining the basic concern of the negative theory, that the subject is still the final authority as to what his freedom consists in, and cannot be second-guessed by external authority. Freedom would be modified to read: the absence of internal or external obstacle to what I truly or authentically want. But we would still be holding the Maginot Line. Or would we?

I think not, in fact. I think that this hybrid or middle position is untenable, where we are willing to admit that we can speak of what we truly want, as against what we most strongly desire, and of some desires as obstacles to our freedom, while we still will not allow for second-guessing. For to rule this out in principle is to rule out in principle that the subject can ever be wrong about what he truly wants. And how can he never, in principle, be wrong, unless there is nothing to be right or wrong about in this matter?

That in fact is the thesis our negative theorist will have to defend. And it is a plausible one for the same intellectual (reductive-empiricist) tradition from which the crude negative theory springs. On this view, our feelings are brute facts about us; that is, it is a fact about us that we are affected in such and such a way, but our feelings cannot themselves be understood as involving some perception or sense of what they relate to, and hence as potentially veridical or illusory, authentic or inauthentic. On this scheme, the fact that a certain desire represented one of our fundamental purposes, and another a mere force with which we cannot identify, would concern merely the brute quality of the affect in both cases. It would be a matter of the raw feel of these two desires that this was their respective status.

In such circumstances, the subject's own classification would be incorrigible. There is no such thing as an imperceptible raw feel. If the subject failed to experience a certain desire as fundamental, and if what we meant by 'fundamental' applied to desire was that the felt experience of it has a certain quality, then the desire could not be fundamental. We can see this if we look at those feelings which we can agree are brute in this sense: for instance, the stab of pain I feel when the dentist jabs into my tooth, or the crawling unease when someone runs his fingernail along the blackboard. There can be no question of misperception here. If I fail to 'perceive' the pain, I am not in pain. Might it not be so with our fundamental desires, and those which we repudiate?

The answer is clearly no. For first of all, many of our feelings and desires, including the relevant ones for these kinds of conflicts, are not brute. By contrast with pain and the fingernail-on-blackboard sensation, shame and fear, for instance, are emotions which involve our experiencing the situation as bearing a certain import for us, as being dangerous or shameful. This is why shame and fear can be inappropriate, or even irrational, where pain and a frisson cannot. Thus we can be in error in feeling shame or fear. We can even be consciously aware of the unfounded nature of our feelings, and this is when we castigate them as irrational.

Thus the notion that we can understand all our feelings and desires as brute, in the above sense, is not on. But more, the idea that we could discriminate our fundamental desires, or those which we want to repudiate, by the quality of brute affect is grotesque. When I am convinced that some career, or an expedition in the Andes, or a love relationship, is of fundamental importance to me (to recur to the above examples), it cannot be just because of the throbs, élans or tremors I feel; I must also have some sense that these are of great significance for me, meet important, long-lasting needs, represent a fulfilment of something central to me, will bring me closer to what I really am, or something of the sort. The whole notion of our identity, whereby we recognize that some goals, desires, allegiances are central to what we are, while others are not or are less so, can make sense only against a background of desires and feelings which are not brute, but what I shall call import-attributing, to invent a term of art for the occasion.

Thus we have to see our emotional life as made up largely of import-attributing desires and feelings, that is, desires and feelings which we can experience mistakenly. And not only can we be mistaken in this, we clearly must accept, in cases like the above where we want to repudiate certain desires, that we are mistaken.

For let us consider the distinction mentioned above between conflicts where we feel fettered by one desire, and those where we do not, where, for instance, in the example mentioned above, a man is torn between his career and his marriage. What made the difference was that in the case of genuine conflict both desires are the agent's, whereas in the cases where he feels fettered by one, this desire is one he wants to repudiate.

But what is it to feel that a desire is not truly mine? Presumably, I feel that I should be better off without it, that I do not lose anything in getting rid of it, I remain quite complete without it. What could lie behind this sense?

Well, one could imagine feeling this about a brute desire. I may feel this about my addiction to smoking, for instance – wish I could get rid of it, experience it as a fetter, and believe that I should be well rid of it. But addictions are a special case; we understand them to be unnatural, externally induced desires. We could not say in general that we are ready to envisage losing our brute desires without a sense of diminution. On the contrary, to lose my desire for, and hence delectation in, oysters, mushroom pizza, or Peking duck would be a terrible deprivation. I should fight against such a change with all the strength at my disposal.

So being brute is not what makes desires repudiable. And besides, in the above examples the repudiated desires are not brute. In the first case, I am chained by unreasoning fear, an import-attributing emotion, in which the fact of being mistaken is already recognized when I identify the fear as irrational or unreasoning. Spite, too, which moves me in the third case, is an import-attributing emotion. To feel spite is to see oneself and the target of one's resentment in a certain light; it is to feel in some way wounded, or damaged, by his success or good fortune, and the more hurt the more he is fortunate. To overcome feelings of spite, as against just holding them in, is to come to see self and other in a different light, in particular, to set aside self-pity, and the sense of being personally wounded by what the other does and is.

(I should also like to claim that the obstacle in the third example, the too great attachment to comfort, while not itself import-attributing, is also bound up with the way we see things. The problem is here not just that we dislike discomfort, but that we are too easily depressed by it; and this is something which we overcome only by sensing a different order of priorities, whereby small discomforts matter less. But if this is thought too dubious, we can concentrate on the other two examples.)

Now how can we feel that an import-attributing desire is not truly ours? We can do this only if we see it as mistaken, that is, the import or the good it supposedly gives us a sense of is not a genuine import or good. The irrational fear is a fetter, because it is irrational; spite is a fetter because it is rooted in a self-absorption which distorts our perspective on everything, and the pleasures of venting it preclude any genuine satisfaction. Losing these desires we lose nothing, because their loss deprives us of no genuine good or pleasure or satisfaction. In this they are quite different from my love of oysters, mushroom pizza and Peking duck.

It would appear from this that to see our desires as brute gives us no clue as to why some of them are repudiable. On the contrary it is precisely their not being brute which can explain this. It is because they are import-attributing desires which are mistaken that we can feel that we would lose nothing in sloughing them off. Everything which is truly important to us would be safe-guarded. If they were just brute desires, we could not feel this unequivocally, as we certainly do not when it comes to the pleasures of the palate. True, we also feel that our desire to smoke is repudiable, but there is a special explanation here, which is not available in the case of spite.

Thus we can experience some desires as fetters, because we can experience them as not ours. And we can experience them as not ours because we see them as incorporating a quite erroneous appreciation of our situation and of what matters to us. We can see this again if we contrast the case of spite with that of another emotion which partly overlaps, and which is highly considered in some societies, the desire for revenge. In certain traditional societies this is far from being considered a despicable emotion. On the contrary, it is a duty of honour on a male relative to avenge a man's death. We might imagine that this too might give rise to conflict. It might conflict with the attempts of a new regime to bring some order to the land. The government would have to stop people taking vengeance, in the name of peace.

But short of a conversion to a new ethical outlook, this would be seen as a trade-off, the sacrifice of one legitimate goal for the sake of another. And it would seem monstrous were one to propose reconditioning people so that they no longer felt the desire to avenge their kin. This would be to unman them.[4]

Why do we feel so different about spite (and for that matter also revenge)? Because the desire for revenge for an ancient Icelander was his sense of a real obligation incumbent on him, something it would be dishonourable to repudiate; while for us, spite is the child of a distorted perspective on things.

We cannot therefore understand our desires and emotions as all brute, and in particular we cannot make sense of our discrimination of some desires as more important and fundamental, or of our repudiation of others, unless we understand our feelings to be import-attributing. This is essential to there being what we have called strong evaluation. Consequently the half-way position which admits strong evaluation, admits that our desires may frustrate our deeper purposes, admits therefore that there may be inner obstacles to freedom, and yet will not admit that the subject may be wrong or mistaken about these purposes – this position does not seem tenable. For the only way to make the subject's assessment incorrigible in principle would be to claim that there was nothing to be right or wrong about here; and that could only be so if experiencing a given feeling were a matter of the qualities of brute feeling. But this it cannot be if we are to make sense of the whole background of strong evaluation, more significant goals, and aims that we repudiate. This whole scheme requires that we understand the emotions concerned as import-attributing, as, indeed, it is clear that we must do on other grounds as well.

But once we admit that our feelings are import-attributing, then we admit the possibility of error, or false appreciation. And indeed, we have

---

[4] Compare the unease we feel at the reconditioning of the hero of Anthony Burgess' *A Clockwork Orange*.

to admit a kind of false appreciation which the agent himself detects in order to make sense of the cases where we experience our own desires as fetters. How can we exclude in principle that there may be other false appreciations which the agent does not detect? That he may be profoundly in error, that is, have a very distorted sense of his fundamental purposes? Who can say that such people cannot exist? All cases are, of course, controversial; but I should nominate Charles Manson and Andreas Baader for this category, among others. I pick them out as people with a strong sense of some purposes and goals as incomparably more fundamental than others, or at least with a propensity to act the having such a sense so as to take in even themselves a good part of the time, but whose sense of fundamental purpose was shot through with confusion and error. And once we recognize such extreme cases, how avoid admitting that many of the rest of mankind can suffer to a lesser degree from the same disabilities?

What has this got to do with freedom? Well, to resume what we have seen: our attributions of freedom make sense against a background sense of more and less significant purposes, for the question of freedom/unfreedom is bound up with the frustration/fulfilment of our purposes. Further, our significant purposes can be frustrated by our own desires, and where these are sufficiently based on misappreciation, we consider them as not really ours, and experience them as fetters. A man's freedom can therefore be hemmed in by internal, motivational obstacles, as well as external ones. A man who is driven by spite to jeopardize his most important relationships, in spite of himself, as it were, or who is prevented by unreasoning fear from taking up the career he truly wants, is not really made more free if one lifts the external obstacles to his venting his spite or acting on his fear. Or at best he is liberated into a very impoverished freedom.

If through linguistic/ideological purism one wants to stick to the crude definition, and insist that men are equally freed from whom the same external obstacles are lifted, regardless of their motivational state, then one will just have to introduce some other term to mark the distinction, and say that one man is capable of taking proper advantage of his freedom, and the other (the one in the grip of spite, or fear) is not. This is because in the meaningful sense of 'free', that for which we value it, in the sense of being able to act on one's important purposes, the internally fettered man is not free. If we choose to give 'free' a special (Hobbesian) sense which avoids this issue, we will just have to introduce another term to deal with it.

Moreover, since we have already seen that we are always making judgements of degrees of freedom, based on the significance of the activities or purposes which are left unfettered, how can we deny that the man, externally free but still stymied by his repudiated desires, is less free than one who has no such inner obstacles?

But if this is so, then can we not say of the man with a highly distorted view of his fundamental purpose, the Manson or Baader of my discussion above, that he may not be significantly freer when we lift even the internal barriers to his doing what is in line with this purpose, or at best may be liberated into a very impoverished freedom? Should a Manson overcome his last remaining compunction against sending his minions to kill on caprice, so that he could act unchecked, would we consider him freer, as we should undoubtedly consider the man who had done away with spite or unreasoning fear? Hardly, and certainly not to the same degree. For what he sees as his purpose here partakes so much of the nature of spite and unreasoning fear in the other cases, that is, it is an aspiration largely shaped by confusion, illusion and distorted perspective.

Once we see that we make distinctions of degree and significance in freedoms depending on the significance of the purpose fettered/enabled, how can we deny that it makes a difference to the degree of freedom not only whether one of my basic purposes is frustrated by my own desires but also whether I have grievously misidentified this purpose? The only way to avoid this would be to hold that there is no such thing as getting it wrong, that your basic purpose is just what you feel it to be. But there is such a thing as getting it wrong, as we have seen, and the very distinctions of significance depend on this fact.

But if this is so, then the crude negative view of freedom, the Hobbesian definition, is untenable. Freedom cannot just be the absence of external obstacles, for there may also be internal ones. And nor may the internal obstacles be just confined to those that the subject identifies as such, so that he is the final arbiter; for he may be profoundly mistaken about his purposes and about what he wants to repudiate. And if so, he is less capable of freedom in the meaningful sense of the word. Hence we cannot maintain the incorrigibility of the subject's judgements about his freedom, or rule out second-guessing, as we put it above. And at the same time, we are forced to abandon the pure opportunity-concept of freedom.

For freedom now involves my being able to recognize adequately my more important purposes, and my being able to overcome or at least neutralize my motivational fetters, as well as my way being free of external obstacles. But clearly the first condition (and, I would argue, also the second) require me to have become something, to have achieved a certain condition of self-clairvoyance and self-understanding. I must be actually exercising self-understanding in order to be truly or fully free. I can no longer understand freedom just as an opportunity-concept.

In all these three formulations of the issue – opportunity- versus exercise-concept; whether freedom requires that we discriminate among motivations; whether it allows of second-guessing the subject – the extreme negative view shows up as wrong. The idea of holding the Maginot Line before this Hobbesian concept is misguided not only because it involves abandoning some of the most inspiring terrain of liberalism, which is concerned with individual self-realization, but also because the line turns out to be untenable. The first step from the Hobbesian definition to a positive notion, to a view of freedom as the ability to fulfil my purposes, and as being greater the more significant the purposes, is one we cannot help taking. Whether we must also take the second step, to a view of freedom which sees it as realizable or fully realizable only within a certain form of society; and whether in taking a step of this kind one is necessarily committed to justifying the excesses of totalitarian oppression in the name of liberty; these are questions which must now be addressed. What is certain is that they cannot simply be evaded by a philistine definition of freedom which relegates them by fiat to the limbo of metaphysical pseudo-questions. This is altogether too quick a way with them.

CHAPTER NINE

THE DIVERSITY OF GOODS

I

What did utilitarianism have going for it? A lot of things undoubtedly: its seeming compatibility with scientific thought; its this-worldly humanist focus, its concern with suffering. But one of the powerful background factors behind much of this appeal was *epistemological*. A utilitarian ethic seemed to be able to fit the canons of rational validation as these were understood in the intellectual culture nourished by the epistemological revolution of the seventeenth century and the scientific outlook which partly sprang from it.

In the utilitarian perspective, one validated an ethical position by hard evidence. You count the consequences for human happiness of one or another course, and you go with the one with the highest favourable total. What counts as human happiness was thought to be something conceptually unproblematic, a scientifically establishable domain of facts like others. One could abandon all the metaphysical or theological factors — commands of God, natural rights, virtues — which made ethical questions scientifically undecidable. Bluntly, we could calculate.

Ultimately, I should like to argue that this is but another example of the baleful effect of the classical epistemological model, common to Cartesians and empiricists, which has had such a distorting effect on the theoretical self-understanding of moderns. This is something which is above all visible in the sciences of man, but I think it has wreaked as great havoc in ethical theory.

The distortive effect comes in that we tend to start formulating our meta-theory of a given domain with an already formed model of valid reasoning, all the more dogmatically held because we are oblivious to the alternatives. This model then makes us quite incapable of seeing how reason does and can really function in the domain, to the degree that it does not fit the model. We cut and chop the reality of, in this case, ethical thought to fit the Procrustean bed of our model of validation. Then, since meta-theory and theory cannot be isolated from one another, the distortive conception begins to shape our ethical thought itself.

A parallel process, I should like to argue, has been visible in the sciences of man, with similar stultifying effects on the practice of students of human behaviour. The best, most insightful, practice of history, sociology, psychology is either devalued or misunderstood, and as a consequence we find masses of researchers engaging in what very often turns out to be futile exercises, of no scientific value whatever, sustained only by the institutional inertia of a professionalized discipline. The history of behaviourism stands as a warning of the virtual immortality that can be attained by such institutionalized futility.

In the case of ethics, two patterns of thought have especially benefited from the influence of the underlying model of validation. One is utilitarianism, which as I have just mentioned seemed to offer calculation over verifiable empirical quantities in the place of metaphysical distinctions. The other is various species of formalism. Kant is the originator of one of the most influential variants, without himself having fallen victim, I believe, to the narrowing consequences that usually follow the adoption of a formalism.

Formalisms, like utilitarianism, have the apparent value that they would allow us to ignore the problematic distinctions between different qualities of action or modes of life, which play such a large part in our actual moral decisions, feelings of admiration, remorse, etc., but which are so hard to justify when others controvert them. They offer the hope of deciding ethical questions without having to determine which of a number of rival languages of moral virtue and vice, of the admirable and the contemptible, of unconditional versus conditional obligation, are valid. You could finesse all this, if you could determine the cases where a maxim of action would be unrealizable if everyone adopted it, or where its universal realization was something you could not possibly desire; or if you could determine what actions you could approve no matter whose standpoint you adopted of those persons affected; or if you could circumscribe the principles that would be adopted by free rational agents in certain paradigm circumstances.

Of course, all these formulae for ethical decision repose on some substantive moral insights; otherwise they would not seem even plausible candidates as models of *ethical* reasoning. Behind these Kant-derived formulae stands one of the most fundamental insights of modern Western civilization, the universal attribution of moral personality: in fundamental ethical matters, everyone ought to count, and all ought to count in the same way. Within this outlook, one absolute requirement of ethical thinking is that we respect other human agents as subjects of practical reasoning on the same footing as ourselves.

In a sense, this principle is historically parochial. This is not the way the average Greek in ancient times, for instance, looked on his Thracian slave. But, in a sense, it also corresponds to something very deep in human moral reasoning. All moral reasoning is carried on within a community; and it is essential to the very existence of this community that each accord the other interlocutors this status as moral agents. The Greek who may not have accorded it to his Thracian slave most certainly did to his compatriots. That was part and parcel of there being recognized issues of justice between them. What modern civilization has done, partly under the influence of Stoic natural law and Christianity, has been to lift all the parochial restrictions that surrounded this recognition of moral personality in earlier civilizations.

The modern insight, therefore, flows very naturally from one of the basic preconditions of moral thinking itself, along with the view – overwhelmingly plausible, to us moderns – that there is no defensible distinction to be made in this regard between different classes of human beings. This has become so widespread that even discrimination and domination is in fact justified on universalist grounds. (Even South Africa has an official ideology of *apartheid*, which can allow theoretically for the peoples concerned to be not unequal, but just different.)

So we seem on very safe ground in adopting a decision procedure which can be shown to flow from this principle. Indeed, this seems to be a moral principle of a quite different order from the various contested languages of moral praise, condemnation, aspiration or aversion, which distinguish rival conceptions of virtue and paradigm modes of life. We might even talk ourselves into believing that it is not a moral principle in any substantive contestable sense at all, but some kind of limiting principle of moral reasoning. Thus we might say with Richard Hare, for example, that in applying this kind of decision procedure we are following not moral intuitions, but rather our linguistic intuitions concerning the use of the word 'moral'.

Classical utilitarianism itself incorporated this universal principle in the procedural demand that in calculating the best course, the happiness of each agent count for one, and of no agent for more than one. Here again one of the fundamental issues of modern thought is decided by what looks like a formal principle, and utilitarianism itself got a great deal of its prima facie plausibility from the strength of the same principle. If everyone counts as a moral agent, then what they desire and aim at ought to count, and the right course of action should be what satisfies all, or the largest number possible. At least this chain of reasoning can appear plausible.

But clear reasoning ought to demand that we counteract this tendency to slip over our deepest moral convictions unexamined. They look like formal principles only because they are so foundational to the moral thinking of our civilization. We should strive to formulate the under-lying moral insights just as clearly and expressly as we do all others.

When we do so, of course, we shall find that they stand in need of justification like the others. This points us to one of the motives for construing them as formal principles. For those who despair of reason as the arbiter of moral disputes (and the epistemological tradition has tended to induce this despair in many), making the fundamental insights into a formal principle has seemed a way of avoiding a moral scepticism which was both implausible and distasteful.

But, I want to argue, the price of this formalism, as also of the utilitar-ian reduction, has been a severe distortion of our understanding of our moral thinking. One of the big illusions which grows from either of these reductions is the belief that there is a single consistent domain of the 'moral', that there is one set of considerations, or mode of calcula-tion, which determines what we ought 'morally' to do. The unity of the moral is a question which is conceptually decided from the first on the grounds that moral reasoning just is equivalent to calculating conse-quences for human happiness, or determining the universal applicability of maxims, or something of the sort.

But once we shake ourselves clear from the formalist illusion, of the utilitarian reduction — and this means resisting the blandishments of their underlying model of rational validation — we can see that the boundaries of the moral are an open question; indeed, the very appro-priateness of a single term here can be an issue.

We could easily decide — a view which I would defend — that the universal attribution of moral personality is valid, and lays obligations on us which we cannot ignore; but that there are also other moral ideals and goals — e.g. of less than universal solidarity, or of personal excellence — which cannot be easily coordinated with universalism, and can even enter into conflict with it. To decide *a priori* what the bounds of the moral are is just to obfuscate the question whether and to what degree this is so, and to make it incapable of being coherently stated.

II

I should like to concentrate here on a particular aspect of moral language and moral thinking that gets obscured by the epistemologically motivated reduction and homogenization of the 'moral' we find in both utilitarianism and formalism. These are the qualitative distinctions we make between different actions, or feelings, or modes of life, as being in some way morally higher or lower, noble or base, admirable or contemptible. It is these languages of qualitative contrast that get marginalized, or even expunged altogether, by the utilitarian or formalist reductions. I want to argue, in opposition to this, that they are central to our moral thinking and ineradicable from it.

Some examples might help here of such qualitative distinctions which are commonly subscribed to. For some people, personal integrity is a central goal: what matters is that one's life express what one truly senses as important, admirable, noble, desirable. The temptations to be avoided here are those of conformity to established standards which are not really one's own, or of dishonesty with oneself concerning one's own convictions or affinities. The chief threat to integrity is a lack of courage in face of social demands, or in face of what one has been brought up to see as the unthinkable. This is a recognizable type of moral outlook.

We can see a very different type if we look at a Christian model of *agapê*, such as one sees, for example, with Mother Theresa. The aim here is to associate oneself with, to become in a sense a channel of, God's love for men, which is seen as having the power to heal the divisions among men and take them beyond what they usually recognize as the limits to their love for one another. The obstacles to this are seen as various forms of refusal of God's *agapê*, either through a sense of self-sufficiency, or despair. This outlook understands human moral transformation in terms of images of healing, such as one sees in the New Testament narratives.

A very different, yet historically related, modern view centres around the goal of liberation. This sees the dignity of human beings as consisting in their directing their own lives, in their deciding for themselves the conditions of their own existence, as against falling prey to the domination of others, or to impersonal natural or social mechanisms which they fail to understand, and therefore cannot control or transform. The inner obstacles to this are ignorance, or lack of courage, or falsely self-depreciatory images of the self; but these are connected with external obstacles in many variants of modern liberation theory. This is particularly so of the last: self-depreciating images are seen as inculcated by others who benefit from the structures of domination in which subject groups are encased. Fanon has made this kind of analysis very familiar for the colonial context, and his categories have been transposed to a host of others, especially to that of women's liberation.

Let us look briefly at one other such language, that of rationality, as this is understood, for instance, by utilitarians. We have here the model of a human being who is clairvoyant about his goals, and capable of objectifying and understanding himself and the world which surrounds him. He can get a clear grasp of the mechanisms at work in self and world, and can thus direct his action clear-sightedly and deliberately. To do this he must resist the temptations offered by the various comforting illusions that make the self or the world so much more attractive than they really are in the cold light of science. He must fight off the self-indulgence which consists of giving oneself a picture of the world which is satisfying to one's *amour propre*, or one's sense of drama, or one's craving for meaning, or any of these metaphysical temptations. The rational man has the courage of austerity; he is marked by his ability to adopt an objective stance to things.

I introduce these four examples so as to give some intuitive basis to an otherwise abstract discussion. But I did not have to look far. These moral outlooks are very familiar to us from our own moral reasoning and sensibility, or those of people we know (and sometimes of people we love to hate). I am sure that some of the details of my formulation will jar with just about any reader. But that is not surprising. Formulating these views is a very difficult job. Like all self-interpretive activity, it is open to potentially endless dispute. This is, indeed, part of the reason why these outlooks have fallen under the epistemological cloud and therefore have tended to be excluded from the formalist and utilitarian meta-ethical pictures. But one or some of these, or others like them, underly much of our deciding what to do, our moral admirations, condemnations, contempts, and so on.

Another thing that is evident straight off is how different they are from each other. I mean by that not only that they are based on very different pictures of man, human possibility and the human condition; but that they frequently lead to incompatible prescriptions in our lives – incompatible with each other, and also with the utilitarian calculation which unquestionably plays some part in the moral reasoning of most moderns. (The modern dispute about utilitarianism is not about whether it occupies some of the space of moral reason, but whether it fills the whole space.) It could be doubted whether giving comfort to the dying is the highest util-producing activity possible in contemporary Calcutta. But, from another point of view, the dying are in an extremity that makes calculation irrelevant.

But, nevertheless, many people find themselves drawn by more than one of these views, and are faced with the job of somehow making them compatible in their lives. This is where the question can arise whether all the demands that we might consider moral and which we recognize as valid can be coherently combined. This question naturally raises another one, whether it is really appropriate to talk of a single type of demand called 'moral'. This is the more problematic when we reflect that we all recognize other qualitative distinctions which we would not class right off as moral, or perhaps even on reflection would refuse the title to; for instance, being 'cool', or being macho, or others of this sort. So that the question of drawing a line around the moral becomes a difficult one. And it may even come to appear as an uninteresting verbal one in the last analysis. The really important question may turn out to be how we combine in our lives two or three or four different goals, or virtues, or standards, which we feel we cannot repudiate but which seem to demand incompatible things of us. Which of these we dignify with the term 'moral', or whether we so designate all of them, may end up appearing a mere question of labelling – unless, that is, it confuses us into thinking that there is in principle only one set of goals or standards which can be accorded ultimate significance. In certain contexts, it might help clarity to drop the word, at least provisionally, until we get over the baleful effects of reductive thinking on our meta-ethical views.

III

Before going on to examine further the implications of this for social theory, it will be useful to look more closely at these languages of qualitative contrast. What I am gesturing at with the term 'qualitative contrast' is the sense that one way of acting or living is higher than others, or in other cases that a certain way of living is debased. It is essential to the kind of moral view just exemplified that this kind of contrast be made. Some ways of living and acting have a special status, they stand out above others; while, in certain cases, others are seen as despicable.

This contrast is essential. We should be distorting these views if we tried to construe the difference between higher and lower as a mere difference of degree in the attainment of some common good, as utilitarian theory would have us do. Integrity, charity, liberation, and the like stand out as worthy of pursuit in a special way, incommensurable with other goals we might have, such as the pursuit of wealth, or comfort, or the approval of those who surround us. Indeed, for those who hold to such views of the good, we ought to be ready to sacrifice some of these lesser goods for the higher.

Moreover, the agent's being sensible of this distinction is an essential condition of his realizing the good concerned. For our recognizing the higher value of integrity, or charity, or rationality, and so on, is an essential part of our being rational, charitable, having integrity and so on. True, we recognize such a thing as unconscious virtue, which we ascribe to people who are good but quite without a sense of their superiority over others. This lack of self-congratulation we consider itself to be a virtue, as the deprecatory expression 'holier than thou' implies. But the absence of self-conscious superiority does not mean an absence of sensitivity to the higher goal. The saintly person is not 'holier than thou', but he is neces-sarily moved by the demands of charity in a special way, moved to recog-nize that there is something special here; in this particular case, he has a sense of awe before the power of God, or of wonder at the greatness of man as seen by God. And a similar point could be made for the other examples: an essential part of achieving liberation is sensing the greatness of liberated humanity – and consequently being sensible of the degrada-tion of the dominated victim; an essential part of integrity is the recogni-tion that it represents a demand on us of a special type, and so on.

Another way of making this point is to say that motivation enters into the definition of the higher activity or way of being in all these cases. The aspiration to achieve one of these goods is also an aspiration to be motivated in a certain way, or to have certain motivations win out in oneself. This is why we can speak of these aspirations as involving 'second-order' motivations (as I have tried to do elsewhere, following Harry Frankfurt).[1]

We can articulate the contrast or incommensurability involved here in a number of ways. One way of saying it is via the notion of obligation. Ordinary goals, for instance for wealth or comfort, are goals that a person may have or not. If he does, then there are a number of instrumental things that he ought to do – hypothetically, in Kant's sense – to attain them. But if he lacks these goals, no criticism attaches to him for neglecting to pursue them. By contrast, it is in the nature of what I have called a higher

---

[1] Cf. Volume 1 chapter 1; and Harry Frankfurt, 'Freedom of the will and the concept of a person', *Journal of Philosophy* 67: 1 (1971), pp. 5–20.

goal that it is one we *should* have. Those who lack them are not just free of some additional instrumental obligations which weigh with the rest of us; they are open to censure. For those who subscribe to integrity, the person who cares not a whit for it is morally insensitive, or lacks courage, or is morally coarse. A higher goal is one from which one cannot detach oneself just by expressing a sincere lack of interest, because to recognize something as a higher goal is to recognize it as one that men ought to follow. This is, of course, the distinction that Kant drew between hypothetical and categorical imperatives.

Or rather, I should say that it is a closely related distinction. For Kant the boundary between the categorical and the hypothetical was meant to mark the line between the moral and the non-moral. But there are languages of qualitative contrast which we are quite ready to recognize as non-moral, even bearing in mind the fuzzy boundaries of the domain which this word picks out. We often apply such languages in what we call the aesthetic domain. If I see something especially magnificent in the music of Mozart as against some of his humdrum contemporaries, then I will judge you as insensitive in some way if you rate them on a par. The word 'insensitive' here is a word of deprecation. This is a difference one *should* be sensible of, in my view.

Of course, I would not speak of this as a *moral* condemnation, but condemnation it would be nevertheless. I do not react to this difference as I do to differences of taste which correspond to no such incommensurability, for example whether you like the symphonies of Bruckner or not.

The criterion for incommensurability I am offering here is therefore not the same as Kant's for the moral. But, as I have already indicated, I do not think that a line can be drawn neatly and unproblematically around the moral. Of course, if someone professes to see no distinction between his concern for the flowers in his garden and that for the lives of refugees faced with starvation, so that he proposes to act in both cases just to the degree that he feels interested at the time, we are rightly alarmed, and take this more seriously than the failure to appreciate Mozart over Boieldieu. We feel more justified in intervening here, and remonstrating with him, even forcing him to act, or subjecting him to some social or other penalty for non-acting. We feel, in other words, that the obligation here is 'categorical' in the stronger sense that licenses our intervention even against his will.

But the boundary here is necessarily fuzzier and very much open to dispute. Whereas the weaker sense of 'categorical' that could apply to the distinction I am drawing above turns on the question whether a declared lack of interest in a certain good simply neutralizes it for you, or whether on the contrary, it redounds to your condemnation, shows you up as being blind, or coarse, or insensitive, or cowardly, or brutalized, too self-absorbed, or in some way subject to censure. This, I would like to argue, is a relatively firm boundary – although the languages in which we draw it, each of us according to his own outlook, are very much in dispute between us – but it does not mark the moral from the non-moral. The languages of qualitative contrast embrace more than the moral.

A second way in which we can articulate this contrast is through the notions of admiration and contempt. People who exhibit higher goods to a signal degree are objects of our admiration; and those who fail are some-times objects of our contempt. These emotions are bound up with our sense that there are higher and lower goals and activities. I would like to claim that if we did not mark these contrasts, if we did not have a sense of the incommensurably higher, then these emotions would have no place in our lives.

In the end, we can find ourselves experiencing very mitigated admiration for feats which we barely consider worthy of special consideration. I have a sort of admiration, mixed with tolerant amusement, for the person who has just downed twenty-two pancakes to win the eating contest. But that is because I see some kind of victory over self in the name of something which resembles a self-ideal. He wanted to be first, and he was willing to go to great lengths for it; and that goal at least stands out from that of being an average person, living just like everybody else. It is only because I see the feat in these terms, which are rather a caricature than an example of a higher aspiration, that the feeling of admiration can get even a mitigated grip on this case.

But we also find ourselves admiring people where there is no victory over self, where there is no recognizable achievement in the ordinary sense at all. We can admire people who are very beautiful, or have a striking grace or personal style, even though we may recognize that it is none of their doing. But we do so only because the aura of something higher, some magic quality contrasting with the ordinary and the humdrum, surrounds such people. The reasons why this should be so go very deep into the human psyche and the human form of life, and we find them hard to understand, but a special aura of this kind contributes often to what we call the 'charisma' of public figures (a word which conveys just this sense of a gift from on high, some-thing we have not done for ourselves). Those who consider this kind of aura irrational, who resist the sense of something higher here, are precisely those who refuse their admiration to the 'charismatic', or to 'beautiful people'. Or at least they are those who claim to do so; for sometimes one senses that they are fighting a losing battle with their own feelings on this score.

In this way, admiration and contempt are bound up with our sense of the qualitative contrasts in our lives, of there being modes of life, activities, feeling, qualities, which are incommensurably higher. Where these are moral qualities, we can speak of moral admiration. These emotions provide one of the ways that we articulate this sense of the higher in our lives.

A third way we do so is in the experience we can call very loosely 'awe'. I mentioned above that a sensibility to the higher good is part of its realization. The sense that a good occupies a special place, that it is higher, is the sense that it somehow commands our respect. This is why there is a dimension of human emotion, which we can all recognize, and which Kant again tried to articulate with his notion of the *Achtung* which we feel before the moral law. Once again, I propose to extend a Kantian analysis beyond the case of the unambiguously moral. Just as our admiration for the virtuosi of some higher goal extends to other contexts than the moral, so our sense of the incommensurable value of the goal does. For this sense, as a term of art translating Kant's *Achtung*, I propose 'awe'.

IV

It is this dimension of qualitative contrast in our moral sensibility and thinking that gets short shrift in the utilitarian and formalist reductions. One of the main points of utilitarianism was to do away with this and reduce all judgements of ethical preference to quantitative form in a single dimension. In a different way, formalisms manage to reduce these contrasts to irrelevance; ethical reasoning can finesse them through a procedure of determining what is right which takes no account of them, or allows them in merely as subjective preferences, and therefore is not called upon to judge their substantive merits.

Now my argument was that a big part of the motivation for both reductions was epistemological; that they seemed to allow for a mode of ethical reasoning which fitted widely held canons of validation. We can now see better why this was so.

It is partly because these languages of contrast are so hard to validate once they come into dispute. If someone does not see that integrity is a goal one should seek, or that liberation is alone consistent with the dignity of man, how do you go about demonstrating this? But this is not the whole story. That argument is difficult in this area does not mean that it is impossible, that there is no such thing as a rationally induced conviction. That so many who have opted for utilitarianism or formalism can jump to this latter conclusion as far as higher goals are concerned is due to two underlying considerations which are rarely spelled out.

The first is that the ethical views couched in languages of contrast seem to differ in contestability from those which underlie utilitarianism and formalism. No one seems very ready to challenge the view that, other things being equal, it is better that men's desires be fulfilled than that they be frustrated, that they be happy rather than miserable. Counter-utilitarians challenge rather whether the entire range of ethical issues can be put in these terms, whether there are not other goals which can conflict with happiness, whose claims have to be adjudicated together with utility. Again, as we saw, formalistic theories get their plausibility from the fact that they are grounded on certain moral intuitions which are almost unchallenged in modern society, based as they are in certain preconditions of moral discourse itself combined with a thesis about the racial homogeneity of humanity which it is pretty hard to challenge in a scientific, de-parochialized and historically sensitive contemporary culture.

The premises of these forms of moral reasoning can therefore easily appear to be of a quite different provenance from those that deal with qualitative contrast. Against these latter, we can allow ourselves to slip into ethical scepticism while exempting the former, either on the grounds that they are somehow self-evident, or even that they are not based on ethical insight at all but on something firmer, like the logic of our language.

But, in fact, these claims to firmer foundation are illusory. What is really going on is that some forms of ethical reasoning are being privileged over others because in our civilization they come less into dispute or look easier to defend. This has all the rationality of the drunk in the well-known story (which the reader may forgive me for repeating) who was looking for his latch key late one night under a street lamp. A passer-by, trying to be helpful, asked him where he had dropped it. 'Over there' answered the drunk, pointing to a dark corner. 'Then why are you looking for it here?' 'Because there's so much more light here', replied the drunk.

In a similar way, we have been manoeuvred into a restrictive definition of ethics, which takes account of some of the goods we seek, for example utility, and universal respect for moral personality, while excluding others, viz. the virtues and goals like those mentioned above, largely on the grounds that the former are subject to less embarrassing dispute.

This may seem a little too dismissive of the traditions of reductive meta-ethics, because in fact there is a second range of considerations which have motivated the differential treatment of languages of contrast. That is that they seem to have no place in a naturalist account of man.

The goal of a naturalist account of man comes in the wake of the scientific revolution of the seventeenth century. It is the aim of explaining human beings like other objects in nature. But a part of the practice of the successful natural science of modern times consists in its eschewing what we might call subject-related properties. By this I mean properties which things bear only insofar as they are objects of experience of subjects. The classical example of these in the seventeenth-century discussion were the so-called secondary properties, like colour or felt temperature. The aim was to account for what happens invoking only properties that the things concerned possessed absolutely, as one might put it (following Bernard Williams' use in his discussion of a related issue),[2] properties, that is, which they would possess even if (even when) they are not experienced.

How can one follow this practice in a science of animate beings, that is of beings who exhibit motivated action? Presumably, one can understand motivated action in terms of a tendency of the beings concerned to realize certain consummations in certain conditions. As long as these consummations are characterized absolutely, the demands of a naturalistic science of animate subjects seem to be met. Hence we get a demand which is widely recognized as a requirement of materialism in modern times: that we explain human behaviour in terms of goals whose consummations can be characterized in physical terms. This is what, for example, for many Marxists establishes the claim that their theory is a materialist one: that it identifies as predominant the aim of getting the means to life (which presumably could ultimately be defined in physical terms).

But without being taken as far as materialism, the requirement of absoluteness can serve to discredit languages of qualitative contrast. For these designate different possible human activities and modes of life as higher and lower. And these are plainly subject-related notions. In the context of a naturalist explanation, one goal may be identified as more

---

[2] Bernard Williams, *Descartes: The Project of Pure Enquiry* (Harmondsworth, 1978).

strongly desired than others, for example if the subject concerned gave it higher priority. But there is no place for the notion of a higher goal, which in the very logic of the contrast must be distinguishable from the strongest motive – else the term would have no function in moral discourse at all.

For those who cleave to naturalism, the languages of contrast must be suspect. They correspond to nothing in reality, which we may interpret as what we need to invoke in our bottom line explanatory language of human behaviour. They appear therefore to designate purely 'subjective' factors. They express the way we feel, not the way things are. But then this gives a rational basis to ethical scepticism, to the view that there is no rational way of arbitrating between rival outlooks expressed in such languages of contrast. This seems to give a strong intellectual basis to downgrading ethical reasoning, at least that cast in contrastive languages. For those who are impressed by naturalist considerations, but still want to salvage some valid form of ethical reasoning, utilitarianism or formalism seem attractive.[3]

But this ground for scepticism is faulty. It leaves undefended the premise that our accounts of man should be naturalistic in just this sense. Purging subject-related properties makes a lot of sense in an account of inanimate things. It cannot be taken as *a priori* self-evident that it will be similarly helpful in an account of human beings. We would have to establish *a posteriori* that such an absolute account of human life was possible and illuminating before we could draw conclusions about what is real, or know even how to set up the distinction objective/subjective.

In fact, though there is no place to examine the record here, it does not seem that absolute accounts offer a very plausible avenue. Put in other terms, it may well be that much of human behaviour will be understandable and explicable only in a language which characterizes motivation in a fashion which marks qualitative contrasts and which is therefore not morally neutral. In this it will be like what we recognize today as the best example of clairvoyant self-understanding by those who have most conquered their illusions. If a science which describes consummations in exclusively physical terms cannot fill the bill, and if we therefore have to take account of the significances of things for agents, how can we know *a priori* that the best account available of such significances will not require some use of languages of qualitative contrast? It seems to me rather likely that it will.

---

[3] For a naturalist attack on the objectivity of value, see J. L. Mackie, *Ethics: Inventing Right and Wrong* (Harmondsworth, 1977).

In the absence of some demonstration of the validity of naturalism of this kind, the utilitarian and formalist reductions are clearly arbitrary. For they have little foundation in our ethical sensibility and practice. Even utilitarians and formalists make use of languages of contrast in their lives, decisions, admirations and contempts. One can see that in my fourth example above. 'Rational' as used by most utilitarians is a term in a qualitative contrast; it is the basis of moral admiration and contempt; it is a goal worthy of respect. The fact that it finds no place in their own meta-theory says a lot about the value of this theory.

V

Once we get over the epistemologically induced reductions of the ethical, the problems of moral reasoning appear in a quite different light. I just have space here to mention some of the consequences for social theory.

An obviously relevant point is that we come to recognize that the ethical is not a homogeneous domain, with a single kind of good, based on a single kind of consideration. We have already noted at least three kinds of consideration which are morally relevant. The first is captured by the notion of utility, that what produces happiness is preferable to its opposite. The second is what I called the universal attribution of moral personality. These can combine to produce modern utilitarianism, as a theory that lays on us the obligation of universal benevolence in the form of the maximization of general happiness. But the second principle is also the source of moral imperatives that conflict with utilitarianism; and this in notorious ways, for example demanding that we put equal distribution before the goal of maximizing utility. Then, thirdly, there are the variety of goals that we express in languages of qualitative contrast, which are of course very different from each other.

The goods we recognize as moral, which means at least as laying the most important demands on us, over-riding all lesser ones, are therefore diverse. But the habit of treating the moral as a single domain is not just gratuitous or based on a mere mistake. The domain of ultimately important goods has a sort of prescriptive unity. Each of us has to answer all these demands in the course of a single life, and this means that we have to find some way of assessing their relative validity, or putting them in an order of priority. A single coherent order of goods is rather like an idea of reason in the Kantian sense, something we always try to define without ever managing to achieve it definitively.

The plurality of goods ought to be evident in modern society, if we could set aside the blinkers that our reductive meta-ethics imposes on us. Certainly we reason often about social policies in terms of utility. And we also take into account considerations of just distribution, as also of the rights of individuals, which are grounded on the principle of universal moral personality. But there are also considerations of the contrastive kind which play an important role. For instance, modern Western societies are all citizen republics, or strive to be. Their conception of the good is partly shaped by the tradition of civic humanism. The citizen republic is to be valued not just as a guarantee of general utility, or as a bulwark of rights. It may even endanger these in certain circumstances. We value it also because we generally hold that the form of life in which men govern themselves, and decide their own fate through common deliberation, is higher than one in which they live as subjects of even an enlightened despotism.

But just as the demands of utility and rights may diverge, so those of the citizen republic may conflict with both. For instance, the citizen republic requires a certain sense of community, and what is needed to foster this may go against the demands of maximum utility. Or it may threaten to enter into conflict with some of the rights of minorities. And there is a standing divergence between the demands of international equality and those of democratic self-rule in advanced Western societies. Democratic electorates in these societies will probably never agree to the amount of redistribution consistent with redressing the past wrongs of imperialism, or meeting in full the present requirements of universal human solidarity. Only despotic regimes, like Cuba and the DDR, bleed themselves for the Third World – not necessarily for the best of motives, of course.

It ought to be clear from this that no single-consideration procedure, be it that of utilitarianism, or a theory of justice based on an ideal contract, can do justice to the diversity of goods we have to weigh together in normative political thinking. Such one-factor functions appeal to our epistemological squeamishness which makes us dislike contrastive languages. And they may even have a positive appeal of the same kind in so far as they seem to offer the prospect of exact calculation of policy, through counting utils, or rational choice theory. But this kind of exactness is bogus. In fact, they only have a semblance of validity through leaving out all that they cannot calculate.

The other strong support for single-factor theory comes from the radical side. Radical theories, such as for instance Marxism, offer an answer to the demand for a unified theory – which we saw is a demand we cannot totally repudiate, at least as a goal – by revolutionary doctrines which propose sweeping away the plurality of goods now recognized in the name of one central goal which will subsume what is valuable in all of them. Thus the classless society will allegedly make unnecessary the entrenching of individual rights, or the safeguarding of 'bourgeois' civic spirit. It will provide an unconstrained community, in which the good of each will be the goal of all, and maximum utility a by-product of free collaboration, and so on.

But Marxism at least does not make the error of holding that all the goods we now seek can be reduced to some common coinage. At least it proposes to bring about unity through radical change. In the absence of such change, commensurability cannot be achieved. Indeed, it is of the essence of languages of contrast that they show our goals to be incommensurable.

If this is so, then there is no way of saving single-consideration theory however we try to reformulate it. Some might hope for instance to salvage at least the consequentialism out of utilitarianism: we would give up the narrow view that all that is worth valuing is states of happiness, but we would still try to evaluate different courses of action purely in terms of their consequences, hoping to state everything worth considering in our consequence-descriptions.

But unless the term 'consequentialism' is to be taken so widely as to lose all meaning, it has to contrast with other forms of deliberation, for instance one in which it matters whether I act in a certain way and not just what consequences I bring about. To put it differently, a non-consequentialist deliberation is one which values actions in ways which cannot be understood as a function of the consequences they have. Let us call this valuing actions intrinsically.

The attempt to reconstruct ethical and political thinking in consequentialist terms would in fact be another *a priori* fiat determining the domain of the good on irrelevant grounds. Not as narrow as utilitarianism, perhaps, it would still legislate certain goods out of existence. For some languages of contrast involve intrinsic evaluation: the language of integrity, for instance. I have integrity to the degree to which my actions and statements are true expressions of what is really of importance to me. It is their intrinsic character as revelations or expressions that count, not their consequences. And the same objection would hold against a consequentialist social choice function. We may value our society for the way it makes integrity possible in its public life and social relations, or criticize a society for making it impossible. It may also be the case, of course, that we value the integrity for its effects on stability, or republican institutions, or something of the kind. But this cannot be all. It will certainly matter to us intrinsically as well as consequentially.

A consequentialist theory, even one which had gone beyond utilitarianism, would still be a Procrustes bed. It would once again make it impossible for us to get all the facets of our moral and political thinking in focus. And it might induce us to think that we could ignore certain demands because they fail to fit into our favoured mode of calculation. A meta-ethics of this kind stultifies thought.

Our political thinking needs to free itself both from the dead hand of the epistemological tradition, and the utopian monism of radical thought, in order to take account of the real diversity of goods that we recognize.

CHAPTER TEN

LEGITIMATION CRISIS?

I want to explore the question of whether we can speak of a 'legitimation crisis' in Western capitalist societies, and how it is to be conceived. I think we have not yet developed the concepts we need to come to terms with this fruitfully, and I want to try slowly and painfully to edge towards them here.

The belief that capitalism destroys itself is, of course, central to the Marxist tradition. *Capital* adumbrates a number of ways in which the system careens towards breakdown owing to the uncontrolled nature of capitalist accumulation. Later this vision has been refined, modified, even abandoned by some. We have had revised theories: that the system tends to increasing arms production, or imperialism, or both; that it tends to export its contradictions to the international sphere. More recently, we have theories like that of James O'Connor[1] which see capitalist economies as generating external costs that they cannot assume, which must be assumed by the political system, thus threatening its legitimacy.

I think this latter type of theory is approaching a theoretically fruitful area, in which we can identify something like 'contradictions' in modern advanced capitalist society.[2] But I think we can only make headway if we focus our attention on the question of legitimation. The breakdown, or self-undermining, of capitalism cannot be adequately understood, I want to claim, if we think of it primarily in economic terms: as a failure of output, or an escalation of costs. Rather, societies destroy themselves when they violate the conditions of legitimacy which they themselves tend to posit and inculcate.

What we need to get clearer, therefore, is the family of conceptions of the good life, the notions of what it is to be human, which have grown up with modern society and have framed the identity of contemporary men. This set of conceptions is, of course, essentially linked to the economic

---

[1] *The Fiscal Crisis of the State* (New York, 1973).
[2] Cf. also J. Habermas, *Legitimation Crisis* (Boston, 1975).

and political structures which have developed in the last centuries, although the link is not the simple one assumed by vulgar Marxism. But it is only by articulating these conceptions that we can identify the conditions of a legitimation crisis of contemporary society. For these will define the terms in which institutions, practices, disciplines, structures will be recognized as legitimate or marked out as illegitimate.

I shall thus try, in the first part of this paper, to sketch an all-too-schematic portrait of the main lines of development of what I want to call the modern identity; and then proceed in the following sentences to trace the features of modern society that reflect and entrench it; and the ways in which this same society may be systematically undermining its own legitimacy.

Before launching into a speculative attempt to define some of the basic features of the modern identity, it might be helpful to look at the moral condemnations and defences that are made of contemporary society, and that give articulacy, as it were, to the underlying legitimacy threat. The ones I want to pick out here are those which centre around the debate about growth. I will try to make a short inventory.

One of the most important streams in the malaise about endless growth is a moral protest, against a society whose motive forces are greed and envy. Schumacher articulates this most eloquently: 'The modern economy is propelled by a frenzy of greed and envy, and these are not accidental features but the very causes of its expansionist success.'[3] Schumacher's is ultimately what one would call a Platonic protest. What is evil in modern society is that it is based on the endless multiplication of desires. 'The cultivation and expansion of needs is the antithesis of wisdom.'[4] The member of modern society is like the figure in Plato's *Gorgias*, Callicles, who preaches the indefinite expansion of wants provided it goes *pari passu* with the expansion of the means to satisfy them.

For Schumacher, speaking out of the Platonic tradition, this is a kind of madness, at least a blindness. Ever-increasing desire is a kind of slavery. It prevents us from turning to higher things, like the contemplation of truth, or beauty, or devotion to some cause greater than ourselves. It also makes us prey to disquiet, internal division, tension and anxiety; and breeds conflict between men, as they are driven to struggle to fulfill their ever-expanding wants.

This Platonic protest is closely related to another stream of contemporary moral resistance to growth, which one might call the Romantic.

---

[3] *Small is Beautiful* (London, 1974), pp. 24–5.   [4] *Ibid.*, p. 26.

Rousseau is the crucial transition figure, since he was deeply influenced by Plato, and a strong proponent of the limitation of needs.

The Romantic sensibility which emerges partly from Rousseau is, of course, profoundly un-Platonic, in that the 'nature' to which it aspires to turn is no longer the Platonic order of ideas, but rather the spontaneous flow of life which runs through us and all things. But its critique of Calliclean man converges very close to Plato's: the insatiable desire to possess things, to dominate them, is a kind of thraldom, interwoven with a blindness (or 'false consciousness') which is both cause and effect of an inability to communicate and receive communication, that is an ability to communicate with others, and to respond to beauty and meaning in nature. The drive to dominate generates compulsive activity, anxiety, inner tension, and eventually aggression and violence. Freedom and vision, as well as harmony, community and peace, are only possible if we somehow liberate ourselves from it.

This strand of critique, which I perhaps too loosely call 'Romantic', was echoed by the early Marx, developed by the Frankfurt school, popularized by Marcuse, and is now very widespread.

A third line of criticism, which often combines with either Platonic or Romantic, lies in the reproach that our society pushes inexorably towards bigness and concentration, and in the process inexorably destroys smaller communities and long-standing ties between people. This is often seen just as another aspect of the price we pay for our Calliclean path. Mobility and concentration have been seen as essential conditions of rapid growth. And perhaps more fundamentally, the true Calliclean man who puts acquisition first would naturally be willing to sacrifice past ties and loyalties; he would constantly readjust his 'relationship,' to suit the demands of advancing fulfilment.

But although linked with the reproach of endless acquisition, the drive to concentrations is separable. A society is conceivable which would concentrate or break up traditional communities in the name of some other goal than rising consumer standards. Indeed some Asian communist societies have seemed to provide a model.

As far as Western capitalist society is concerned, however, the protest against concentration is part of that against endless growth. What is being fought here is not just concentration with its evils of crowding, impersonal relations, loss of public accountability; but also mobility: the breaking up of older communities, of long-standing ties. At a deeper level, it is the liquidation of the past which is seen as terrible. The protesters have a different model for how man inhabits time. In a perspective of desire-fulfilment, only the future counts; whatever can affect my happiness must lie in the future, fulfilment or frustration. But on the alternative view, men can only come to understanding themselves by finding some unity in their whole lives, and that means uniting their past to their future.

From this standpoint, one of the most profoundly objectionable features of modern society is its encouragement of the 'throw-away' style of life, in which everything which surrounds us suffers perpetual obsolescence. No external expression is left of the unity of life, of its continuity. The urban environment is constantly being transformed in the pursuit of profit or greater utility.

This third line of attack is thus levied against concentration and mobility, seen as linked. A fourth line of attack centres on the irrationalities of modern society. Because of the bent of this society, we find ourselves doing things, it is claimed, which we would never choose to do if we set about dealing deliberately.

Thus we sacrifice such goals as the humanization of work, or an undamaged environment, or communities rich in tradition, or genuine leisure, for the sake of continued growth in the number and variety of consumer goods and services, and continued increase in the level of technological sophistication. It is absurd, for instance, to endanger the ozone layer around the atmosphere, and the ear-drums of countless people, for the sake of shaving a couple of hours off the time it takes to fly from London to New York; particularly when the snarl-ups that accompany fast transit on either end eat heavily into the gain anyway. No one sitting down to such a decision, with a fresh mind, as a free agent, would make such a choice. But the bent of our technological civilization seems powerfully set in this direction; so that it takes immense effort to stop us hurtling ahead mindlessly towards higher technology.

This reproach of irrationality is separable from the moral critique above. One could agree that our society structures our choices irrationally, even if one did not share the Platonic/Romantic moral sense of the good. But for those who accept the moral critique, the irrationalities of contemporary society are not unconnected with its moral distortions. The drive to continuing expansion of needs is connected to the favouring of increased quantitative production and more intense technology, and all this makes us find this extraordinary bias normal most of the time. Marxist thought also sees a connection between irrational priorities and the ideological consciousness of capitalist society.

This fourfold criticism of the growth–concentration–mobile society strikes a chord in great numbers of people in our society. But what is significant is that the same people are ambivalent: they also respond to the defences put up for this society. The Calliclean life can also be defended. We can argue that restless ambition, the search for new fields to conquer, brings continued vitality and creativity, that concentration and mobility widen our horizons, that a society of vital, striving, ambitious, mobile people is an exciting and creative place to live. That is why, indeed, people are drawn to such centres as New York, Los Angeles, and other ag-glomerations of the Western world (including, and especially, liberal intellectuals who articulate the case against growth).

More soberly, we could defend this society by denying that the Callic-lean image fits. For after all, what has consumer society brought about? For millions of people, whose forbears were the factory fodder of the industrial revolution, who may have been packed in over-crowded, insanitary, hastily-built workers' housing, sweated twelve hours and more a day, without privacy or a decent family life in the other twelve, barely able to scrape a living, with an appalling rate of desertion of women by their men, with children growing up stunted physically and emotionally; for these millions there now is the chance for a home, de-cently furnished, space, family life, the creative use of leisure, the building of a private space in which they can bring up a family, practise hobbies, see friends, as well as being plugged into a world-wide network of communications (admittedly only one-way).

From this point of view, many of the things that count against the consumer society of the Platonic/Romantic critique turn out to count for it. For instance, much of the effort of acquisition in consumer society is directed to acquiring and furnishing and equipping private space in which the nuclear family can operate: house, car perhaps garden, perhaps a house in the country. Instead of seeing these acquisitions as stages on the road to the disintegration of a wider community through the privatiz-ation of its members, we could seem them rather as the facilitators of greater integration of masses of people whose ancestors were swept up in the great migrations which accompanied and still accompany the con-tinuing industrial revolution, and whose family life was often cramped and strained, and threatened with the vicissitudes of unemployment and pauperization.

We can take this line of thought further and reflect that the places in the Western world where some kind of local community can flourish all seem to share the feature that the private space of each of the constituent families is felt as adequate, whatever difference they may be in absolute levels. In the places where this is not felt to be so, such as the ghettoes of city centres in the USA, we find the most frightening examples of the breakdown of community, and sometimes of the most basic rules of civilization. In our society, no one seems to be induced to participate in community life through a *lack* of private space.

It is considerations of this kind that left-wing opponents of the moral protest to growth have in mind when they accuse their adversaries of reflecting purely middle-class concerns.

I daresay great numbers of us feel the pull of both these orders of considerations. My aim here is not to arbitrate, but to try rather to explain what underlies this ambivalence by digging down to those basic underlying features of our conception of human life which have helped shape both the growth of society and the protest to it. It is this modern identity which can help to explain the legitimacy of modern societies and the threat to it.

II

We can start exploring the moral notions underlying consumer society if we ask how it avoids the stigma which traditionally attaches to endless acquisition. For Schumacher's strictures are those of the perennial moral tradition in our civilization. At any time previous to the modern era, it would have seemed evident that a way of life involving endless accumulation was at best morally suspect. We might ask, how did it ever come to seem otherwise? How did we break from the Platonic mould? It may seem odd today to frame the onus of the question in this way. But from a broader perspective, it is our modern society which stands out as different from the perennial norm.

We are given some help towards an answer if we look at what we value in consumer society. Over the last sixty years or so there has developed in the capitalist world a modern society in which masses of people have acquired the durable consumer goods necessary to possess an adequate private space, to mechanize much of the labour involved in living in it, and to have communications access through the media to the society at large. There are substantial minorities in all Western societies who are still outside, but the magnitude of the achievement is staggering. Millions of people are living on a standard of comfort that only a minority could hope for in the past, those who could command the service of others.

Compared to the condition of masses of urban dwellers at any earlier stage of the industrial revolution, that is more than a great material improvement. It offers vastly superior conditions of personal development and family life.

What is special about it, and what many of its citizens have seized on, is that this way of life is in a sense more individualistic than previous ones. The family can live on its own, bringing in what it needs through its own transportation from shops which are often large and impersonal, doing the labour required for the home in the home, and even keeping in contact with the larger society and the world events within the home, thanks to the electronic media and the press. Relative to its neighbours and immediate surroundings, the family is much more self-contained than the great majority of any previous generation of urban dwellers, and incomparably more so than most villagers of previous ages. In another way, of course, the modern family is wide open all the time to the large currents of our civilization, because of modern communications. But it is open through a channel which by-passes the immediate community, and which intensifies its privacy.

This self-contained life has been attacked by critics as a negation of previous community. But what these critics often fail to appreciate is how much this self-containedness is in line with the identity which has developed in Western civilization.

Historians have shown the extraordinary development in modern times of a new ideal of family life.[5] Starting among the wealthier classes in Anglo-Saxon countries in the late seventeenth and eighteenth centuries, we see a growing idealization of marriage based on affection, of true companionship between husband and wife, and devoted concern for the children. Affectionate marriage and family life comes to be seen as an important part of human fulfilment, and the sentiments of love, concern, affection for one's spouse come to be cherished, dwelt on, rejoiced in, and articulated. Experiencing certain feelings is henceforth an important part of a fulfilled life, and important among these is love. This was naturally the age, too, when childhood comes to be seen as a separate phase of the life-cycle, with its own feelings and needs, and child-rearing becomes a subject of absorbing interest to the literate public. The spiritual age of Dr Spock begins.

This new mode of life/feeling centres on the nuclear family, and goes along with the building of a private space for this family. This can be seen

---

[5] See, for example, Lawrence Stone, *The Family, Sex and Marriage in England 1500–1800* (London, 1977); and E. Shorten, *The Making of the Modern Family* (New York, 1975).

literally in the new organization of space in the home: for example, the building of corridors allowing servants to circulate without disturbing the privacy of the family, the installation of private dining rooms, and so on. But it also meant a withdrawal from the control, supervision of, or even subordination to wider groups, like the kinship lineage, or the village community. Moderns are appalled to learn, for instance, how much the pre-eighteenth-century village presumed to control, even of its members' intimate family life. One has only to think of the 'charivari' that henpecked husbands had to undergo, not to speak of fornicators.

These two changes, affection and privacy, obviously went together. The family based on affection had to be formed by affinity; it could not be the fruit exclusively of the dynastic and property arrangements that were so important for the old lineage. And it could only flourish in intimacy, which ruled out the open, goldfish-bowl world of traditional society.

Now what began with the wealthier classes of England and America spread in the course of the nineteenth and twentieth centuries through the rest of the Western world, and through the other classes of all Western societies. The achievement of consumer society that I have been describing is in a sense the (virtually) final universalization of the conditions of affluence-in-privacy which will allow (almost) everyone to live this ideal to the full without sacrifice and in comfort. Hence the minority which has not yet got these conditions sees itself as terribly deprived. For instance, ghetto negro families in the USA, sometimes idealized by critics of the modern family for their deviance from its norms, seem to aspire to nothing else than the western affectionate nuclear family.[6]

Thus what we value in consumer society is that it has put at (almost) everyone's disposal a mode of fulfilment which has been seen as central in our civilization for a couple of centuries, if not more. What lies behind this ideal, and how is it connected with lifting the limits to endless accumulation?

I think we can find the answer to this in what I want to call the modern identity, a new conception of what it is to be a human subject which entrenches itself in our thought and sensibility from the seventeenth century on. This in turn leads to a radically new understanding of nature. The development of this new identity emerges in a host of ways: in the new natural science, in the growth of atomism, in the new emphasis on sentiment, and so on. But perhaps we can trace it most easily through a

---

[6] See Lee Rainwater, *Behind Ghetto Walls* (Chicago, 1970), quoted in Christopher Larch, *Haven in a Heartless World* (New York, 1977), p. 218.

highly intellectual issue, that of cosmology, trying all the time to read the deeper changes underlying the transformations of doctrine.

Before the seventeenth century, the dominant cosmologies saw the universe as a meaningful order. By a 'meaningful' order, I mean one which can only be explained or understood in semiological categories, as an order which 'makes sense'. Consider what Lovejoy called the 'principle of plenitude', which was common property of all the pre-modern cosmologies. This was the principle that in the cosmic order all the possibilities are realized. But the very notion of 'all the possibilities' requires some background conception of a closed order. There must be a scheme in which everything has a place, because there are just a certain number of places and no more. Otherwise no determinate sense can be given to the idea of a totality of possibilities. And this scheme can only offer a determinate totality, because in some way it makes sense that there should be just this range of places, no more and no less.

Pre-modern cosmologies thus saw the world as the embodiment of an underlying scheme which made sense; one could say that they saw the different levels and types of existents as expressions of this scheme. For instance, following a Platonic formulation, we might see the things that exist around us as embodiments of the Ideas; where these Ideas themselves are not just a random collection but form an order in which each has a necessary place. Or we can take the medieval-Renaissance notion of the correspondences. The lion represents in the kingdom of animals what the eagle does among the birds, the king in the realm, etc. The parallelism here is not an interesting *de facto* resemblance; it exists not by chance, but by a necessity of things. These slots have to be filled because they make up an order which makes sense, and which in virtue of this is pressing for realization.

Compare a modern notion which might look analogous, the conception of an ecological order with a number of 'niches', also exhibiting relations of analogy, and which also tends to fill all its niches. Now this system is a whole, just in that it is an interlocking, self-sustaining system. Its wholeness is its being self-sustaining; this is the criterion by which it could be said to be missing something, or something could be said to have a place in it, and so on. Once it exists, it will tend to sustain itself, within certain limits. If the holder of one ecological niche becomes extinct, some other may take its place. But this is because of the *de facto* operation of the rest of the system; for example, there is food of a certain kind going begging. There is by contrast no reason why the whole system has the contour that it has; this is just what has evolved. There is only an explanation of why certain species have the form they have in terms of the rest of the system, and hence the niches it offers. Here there is a quite other kind of 'making sense', if one wants to use this expression at all. Things make sense when they cohere as an interlocking, self-sustaining system. By contrast, the pre-modern view does have some account of why the whole system is as it is; the scheme of the totality of places is prior to the empirical embodiment of the system. It makes sense as an order of ideas, or archetypes, or modes and levels of being.

Now these two outlooks embed very different views of what 'nature' is. On the old outlook, the nature of something is the idea it instantiates. And each idea is intelligible against the whole order. The modern is more ready to identify the 'nature' of a thing with the forces or factors which make it function as it does, and these can no longer be seen as existing independently of the particulars which function this way. Nature is within.

At the same time, there is a radical change in the locus of thought. On the old view, there is a *logos* in things. But the modern view, rejecting meaningful order, understands thought as what happens within subjects. Thought is always in a mind.

These two changes helped to transform our notion of what it is for us as rational beings to discover our nature. Both my own nature, and the process of thinking whereby I define it, are within in a new sense. In the post-Cartesian age, we can aspire to understand ourselves even while abstracting from all the rest. (Descartes makes the crucial step in self-clarity, even while the existence of everything else is in doubt.)

In the twentieth century, we may no longer believe, like Descartes, in the soul or mind as an inner space open to transparent introspection. We now are more ready to treat ourselves like other natural objects. But we retain the idea that self-understanding is getting a clear view of the desires, aversions, fears, hopes, aspirations that are within us. To know oneself is to get clear on what is within.

This seems so normal and inescapable to us, that we can hardly imagine an alternative. But let us try. If only I can understand myself as part of a larger order; indeed, if man as the rational animal is just the one who is rationally aware of this order; then I only am really aware of myself, and understand myself, when I see myself against this background, fitting into this whole. I must acknowledge my belonging before I can understand myself. Engaged in an attempt to cut myself off, to consider myself quite on my own, autonomously, I should be in confusion, self-delusion, in the dark.

Let us try to articulate the sense of self that lies respectively behind these two notions of self-understanding. For the modern I am a natural being, I am characterized by a set of inner drives, or goals, or desires and aspirations. Knowing what I am really about is getting clear about these. If I enquire after my identity, ask seriously who I am, it is here that I have to look for an answer. The horizon of identity is an inner horizon.

For the pre-modern, I want to argue, I am an element in a larger order. On my own, as a punctual existence outside of it, I should be only a shadow, an empty husk. The order in which I am placed is an external horizon which is essential to answering the question, who am I? I could not conceivably answer the question with this horizon shut off. If I try to occlude it, I fall into a kind of nullity, a sort of non-existence, a virtual death.

The notion of 'identity' as I am using it here, somewhat Eriksonianly, can be understood in this way: to define my identity is to define what I must be in contact with in order to function fully as a human agent, and specifically to be able to judge and discriminate and recognize what is really of worth or importance, both in general and for me. To say that something is part of my identity is to say that without it I should be at a loss in making those discriminations which are characteristically human. I shouldn't know where I stood, I should lose the sense of what constituted beauty, what nobility, what truly worthwhile fulfilment, and so on. It helps constitute the horizon within which these discriminations have meaning for me.

This horizon is, of course, never fully defined. We find ourselves recurrently engaged in defining and exploring it further. But we have a general sense of where it is to be found. Now my claim is that for the modern, the horizon of identity is to be found within, while for the pre-modern it is without. What I call the modern identity is the modern understanding of what the question of identity amounts to, where one looks for an answer; it is, if you like, a general map of the paths of self-understanding.

These are, of course, two rather abstract ideal types. They provide rough sketches of a whole family of self-understandings on each side. But I believe that something like a shift from one of these families to the other occurs in our history during the last centuries, perhaps pivotally in the seventeenth century. It is this massive shift in self-experience which is reflected in, and partly defined and promoted by, the revolution in cosmology I adverted to above.

An identity shift of this kind involves a change in the basic categories of self-understanding and hence experience. For instance, it transforms our understanding of what it is to live a proper or successful human life. For a modern, successful life, humanly speaking, is one where I have fulfilled the important drives, goals, aspirations which make up my nature. 'Fulfilment' is a natural term which comes often to our lips in this connection. But in the context of the pre-modern identity, to make something of one's life is to realize in one's person a place in the pattern, well, fully, with *éclat*.

This by no means implies unselfishness. That is to see it in a modern perspective which distorts. It is rather a matter of a wholly different way of conceiving human satisfaction, including the most egoistic. On one side, this can be seen as the fulfilment of desires which inhere in me; on the other, it comes from establishing my position in the order of things. Since this order underlies what is, to occupy a place in it firmly, fully, is to live a full life; one might say to achieve a greater fullness of being; to fail to do so is to sink towards the status of a shadow. A limpid everyday image of one kind of satisfaction is the fulfilment of a felt desire for an object, like hunger or thirst; an image for the other would be rather that of approaching a source of light or warmth, for example getting close to a fire.

It is evident that the latter kind of satisfaction can be just as much the goal of ruthless, egoistic ambition as the former. Thus an extremely important part of the pattern for most people in pre-modern society was that they belonged to a lineage, a *domus*. This was not only the case for aristocrats, but also for peasants. They strove to keep the family line going, to preserve its property, to keep the family land from being broken up. The identity of a man was bound up with his belonging to his lineage, a broader pattern which had to be maintained, and hence imposed goals. The successful life was one in which these goals are achieved in a high degree and in exemplary fashion. But one could apply a great deal of ruthless effort, of immorality and egoism to this task. This stands out more clearly in the life of aristocracy, who were constantly fighting each other for land, place and honour; for position in a pattern of order which was never itself challenged.

We are still close enough to this, or perhaps it is that it corresponds to something perennial in man, that we can understand the satisfaction of having been, for instance, an exemplary father, or a successful general. We have realized an archetype in striking fashion. But as moderns, we have been taught to reinterpret these satisfactions. I am happy to have been an exemplary father, because that was my aspiration; that was my 'thing'; or perhaps even, I consider it to be an aspiration found in all men. What is lacking is the idea that in doing so, I come close to the order of being, that I myself exist more fully; that this life does not depend for its value on the shape of aspirations in me or in men, but rather on an order which defines what it is to be human.

We live with patterns today, and we are constantly rebelling against them. We can see this with contemporary women's liberation, which involves a rebellion against the former definition of the role of housewife: a 'homemaker', who sees to the running of the house, and even more to the warmth and emotional fullness of the home. This is attacked in the name of an ideal of self-realization, where each woman, *qua* does her own thing, realizes her talents, and does not exist simply to create the environment in which others can do so. Now in rejecting the pattern, women's liberation is continuing the movement of modernity. But the pattern itself is only a pale reflection of pre-modern ones. For it itself is based on the ideals of an earlier wave of modernity, that of the affectionate nuclear family.

We might say that we continue to create patterns, and to seek satisfaction in exemplifying them; but the shift to the modern identity means that we have difficulty seeing these patterns as ultimate. They are grounded for us in notions of fulfilment, or ought to be. Patterns should be subordinate and derivative. For an earlier identity, it was inconceivable that they be anything but ultimate.

Now the sense of enhanced life which comes from exemplifying a pattern in things is inherently bound up with life in society. The pattern is not relevant to me alone, but to all men. Consequently, society has to be ordered according to it; and it is indeed what binds men together in society. One cannot live the cosmic order in isolation from others. At the same time, realizing the pattern involves recognizing it; and realizing it together involves a common, public recognition of it. If our society exemplifies a cosmic order, then this is something realized in common and in public space, not in isolation.

And so realizing one's place in the pattern is bound up with being recognized as having done so, for it is a place in public space. And by the same token, living up to one's place is not just one's own affair; it is everyone's business. For each one of us helps to sustain the order by which everyone lives, as essentially public order. Thus the incredible (to us moderns) degree of social control of mores in pre-modern society, and the striking lack of privacy. The wider kin dictated so much the individual's life pattern, often when and whom he/she married. And the village community exercised an extraordinary surveillance over the lives of its members. The charivaris, manifestations of public collective ridicule, illustrate this very well. In France, as mentioned above, a husband who has beaten his wife, or who did women's work, or who was cuckolded, was subject to charivari; presumably because he was allowing an inversion of the proper, patriarchal order. This could not be seen just as a matter between himself and his wife; the order concerned was everybody's. Sanctions had to be taken.

What is also significant in the charivari is the use made of shame. The experience was probably frightening; certainly difficult to live with, but above all humiliating. Shame plays an important role in societies which live by a public pattern; for whether the pattern is realized or not is always a public affair. One's life was led before everyone else, and hence shame and its avoidance played a big role in people's lives. There was no space, not just physically but psycho-socially, to withdraw into the privacy of one's own self-estimate, or the opinions of a circle based on affinity.

With the rise of the modern identity, this intensely public life withers. The community retreats, and the nuclear family achieves privacy. For the subject with a modern identity is looking for fulfilment. What this amounts to, he will discover in himself. This requires privacy, not, of course, the life of a man alone, but a life of relations founded largely on affinity: it is through our affinities that we largely come to discover ourselves. And this life cannot be subject to the constant scrutiny and judgement of the whole, nor submitted to the structures of a fixed pattern, without being inhibited and stifled. The modern man must be to this degree autonomous, that he can find himself; and autonomy for this end requires privacy.

So the growth of the modern identity involves the withering of community; communities of common life and ritual; of which the villages of traditional society are among the most important examples; and of which extended families tend to be another instance. In the new perspective, they are deprived of their importance, their status as indispensable matrices of order. But more, the modern subject is bound sooner or later to find their common rhythm irksome. In such a community of life and ritual, the whole group in principle moves through the stages of labour, achievement, and rest; of fasting, abstinence and then rejoicing; or mourning and celebration; together as a group.

But as the modern identity develops, and each tries to find himself, it becomes harder to maintain this coordinated rhythm. Rather, it comes to be seen as a constraint external to one's own rhythms, the shapes of one's feelings and aspirations which one strives to define. The modern literature of self-discovery is full of accounts of the adolescent or young person, for whom the rituals of his society go dead, and of a self-finding won out of this moment of inward separation. 'J'ai eu raison, puisque je m'évade', as Rimbaud put it. Hence the ritual community first loses its essential status, then comes to seem irksome, and men break from it. The extended family goes the same way. The worrying thing is whether the movement is not going further and undermining the stable nuclear family as a life-long community.

Negatively the modern identity brings the withering of community, positively the goal of fulfilment of my own nature. But we should now try to see why this takes the form of emotional fulfilment, and specially emotional fulfilment in family life.

Feeling becomes important, because the fulfilment of my desires and aspirations must become evident in feeling. For it is not a matter of matching a cosmic pattern, but of answering my inner needs and desires. Whether they are fulfilled or not is ultimately a matter of my emotional life. And this therefore becomes a crucial factor in the good life. The good life is defined in terms of emotional satisfaction.

We can begin to see the background connection between the modern identity and the modern ideal of family life, the withdrawal of the nuclear family from the larger community, and its concentration on the sentiment and emotional fulfilment of its members. For the development of the modern sense of self involves both a pull towards privacy, and a focus on the fulfilment of drives, desires, aspirations which we find in our own natures. Once one takes this perspective, it is inevitable that the life of the family will take a central place; for what is more basic to human nature, seen as the ensemble of purposes and desires within each one of us? So to identify those purposes within us, be aware of them in feeling, and to fulfil them, becomes a central part of the good life. This life requires privacy, that one's life no longer be mediated by the larger group and the pattern that it embodies, for each finds his nature in himself.

The modern consumer society can be seen as the ultimate flowering of this ideal, a society in which (in principle) everyone has adequate private space for a full family life. This is central to the fulfilment of the man and wife, as companions and lovers, and also as parents. And it is also the locus in which the next generation is nurtured, so that the children in turn will be able to discover and seek their own kind of fulfilment, including the formation of marriages based on their own affinities. The contemporary family ideally has not only the space to live an unmediated existence unhampered, but also the means to foster the development and self-discovery of its children.

III

In the last pages, we have been able to see more fully what lies behind the modern ideal of family life and fulfilment, which is central to the consumer society. In some respects it is a culmination of the modern identity, the new sense of what it is to be a subject which develops with modern society. But is this connected with a lifting of the traditional sense of moral limit to endless accumulation?

In order to see this, we have to look at some of the shifts in moral consciousness and the definitions of moral aspiration which flow from the modern identity.

The modern subject must find his purposes in nature, that is in himself, as nature is now understood. He cannot expect to find them any more in a cosmic order of which he is a part. Of course, in a crucial phase of the modern revolution of identity, the focus was on God, not man. For an important element in the original impetus to reject the old cosmology came from a sense of the majesty of God. The idea of a sovereign God had always sat uneasily with the Greek-derived notion of a hierarchy of levels of being, an ordered cosmos which seemed independent of his will. Already medieval nominalism had expressed the unease of a strand of Christian thought. The semi-pagan embroideries of the notion of cosmic order by thinkers like Bruno awakened this reaction even more strongly. Arguably, this stress on the majesty of God was more important among Protestants, especially among Calvanists. But it also figures in the rise of modern conceptions of subject and science in Catholic countries. One thinks of the role of a monk like Mersenne in the circle of thinkers contemporary with Descartes.

One could therefore, and people did, look on the universe in mechanistic terms for the glory of God. But the result was in the end to turn men inwards. In either case, our purposes were no longer to be found in a cosmic order; but either in the vocation which God prepared for us, or in our own natures. But in a mechanistic conception of the universe, as a creature of God, his purposes could at least partly be discovered by examining the nature of what he had made; provided that one could discern it without presumption and false imaginings.

And so the theological motive for the modern revolution ends up reinforcing what one might call the humanist-naturalist motive. The modern subject is to find his purposes in himself, as a natural being. A good example of the dove-tailing of the two is Locke, a Christian thinker with a modern Christian consciousness: we are the workmanship of God, and thus must follow his purposes. But these purposes are then read off our natural bent: to life, and to acquire through labour the means thereto; and they become the basis thereby of inalienable right.

A major consequence of this is that the modern subject demands autonomy. He is not part of a larger order, but must discern his own purposes. Perhaps what he has to discern is God's purpose in him, but again *he* is called on to do it. Thus relative to any social ordering, or supposed 'natural' ordering of society, he is seen as originally free. The ordering can only be legitimate, if it issues from his consent.

Hence the extraordinary seventeenth-century idea of a state of nature as the original condition of mankind. It was not that the solitary state was seen as optimal for men. On the contrary: God destines man for society. But this social condition is a purpose, which like all other purposes men have to discover in themselves and bring about. Thus society must be brought about by consent. The most basic function of man is discovering the purpose of God/nature in himself; in this basic function, he acts as an individual. Hence the image of the state of nature as the original condition.

Autonomy is therefore one facet of moral life. The second is discernment, the ability to identify what nature calls for in me, without illusion or presumption. Once again, there is theological precedent for modern naturalism. The Reformation placed particular stress on the notion that ordinary life was sanctified by God. This was stressed in polemic against the Catholic notion that there are special vocations of particular holiness which involve the renunciation of ordinary fulfilment, in particular family life. This was seen as part of the old notion of the sacred which the Reformation rejected as idolatrous, for fundamentally the same reason as it rejected the mass. On the contrary, ordinary life, including marriage, was hallowed by God, as long as it was lived in a spirit of humility, thankfulness and worship. But in living a sanctified life in fulfilment of my ordinary needs, I must see them for what they are: needs that God has put in me for his purposes, the maintaining and continuance of the human race. I must avoid the idolatry involved in giving them a special aura of significance, as the old monastic tradition demanding chastity tends to do for sexuality, for instance, treating it as though it had the numinous power to stand between us and a closer union with God. The Reformation sanctification of ordinary life involved its desacralization, emptying it of all magic and sacremental aura. This is one of the antechambers, I should like to claim, to the modern ideal of fulfilling nature in myself. And our contemporary ideal of family love has its roots partly in the puritan exaltation of 'holy matrimony'.

But the important thing to focus on for our purposes is that this notion of ordinary life, of fulfilling one's needs, describes an ideal, even a difficult one. It is not just a matter of following impulse. Rather it requires that we live our life in a certain spirit, a discernment which requires that we fight free of the presumptious illusions that sinful man is prone to. We have to live our ordinary life, while seeing our needs and desires in a certain light, as God-given, and hence free both from the aura of idolatry and the obsessive involvement of libertinism. The sanctified ordinary life is a spiritual condition, involving discipline and discernment. In using the things of this world, it is also asserting the supremacy of the spirit.

Now I should like to claim that the modern conception of fulfilling my nature, which partly grows out of this religious ideal, shares something important with it. Being in touch with the demands of nature is not something which comes of itself. It is an achievement. It requires control and clairvoyance. And thus it is an achievement which engages the peculiar excellence of man, that he is a rational animal. I have to be able to see nature as it really is, and that means strip off the false prestige of an order projected on to it by unthinking irrationality. I have to be able to set aside what Bacon called 'the Idols of the mind', as well as the illusions generated by concupiscence, vanity, greed. Men easily fall prey to illusions, to the false prestige of supposedly sacred order and hierarchies, to the infantile craving for magic, and hence to superstitions and imposture. It takes courage and vision to discern nature aright; or else education.

Hence what is humanly satisfying about this life is not just that natural impulses are fulfilled, but that men in doing so are exercising their reason and affirming their autonomy. The life according to nature satisfies the demands of the spirit as well, if I can so refer to what men sense as a higher goal, an object of strong evaluation. This is life according to nature, in its first version, as it emerges in modern society. As a conception of the good life, it flows out of the modern identity; so that what matters now is that I determine autonomously what my purposes are out of my own nature. But it recognizes this as an achievement; it sees this discernment as something to be attained, and which in certain respects runs against the slope of human weakness.

Thus the human excellence shown here resides in the ability to recognize and follow nature, not specifically in the natural impulses themselves. For what is specifically human about this life is not so much the desires, which are similar to those of animals for a good part, but the ability by reason to discern them and follow them as so discerned. It is reason and control which matter (as earlier, it was the worshipful spirit of the God-fearing man): the rational identification of desire, and the rational fulfilment; and the control to do both. The latter branch of rationality is what we call instrumental rationality, and this became for many thinkers in the modern world synonymous with rationality itself.

This claim that the excellence of man consisted in reason and control, and not just the fulfilment of desires, may seem strained when we think of some of the variants of modern Enlightenment naturalism. This is because this naturalism developed in some versions an objectified account of human life, which had no place for a notion like excellence at all. This is the case, for instance, with utilitarianism, which claims to settle all normative questions with the aid of a single yardstick, that of happiness, i.e., desire-satisfaction, presumably something completely naturalistically determinable and measurable. My claim is that even this hardboiled variant meets the description that I have drawn. Only in this case, the stress on excellence is unadmitted. It is, however, very much present, as one can see in the utilitarians' stress on rationality, their admiration of it as a human quality; their exhortations to it, their attempts to develop it or inculcate it. The man of reason, capable of making a dispassionate calculus of human happiness, achieves an excellence that the self-indulgent believer in metaphysics and superstition does not have. Rationality is a virtue-term for utilitarians. The fact that this kind of judgment has no place in their philosophy just shows its inadequacy as a vehicle of self-understanding.

This is according to nature, in a first version. There is a second which grows out of it in the eighteenth century. But before talking about this, I want to draw out a bit farther the importance of control for this first version. Control of myself, and of my environment: these are important, because they make us able to effect our desires. But control is also important for another reason. To see nature as it really is, not under the illusion of a supposed cosmic order, is to see the things around us as potentially raw material for our purposes. They no longer exhibit a purpose in themselves, in virtue of their place in a meaningful order; their relevance to purpose can only be to *our* purpose. The new modern naturalism inculcates an instrumental stance towards the world. That is why instrumental reason becomes so easily the whole of reason.

And that is why also taking an instrumental stance towards nature is important for more than its results. It is important itself, because it affirms the autonomy and the freedom from illusion/imposure of the one who takes it. Thus the famous quote from Bacon, that the fruits of control of nature were more important as gauges of our having the right vision, seeing nature without superstition or imposture.[7] To use Max Weber's term, the instrumental stance to nature is the stance of disenchantment. This gives it intrinsic value, as well as the instrumental value that it has in producing goods.

Once again, we may demur here, because the self-image of much modern naturalism forbids our talking in these terms, and even raising such issues. But if one examines the rhetoric of naturalists, pays attention to their praise of rationality, the scientific stance, their portrait of their opponents as having taken a path of facility, having too easily surrendered to consoling myths, it is evident that their almost perverse joy in showing that man is only a machine in a meaningless mechanistic universe has a root in some sense of spiritual achievement involved in disenchantment and objectification. One wins through thereby, through austerity and courage, to autonomy, contact with reality, and hence efficacy.

But then efficacy, one's ability to get things done, is not valued only for the fulfilments of desire it makes possible. It is also valued as a sign of spirituality, of the correct stance of disenchantment to the world. It is a fruit of that which serves as its sign. In a curious way, we find another continuity with an earlier religious spirituality. Max Weber held that the Puritan saw in worldly success a sort of sign of election. I think there is much in this, though I would like to trace the route somewhat differently from Weber. Because the Puritan felt called upon to treat the world as a disenchanted one, for the greater glory of God, the stance of rational work had a high value, since this is one of disenchantment *par excellence*. The prospering of one's labours was the fruit of what was at base the right spiritual stance. What more understandable than that God should reward those who are faithful to him? This sense of the link between prosperity and godliness was very common in early America.

I want to suggest that the value put on efficacy in modern life according to nature is a kind of secular transposition, in some regards a continuation of this religious sense. For modern naturalism continues to value its own variant of the disenchantment of the world; now to the glory of man and his freedom. In the context of this outlook, it is quite rational and understandable that the instrumental stance to nature, which is that of radical disenchantment, should also pay off in happiness and prosperity. Thus the earlier religious belief in prosperity as a sign of godliness shades easily into a later secular variant in America. The chief sign of goodness is success.

We can now understand some of the background to the lifting of moral

[7] *The New Organon*, I, cxxix.

limits on accumulation. The modern notion of following nature, of life according to nature, at least in what I want to call its first version, lifts the curse of the Calliclean way of life. Modern man accumulates through productive labour. And this labour is the result of discipline and control, the discipline of an instrumental stance towards the world. In producing, we are not only meeting our needs, but we are also realizing our status as autonomous, rational agents. We are affirming ourselves spiritually, and not just fulfilling our material needs – using this term 'spiritual' again to designate the goals and aspirations which we recognize not only as ours *de facto*, but as having an intrinsic worth in our lives.

From a Platonic perspective, a life of endless accumulation is one of vice, because it represents a kind of slavery, an obsessive craving for what is purely material, leaving no place for what is higher, what is truly important, what has intrinsic worth, that is worth not just dependent on its being in fact desired by us. An object of mere desire, say, a succulent fruit, has worth only because it happens to give us pleasure. This is in virtue of a purely contingent fact about our make-up. But the contemplation of beauty and truth has an intrinsic worth, independent of whether men have the discernment to see it, and desire it. To be concerned with the endless accumulation of things is to be totally occupied with the goods which are merely so *de facto*, at the expense of those which are so intrinsically. But this is to miss the point of a specifically human life. Man is the being who is sensitive to the good, in the sense of the intrinsically good, the goodness founded on Being, and not on mere appearance. If we call this the spiritual dimension, then the Calliclean man's life is a perversion, because he systematically sacrifices the spiritual dimension to the pursuit of mere *de facto* goods. To escape this must mean to put a limit on accumulation.

But in this modern perspective of the life according to nature, this no longer holds. The accumulation of goods through productive activity is an exercise of our spiritual capacity, that in man which has intrinsic worth; it is an affirmation of spirituality. The greater its extent, the more forceful the affirmation. Continued accumulation bespeaks consistent, disciplined maintenance of the instrumental stance; hence is not a deviation, or a form of decadence, but a realization of man's spiritual dimension. Far from being an obsession with things, or a sort of entrapment in them, it is an affirmation of our autonomy: that our purposes are not imposed on us by the supposed order of things, but we develop them ourselves through our discernment of nature. The instrumental stance towards nature is a spiritual declaration of independence from it.

Seen in this light, the ideal of life according to nature represents a revolution from the traditional moral outlook. But it is not quite the revolution it is commonly represented as being. Frequently those who defend a naturalist outlook speak of the modern moral revolution as an affirmation of hedonism, that its central value is pleasure, or happiness, or the fulfilment of desire, and that it rejects a Platonic morality as irrationally ascetic. And this line is taken up by the revolutionary hedonism which is one of the strands of the contemporary New Left.

But this is the same error of perspective as we saw above with utilitarianism. The metaphysic has no place for any notion of worth beyond *de facto* desire-fulfilment. But in this it is less than self-clairvoyant; because in fact it operates with a stronger notion. And indeed, I would argue that it is next to impossible for human beings quite to do without some conception of intrinsic worth in their moral reflections. The sense of the moral superiority of rational utilitarian policies, of policies of universal happiness, stems from the unspoken appreciation of the rational autonomy and altruism which they express. The mere fulfilment of desire could never be a value sufficient to ground our moral categories. It could never be the basis of moral admiration, for instance, or of indignation.

Hence the curse on the Calliclean way of life is lifted, endless accumulation is not seen as vice, because the autonomous rational accumulator is not a prisoner of the things he accumulates; he is not in thrall to his desires, as Calliclean man was painted by Plato. We begin to descry now the conditions in which a modern society could lose faith in itself. But before we go on to this, we should look at a second version of life according to nature which emerges later, in the eighteenth-century. For this in some respects provides the antidote, the ground of criticism of modern society.

In this second version, it is the voice of nature which sets our highest goals, those that have intrinsic worth. That is, the specifically human excellence does not lie in the autonomy and rationality with which men discern and fulfil desires, which desires themselves are for things of mere *de facto* worth; rather it lies in the tender and noble sentiments which he has, which flow from an undistorted or unsullied nature. It is not calculating reason which tells him that he ought not to harm his fellow man, or that he must be industrious and sober, but the voice of nature, a pure unsullied impulse which carries him towards benevolence, industry, sobriety, frugality, the enjoyment of simple pleasures, and the like.

The great protagonist of this second version is Rousseau, as in a sense the utilitarians were a good, if largely unself-clairvoyant, example of the first version. For the utilitarians, the excellence of the good man does not lie in the quality of his desires; these are the same as those of the bad man; it lies in the rationality and control with which he identifies and carries out the desires.[8] But for Rousseau, the important difference lies precisely in the quality of the motivation. The good man is moved by the pure voice of conscience/nature, which truly comes from him; the bad man by heteronomous passions. The motivations of good and bad are not homogeneous, but qualitatively different.

So living according to nature, version I, means exercising rationality and control to follow the demands of nature, which are themselves of no more than *de facto* worth. In version II, it is following the voice of nature, a source of pure, higher desire within us which induces us to act well. Sentiment thus comes into its own; and the eighteenth-century cult of feeling was bound up with this new conception of nature which Rousseau did so much to articulate.

Now this second version can turn and challenge some of the most important values of the first. The first puts great value in an instrumental stance, a stance of disenchantment towards the world, with the consequent control. Disenchantment is the condition of a true grasp of nature. And because of the importance of an instrumental stance, reason is identified with instrumental reason.

But for version II, discerning the demands of nature involves identifying my true sentiments, setting aside the false (because unnatural, heteronomous) passions. It requires a kind of intuition, of attunement. If we want to speak of reason in this context, it cannot be instrumental reason, but a form of rationality which can grasp intrinsic value. It is not *Zweckrationalität*, but a kind of *Wertrationalität*, to use Weber's terms. Further, in a stance of disenchantment, we seek only *de facto* goods, things that are satisfying to our *de facto* desires. But what we are looking for in version II is our yearning for the intrinsic good.

So the second version can turn critical of the first. The stress on instrumental reason and a stance of disenchantment can be taxed as a blindness, an insensitivity to the crucial distinction between virtue and vice, an incapacity to discern what truly comes from nature. And from this perspective, the striving after control and efficacy, that is, the domination of

---

[8] In the more objectifying variants, it can lie in the associations he has been trained to make, the shape his self-love has been conditioned into; this is standard fare for the social engineering of the Enlightenment, e.g., Helvétius; but it is never possible as an understanding of *moral* predicament; just because it only portrays men as *objects* of social policy.

nature, can seem like a wilful refusal to listen, a kind of flight forward, an attempt to still with material success the demand for an insightful reflection on the intrinsic value of one's ends.

For if our ends are depraved, that is, not according to the voice of nature, the successful use of instrumental reason in encompassing them will not improve them; rather it will make us worse in committing our lives more fully in this deviant course.

In this way, the second, Rousseauian version of modern life according to nature re-introduces another form of the ancient moral critique of limitless striving, and endless accumulation. It is now seen again as a deviation, as a form of enslavement to what is secondary which blinds us to what is primary. Rousseau rounds on the utilitarian mainstream of the Enlightenment with a Platonic condemnation and Platonic-inspired vision. For him the good life essentially involves frugality, the limitation of needs; their continued extension is a fact of heteronomy, of a loss of centre; a drowning of the voice of nature.

But the condemnation of endless accumulation which comes from the modern doctrine of life according to nature, second version, is more thoroughgoing than the ancient one. Where the ancients see only the headlong rush of uncontrolled desire in the striving to accumulate, not recognizing the spiritual dimension which the first version implicitly claims for it, the modern critique recognizes and condemns just that form of spirituality. The ascesis of disenchantment-control is seen as a kind of loss of contact with nature, humanity, the self. It is not just vice but a kind of wilful blindness. Its strength turns out to be its greatest evil. The full development of this critique is not found in Rousseau, but will develop later.

But although it rehabilitates something like the Platonic critique, the second version is a very modern theory. The higher source, which the good man must be in touch with, is not a cosmic order, but nature within. Virtue is understood as identical with freedom, with the following of purposes which are truly mine. Rousseauian moral theory is centrally a theory of freedom. A theory of this kind emerges from the modern identity, could only emerge when it was becoming firmly established. More, we might claim that a theory of this kind had to emerge, that version II could not but follow version I; that once we reject the cosmic order as a source of value, and develop the modern notion of nature, we cannot avoid finding an alternative source in this nature; that is, images of nature as a healing force, as a source of goodness, cannot but have appeal, even if not all of us give intellectual assent to them, even, indeed, if some strive against them.

So versions I and II have strong inner connections; and yet they animate very different judgements and feelings about modern society. Version I provides an important part of the justification of modern consumer society, as we can already see and shall spell out further in a moment; whereas the second version underpins much of what I have called the Platonic/Romantic critique. This is why, as I mentioned earlier, so many of us feel ambivalent about the dispute over growth, and the direction of our society. The battle is in a sense an intra-mural one for the modern identity.

This will perhaps become more evident if we note the developments of version II. For it has gone through more than one phase. In its beginning, with Rousseau, the voice of nature is to be recovered, but what it says is relatively simple, and in a way everyone knows what it is; it is the voice of conscience and goodness. But with the Romantics – properly earlier, with what one might call 'expressivism' – we have a shift. We come to the idea that each man (and also nation) has a nature within him (it) that has to be explored and revealed. This only comes to light in its articulation, and it is entirely original and peculiar to the man (or nation) concerned. Now not only do we need to turn away from other-dependence and false passion; but we have to be able to find ourselves, to articulate what we are. In a further development this turns into the notion that our fulfilment requires an inner exploration. From the second version emerge the ideas of self-exploration and fulfilment which play such an important part in our time; the need for self-expression which is also self-realization.

All this has become part of our civilization, and underlies the present malaise about the growth society; and in more than one way. The later, expressive-Romantic variants of the second version are deeply interwoven into our love/family lives. They have helped to transform the original eighteenth-century model of the affectionate marriage. As Stone points out, in this ideal, the companionate marriage was meant to be founded on affection, affinity, growing into love. But Romantic passion was decried as a very dangerous basis for it, as much as was lust. But with the developing models of self-realization, this is no longer so. Love relations are meant to meet the strongest passions of emotional fulfilment, which may no longer be called Romantic, but would unquestionably have been stigmatized as such by our eighteenth-century forbears, if they were not frankly condemned as lust. Indeed, our contemporary sense of the importance of this kind of fulfilment even threatens the stability of marriage, which we seem increasingly willing to sacrifice to it.

In this and other ways, the Romantic-expressive aspirations are woven into our understanding of the good life in modern society. And in a sense they combine with contemporary variants of version I, which value instrumental rationality and efficacy. Expressive aspirations help constitute the ends for which we are being highly *zweckrational* and efficacious, for instance, in consumer society, where rationalized production is seen as aimed to make fulfilment in family life available to the many. Both versions of living by nature are thus entrenched in our contemporary civilization.

And yet they are also at odds, as we have seen. This comes out most obtrusively today in their stances towards our natural surroundings. Version I tends to encourage a purely instrumental stance, even exploitative. Even in this tradition, there has been a sense that the whole panoply of the natural world, and particularly of living things, provided a vast object lesson in natural existence; so that looking at it, contemplating it, would enable us to break free of false perspectives and see nature as it really is. So even in version I, our natural environment cannot just be treated as a garbage heap.

But this sense is transposed and becomes much stronger with the expressive-Romantic variants of version II. For some of them, we only come to our natural selves when we are in tune with the whole of nature. Man has to be in a relation of communication with nature. The exploitative, *zweckrational* stance denies this, and makes it impossible. The resulting 'domination' of nature involves a distortion of human life, a repression of our own natures, and oppression and exploitation one of another.

Life according to nature underlies almost inescapably our conceptions of the good life just because it is so bound up with the modern identity. And this in two versions, with their families of variants. They are both operative in our civilization, are interwoven in our ideals, and yet are also at odds. Their conflict underlies some of our most profound divergences in social outlook. And yet on these issues, we are frequently torn, feel affinity for both sides. We sense here just how much these disputes are intra-mural to the modern identity.

IV

This conception of life according to nature, in its two versions, has grown up with modern society. It has been embedded in the structures, practices and institutions of this society; in our relations of production, in our application of technology to production on a massive scale, in our sexual relations and family forms, in our political institutions and practices.

Certain of these institutions and practices have been of crucial importance in sustaining this modern identity. This has generally been lost to sight, because the modern identity itself (in phase one) has stressed individual autonomy to the point where the necessity of social mediation has been lost to view. The modern identity has too easily bred myths of social contract – and is still doing so today, in a transposed way.[9]

But we can single out four features of modern society which have played a vital part in developing and sustaining our sense of ourselves as free agents. The first is equality. Clearly, the modern identity is incompatible with the status of serf or slave. But the requirement is stronger than this. The identity of the free subject establishes a strong presumption in favour of equality.

Hierarchical societies are justified on the old conception of a cosmic logos. Different groups can be seen as expressing complementary principles. This has been the traditional justification of hierarchy everywhere; different classes and functions correspond to different links in the chain of being. Each was necessary for the other, and for the whole; and the place of each relative to the others is thus natural, right, according to the order of things.

Once this view is swept aside, the basic justification of hierarchy disappears. All self-determining subjects are alike in this crucial respect. There is no further valid ground for hierarchy as an unquestionable, unchanging order of precedence.

Equality is thus one dimension of the free subject's relation to society. Another very obtrusive one is that he must be the subject of rights. As a free subject, he is owed respect for his rights, he has certain freedoms guaranteed. He must be able to choose and act within limits free from arbitrary interference of others. The modern subject is an equal rights-bearer. His having this status is part of what sustains his identity.

Perhaps these two conditions express the basic minimum status of a modern subject in society; that without which his identity must either flounder, or his predicament is experienced as intolerable. But there have been two other important features of this status which are worth mentioning. One of the important faculties of the modern subject is his

---

[9] See J. Rawls, *A Theory of Justice* (Boston, 1971); R. Nozick, *Anarchy, State and Utopia* (Boston, 1974); although Rawls himself is by no means a prisoner of the atomist perspective.

ability to effect his purposes, what I called above 'efficacy'. Someone without efficacy, unable to alter the world around him to his ends, would be incapable of sustaining a modern identity, or else would be deeply humiliated in his identity. Now to some considerable degree, each can have a sense of efficacy in his own individual action: getting the means to live, providing for the family, acquiring goods, going about his business, and so on. The very fact that we command so much private space is most important for our sense of efficacy; in particular, the ability to move around on our own, which the car gives us. The car notoriously gives many people the sense of power, of efficacy, of being able to do things and get places, on their own. Admen recognize this, and also its affinities in us with a sense of sexual potency.

But important as private efficacy is, it is not possible to make it the whole: to give no thought at all to my efficacy as a member of society, to affect its direction, or to have a part in the global efficacy that society possesses relative to nature. So along with the sense of being equal rights-bearers, there are two other important features of our status in society which have played a role in sustaining the modern identity.

The first is our status as citizens, that collectively we determine the course of social events. The modern West has taken up this ancient tradition, that only the citizen is a full man, capable of acting and making a name for himself in men's memories; and has made this an integral part of our sense of efficacy. It is an important part of our dignity as free subjects that we govern ourselves.

The second dimension is that of production. As producers, in the broadest sense, we belong to a whole interconnected society of labour and technology, which has immense efficacy in transforming nature. Every day it produces even more astonishing wonders in this regard. In so far as we belong to this society, work in it, take part in it, contribute to it, we have a share in this efficacy; we can think of it as partly ours, as a confirmation of ourselves. This is an important part of our self-consciousness in advanced industrial society. And symmetrically, it is an important source of malaise, of a creeping sense of unavoidable inferiority among Third World elites.

The modern subject is therefore far from unmediated in fact. He may be, relative to the local community; but he cannot be, relative to the whole society. On the contrary, he is sustained on one hand by the culture, which elaborates and maintains the vocabulary of his self-understanding; and on the other by the society in which he has a status commensurate with free subjectivity: a status of which we have isolated four dimensions, the equal bearer of rights, who is producer and citizen. All this underpins my identity as free individual, which could not long survive a state of nature.

The set of practices by which the society defines my status as an equal bearer of rights, an economic agent, and a citizen – practices such as the operation of the legal system, the political system of voting and elections, the practices of negotiation and collective bargaining – embeds a conception of the agent and his relation to society which reflects the modern identity and its related visions of the good. The growth of this identity can help explain why these practices have developed in the direction they have; why, for instance, voting and collective adversary negotiation take a bigger and bigger place in our societies. But this connection may also help explain why we experience growing malaise today.

It is perhaps not hard to see how our contemporary society satisfies the modern identity. The first version of the modern identity stressed three things: autonomy, fulfilment of our nature, and efficacy; the last being a confirmation of our control, our productive power, and hence our freedom from things. Modern consumer society satisfies these three demands, or appears to. It affords privacy, treats us as autonomous beings, who are efficacious as producers and citizens, seems aimed towards providing us a fulfilment which we determine, along with those with whom we have knit ties of intimacy. It also appears to satisfy some of the variants of natural fulfilment, second version, particularly the Romantic-expressive ones. For much of our private fulfilment, in our relationships, in our artistic and expressive life, is drawn from expressive models. In a sense, we are Romantics in our private existence, our love lives are drawn by a notion of Romantic mutual discovery, we look for fulfilments in our hobbies, in our recreation; while the economic, legal and political structures in which we coexist are largely justified instrumentally.

But then this compromise between versions I and II, which at times seems so stable, at others seems racked with tension. Now is one of those times. In a sense, we can understand some of the background to this too. We have seen how version II of our ideal of natural fulfilment can be turned into a powerful critique of the first version. So we immediately understand the strictures which are flung at our political and economic and legal structures: that they are merely instrumental, that they deny community, that they are exploitative towards man and nature, and so on.

We can see how closely interwoven both the affirmative and critical stances are to our contemporary society, how much they are from the same roots, and draw on the same sources. But perhaps we can also hope to gain some insight into the dialectic between the two, how the balance tips now one way, now another.

What the efficacious industrial, consumer society has going for it is presumably that it delivers the goods. But if we examine this society in the light of the modern identity, we can see that this achievement is not just a matter of meeting quantitative targets. Rather we see that in version I efficacy is valued as the fruit and sign of rational control. Increasing production originally became a value in our civilization, against all the temptations to sloth, and all the blandishments of traditional ethics, because in producing we came to see ourselves as not just meeting our needs, but also realizing our status as autonomous, rational agents. Continued accumulation bespoke a consistent, disciplined maintenance of the instrumental stance to things; it was a realization of man's spiritual dimension. Far from being an obsession with things, an entrapment in them, as it might be stigmatized on a Platonic conception, it is an affirmation of our autonomy; that our purposes are not imposed on us by the supposed order of things. The instrumental stance towards nature is meant to be a spiritual declaration of independence from it.

From this we can understand the potential vulnerability of this kind of society and way of life. The ways and forms of its accumulative life have to go on appearing as affirmations of freedom and efficacy. Should they be seen as degenerating into mere self-indulgence, then the society undergoes a crisis of confidence. It is a moral crisis, but which is inescapably also a political one; because what is impugned is the definition of the good actually embedded in our practices. Should we come to repudiate this, our allegiance to these practices is threatened, and therefore our society itself.

It follows that our society has always been vulnerable to a certain moral critique. It is in trouble if it stands self-convicted, convicted that is, in the eyes of its members of pure materialism, that is, aiming purely at material enrichment. This may not be evident, because of certain commonplaces of sociological comment, such as that we are allegedly more hedonistic in outlook than our forbears. There are some ways in which this is true, but it does not make the underlying sense that our dignity consists in our capacity to dominate, and not be dominated by things, any the less important for us. For this is rooted in the modern identity. If more people are willing to accept a 'permissive' society today, it is because they see such self-indulgence as combinable with the free self-direction whereby we determine our own purpose and fulfilment; and in this they lean partly on certain post-Romantic notions of emotional fulfilment. Those who find this combination hard to accept are precisely those who are most worried and rendered most anxious by the permissive society. Even the revolutionaries, who call for a total rejection of the work disciplines of the 'Protestant ethic', can do so because of a conception of freedom, which is allegedly the fruit of such total abandonment. That this is not a realistic hope should not blind us to the kind of hope it is – one still very much in line with modern identity.

Indeed, one could argue that the more a society is founded on the modern ideal of life according to nature in its first version, the more it should be vulnerable to doubts about its moral standing; that is, the more these doubts are unsettling. It is not surprising to find that this kind of worry is a very old one in the USA. Fred Somkin has shown how the prosperity of the Republic in the early-nineteenth-century raised soul-searchings.[10] On one hand, it was just what one might expect, a proof of efficacy and hence the spiritual excellence of America. On the other hand, it seemed to threaten vice, self-indulgence, a forgetfulness of republican virtue and the demands of the spirit. As Somkin showed, it was essential for many Americans of the time to prove that the prosperity was indeed a fruit of the spirit. The alternative was too unsettling to contemplate.

My claim is that we have left this era behind, when we could be shaken by this kind of doubt. It is not a relic of an earlier 'puritan' era. In a transposed way, many of the features of the puritan era have been recreated in our contemporary variant of the modern identity. Only now the relevance of this has spread well beyond the United States, beyond the Anglo-Saxon world; just because so many societies have been made over so that their dominant practices, those not only of their economic and public life, but also of their family life, reflect the modern identity. With this in mind, let us look at the features of contemporary society which tend to undermine our confidence in it as moderns.

V

I

The first feature is work. For a great many people work is dull, monotonous, without meaning, 'soul-destroying', to use Schumacher's word.[11] And, connected with this, in work relations, most men are far from the equal autonomous subjects that they are at home, or that they feel to be as consumers. For the most part, they stand very much as subordinates in

---

[10] In *Unquiet Eagle* (Ithaca, 1967).   [11] In *Small is Beautiful*.

command relations, and have very little say in how they will work, or in what conditions.

We enter here on to Marx's terrain. It is impossible to make a sensible critique of consumer society without invoking Marx. But there is one very important amendment which I want to make at the outset. I want to see the present formula of consumer society, with its mix of fulfilment and distortion, as a kind of historic compromise which we have, most of us, acquiesced in. Orthodox Marxists, however, are committed to seeing it as an alienating (provided they want to use this word) formula imposed on the working masses by the ruling class, through a mixture of force, mendacious persuasion, propaganda, control of information, divisive tactics, and so on.

This seems to me very wrong. The working class of early industrial society was certainly pitched into the proletarian role against its will. It had the terrible conditions of sweated labour and blighted townscape thrust on it. It was held in place by force where it tried to resist. But in the 150 years since then, our societies have become mass democracies; the conditions of work under capitalism have been profoundly modified; the remuneration of workers has become much greater; they have some substantial control over conditions through trade unions and political power. It is difficult to argue that what remains unmodified in capitalism remains so because of force and fraud, when so much else has been changed, often in the face of bitter resistance from industrialists.

Rather the compromise of affluent society must be seen to represent a tacit acquiescence – for the present anyway – in subordinate relations of labour, on the part of the mass of workers. The compromise consists in accepting alienated labour in return for consumer affluence. This compromise can seem to make sense in the lives of many people, not only because the one can be represented as the necessary condition of the other: by not demanding citizenship in the work-place, the worker allows the provident engine of industry to run untrammelled and generate ever-growing prosperity. But also it can appeal, because alienation is the obverse of non-involvement, the condition then of complete mobility. To become a citizen at work would require some commitment to the enterprise, the devotion of some of my life-energies to this community and its plans and decisions; else the participation becomes a mere sham, or the manipulated instrument of active minorities. But this devotion is a price that the aspiring consumer-citizen may be unwilling to pay, a limitation on the self-contained life he has no desire to take on.

The development of the affluent society, in which the majority can preside over a self-contained life in adequate private space, has thus gone along with a tacit reluctance to challenge the regime of alienated, subordinate labour. This is the first distortion; the fact that it is connived in by the majority, rather than brutally imposed on them, does not make it any more healthy.

2

The sense of the common interest that underlies this compromise is: that the machine must run on. But the machine that we find ourselves with in our societies is a capitalist one, that is, it consists mainly of enterprises whose institutional goals are to grow through the accumulation and re-investment of profit. They have become immensely effective in some ways in the application of technology to this end. But they cannot easily tolerate interference which attempts to set priorities for the production process. A modern capitalist economy can take, indeed, requires much intervention to keep it going: fiscal, monetary controls, subsidies of all sorts. But basic to its operation are the principles that firms must be masters of their own investment, and that they must be able to invest where they can accumulate the greatest profits, or foster the greatest overall growth, or most effectively maintain market share, or some such objective. The condition of the machine running effectively is that no one tries to control too closely its priorities.

And so we get the culture that moral critics object to: the fixation on brute quantitative growth, unalloyed by judgements of priority. The justification of this has to be an image of the good life, in which the acquisition of more and more consumer goods – what the system is good at producing – is seen as a central purpose of life.

Once again, the majority of us acquiesced in this historic compromise for similar mixed reasons as with alienated labour above: on one side, the non-imposition of priorities seemed to be the condition of the machine's running on, on the other, the resultant mode of life satisfied us as modern subjects in certain ways. First, the disinvolvement, our collective silence on priorities seemed the condition of our freedom severally to 'hang loose', each to go our own way, build his own private space, live his self-contained life.

Secondly, the definition of the good life as continuing escalation in living standards has an inescapable appeal to unregenerate men, which we all are. This Plato well knew. Appetite tends to run on to infinity, unless controlled by reason. The consumer society appeals to the lowest in us. But this, just put like that, is only a half-truth. It is also the case that the consumer society comes to us dressed up in a form that meshes with some of the aspirations of the modern subject.

Thus we are invited as consumers to acquire and furnish a private space, which is the condition of an autonomous, self-contained, unmediated existence. We need this space so that we and our family can grow, so that we can be close to nature (a garden, a house in the country). Much advertising plays on this aspiration to private space: the advertisements always show happy families filling those interiors, driving away in those cars, surrounding those barbecues, and so on. Of course, what is not justified is the continued increase; why should the mobile private space we travel in become ever more rapid and high-powered? Why must labour-saving mechanization continue without stop, even up to electric tooth-brushes and similar absurdities? This could never be justified intellectually, but somehow the implication is that more and more powerful accoutrements mean more of the fulfilment that they are meant to make possible. The commodities become 'fetishized' in a non-Marxist sense, endowed magically with the properties of the life they subserve: as though a faster car might actually make my family life more intense and harmonious.

There is a third reason why this compromise appeals to us; and which also aids in fetishization of commodities. The runaway machine, doing prodigies of technological mastery of nature, satisfies our sense of collective efficacy. The member of this society can feel that participative efficacy as producer that I spoke of above. At the same time, personal efficacy is a theme often played on to fetishize commodities. That is what is appealing about high-powered cars, and powerful engines generally. And this in turn taps feelings of machismo and sexual potency. Admen are aware of this.

And so we acquiesce in the consumer goods standard of welfare; and we accept the suspension of our sense of priorities, which allows us to see as normal some truly absurd inversions, such as supersonic flight; until we break the thrall, and look afresh and astonished at what we are doing.

VI

These features of industrial society, the meaninglessness and subordination of work, the mindless lack of control of priorities, above all the 'fetishization' of commodities, all represent a challenge to our image of ourselves as realized moderns, determining our purposes out of ourselves, dominating and not being dominated by things. To the extent that we let these negative features impinge on our self-understanding, we cannot but feel a fading confidence, an unease, a sense that the continued sense of efficacy by which we sustain our self-image within the modern identity is a sham. If we see ourselves as the playthings of mindless impersonal forces, or worse, the victims of a fascination with mere things, and this in the very practices which are supposed to sustain our identity and our conception of the good, then we cannot but lose confidence in these practices. We are threatened with a kind of anomie, in which we cease to believe in the norms governing our social life, but have no alternative but to live by them nonetheless. There is a crisis of allegiance to our society.

I believe this is part of what underlies our present malaise. And to understand why it arises now, we have to see why in recent years these features have begun to press themselves on us. Our consumer society is in several ways the victim of its own success; and these ways compound to put it in crisis.

I

First, the very prosperity of this society cannot but produce doubts and hesitations around its fetishization of commodities. When the society was still struggling to make decent housing and basic consumer durables widely available, the connection of all this effort and production with the goal of securing private space for all was clear enough. But now that most have this space, the refinements, the introduction of higher power, more speed, new models, frills, and so on, begin to look more and more disproportionate. It is harder to believe in all this as a serious social purpose.

Of course there is still a substantial minority which has not yet entered the affluent society. Production for them would make sense. But the continuation of the consumer boom does not seem to be very effective in helping these 'pockets of poverty'. The wealth does not 'trickle down' very adequately. This is partly because the continued boom goes with an upping of the ante, a whole range of new products which one has to get to be well-equipped at home, in the car, and so on. Much of each year's growth is pre-empted by the already affluent who expect a rise in their standard of living. It is very hard to prise some off to redistribute to the poor. This is even more so, of course, when growth slows down or stops, as we have seen in recent years. Then the resistances to redistribution get greater. We can think of the ugly mood of the California electorate, enacting Proposition 13, setting a limit to property taxes, something which will certainly involve cutting drastically programmes for poor and ghetto areas.

At the same time, the replacement of lower by higher technology can make things actually worse for poorer people. It ups the cost of being poor, so to speak. If all of society moves over from the bicycle to the automobile, so that cities are laid out to service it, and the availability of housing to jobs presupposes that people can travel for miles with a car; then you have to get a car to get around, and you may have to get around to hold a job, at least a good job. So you have to have a car. On a bicycle, you will get gassed, perhaps killed, and anyway cannot go the distances. So it ends up costing much more to be poor in New York, than to be middle class, say, in Madras. Growth can thus make the lot of poor people worse.

Now all this – the increasingly evident fetishistic character of the consumer standard, plus the fact that its steady rising does not seem able to alleviate suffering where it counts, or improve what is crying out for improvement – contributes to a loss of faith in the consumer standard, in the value of indefinite increase in consumer goods and services, in indiscriminate growth. This may have less effect on older people, but it visibly emerges in scepticism, questioning, rejection by younger people.

2

Among the things which may be cast into doubt in this crisis is the value of family life itself. This is particularly critical, because the version of the modern identity predominant in our society is one which aims towards a mobile subject, who loosens the ties of larger communities, and finds himself on his own in the nuclear family. But this gives a tremendously heightened significance to the nuclear family, which is now the main locus of strong, lasting, defining relations; and it has given family life and the emotions of family love a uniquely important place in the modern conception of natural fulfilment. The eighteenth century already sees this positive valuation of family life, family ties, and family feelings.

For this to be challenged is thus critical for the identity which has been dominant in our society. But it is not only under threat because it is associated with (to some) discredited consumer way of life. It is also threatened by the very scope of the development of the modern identity. In effect, if the business of life is finding my authentic fulfilment as an individual, and my associations should be relativized to this end, there seems no reason why this relativization should in principle stop at the boundary of the family. If my development, or even my discovery of myself, should be incompatible with a long-standing association, then this will come to be felt as a prison, rather than a locus of identity. So marriage is under greater strain. This is all greater in that the same aspiration to self-development and self-fulfilment leads women now to challenge the whole distribution of roles and emotional give-and-take of the traditional family.

3

The degree of concentration and mobility are beginning to have social consequences which produce tension for our society. For instance, the concentration of people in large cities begins to have negative consequences beyond a certain threshold. Unless they are well-designed, with multiple centres, it tends to make life and getting about more time-consuming and stressful, and relations more full of tension.

In addition, large cities cost more per head to run. As Hugh Stretton puts it, 'They generate more travel, congestion and local pollution per head. They force wasteful rates of demolition and rebuilding on their inner parts. Intense competition for central and accessible locations makes it harder to solve problems of density, shares of space and – above all – land prices.'[12] So concentration begins to raise the overhead costs of social existence.

Concentration/mobility does this in other ways too. The bleeding of local communities for the megalopolis forces a write-off of the excess unused stock of housing and public capital in the declining communities. The decline of the extended family means that society must pick up the pieces for the old, the abandoned, the chronically sick, and so on. In all these ways, the concentrated/mobile life virtually forces an expansion of the public sector. The prevailing doctrines about the efficiency of concentration and giant organizations ensure that the state will compound the error by over-bureaucratizing the public sector.

But the enlarged public sector, both as cost and as bureaucracy, creates great malaise. As a cost, it forces higher taxes. But these are resisted by citizens who have come more and more to see themselves as independent individuals. The link between their high mobility, that is, their 'hanging loose' from all partial communities, and the higher overheads of society is generally quite invisible to them. Ironically, it is just this pattern of life of hanging loose that makes them less capable of seeing it, and makes them look on the public sector as a barely necessary evil. So as they increase the need of the public sector, they decrease their own readiness to assume the burden. This thoroughly irrational state of affairs leads to all kinds of tensions and eruptions, of which the recent California tax revolt is one example.

---

[12] *Capitalism, Socialism and the Environment* (Cambridge, 1976), p. 224.

What further justifies the revolt is the over-bureaucratization of the public sector, which not only makes it unnecessarily costly, but also makes it very unresponsive to the public. This helps to make the process even less transparent, whereby we meet our needs through public mechanisms of our own providing. And this lack of transparency increases the alienation.

What is even worse is that the movement towards concentration and the break-up of partial communities is not entirely voluntary. Once the process goes a certain way, it acquires an élan which is sometimes hard to resist. One may want to stay in a smaller farming community; but as the services move out and concentrate in larger centres in response to earlier movements as well as general concentration, one may find it impossible to function. So more and more people follow the trend, and more services, move, schools, suppliers, outlets, etc.; and more people move; and so on.

4

Thus three 'successes', or hypertrophies, of the consumer society are increasing malaise: the very success of the consumer growth tends to discredit the consumer standard, the development of the identity of self-fulfilment tends to fragment the family which was previously its privileged locus, and the increase of concentration alienates us from government. But besides a loss of faith in the consumer standard, tension in the family and the state, the danger of identity crisis, these strains also undermine that sense of our status within the larger society which is supportive of our identity. Unresponsive bureaucracies make us less sanguine, or frankly cynical, about citizenship; and sometimes even fearing for our rights. The discredit on the consumer standard makes us feel less positive about the efficacy of the whole society in which we have a part as labourers.

But the hypertrophy of this sense of collective efficacy is itself a fourth cause of malaise. As our awareness of belonging to an organized, technological, productive society grew, so did the confidence that we could solve any problem given the will and the concentration of resources. This sense of bullish confidence probably reached its high point in the post-war period in the Kennedy era in the USA, when intelligence, good will and organizing science were set to tackle the age-old problems of poverty, inequality and facial alienation, through the New Frontier. The sense of new creation was heightened by the symbolism of an attractive young man at the head of the enterprise. But since then, things have gone sour. We are more and more made aware that some problems, including the most grievous social ones, like intractable poverty, and racial division, resist even immense resources. They are more than problems, they are human dilemmas. The sense of our efficacy has taken a serious blow.

In sum, by this combined effect, we have been led partly to lose confidence in our definitions of the good life, partly to feel alienated from and even cynical about our governmental institutions, partly to feel uncertain and tense about our social relation and even about our family life, partly to feel unsupported by the larger society in our identity as modern subjects.

5

All this is likely to make for strains, tensions, mutual aggressivity. But as it happens, a bout of social conflict was probably coming our way after the halcyon decades of steady consumer growth of the post-war period. This was partly because of the growth of the public sector and its consequent burden on the productive sector and on tax-payers, which I mentioned above. But it is also because we live in a society which has become more equal and 'classless' in style and spirit, in which workers and the less well-off have acquired greater bargaining muscle through trade unions, in which the general standard of education has risen, and in which there is a prevailing belief that government can do anything, so that age-old poverty, or underdevelopment, or inequality, formerly seen as in the order of things, is now removable. Such a society will sooner or later make more and more insistent demands on government and the economy, which by their very nature and number will be incompatible.

To face this, a society needs an even higher degree of cohesion, self-confidence, and mechanisms of effective self-management. But instead, we affronted this period with lowered confidence, inner tensions, and in greater alienation from our institutions than before. The result has been a scramble for income and advantage in which powerful forces competed and maintained their position, but at the expense of the unorganized, through inflation. We are being forced to return to more orderly consensus through the disastrous experience of inflation. But it is a slow and reluctant business, and leaves many burning resentments and sense of grievance without vent.

This is because the consensus is forcing us to decide something that has previously been let happen, viz., the distribution of income. We are being forced to take a greater hand in the collective direction of our economy. But any agreement on this, hard enough at any time, is only possible within some common sense of purpose. We would have found it much easier to agree on a wages policy in the 1950s. But that is exactly why, of course, we did not need one then. Because of our uncertain purpose, and our faltering confidence in the over-riding value of the society we are evolving through our economic efforts, the disciplines imposed by any incomes policy will often be felt as an imposition, a rip-off. And the angry reaction of one group, tearing through the limits, will stimulate others to do the same. High wage-claims in one sector prompt them in others. Tax-payers' revolts increase the bitterness of the poor. Inflation is the visible sign of our disarray, and itself an object of anxiety. It compounds our self-doubt.

So to sum up the argument: the modern identity, and the accompanying moral visions, give the background both to the affirmative and critical stances to our society. They show them to be closely related. But they also help us understand the balance between the two.

For in fact the affirmative view does not just praise endless accumulation; this is understood as an affirmation of efficacy, productive power, which in turn is a sign of autonomy, and of our domination over things. Thus the affirmative view is vulnerable to whatever presses on us an understanding of our plight in which we are not in fact autonomous, are not dominating, but enslaved to things. The word 'fetish' is redolent of this. It connects with the earlier rejection of idolatory, and the modern's sense of superiority over the primitive, of having won free from an obsession in things, an immersion in them, a shaping of his life on their model.

In fact we live in a society whose practices embody a certain notion of identity, and the human good. This must be ours, or we cannot give this society our allegiance; we are alienated from it. At the time, we rely to a great extent on these practices to maintain this sense of identity. If these practices which supposedly embody the modern identity can be shown to lead in fact to some such failure to achieve it, as we mentioned in the last paragraph, then our allegiance to them is shaken; and perhaps our faith in the conception of the modern identity is shaken as well. We turn to other models.

In the balance between affirmative and negative stances to our society, the affirmative relies largely on the first version of life according to nature, as this has become embedded in the political and economic, largely market-atomistic practices of our society. If we become convinced that we are dominated by mindless forces, or enslaved to commodities which we make into fetishes, then we will withdraw allegiance from these practices, and obviously from the first version, or at least this way of expressing the first version institutionally.

VII

If something like the story in the preceding pages is true, then we can understand why modern capitalist society will be prey to recurrent 'legitimation crises'. It has a fateful tendency to sap the bases of its own legitimacy. The very institutions and practices which express and entrench the modern identity in its successive phases – the capitalist industrial economy in a liberal polity – are also undermining participants' faith in this identity, or in these institutions as fit carriers of this identity, or both. This society is in a sense in 'contradiction', the full extent of which is not evident if one looks simply at the economic irrationalities, or the galloping externalization of costs, which provoke a fiscal crisis – though these may be grievous enough dangers. The most lethal tension only comes into view when we try to understand the society in the light of the sense of the human good which it presupposes and helps to inculcate – what I have been calling the modern identity.

But then the further question arises: is this a contradiction just of *capitalism*? The uncontrolled drive to growth, concentration, mobility; the exaltation of instrumental reason over history and community; these have been features of most hitherto attempted models of socialism. Political theory has yet to come seriously to grips with this crisis.

CHAPTER ELEVEN

THE NATURE AND SCOPE OF DISTRIBUTIVE JUSTICE

I

I

A vigorous debate is raging today about the nature of distributive justice. But the controversy concerns not only the criteria or standards of justice, what we would have to do or be to be just; it also touches the issue of what kind of good distributive justice is. Indeed, I would argue that as the debate has progressed, it has become clearer that the solution to the first kind of question presupposes some clarification on the second. In any case, recent extremely interesting works by Michael Walzer and Michael Sandel raise fundamental questions in the second range.

I want to take up both issues in this paper. In the first part, I raise questions about the nature of distributive justice. In the second, I want to look at the actual debates about criteria which now divide our societies.

First, what kind of good, or mode of right, is distributive justice? Rawls helps us by giving us a formulation[1] of the circumstances of justice: we have separate human beings who are nevertheless collaborating together in conditions of moderate scarcity. This distinguishes it from other kinds and contexts of good. For instance there is a mode of justice which holds between quite independent human beings, not bound together by any society or collaborative arrangement. If two nomadic tribes meet in the desert, very old and long-standing intuitions about justice tell us that it is wrong (unjust) for one to steal the flocks of the other. The principle here is very simple: we have a right to what we have. But this is not a principle of *distributive* justice, which presupposes that men are in a society together, or in some kind of collaborative arrangement.

Similarly we have to distinguish distributive justice from other kinds of good or right action. If in the above case one of the tribes were starving,

---

[1] In *A Theory of Justice* (Cambridge, Mass., 1971); following Hume. I am aware of the difficulties which this formulation makes for Rawls, which Sandel has so well explored in *Liberalism and the Limits of Justice* (Cambridge, 1983), chap. 1.

the other would, according to a widespread moral tradition, have a natural duty to succour it; and by extension, it is usually held that the starving tribe could legitimately steal from the other if it refused to help. But acting according to this natural duty is not the same thing as acting according to justice – although the demands of natural duty can have moral repercussions on justice, as we see in the second case: the necessity in which the starving tribe finds itself, and the refusal of the better-off, cancels what would otherwise be the injustice of the act of stealing.

Nomadic clans of herders are rather far removed from our predicament. They only enter here as exemplars of man in what is called 'the State of Nature'. The basic point is that there is no such thing as distributive justice in the State of Nature. Everyone agrees with this truism; but beyond it agreement stops. The really important question is: in what way do the principles of distributive justice differ from those of justice among independent agents (agents in the State of Nature)? And what is it about human society that makes the difference?

This second question is not even recognized as a question by many thinkers. But I want to claim that it is the fundamental one. To argue or reason about distributive justice involves giving clear formulations to strong and originally inchoate intuitions; and attempting to establish some coherent order among these formulations. In the process, as Rawls points out in his excellent discussion of this question, both formulations and intuitions can undergo alteration, until that limiting stage where they are in 'reflective equilibrium'.

Now our intuitions about distributive justice are continuous with our basic moral intuitions about human beings as beings who demand a certain respect (to use one moral language among many possible ones, but it is not possible to *talk* about this without using *someone's* formulations). It is because men ought to be treated in a certain way, and thus enjoy a status not shared by stones and (some think also) animals, that they ought to be treated *equally* in collaborative situations (using the term 'equally' in its wide Aristotelian sense, where it includes also 'proportionate equality').

If we introduce the Kantian term 'dignity' as a term of art to describe this status that men enjoy, then it is plain that there has been widespread disagreement on what human dignity consists in. But, I would like to add, this disagreement lies behind the disputes about the nature of distributive justice. We cannot really get clear about these without exploring the different notions of human dignity.

Our notion of human dignity is in turn bound up with a conception of the human good, that is, our answer to the question, what is the good for man? What is the good human life? This too is part of the background of a conception of distributive justice. Differences about justice are related to differences about the nature of the good (if I may be permitted this Aristotelian expression). And they are related in particular to a key issue, which is whether and in what way human beings can realize the good alone, or to turn it around the other way, in what way they must be part of society to be human in the full sense or to realize the human good.

The claim I am making could be put in this way: that different principles of distributive justice are related to conceptions of the human good, and in particular to different notions of men's dependence on society to realize the good. Thus deep disagreements about justice can only be clarified if we formulate and confront the underlying notions of man and society. This is the nature of the argument, and it also underlies the actual disputes we witness in our society.

The above paragraph would be a crashing truism but for two related factors. The first is the tendency of much Anglo-Saxon philosophy to shy away from any exploration of the human subject. Seventeenth-century epistemology started with an unexamined and unexaminable subject – unexaminable, since any examination deals with data, and these are on the side of the known, not the knower. In a parallel way, seventeenth-century theory of natural right started with the unexamined subject. Much Anglo-Saxon philosophy seems to want to continue in this direction. Rawls is a partial exception, since he speaks of a Kantian basis for his principles of justice, expressing as they do our nature as free and equal rational beings; but even he does not bring this foundation out as an explicit theme. Nozick is an extreme example. He argues from our current conception of individual rights, and reasons as though this conception were sufficient to build our notion of the entire social context. The question is never raised whether the affirmation of these rights is bound up with a notion of human dignity and the human good which may require quite another context. In short the question is never raised whether man is morally self-sufficient as Locke thought, or whether perhaps Aristotle is not right about this. An argument which abstracts from this, and which is insensitive to the social nature of man, naturally produces the most bizarre consequences.

I really want to argue here for an Aristotelian way of putting the issue about distributive justice. But Aristotle not only has a substantive view about man as *zwon politikon* which conflicts with Locke. He also has an implicit metaview (a view about what is at stake in the argument). And this conflicts with that of a philosophical tradition of which Locke is one of the patrons, which wants to make questions of the nature of man irrelevant to morals and political philosophy, and to start instead with rights. This means that it is, alas, not just platitudinous to restate Aristotle's way of putting the issue. From this naturally follows a second reason for re-editing Aristotle: that the precise way in which different notions of distributive justice are related to their foundation in a view of man needs to be re-stated.

The Aristotelian meta-view I want to put forward here as a background to discussing principles of distributive justice is that these principles are related to some notion of the good which is sustained or realized or sought in the association concerned.

We can illustrate this first with a very un-Aristotelian theory as an example, the atomist view of Locke. For the purposes of this discussion we can describe as atomist views of the human good for which it is conceivable for man to attain it alone. On these views, in other words, what men derive from association in realizing the good are a set of aids only contingently, even if almost unfailingly, linked to this association. Examples of this are: protection against attack from others, or the benefits of higher production. These always require association, or almost always. But there are imaginable circumstances in which we could enjoy security, or a high living standard, alone: for example, on a continent in which there were no others, or in a land of paradisiac natural abundance.

By contrast a social view of man is one which holds that an essential constitutive condition of seeking the human good is bound up with being in society. Thus if I argue that man cannot even be a moral subject, and thus a candidate for the realization of the human good, outside of a community of language and mutual discourse about the good and bad, just and unjust, I am rejecting all atomist views; since what man derives from society is not some aid in realizing his good, but the very possibility of being an agent seeking that good. (The Aristotelian resonances in the above sentence are, of course, not coincidental.)

To put the issue in other terms, social views see some form of society as essentially bound up with human dignity, since outside of society the very potentiality to realize that wherein this dignity consists is undermined; whereas atomist views see human dignity as quite independent of society – which is why they have no difficulty ascribing *rights* (as against just the status of being an object of respect) to a man alone, in the State of Nature.

Now the issue of the principles of justice is quite differently posed within these two views. For the atomist, there is such a thing as the aims of society, that is, purposes which society fulfils for individuals, who are morally self-sufficient in the sense that they are capable of framing these purposes outside of society. Thus Locke's thesis that 'the great and chief end ... of men's uniting into Commonwealths ... is the preservation of their property'[2] is posed against the background that men acquire property outside of society, by mixing their labour with it 'without the assignation or consent of any body'.[3]

But outside of society, human beings are in the predicament of our nomad tribes above; and the rules of justice which prevail are not those of distributive justice, but those of independent possession. Consequently, an atomist view gives one the basis to argue that what we have a right to under these original rules cannot be abrogated, since the purpose of entering society cannot be to jeopardize these, but rather to protect them. And from this one can derive an absolute right to property, which no society can infringe.

What then does entering society change? What does it add to original justice in the specific form of distributive justice? This depends on the aims of the association. Let us take Locke's aims as our example. The aim of the association is to preserve property, which of course includes life, liberty and estate. But if all enter into society freely, then all should benefit from the association. This is the basis of a principle of equality, the principle of equal fulfilment, that is, the principle that society's aims should be equally fulfilled for each of its members; for otherwise some in joining would be giving more than they get, would be sacrificing themselves for others; and there is no ground why they should do this (outside of a special context where a natural duty might come into play, for example where someone was starving).

In the Lockeian case, the principle of equal fulfilment requires that the government protect equally effectively the life, liberty and estate of each of its subjects. Of course, this equality is not only compatible with, but one might argue even requires inequality of another sort. The state would have to protect the legitimately arrived-at distribution of property, no matter how unequal this was. (And on some plausible thesis about the hazards of many transactions, the distribution could not help but be unequal, as Nozick argues.) But this would still be equality of equal *fulfilment* of the aims of the association, and hence would be justice.

We thus see two kinds of arguments for principles of distributive

---

[2] *Two Treatises of Government*, II. 124.   [3] *Ibid.*, II. 28.

justice which are apposite in an atomist perspective. The first invokes the context-less justice of the State of Nature, and argues for the (partial) preservation in civil society of some of its features. This is the basis for one of the arguments for inalienable rights. It can also be seen as the basis for Nozick's entitlement theory of justice, where all that enters into account is the series of permissible transactions between independent agents.

But one might object that this is not a principle of distributive justice at all, which becomes relevant when men are associated together in society, and have to share in some sense. Now it can be argued that the underlying notion of distributive justice is equality, that men associated together for the good have to share in some way in this good, or else a wrong is being done. (The notion of equality here is Aristotle's of *Ethics* V, as I mentioned above.) But the question is, what is the relevant kind of equality? And here an atomist view can give us an answer by invoking the aims of the association. The fundamental notion of equality as basic to distributive justice is interpreted here to mean that there should be equal fulfilment. So that what equality means in society is directly dependent on what are seen to be the aims of the association; for equality is just the fulfilling of these aims for everyone alike.

These two kinds of argument, on the other hand, have no weight in the perspective which sees man as a social animal. Rather two other kinds of argument are invoked which offer only a distant parallel to the atomist ones.

First, any social view sees a certain kind or structure of society as an essential condition of human potentiality, be this the polis, or the classless society, or the hierarchical society under God and king, or a host of other such views which we have seen in history. This structure itself, or order, or type of relation thus provides the essential background for any principles of distributive justice.

This means of course, that the structure itself cannot be called into question in the name of distributive justice. Within the bounds of a hierarchical conception of society in which the political order is thought to reflect the order in the universe, it makes no sense to object to the special 'status' or 'privileges' of king or priesthood as violations of equality. When this objection is made, it involves a challenge to the entire hierarchical conception.

This point is generally recognized, and might be thought to be of no relevance to our age. But although such hierarchical conceptions belong now to an irrevocable past, the underlying form of argument does not. For if we have a conception of a certain structure which is essential for human potentiality, or for the fullness of human potentiality, it defines for us the kinds of subject to whom distributive justice is due. It is not just that the normative structure is untouchable, but also that it is men-within-the-normative-structure between whom justice must be done.

To take an example from a peripheral discussion of John Rawls' book. In section 77, he takes up briefly the question whether a real equality of opportunity wouldn't have to equalize the advantages people derive from their family backgrounds. Obviously, there is a potential thrust to the argument for individual equality which taken to its limit would have us break up families, perhaps even bring children up in state institutions, in order to bring about true equality of condition. Why do we shrink from this? Because we have the intuition that growing up in a family is linked with an important aspect of the human potential; or to use the ancient language, that forming and living in families is 'natural' to man. To those who think like this, the argument seems absurd that we should break up families in order to do justice between individuals. The absurdity arises from the sense that the proposed break-up would no longer be doing justice between full human beings, but between truncated people. So that the very ground for justice as equality, that it is bound up with the respect due to human dignity, would give way under the argument.

But of course, this idea that families are natural to man can be challenged; and naturally is by the more extreme offshoots of the modern tradition of 'absolute freedom', for example some variants of contemporary 'women's liberation'. From this point of view, the family is an imposture, an oppressive structure masquerading as a natural form. And we have a parallel argument to that around the hierarchical society of the *ancien régime*.

We can take another example which brings us to a more central dispute in modern Western politics. Within some general agreement (at least avowed agreement) that the life chances of people in different regions and classes ought to be equalized, there is an important disagreement as to what this means. For some regional equalization means, where the economically most efficient solution is to encourage out-migration, that one take this most efficient route to the goal of equality between *individuals*. For others, on the contrary, it means bringing about comparable living standards for the different regional societies, as *communities*. Whatever the political rhetoric, the underlying philosophical issue is this: is living in the kind of community which one sees, for example, in Cape Breton Island, or the Gaspé, essential to (an important) human potential?

If so, then equality must be between men-in-such communities, and this means we must adopt the second solution. But if, on the contrary, we look on this sense of community belonging as simply a taste that some people have, then there is no reason why it should be subsidized by the rest of the society; our duty is rather to take the cheapest road towards equal living standards for individuals. To spend more resources refloating the economy of a region so that it need not suffer out-migration is then to give people in the disfavoured regions *more* than their due.[4]

From a social perspective there is a first kind of argument, therefore, which spells out the background against which the principles of distributive justice must operate. There is no comparable notion of background on an atomist view. Or, if one wants to discover one, the nearest thing to it would be the State of Nature, the original predicament of justice between independent beings, where justice is not yet distributive justice.

But this conception of the background generates its own parallel to the notion of inalienable rights: types of relationships that men should be able to enter into and remain in, and which cannot be normatively overridden by other considerations such as distributive justice.

In the above examples I have spoken of the background as being set by certain considerations about the human good or potentiality as such. But this is perhaps an over-essentialistic, and certainly a too restrictive, perspective. The framework for distribution can also be determined for a given society by the nature of the goods they seek in common. It can vary historically.

I could, for instance, have put the second example above in these terms. One could make the claim that equalization ought to be between regional communities, because the nature and purpose of the association in question (here the Canadian federal union) was to secure together the health and flourishing of its constituent regional communities. We could prescind altogether from issues of human (trans-historical) nature, whether man was by essence a community animal; we would just argue that the very nature of the common good defining our association precludes our conceiving equalization in purely individual terms.

Michael Walzer's brilliant *Spheres of Justice*[5] offers a whole series of

---

[4] Of course, in politics you have to muddy the waters. Those of us who are in favour of the second policy *also* argue that it is overall the cheapest, particularly because of the cost of writing off the stock of houses, schools, etc. in the declining areas. We cannot afford to ignore the atomist vote. But our philosophical grounds are not revealed in these (we hope politically persuasive) arguments.

[5] New York, 1983.

arguments purporting to show the justified distribution of different goods which we in a certain sense produce or provide in common, reasoning in each case from the nature of the good provided, and the character of the agents who have associated for its provision. Thus he argues that the character of universal citizen self-rule which has become central to modern Western democracies renders illegitimate the exercise of essentially political power which is based on the ownership of property.[6] This justifies a condemnation of the famous Pullman experiment, but also, he thinks, tells in favour of workers' control at least of large-scale economic units.

Again, he argues for certain principles governing the provision of welfare – especially that goods be distributed in proportion to need, and that the distribution recognize the underlying equality of membership[7] – on the basis of the nature of the goods, and our common understanding of membership in a democratic society.

Analogous arguments are put forward for a redistribution of the burdens of hard and dirty work – involving even a republican version of the *corvée*.[8]

Now what all these examples have in common is that they involve a fixing either of the forms and structures of distribution (e.g., that goods should be partitioned between people-in-families as against people-as-individuals), or the actual shape of the distribution (e.g., welfare should be provided according to need), from considerations of human good or the nature of association as such, or at least from a consideration of the particular goods sought in an historical association. There is no question as yet of the differential merit or desert of the members. Rather arguments of the kind I have been considering here purport to set the framework in which considerations of desert can be allowed to arise, if they are allowed to arise at all, and determine distributions. The framework ought to be given priority over other criteria of distribution because whatever transgresses its limits would allegedly be in violation of the nature of the goods distributed or of the agents to whom they are distributed. And to propose an allocation of this kind in the name of distributive justice has to be absurd.

The second form of argument which arises in a social perspective concerns the principles of distributive justice themselves, and not just the framework. Granted a certain view of a common good, in the sense of an indivisible good, which a social perspective necessarily offers us, since it

---

[6] *Ibid.*, chaps. 4, 12.   [7] *Ibid.*, chap. 3, p. 84.   [8] *Ibid.*, chap. 6.

sees men as realizing their potential only in a certain common structure, it may appear evident that certain people deserve more than others, in the sensè that their contribution to this common good is more marked, or more important.

We could put it this way: for this common good of living in a family, or a community, or whatever, we are all in each other's debt. But we might see the balance of mutual indebtedness as not entirely reciprocal. Some people, who especially contribute to the animation of the community, or the common deliberative life of the society, or the defence of its integrity, or whatever, deserve more, because we are more in their debt than vice versa.

This is the perspective of Aristotle's discussion of distributive justice in books III and IV of the *Politics*. He closely links together what the principle of distribution of offices and honours ought to be, and what the common good is which the polis is for.

Now in Aristotle's society, particularly given the importance of honour, and its being one of the key goods at stake in the issue of who could have a political career, this type of argument was naturally used to justify certain inequalities (or as Aristotle put it, certain 'proportionate' equalities). But the argument form can serve also as a ground for equality, and does in the modern world. For it can be used to rebut the claims for unequal distribution based on some other criterion, say economic contribution. The argument here runs along these lines, that although men's economic contribution to a society may be of very unequal value, nevertheless as members of a community who sustain together certain kinds of relations, of civility, or mutual respect, or common deliberation, their mutual indebtedness is fully reciprocal; or close enough to this so that judgements would be impossible and invidious. We shall return to this below.

This second type of argument can be applied in two different ways, both of which we find in Aristotle. The first way, illustrated in the preceding paragraph, is to hold that because of a common good which in fact is sustained by the common life of our society, we ought to accept certain principles of distribution which take account of the real balance of mutual indebtedness relative to this good. For instance, that we owe each other much more equal distribution than we might otherwise agree to on economic criteria, because in fact we are involved in a society of mutual respect, or common deliberation, and this is the condition for all of us realizing together an important human potential.

Or else we can apply it in another way: recognizing that a certain kind of society, for example, one of common deliberation in mutual respect, represents the highest realization of human potential, we might nevertheless judge that certain, or most societies, have not yet arrived at the point where this is fully embodied in their common life. If this is so, then for certain societies which are still far from the best, it would be wrong to apply the principles of justice which belong to the best. Thus if a society is in fact much more fragmented than the ideal of common deliberation, much closer (at its best, that is, freed of the savagery and exploitation it may contain) to a society of mutual protection, be this because of its history, its mode of economic life, its cultural diversity, or whatever, then it may be wrong to demand, say, the degree of equality that we can justify between those in a true community of common deliberation.

Of course, we would still consider the latter as a better society, and try to move our society closer towards that goal. And we will probably judge our society harshly for all sorts of injustices which are such on its own terms. But it may nevertheless be wrong to demand *in the name of justice* a standard of equality from this society unchanged which we would think normal and enjoined on us in the best society. We may judge for instance that the tenuous relation of semi-alliance between two cultural groups in a state does not justify the equal sharing of all benefits and burdens that is indispensable in the polis.

We can thus see two kinds of arguments in the social perspective, paralleling the two kinds of argument in the atomist perspective. The first, as it were, sets the framework for the principles of distributive justice from the notion of the common good which we are involved in. The latter tries to derive these principles from this same notion.

There are limit cases of social perspectives where the second argument is lacking altogether. These are cases where, once the structural demands for the common good are met, there is no further room for questions of distribution. The two most famous cases which (it can be argued) are of this kind are the views of Plato and Marx. To take the latter case, this may help explain what has been found rather odd by many, that there seems to be no doctrine of distributive justice in Marx. This can be explained I believe by the fact that the conception of the communist society in which alone the human potential is fully realized contains a principle of distribution (to each according to his need) as a structural feature, essential to it as community. So that all questions of distribution are decided by the framework argument. There is no room left for arguments which we recognize as being properly about distributive justice, that group A or group B deserve or merit more or the same, in virtue of the balance of mutual indebtedness. A parallel argument might be made in the case of Plato.[9]

2

What emerges out of the above discussion is above all two major points about the nature and scope of distributive justice, confusion about which bedevils discussions today. The confusions arise from conflating distributive justice with other virtues, so that it is no longer clear just what is being demanded or advocated. This is not a merely 'academic' question, as I hope to show; rather the confusions may hide from us important political choices.

First, Aristotle in distinguishing particular from general justice points out that the former is a virtue whose opposite is 'pleonexia', grasping more than one's share. Criteria of distributive justice are meant to give us the basis for knowing what our share is, and therefore when we are being grasping. But what falls out of the above discussion is that there are two rather different kinds of argument that do this. There are arguments about the nature of the framework, from considerations of the goods sought and the nature of the agents associated; and these can sometimes tell us that certain distributions are wrong, and those pushing for them are 'grasping'. And then there are arguments about the balance of mutual indebtedness which justify some distributions within the framework and rule out others.

Both of these arguments concern distributive justice in a sense; but in another sense, only the latter do, because only they tell us how to resolve

---

[9] What is interesting in the highly original work of Michael Walzer is that he seems to be attempting a similar feat, but in an infinitely more supple and pluralistic fashion than either Plato or Marx. By a similar feat, I mean a theory which will determine all the questions normally thrown up for distributive justice by considerations of the framework type, without recourse to questions of desert, or what I have called the balance of indebtedness. The principles are of course utterly different from the Procrustean one we see in Plato: indeed, the theory is in a sense the ultimate anti-Procrustean social theory; and this, I believe, is what is tremendously valuable in it. But the question may still arise whether one can do altogether without any principles of distributive justice in the narrow, intra-framework sense. It is not that Walzer is trying to tie down the distribution of every good by some antecedent criterion. On the contrary, the whole thrust of the work is to limit the scope of distributive criteria to their proper domains. It is just that where distributions are not determined by some framework considerations they are left quite unrestricted. The market is an example. Its operations have to be restricted at certain places in the name of other goods; but within its legitimate scope the allocations brought about through it are legitimate without being deserved. People are entitled to what they get, but there is no place for considerations of desert, or the balance of mutual indebtedness in determining, say, incomes policy.

questions of distribution which can be considered as open and allowable questions in the light of the framework. They help us decide the distributive questions which we can legitimately allow as questions without subverting the good or the very basis of our association. However, the issue of how to use the term is not vital; so long as these two levels are not confused.

Secondly, both framework questions and the criteria of distribution are derived at least in part from the nature of the association and that of the goods sought in common. But that means that the demands of distributive justice can and will differ across different societies and at different moments in history. This is a crucial point which is hammered home so effectively in Walzer's book, for instance. As a matter of fact, the variation may take us beyond the range of distributive justice altogether, as Michael Sandel has shown in his penetrating work. Certain associations, for example, families, may be such that the presumption of independent interests implicit in demanding distribution by entitlement may be destructive. The good of these associations may exclude distributive justice.[10]

But even restricting ourselves to those societies where some form of distributive justice is appropriate, it is clear that they may be widely different; and even that some may require principles of justice which are wrong – principles which we can even call unjust in another sense. The fight between Agamemnon and Achilles over Briseis was a dispute about distributive justice. Both parties justify their behaviour in terms of a principle (Achilles holds that she was part of his share; Agamemnon holds that the ruler cannot be left with less than the followers). Let us say only one of them was right in terms of Mycenean warrior society. Nevertheless, as far as we are concerned people should not be allocated like this as spoils of war.

If we ask why we think this, we will recur to the discussion above about the atomist perspective. We believe that there are some ways we should and should not treat each other quite irrespective of whether we are associated together in society or not. In the State of Nature, people should not treat others as booty. This is unjust, in a sense which has nothing to do with distributive justice within a society. The fact that we see that the social perspective is necessary to raise questions of distributive justice does not mean that we cease to believe in certain inalienable rights. The error of atomist writers like Nozick was to try to make the right of this

[10] Sandel, *Liberalism and the Limits of Justice*, chap. 1.

asocial context the *sufficient* basis for distributive justice in society, which it can never be. But avoiding this error does not mean that we abandon all trans-societal criteria of right.

So we can say that Briseis was justly Achilles' (let us side with him); but the whole operation was unconscionable and wrong. In less dramatic fashion, we might consider some society in which the degree of solidarity was low as morally inferior to another; or one in which the goods sought were defined in a narrowly material fashion, excluding the cultural development of the members. Certain distributions might then be just in terms of the society, but repugnant to us.

This suggests that it might be important to distinguish in our moral condemnation of a society the case where we attack it specifically for failing in distributive justice from the case where we see it is failing in absolute justice (to use this term for the good violated in the Mycenean case), or some other good. Nor would this distinction be necessarily a purely pedantic exericse. To try to make a society more distributively just is to try to make it conform more to the constitutive understandings shared in its membership. To try to make a society absolutely just, or bring it closer to absolute justice, or some other good, may well be to subvert and destroy the constitutive understandings. Agamemnon and Achilles would have had to be totally re-educated, their economy and way of life largely abolished, before they could have renounced what we find utterly unacceptable in their conduct. But there are costs, sometimes terrible costs, in such transformations, as is evident to us once the hold of imperialist politics and atomistic philosophy on us weakens.

This means that the revolutionary critic of injustice can be in a political dilemma: should he break altogether with the regnant standards of distributive justice, in order to bring people up to a higher type of association, more in line with the good or with absolute justice; but then risk the dangers of deracination, the breakdown of civility, the debilitating effect of whatever vanguard tutelage is necessary, and the like: or should he respect the dominant culture, even at the cost of renouncing the higher good? There can, of course, be no simple answer to this dilemma. In cases where slavery and ritual murder are involved, we might easily agree to take the revolutionary road; while with a society which failed to some degree with regard to solidarity and a concern for the better things of life, we might more readily feel bound to work within.

A dilemma of this kind might be thought to exist for us now, at least in principle, in the international arena. We might argue that the present distribution of the world's resources between rich and very poor is scandalously unjust, judged by the standards of absolute justice we acknowledge in the state of nature. No one would be right to leave another in such need should they meet in the desert, for instance. And yet the degree of sacrifice which would have to be imposed on rich countries to effect the required transfers might be impossible short of despotism. International justice might not be combinable with democratic rule in the developed countries. Absolute justice here would require that one violate distributive justice in these polities, and indeed, smash the present matrices in which existing standards of distributive justice have grown.

I think we also face this dilemma in more immediate and less dramatic forms in our societies, as will be indicated in the sequel. But much of the contemporary discussion about distributive justice ignores its very possibility. It could be argued that Rawls, for instance, is presenting us a highly revisionary standard of justice in his difference principle. I shall try to show how this is so below. But the question whether it is cannot even arise, as long as one sees the task of defining the principles of justice as an ahistorical one; a single question to be asked and answered for all societies irrespective of their culture and traditions and self-understandings.

II

I

After this long discussion of the nature of the argument, I want to look at the issues about distributive justice that are current today. There are two areas in which these constantly arise. One is that of 'differentials', the question of the allowable differences between wages or income received for different kinds of work. This is becoming a particularly acute question as Western societies find themselves experimenting with incomes policy more and more.

The second major area is one that we can designate roughly as equalization policies. This covers the whole gamut of policies which attempt in some way to redistribute income or economic prosperity, or life opportunities; either by transfer payments, or by special programmes to develop certain regions, or to allow certain disfavoured groups to catch up in one way or another (e.g., in education opportunity). These policies are the object of sometimes bitter controversy today, and one which gets to the heart of the issues about distributive justice.

In both these spheres, the issue is about equality, and this might be schematically introduced in the following way: equality is a powerful ideal in Western society just because we have put behind us all views of society as embodying some kind of differential order, views which formerly justified unbridgeable differences of status. There are no longer any reasons in the order of things why one group should perpetually and systematically have a different lot than another.

At the same time the growth of technology and the modern industrial economy has given us (the sense of) unprecedented power to alter our natural and social condition at will. So that not only the ancient class inequalities based on the 'order of things' are no longer justifiable, but also other inequalities, such as those between regions, which used to seem just inevitable and beyond remedy. Now, for instance the difference in standard of living between southern Italy and the rest of Europe is not seen just as a consequence of the hazards of history and natural endowment, but as a problem to be solved. The same goes for other pockets of poverty within favoured regions, which were formerly thought of as unalterable.

All this means that on the one hand there is a growing pressure towards equality, a growing impatience with long-standing and stubborn gaps in living standards. But on the other hand, there is a powerful resistance to equalization. This needs no special explanation; when have the comparatively better-off *liked* redistribution? Nevertheless, the resistance takes place in a certain climate, which has important consequences. Western industrial society, having done much to break up the old local communities which were previously important in people's lives, has brought about a 'privatization' of life. By this I mean here a generally accepted picture of happiness and the good life as that of a man alone, or more exactly, a nuclear family alone. The promise of greater control over nature which our civilization holds out is naturally translated in this context into a promise of increased individual control, which means disposing of an increasing number of individual consumer goods. The aspiration to perpetually rising consumer standards has become very powerful in all Western societies.

Privatization naturally makes us tend to look at society as a set of necessary instruments, rather than as the locus in which we can develop our most important potential. This is by no means the only way we look at it, but it is an important part of many people's consciousness of society. And privatization tends to be self-reinforcing; since a society whose institutions are mainly seen in instrumental terms is one which offers very few intrinsic satisfactions, and which men naturally tend to withdraw from whenever feasible to their own private space. This is well illustrated by the face of modern cities, whose cores become progressively less agreeable places to be, with a consequent flight to the suburbs, which in turn – and so on.

All this is well known, and much commented on. Its relevance for the discussion here is that these conditions ensure a continued vogue to atomist views. In a way it might seem strange that in such an unprecedentedly interdependent society, where we are farther away than ever from the original human condition of self-subsistent clans, people should still think in such atomist terms. Locke might be excused for such a view, in a still largely agricultural society, and even more the farmers of the American Republic in the late eighteenth century. But how can such views survive today?

In a sense, of course, they don't. No one can believe the fables about a state of nature. But in our moral reasoning these atomist views do; and this is because the experience of so many in modern society is one which atomist views seem to make sense of. Not that it is ever conceivable that we might have put society together from scratch; but rather that society and its institutions are seen as having only instrumental significance; that what we need to acquire the full range of human purposes we already possess as individuals, or develop in close, intimate relations with others, while the larger society merely provides us with the means to carry them out (while also, alas, putting obstacles in our way).

Hence, we find atomist forms of reasoning about distributive justice which have a certain currency. Of course, the original Lockean form is not too plausible for most people in modern society. On this view, men already had outside of society an independent capacity to exploit the resources of nature, and their so doing (mixing their labour with nature) founded property. This kind of myth about property is still important in some parts of the USA for historical reasons. But it obviously is implausible for the life experience of the vast majority in Western society which is rather that of working within large and complex structures.

But there is another starting point for an atomist view which is the individual not as possessor of property, but as an independent being with his own capacities and goals. The aims of association are here not so much the protection of property, but the combination of our capacities which allows each of us to be much more productive than we would be alone. Our capacities, what we bring to the association, are however of very unequal value. Thus on the principle of equal fulfilment of the aims of association, those of us with especially useful capacities, and who really use them to the full in our collaboration with others, ought to receive a greater share of the resultant product.

This is not a doctrine which is anywhere spelt out. Rather what I am trying to do in the preceding paragraph is sketch what I think is the implicit background to a widely held principle of distributive justice in our society, which we can call the contribution principle. This is (at least partly) what lies behind the widely felt intuition that highly talented people ought to be paid more than the ordinary, that professions requiring high skill and training should be more highly remunerated, and in general that complete equality of income, or distribution according to need, would be wrong.

Of course, there are many other reasons why people oppose equality of income, one of the principal ones being the sense that it would dry up the stream of outstanding contributions. But I am trying to account for the intuition not just that such equality might be disastrous, but that it would be *unjust*, and this is based on what I have called the contribution principle. It matters not at all that in fact the task of applying the contribution principle with certainty, of assessing the real relative value of the contributions of doctors, lawyers, orchestra conductors, garbage collectors, welders, ship pilots, and so on, would be next to impossible; that any solution requires countless arbitrary stipulations. What matters here is that people have an intuition about relative values at least in 'obvious' cases (surgeons versus garbage collectors, for instance), and this alleged difference of contribution justifies differential remuneration.

If we take the underlying reasoning of the contribution principle, it is evident that some differentials are just on the principle of equal fulfilment, and it may even appear that equal payment would be a kind of denial of an 'inalienable' right, treating me as though my exceptional capacity were not my own, but in some way belonged to society. But I identify with this capacity, and feel expropriated in my being. (For a parallel type of reflection, see Nozick's discussion of the equivalence between taxation for transfer payments and forced labour.)

There is great strain in many Western societies between the drive for equality on one hand, and the sense of justified differentials which the contribution principle yields on the other. On one side it is felt that in a highly interdependent society, whose arrangements can be remade virtually at will (this sense of omnipotence is probably illusory, but that is another matter), that the less-favoured have a justified sense of grievance. On the other side, as the measures designed to redress these inequalities become more expensive (and they include more than transfer payments, but also programmes designed to develop regions, classes, as well as certain universal programmes), the middle classes, or in some cases the affluent in general see their aspiration to continually rising consumer standards being jeopardized. But the redistributive measures seem to be in favour of the less endowed and the less hard-working. And since our contribution is a joint function of capacity and effort, massive redistribution violates the contribution principle. The affluent now have a sense of justified grievance.

If we take these two perspectives alone, there is no reason why the tension should not build up almost indefinitely, until continued democratic politics become impossible. But Western society has managed to stave off any such reckoning in the post-war period by sustained rapid growth. Growth enabled them to meet the higher demands of public expenditure to redress the most politically pressing inequalities and provide certain services universally (the pressure for the latter type of programme came of course also from the middle classes), and at the same time to ensure rising consumer standards to the affluent. Now that continued growth is becoming more difficult, tensions are beginning to rise. Uruguay may provide a terrifying preview of the fate of many Western politics.

As the tension builds up, the sense of grievance on both sides increases, and the sense of society as having a legitimate claim on our allegiance, or making legitimate demands of social discipline, declines. From both sides, the 'system' comes to seem irrational and unjust. When the unskilled see how the doctors are able to command a large raise on already (to them) astronomical incomes, they conclude that the operative principle of distribution is according to blackmail power. This feeling is intensified when they discover the tax concessions that middle class and the self-employed can often take advantage of. But from the other perspective, these raises and these concessions are seen as an all-too-grudging recognition of superior contribution, enterprise and effort. On the contrary, from the standpoint of these privileged, their just differential is constantly being eroded by excessive taxation, because politicians succumb to the power of the mass vote.

So on both sides there grows the sense of being imposed on by sheer force, and the principles of justice invoked seem sham. This kind of belief is, of course, self-fulfilling, in that feeling the victims of force, people respond with force, and so on in a spiral. A reasoned debate about distributive justice becomes impossible.

This impossibility is all the greater if the sense of being imposed on by force finds expression in a coherent belief. For instance, the Marxist belief that capitalism systematically distorts and frustrates human potential, and that it can only live on exploitation, entails the view that there is no valid answer to the question, 'what is just?' without the purview of capitalist society. It is irremediably a domain of force. There is no point even discussing about the 'right' differentials; the whole system has to be brought down. From this point of view, no incomes policy can be the right one; but all have to be sabotaged.

2

How can a philosopher enter this debate? The justly famous work of John Rawls would seem to provide us with a paradigm example. And yet the drift of the above argument is that his theory is in a sense answering the wrong question. Or perhaps better, it is eliding two questions into one. Rawls is trying to establish for us *the* principles of justice, almost without heed to historical and cultural variations in the kinds of associations we form and goods we seek (at least among developed societies). But this is, I believe, based on a confusion. Rawls' two principles might be seen as the legitimate answer to *another* question, viz., what principles of distribution animate the truly good society?

If I can take the liberty of reading Rawls' very rich text through my own interpretive grid, I would see it as a powerful plea for a certain kind of society. Perhaps the fullest description of this society is to be found in section 79 of *A Theory of Justice*, where Rawls describes it as 'the social union of social unions'. If this Humboldtian vision were correct about the nature of our mutual involvement in society, and the kinds of common good we seek, then indeed, (a) equal liberty would be an essential background feature (and hence would have priority), and (b) we would be bound to accept the more far-reaching equality Rawls prescribes.

But a question arises about the relation of Rawls' two principles to our present societies. As I read it, Rawls' difference principle is, at least in intent, much more egalitarian than, say, present American practice. Specifically, it wants to set at naught what I have called above the 'contribution principle'. In a famous passage, Rawls argues that 'no-one deserves his greater natural capacity nor merits a more favourable starting place in society'.[11] Rather, 'the difference represents, ... an agreement to regard the distribution of natural talents as a common asset and to share in the benefits of this distribution whatever it turns out to be'.[12] This 'socialization' of our capacities is directly contrary to the view of man and society which underlies the contribution principle.

But the defender of the contribution standard could object that this

---

[11] *A Theory of Justice*, p. 102.   [12] *Ibid.*, p. 101.

difference principle is designed for a quite different world. He could deny that our actual society bears any relation to the vision of a social union of social unions, and protest that he was being asked to accept a principle of equality which would be apposite in a quite different environment. On my view, this objection raises a difficult question, one which cannot just be waved away.

Philosophical reflection ought to bring us to the point where we are able to come to grips with this question. One possible route to that end lies through a critique of currently accepted standards. Broadly speaking, we can identify four main families of views about distributive justice in our society. Starting from the 'right', they are: (1) a 'Lockean' atomism which focusses on the inalienable right to property; (2) the contribution principle; (3) the family of liberal and social-democratic views which justify egalitarian redistribution; and (4) Marxist views which refuse the issue of distributive justice altogether, on the grounds that the question is insoluble here, and unnecessary in a communist society. (Rawls' theory falls somewhere in (3).)

It is perhaps easiest to start with a critique of atomist views, both of the more radical form underlying (1), and of the more sophisticated type which is invoked in the more pugnacious affirmations of the contribution principle.

The basic error of atomism in all its forms is that it fails to take account of the degree to which the free individual with his own goals and aspirations, whose just rewards it is trying to protect, is himself only possible within a certain kind of civilization; that it took a long development of certain institutions and practices, of the rule of law, of rules of equal respect, of habits of common deliberation, of common association, of cultural self-development, and so on, to produce the modern individual; and that without these the very sense of oneself as an individual in the modern meaning of the term would atrophy.

Atomist thought tends to assume that the individual needs society, democratic institutions, the rule of law, only for the Lockean purpose of *protection*; the underlying idea being that my understanding of myself as an individual, my sense that I have my own aspirations to fulfil, my own pattern of life which I must freely choose, in short the self-definition of modern individualism, is something given. In a sense, if I look only at this instant of time, there is some truth in this; since the conditions of civilization which have helped to bring this about are already behind me. I have now developed the identity of an individual, and a fascist coup tomorrow would not deprive me of it, just of the liberty to act it out in full. Indeed, once this identity has developed it is hard to stamp it out, as modern tyrannical regimes have discovered.

But over time this identity would be reduced if the conditions that sustain it were to be suppressed. First by all the ways in which our sense of our own goals is nourished by free interchange with others and which would no longer be possible; second, by the loss of responsibility for the direction of public affairs, without which our moral reflection on these affairs would tend to lose the seriousness of deliberation over real options (although the story of Soviet dissidents shows how a minority will never lose this).

Under conditions of prolonged tyranny, individualism for the majority of the succeeding generations would become something quite different: a sense of one's private tastes, a world of relationships cut off from the public world, a great desire to be left alone by the powers, whoever they are. And even here one's tastes might be severely limited by the cultural proscriptions imposed by the powers.

For some atomists this might be sufficient as a sense of the individual; all that would be missing would be liberty to act it out. But if we follow the tradition of Montesquieu, Tocqueville, von Humboldt and J. S. Mill in seeing it as a truncated version of the aspiration to liberty, then something follows for the theory of justice. For we have not only to maintain these practices and institutions which *protect* liberty but also those which sustain the *sense* of liberty. For this is to accept the (social) perspective that the very potential for the good (here liberty) is bound up with a certain form of society.

To the extent that we think of ourselves as already formed by the past development of these institutions and practices, our obligation to maintain them springs from a principle of justice between generations, that the good we have received we should pass on.

This has an important effect on the principles of justice we will accept. If we think of the public institutions as just existing to protect liberty, they can consist with almost any degree of inequality, as we can see from Locke's theory. But if we think of these institutions as nourishing the sense of liberty, and in particular through interchange and common deliberation, then great inequalities are unacceptable. This point has been continually made in that branch of the modern liberal democratic tradition which was inspired by ancient republics; we can see it, for instance, in Montesquieu, Rousseau and Tocqueville.

If we see ourselves as engaged together in a society which not only defends liberty but also sustains the sense of liberty, then the two forms of argument of the social perspective become relevant. First a certain degree of equality is essential if people are to be *citizens* of the same state, and so this degree of equality becomes a background feature which any principle of distributive justice must conform to. And secondly, it can be argued that as citizens, maintaining together institutions of common deliberation, the balance of our mutual debt is much more equal than is that of our economic contribution.

Hence we can see that undermining the atomism which underpins the pure contribution principle also ends up at least severely limiting this principle. But does it do away with it altogether? Have we found in the conception of a society sustaining liberty the single source of a coherent set of criteria of distributive justice? If we think so, then we will argue for a highly egalitarian society. Indeed, it would be difficult to argue for any inequalities at all, except, for example, those which might be allowed by the difference principle, which are precisely such as do not cost anyone else anything. Or they might allow for inequalities of a non-economic sort: a just distribution of honour in a republic can never be egalitarian; indeed, honour equally bestowed (unlike respect) is not honour; and some people will arise who serve the society sustaining freedom in an outstanding way; these deserve honour. (These considerations are, of course, squarely in the ancient republican tradition.)

It would be tempting to argue in this way, particularly for those modern socialists who are nourished on the tradition I have just mentioned. But the protagonists of the contribution principle could protest that it was wrong, on exactly the grounds mentioned above, that it assumes a society we have not yet got.

Defenders of a mitigated contribution principle could argue that although we have indeed a society which aims to sustain liberty, this is not the only good we seek in society. We are not citizens of an ancient polis with our lives entirely focussed on Montesquieuian *vertu* or Hegelian *Sittlichkeit*. For us society is *also* valuable as a collaborative enterprise whereby the contribution of each can be multiplied through coordinated activity. Consequently, the atomist perspective is not just an error; it corresponds to one dimension of our social experience.

In other words, on this view, our contemporary society is such that it cannot be understood within the bounds of a single theory. It has aspects of the republic in it, sustaining liberty, as well as of the collaborative enterprise serving private purposes. This complexity, or plurality of focus, becomes the more evident when we reflect that the boundaries of society for one or another purpose are not necessarily the same, and are indeed perhaps not altogether clear.

As collaborators in an economy, we are linked together in one sense with virtually the whole human race, now that the world economy has penetrated virtually everywhere. That is why there are certain questions of distributive justice which arise internationally (as against the obvious issues of retributive justice, where restoration is due for plunder, rapine, conquest, spoliation, etc.). So that our obligations by the contribution principle may go beyond the boundaries of our political society.

By contrast it may be argued that in certain cases the community within which we sustain our sense of liberty, personality, individuality is smaller than our political society. This may be most palpably the case in multi-cultural societies. But an analogous point might even be made in homogeneous but large societies. At least it might be argued that the more intense or culturally vital relations of a local community give rise to more far-reaching obligations of distributive justice. For instance, the level of equality one can demand might be more far-reaching within a local community than between such communities.

What all this means is that we have to abandon the search for a single set of principles of distributive justice. On the contrary a modern society can be seen under different, mutually irreducible perspectives, and consequently can be judged by independent, mutually irreducible principles of distributive justice. Complexity is further compounded when we reflect that there is no single answer to the questions of the unit within which men owe each other distributive justice; that even within one model of society, there are different degrees of mutual involvement which create different degrees of mutual obligation. So that we may have to think both of justice between individuals, as well as between communities, and also perhaps within communities.

If this all means that there may be no such thing as *the* coherent set of principles of distributive justice for a modern society, we should not be distressed. The same plurality emerges in Aristotle's discussion of justice in *Politics* III and IV. Those who adopt a single exclusive principle, Aristotle says, 'speak of a part of justice only' (*meros ti tou dikaiou legousi*, 1281a10).

3

This need not reduce us to silence, but it means that there are no mathematical proofs about distributive justice. Rather the judgement of what is just in a particular society involves combining mutually irreducible principles in a weighting that is appropriate for the particular society, given its history, economy, degree of integration. It is hard to set out knock-down proofs of such judgements.

But some things can be said in general about Western societies. All or most are or aspire to be republican societies sustaining the sense of individual liberty and common deliberation; and at the same time all or most are also experienced by their members as collaborative enterprises for the furtherance of individual prosperity. The first aspect is the basis for a principle of equal sharing, the second for what I have called the contribution principle.[13]

Justice involves giving appropriate weight to both of these principles. And this means, on one hand, that we cannot envisage a society of completely equal shares, that is, one in which the contribution principle would have no place, unless we can alter our society very fundamentally in a socialist direction. And this means not just towards public ownership of the means of production, which could after all be introduced just as a more effective and/or fair way of encompassing everyone's (individual) prosperity (and this is how it is ending up in Eastern Europe, whose societies are no closer to equality of income than ours). It would mean a society in which the major good sought by the majority in engaging in economic activity was no longer individual prosperity, but, for example some public goal, or the intrinsic satisfaction of the work itself; or else a society where people's needs were few and limited, and where production for the means to life had no interest beyond a certain modest level of prosperity, but where all surplus energies were devoted to other things, that is, the kind of society of which the ancients talked and Rousseau dreamed. In such a society, people would seek a greater share of honour, or of public office (which Aristotle lists as the major goods about whose distribution justice is concerned), and would be less concerned with a greater share of income or wealth.

In short it would take some major institutional-cum-cultural change in our society, so that one of the major goods sought in common was not individual prosperity, for the contribution principle to cease to be a valid principle of distribution of income. Of course, strictly speaking, in any society which is inter alia an enterprise of economic collaboration, and

---

[13] This latter, incidentally, can be separated from its illusory atomist mode and can be put in a social perspective: that one of the goods sought in common is prosperity, and that in relation to this the balance of mutual indebtedness is not strictly reciprocal, but that some make bigger contributions than others, and thus *as far as this criterion is concerned* deserve greater shares.

that is any society outside of Arcadia, and in which the economic contributions are not equal, as they cannot be in an advanced, technological society, some form of the contribution principle is valid. But in some society which had undergone one of the cultural mutations referred to above, where individual prosperity was not the principal goal, signal contribution would entitle one to something other than greater income; for example, public honour, or more meaningful work, or perhaps greater leisure, or sabbatical leaves (the intellectual's dream).

But if the contribution principle seems irremovable prior to such a transformation, it remains generally true on the other hand that it is invoked in an obsessive and one-sided way in our societies. Because of the privatizing features of our culture mentioned above, atomist illusions continually arise; that is, there is a tendency to forget the ways in which we depend on society to be full human agents, and also to be capable of the contribution we are making. Taking account of these would require that the contribution principle be combined with other more egalitarian considerations.

One of these, mentioned above, is the requirement of what we can call for short a republican society, where a common citizenship requires a certain degree of equality, or to put it negatively, cannot consist with too great inequalities. This is the background condition. A second, also mentioned above, is the principle of distribution which arises out of our republican society, and in which the balance of mutual indebtedness is much more equal, except in so far as some who make a signal contribution to public life deserve special consideration.

4

What does all this tell us about the politics of distributive justice in our societies? There are in fact two major directions one can go in if one accepts the argument so far. The first is to take the principle of equality implicit in our society *qua* republican and seek to transform our society so that it can be integrally carried out. This means undertaking one of the transformations mentioned above. The Marxist vision of the classless society offers one such, but there are others, for example, the ideal of a commune life based on limited needs in some balance with nature. And there are more. In most cases the incentive to pursue these revolutionary changes is strengthened by the belief that the present structures are corrupt or distorted or contradictory to the point where there is no valid answer to the question of distributive justice as things stand. But in one way or another, the goal is held up of a society which would be beyond the contribution principle and which could thus be a fully equal society.

The other major road would be to accept that some version of a contribution principle society is here to stay, and concentrate rather on making the other considerations palpable enough to the society at large so that equalization measures will be readily accepted. This is the politics of the majority Left in a great many Western countries today.

Income differentials are thought to be justified to some degree by the contribution principle; and then alongside these equalization measures are taken: for instance, certain minima are assured to everyone in virtue of being members of a republican society, and measures are taken following the principle of redress/development to help poorer regions.

The difficulty is today that neither of these roads seems satisfactory. The first banks on a transformation of culture and aspirations which is too far-reaching to hope for. But the second runs into the fact that the two principles of modern societies, let us call them for short the contribution and the republican principles, are in great and increasing tension, as I discussed in the first section. The privatizing features of modern culture, which include greater mobility, the decline of traditional communities, the growth of megalopolies, the pressures of consumer society (itself partly a result of privatization), tend to give rise to an atomist consciousness, and make people less aware of or make them have less belief in the republican dimension of our society. The growth of large-scale, highly interdependent, bureaucratically run, big-city societies is exercising the destructive, alienating effect on our republican life which the writers of the tradition always predicted.

The result may be that the two principles will be pitched against each other, that is, they will cease to be recognized as necessarily complementary for our society; but each will be put forward exclusively and will see in the other a pure exercise of force (the blackmail power of those with indispensable skill on one hand, or the naked, levelling force of the mass vote on the other). Strangely enough, for this to happen we do not even need society to divide into two mutually exclusive groups. The astounding thing is how many people while being ambivalent, and invoking now one, now the other of the major principles, nevertheless interpret each in its exclusive, polemical form; for example, affluent workers indignant about 'welfare bums' (a real myth bred by the contribution principle, since studies show that the amount of cheating on the welfare system or on unemployment insurance is not that great) on one hand, and about the too great pay rises of doctors, or even other branches of skilled workers, or else various middle-class tax concessions, on the other. Societies can break up because people develop a general sense of being systematically 'ripped off', even if this is not based on a single consistent principle.

The result of this radical polarization would be a society in which atomist illusions would grow apace while feeding in the opposite camp unreal dreams of transformation to an equal society; while on both sides there is an overwhelming sense of living in a society where mere force, or political muscle, but not justice, makes the law. In this kind of society policies of true distributive justice become impossible politically, and they become above all unrecognizable as just by any of the parties. And indeed at a certain point in the decay of a republic into the rule of force or tyranny, the question may arise whether the very basis of any principle of distributive justice, which is association for the good, has not been undermined. Argentinians or Uruguayans may be asking this question today. I hope we will not be asking them tomorrow.

Here is where the rather academic-sounding distinction between questions I proposed above becomes highly relevant. Or to put the same point negatively, the costs of intellectual confusion may be high. As long as we see ourselves as concerned to find and defend *the* principles of distributive justice, both Left and Right are not only locked into a debate to which there is no satisfactory intellectual resolution (because it is cut off from the considerations about our real cultural and historical predicament which could resolve it); they are also engaged on a terrain which is bound to maximize frustration and resentment, as each is encouraged to experience every distributive defeat as a 'rip-off', a violation of fundamental right, a flouting of justice itself. Our present reading of things, which philosophy has generally endorsed, encourages ever-rising indignation on both sides of an issue unresolvable by rational discourse.

But if I am right, the real nature of the critique levelled by both Left and Right against our present society concerns as much if not more its failure to embody or allow for certain excellences of the good life, as it does its alleged unfairness. What is involved in each case is the project of a different society – one which will supposedly liberate the self-reliant individual in one case, or one which will realize greater solidarity and collective self-management on the other. To get this intellectually straight will not resolve the political tension; it will if anything show us more clearly how far apart we are. But I believe that this clarity can be very beneficial, if some political energy can be drained from displaced indignation at the adversary's alleged sins against justice, and directed instead at a defensible and persuasive definition of one's own project of society. Maybe the social climate will not be more serene, but at least we will be fighting over what matters, as we are forced to be clearer and franker about our ultimate allegiances.

Distinguishing the issues of distributive *fairness* from those of political *transformation* should bring the debate closer to reality on both. It would make us defend our views about the former in relation to our actual culture and history; and that will make it at least somewhat harder to espouse dogmatically one principle in utter blindness to the relative claims of the others. And with luck, it could greatly improve the discussion of the latter as well.

For perhaps some projects will not stand up all that well, once they are openly defined, as against being smuggled in under the mantle of doctrines about property or fair shares. I believe this to be true of some cherished doctrines of both Left and Right – for example, the various atomisms, or highly centralizing variants of socialism. They crumble under direct intellectual scrutiny. It would be truly liberating to clear this old lumber out of the way, and open the road to projects which were at once more imaginative and more realistic, particularly those which lie in the direction of decentralization and self-management. This might restore to contemporary society a credible horizon of hope. I am getting perilously close to a utopian dream, but we cannot even approach this condition unless we see that these issues take us beyond justice. And to this insight philosophy can contribute.

CHAPTER TWELVE

KANT'S THEORY OF FREEDOM

I

We live in an age of liberation movements. This is a sign of the degree to which freedom has become the central value of our culture. All sorts of demands are made from all sorts of quarters in the name of liberty. People seek recognition, equality, justice, but all as corollaries of 'liberation'. This is something which has evolved in our civilization over the last three centuries. The process has been punctuated, and partly shaped, by paradigm statements by major thinkers, although it has amounted to much more than these: the movement of a whole culture. Among these statements, Kant's has been very important. It marked a crucial step on the way.

It would help to place Kant's theory of freedom in relation to other conceptions which developed before him. And for this purpose, I want to engage in some very schematic intellectual history, and contrast an influential ancient notion of freedom with a family of modern ones, following Benjamin Constant's *De la liberté des anciens, comparée avec celle des modernes.*

A notion of freedom quite common in the ancient world saw it as consisting in the status of the citizen. The citizen was free in one sense by contrast to the slave in that he was not servile; and in another sense in contrast to the metic or disfranchised, in that he could act as a citizen. Freedom, on this view, consisted in a certain place within society.

There are three features of this conception which contrast with modern ones. First, it only makes sense to ask whether people are free or unfree within society. The political matrix must exist before people can either enjoy freedom or fail to have it. Second, it is considered quite normal that not all men have freedom. It is a privilege that only certain people can attain, for example, Hellenes as against barbarians; in some views, aristocrats as against commoners; always men as against women. And third, this is a conception of political freedom, relatively unconnected to a metaphysical theory about what freedom consists in, or about human freedom as such.

The modern views which arose in the seventeenth century contrast with this ancient one on all these heads. They emerged out of a rejection of various earlier conceptions of the cosmic order in which men were thought to be placed. Man is a free being in the sense that he is meant by God to find his paradigm purposes within himself, and not out of the order in which he is set. Hence, in the political realm, human freedom is prior to legitimate order, in that legitimate authority can arise only as the creation of human agents through consent. Freedom is part of the natural condition of man, the 'state of nature'; political structures come later.

So the modern views represent a rejection of all three features of the influential ancient view. It does make sense to speak of freedom outside of all social contexts; indeed, that is the place of 'natural liberty'. This kind of freedom belongs to man as such, it is not the appanage of some classes or nations. And modern conceptions are linked with metaphysical views about the nature of man.

There were, of course, several variants of this modern approach. I should like to single out two. One, for which Locke could stand as the representative figure, associates this freedom with law. Men are free only as rational beings, and that means in so far as they recognize natural law. So, in a sense, freedom requires that men recognize themselves as part of some order; only now it is no longer a political one. It is a moral order, and freedom cannot be separated from morality.

According to the second view, of which Hobbes is the most famous early proponent, freedom has nothing to do with law. Freedom can be characterized purely naturalistically. A man is free when there are no obstacles in his path. In the strict sense, we should take account only of physical obstacles, so that you are free if you can in fact move. But Hobbes recognizes an extended sense, in which we can speak also of freedom as the absence of legal prohibitions ('the silence of the law').

This unhooking of freedom from any link with the idea of a moral order went along also with a new view of morality, initiated by Hobbes and developed by his utilitarian successors, according to which good and bad conduct are no longer distinguished by the qualities of the motivation which inspires each. There is only one kind of motive recognized as lying behind all human action: a kind of self-love. It produces good or ill, depending on how it is canalized by training or reason. Virtue and vice no longer have a proper place in moral vocabulary, at least in so far as they are meant to distinguish qualities of the will.

This naturalistic variant could be seen as a more radical notion of freedom than its natural law cousin; that is, as offering in more uncompromising form what all modern views see as essential to freedom, that is, that men determine their purposes out of themselves, unconstrained by external demands or hindrances. For it allows no limits on what a man may legitimately want, on the desires the unconstrained fulfilment of which represents freedom. Whereas a doctrine linking freedom to morality cannot allow that we are truly free when we are in violation of natural law, when we 'quit reason', in Locke's phrase.[1] And this uncompromising stand on freedom has been part of the appeal of the naturalistic doctrine then and now. We see in the eighteenth-century Enlightenment a growing movement of thought against paternalism, the claim on the part of governments or other authorities to determine for their charges what the good life was for them, or in what their happiness truly consisted. On the contrary, argues Bentham, each man is best judge of his own interests. The naturalistic view, according to which there are just desires, and no higher moral impulses about which the ordinary man could be mistaken, seemed a safer bulwark for this radical endorsement of individual choice than any moral theory of true freedom distinguished from licence. And so it does to many people today.

It was Rousseau who turned the tables on the naturalistic theory. He rehabilitates the distinction between virtue and vice. The quality of the will is once more relevant to ethics. But this in no sense places limits on freedom. On the contrary, virtue and vice themselves are given a new interpretation in terms of freedom. For the key to vice is other-dependence, a failure to be determined by one's own internal purposes; and virtue is nothing other than the recovery of this self-determination. Morality is criterial for freedom. But that is no restriction, because morality is itself defined in terms of freedom. To be virtuous is to be able to listen to the inner voice of nature, to be dependent on oneself.

It was with Rousseau that the important feature of modern culture which was my starting point emerges. Freedom becomes the central value. It becomes the central concept of morality, in that all other ethical goals are expressed in terms of it, and are explicated by it. And thus, in linking freedom again with morality, Rousseau appeared to be offering an even more radical view of freedom than the naturalistic Enlightenment. I mean 'radical' in the same sense as above, that is, offering a more uncompromising form of the same basic conception of

---

[1] *Second Treatise of Civil Government*, XV. 172. See also IV. 22.

freedom as self-determination. For what was the acme of freedom on the naturalistic construal, carrying out my desires unhindered, could now be represented as a kind of slavery, in so far as these desires are themselves the fruit of other-dependence. To be really self-determining I must recover contact with my own authentic self, with the voice within, which is also the voice of conscience.

The extraordinary power of Rousseau's theory comes partly from the fact that he recovers this link between freedom and moral order, in the context of what nevertheless appears as a more radical notion of freedom. And not only the moral order; he also recovers the links with the ancient view of republican freedom. The doctrine of the *Social Contract* shows us as being truly free only within a citizen republic. And yet here, too, Rousseau manages to reconcile this somehow with the modern ideal of freedom, through his notion of the general will, or the 'common self' (*moi commun*). Whether this whole doctrine is ultimately consistent or not is a moot point, but its power clearly comes from what it synthesizes, even illegitimately.

Kant follows Rousseau in offering another theory of freedom as reconnected to morality, and just for that reason as putatively more radical than the naturalistic Enlightenment. But what is still relatively implicit in Rousseau is worked out in a clear philosophical doctrine by Kant.

The centre-piece of Kant's doctrine is the notion of rationality. The error of the naturalistic Enlightenment for Kant is that it sees rationality as having a purely instrumental role. Reason is, and ought to be, the slave of the passions, as Hume put it. Our goals are set by nature, or by conditioning. In either case, they are beyond rational criticism. The office of reason is to determine how to achieve these goals. A plan can be thought of as deficient in rationality if it is insensitive to the available information relevant to the attainment of our goals. But unless the goal is given, plans can be neither rational nor irrational.

Kant utterly rejects this doctrine. He concurs with Rousseau in holding that if reason were merely instrumental it would be of little value. Its real function is to set our ends:

Reason is not, however, competent to guide the will safely with regard to its objects and the satisfaction of all our needs (which it in part multiplies), and to this end an innate instinct would have led with far more certainty. But reason is given to us as a practical faculty, i.e., one which is meant to have an influence on the will.[2]

---

[2] *Foundations of the Metaphysics of Morals*, p. 396. I have quoted from the Lewis White Beck translation (Indianapolis, 1969). But page references are to the Berlin Academy edition, usually given in the margin or in square brackets in translations of this work.

But how can reason be practical in Kant's sense, that is, determine our ends? Kant holds that our instinctive moral reactions already have an inkling of this. We distinguish actions which we do from duty from those to which we are merely inclined. But, Kant argues, the distinction cannot repose on a difference in the outcome sought in the two cases. For, given any outcome which we might qualify as good, we can imagine it being sought by one man out of duty, and by another for some interested motive. The morality of an action cannot therefore reside in its having a certain intended outcome, but rather in the quality of the motivation which inspires it.

But what is this feature of motivation, which cannot be equated with any particular class of intended outcome? It must be, says Kant, purely formal, where this word at first simply means: not determined by the content of the act. The formal feature which is the essence of moral motivation turns out to be this: that I will above all that the intention with which I act ('the maxim of my action', in Kant's phrase) be selected by the canons of reason. Thus, when I act morally, what is of ultimate importance is not the particular outcome sought, but the fact that willing an act with this outcome conforms to the canons of reason in this predicament.

We could put the thesis this way: acting morally is acting with a certain goal, that of conforming my will to reason. But this is not a goal like any other, which could be identified with a certain class of external outcomes of action. Rather we have to think of it as a formal goal. I act morally only when this formal goal is what moves me to action. If it is merely the outcome itself which moves me, then I am acting simply out of desire, not out of duty.

Thus we can see what it is for reason to determine our ends, or for reason to be practical. It sets our ends when it *is* our highest end, when willing rationally is what we above all seek.

Why should this be thought to be the essence of morality? Partly because of the link Kant sees between rationality and law. Acting morally is acting according to (the moral) law. But this notion of law unites two features. To act according to law is to act under obligation, to act as you ought. But it is also to act under obligation which does not just bind you, but which binds agents generally. Laws are by their nature general. Now the link between obligation and generality, which the notion of law involves, is assured by rationality. In so far as obligation is for a reason, then not just I am obliged, but any agent in like circumstances is.[3] An

---

[3] This connection has been clearly established again in contemporary moral philosophy, notably in the work of Richard Hare. See *The Language of Morals* (Oxford, 1952), and *Freedom and Reason* (Oxford, 1963).

agent who is obligated by laws is therefore an agent who is bound by reasons, that means a rational agent. So in so far as we see being morally obligated as equivalent to being obligated by law, we are recognizing an essential link between morality and rationality. Morality is addressed to the rational agent.

This means that it is at least a necessary condition of any moral obligation that it be based on a reason; and it is an essential feature of a reason that it be valid for everyone, for all rational creatures alike. That is the basis of the first form of Kant's categorical imperative: that I should act only according to a maxim which I could at the same time will as a universal law. For if I am *right* to will something, then everyone is right to will it, and it must thus be something that could be willed for everybody.

But although we might easily accept that it is a necessary condition of any command being moral that it be rational, we might still not accept that rationality is the basis of morality. The insight which led Kant to make this stronger claim is something of this kind. Moral ends are higher ends. To be aware of moral demands is to be aware of ends of my action which are not on the same level as my ordinary goals, those which are mine in virtue of the bent of my desires, or the choices I have made. These ends are unconditionally valid for me, and in this they have a higher status. They command respect.

Now what could be the source of this higher status? What could command respect in this way? In particular, what could lay such demands of respect on a rational agent? For Kant, the answer to this question can only be: his own rationality.

First, Kant holds that rationality does lay such demands. This is because rationality is something unique in the world. It transcends nature. 'Everything in nature works according to laws. Only a rational being has the capacity of acting according to the conception of laws, i.e., according to principles.'[4] We could put it that everything else in nature conforms to law blindly. Only rational creatures conform to laws that they themselves formulate. This is something incomparably higher. It follows that a rational agent ought to determine his own action in this way. If he slips away from this, if he becomes simply another being merely conforming to natural law, then he is living below his status, he is acting in a way which is unworthy of what he is as rational agent. And this is what he would be doing if he acted merely out of desire. For our desires are determined in us by purely natural processes. It is only when our

---

[4] *Foundations*, p. 412.

actions are rationally determined, when we act out of principles, that we are living up to our true status.

Rationality thus imposes obligations on us. Being rational agents, that is possessing a capacity so much higher than nature, puts us under an obligation to live up to this status. We could say that the fundamental principle underlying Kant's whole ethical theory is something of this form: live up to what you really are – rational agents. Because it is something higher, rationality commands our respect. That is why we experience the moral commands as higher than the demands of nature. We recognize that the moral law is something that commands our respect (*Achtung*).

That rationality transcends nature enables Kant to establish another way of providing content for his fundamental moral principle to supplement the universalizability criterion mentioned above. Any thing we desire, or end we seek, can be said to have worth. But its worth is conditional on our desiring or seeking it. One and only one thing, how-ever, has an unconditional, or absolute worth. That is rational agency. This encompasses a set of ends to be fulfilled regardless of whether they are in fact sought by men or neglected by them. The ends of rationality retain their validity regardless. 'Rational nature exists as an end in itself.'[5]

But this means that rational agents enjoy a special status. Everything else in the universe can be treated as a mere means to our goals, whatever they are. For these other things have no unconditional worth. They have worth only as means, and hence we are right to treat them as such. But

man, and, in general, every rational being exists as an end in himself and not merely as a means to be arbitrarily used by this or that will. In all his actions, whether they are directed to himself or to other rational beings, he must always be regarded at the same time as an end.[6]

Beings of absolute worth, in other words, have their own intrinsic ends, and they lay the demand on us that we treat them with these ends in view, and not just in the light of extraneous ends that they might serve. Or as Kant puts it later, other things have a price, but only rational agents have dignity.[7]

So rationality lays demands on us. But, Kant holds, *only* rationality can lay such demands on us. Rational agents, as being obligated by their own rationality, cannot be obligated by anything else in the universe. They are called on to live up to their status as rational; and that means to direct

---

[5] *Ibid.*, p. 429.   [6] *Ibid.*, p. 428.   [7] *Ibid.*, p. 434.

themselves by principles, that is, by laws that they formulate themselves, that they find rational. But the nature of this demand is that they cannot be guided by anything but their own rationality. The moral law is thus essentially a law we give to ourselves. It cannot be, properly speaking, the moral law if it is imposed on us from outside.

In Kant's term, the moral will is necessarily autonomous. The law it follows is its own, what reason and reason alone has dictated to it. And so Kant, like Rousseau, makes freedom central to morality. Being good and being really free are one and the same. It is impossible to state what morality really consists in without making clear that it consists in freedom. So while morality is central to freedom, this involves no limitation of our possible freedom, because moral life *is* essentially freedom. Kant has established the basic Rousseauian equation, but he has done so by means of his concept of rationality, a notion of rationality as practical. We are good when reason is sovereign, and hence when we as rational beings are free.

And, as with Rousseau, this presents itself as a more radical doctrine of freedom than the naturalist one. In following unhindered desire, I am more free as an agent of inclination. But as a rational agent, I am still fettered. As long as inclination determines my actions, I have not really determined them out of myself. This I do only when what I really am, that is reason, becomes practical; when the principles I formulate are decisive. Now I have a truly exalted freedom, in which I break loose from what is merely given by nature, including the brute facts of my inclinations, and direct my life by principles which I generate myself.

The Kantian appeal to a more radical freedom has been powerful because it seems to offer a prospect of pure self-activity, where my action is determined not by the merely given, the facts of nature (including inner nature), but ultimately by my own agency as a formulator of rational law. This is at the point of origin of one of the most influential streams of modern thought, developing through Fichte, Hegel and Marx, which refuses to accept the merely 'positive', what history, or tradition, or nature offers us as a guide to value and action, and insists instead on autonomous generation of the forms we live by out of our own self-activity. There is an aspiration here to total liberation, which Kant helped to awaken and define for the modern world.

II

Kant's notion of freedom is recognizably that of a modern. It is concerned with self-determination. Freedom is a property of, and hence a demand on, all men, indeed on all rational agents, whether human or not. And his conception is linked to a metaphysical theory of what man is.

But, like Rousseau, Kant essentially integrates the free subject into the community of men. The Hobbesian subject does not need other men to be free. On the contrary, he would be most securely free alone. Rousseau's proto-man in his state of nature can also exist alone. But he is not yet fully human, and hence not free in the human sense. For that he needs others.

Kant follows Rousseau in this, and once more offers a clearer doctrine. If to be free is to follow the moral law, and to act morally is to see that the maxim of my action could be willed universally, then freedom requires that I understand myself as a human among other humans. I have to understand myself as standing under a law that applies as well to others, one that is not addressed to me alone, but to rational subjects as such.

So being free is standing in a certain kind of moral order; although once again this is no limitation on my freedom, because being related to this order is integral to freedom. Kant gives a name to this moral order: the 'kingdom of ends' (*das Reich der Zwecke*). Kant speaks of this as 'a systematic union of rational beings through common objective laws'.[8] It is the ideal of a society of rational agents whose common life is shaped only by those goals which rationality allows. We can think of it as 'a whole of all ends in systematic connection, a whole of rational beings as ends in themselves as well as of the particular ends which each may set for himself'.[9] The ends form a coherent set, directing the common life in a harmonious way. This ideal offers another route whereby we can work out just what morality demands of us.

But this order is, of course, not yet realized. It is an ideal. Nevertheless, being free is recognizing that this is our ideal, and hence that we belong in an order with all other human beings.

And, as with Rousseau, this principle is obviously decisive for Kant's doctrine of political freedom. But not at all in the same way as with Rousseau. One might be tempted to take the kingdom of ends as a *political* ideal, the formula for the perfect political society. And in this we would be helped by the obvious echoes of the *Social Contract* which recur in Kant's account of the kingdom of ends in the *Foundations*:

A rational being belongs to the kingdom of ends as a member when he gives universal laws in it while also himself subject to these laws. He belongs to it as sovereign when he, as legislating, is subject to the will of no other.[10]

---

[8] *Ibid.*, p. 433.   [9] *Ibid.*   [10] *Ibid.*, pp. 433–4.

But Kant precludes this by marking a sharp distinction between the moral and the political realms. The political is a realm not only of law, but of law coercively applied. But the essence of the moral is in the quality of the motivation. It is not the outcome that makes an act moral, but the motivating ground. And what makes an act moral also makes it free.

Now what cannot be coercively enforced is the quality of motivation. I can be forced to comply with rules of behaviour, but not forced so to comply out of the right motive. Indeed, force will be effective in bringing about my compliance only if I act out of an amoral motive, i.e. fear of punishment. Hence the moral condition of men is beyond the scope of politics. Political society cannot take as one of its goals making men become moral beings.

Not only is this goal impossible, it is highly dangerous to try to achieve it. The result would be a suppression of freedom that would be potentially unlimited just because its goal would continually elude it. Thus Kant:

For [a political community] to coerce its citizens to enter an ethical community with each other would be a contradiction in terms, for the latter involves in its very concept freedom from coercion.

And he adds below:

But woe to the legislator who would wish to bring about through coercion a constitution directed to ethical ends. For he would not only bring about the exact opposite of his ethical goals, but also undermine his political goals and render them insecure.[11]

At times Kant can sound almost Augustinian in his insistence that the moral and spiritual salvation of man is beyond the reach of the earthly city's legislation, which can deal only with external compliance.

But if the notion of a moral order inseparable from freedom is not of direct relevance to his political theory in setting a goal for legislation, it nevertheless does determine the very foundations of this theory, in two related ways.

First, it means that living in a political society is a moral obligation for men. It may seem strange that being a member of political society should be a moral obligation when it cannot in turn aim to improve us morally. But there is no contradiction. Political society, by regulating external conduct, does keep the peace between men, and can establish justice; and all this we are plainly obligated to further.

But political society is more directly relevant than that to our moral

---

[11] *Religion within the Limits of Reason Alone*, Berlin Academy Edition, vol. VI, pp. 95–6.

life. In entering this society we put ourselves under law. This does not mean only that we are now under constraint to conform our actions to certain standards. It also means that we recognize, in accepting membership, that we stand together under law. Moreover, this is not just a recognition that each makes on his own. Being in society, under common rules, represents a common recognition of our common subjection to law. The recognition is in public space, as it were.

But this kind of common recognition is essential to the kingdom of ends. This entails not just that *each* of us recognize that he stands as a human among humans, something we each severally have to do to be moral agents at all, that is recognizing that we are under the same law. It also entails that we recognize this *together*, that this law is what coordinates our lives, and shapes the public life of our society. For the goal of morality, the demand that rationality puts on us, is obviously not just that each of us be moral on his/her own, but that we be moral beings together. Rational demands are universal, and they thus require universal recognition.

So entering civil society, in its aspect of recognizing our allegiance to a common law, is not just binding on us because of what it is conducive to instrumentally, for example peace and justice. It is also constitutive of moral agency. It involves acknowledging what we cannot be moral agents without acknowledging; that is, our common law. To want to stand outside is to refuse to enter into the moral order altogether. That is why this obligation – to join, and once in, to obey – is, among all our political duties, the most unconditional.

Of course, none of Kant's ethical injunctions is consequentialist, in the sense that an act would be binding on us just in virtue of its consequences. Kant's theory is thoroughly deontological; indeed, it is the paradigm case of a deontological theory. But that does not exclude the possibility that consideration of the consequences can play a role in determining what is right. We may have to determine the consequences of everyone's doing a certain act in order to see that we cannot will it universally. This would be the case, for instance, of an obligation to join/obey a polity because the consequences of all refraining from this would be war and injustice.

But Kant's injunction that we join/obey the polity is not consequential even in this limited sense. The universal recognition of law is not just *conducive* to something we are obliged to bring about. It is *constitutive* of it.

Thus Kant argues that, though experience teaches that men tend to act in a violent and malevolent manner, nevertheless it is not experience or any kind of factual knowledge which makes public legal co-ercion necessary. On the contrary, even if we imagine men to be as benevolent and law-abiding as we please, the *a priori* rational idea of a non-lawful state will still tell us that before a public and legal state is established, individual men, peoples and states will never be secure against acts of violence from one another, since each will have his own right to do *what seems right and good to him,* indepen-dently of the opinion of others. Thus the first decision the individual is obliged to make, if he does not wish to renounce all concepts of right, will be to adopt the principle that one must abandon the state of nature in which everyone follows his own desires, and unite with everyone else (with whom he cannot avoid having intercourse) in order to submit to external, public and lawful coercion. He must accordingly enter into a state wherein that which is to be recognized as belonging to each person is allotted to him *by law* and guaranteed to him by an adequate power ... In other words, he should at all costs enter into a state of civil society.[12]

The unconditionality of this demand is expressed in the clause: 'if he does not wish to renounce all concepts of right'. What this clause conveys is that entering civil society is equivalent to recognizing the moral order. Kant sees the leaving of the state of nature in the way that Rousseau did as the step (of course a purely notional step, not an historical one) whereby man becomes human and acquires a moral dimension. That is why the properly moral properties, for example rights and duties, apply only within society. Hence possession becomes lawful property only when men stand under law together.

And that is why freedom, in the properly human sense, applies only to man within society. Kant amends the canonical account of the contract, whereby we give up some of our natural liberty in order to preserve the rest more securely:

By this contract, all members of the people ... give up their external freedom in order to receive it back at once as members of a commonwealth ... And we cannot say that men within a state have sacrificed a *part* of their inborn external freedom for a specific purpose; they have in fact completely abandoned their wild and law-less freedom, in order to find again their entire and undiminished freedom in a state of lawful dependence ...[13]

Freedom for humans, as against the 'wild and lawless' freedom of animals, is essentially within a moral order; and this in turn is constituted by a common recognition which is essentially brought about in a political order.

[12] *The Metaphysics of Morals,* as translated in Hans Reiss (ed.), *Kant's Political Writings* (Cambridge, 1970), p. 137.
[13] *Ibid.,* p. 140, original emphasis.

That is why Kant, although far from indifferent between various forms of political order, and although he could derive from his own principles a justification of a republican polity – as we shall see – nevertheless sternly set his face against any revolutionary action against an established order, even directed against a bad order in the name of a much better one. This injunction was not a prudential one for Kant, though he may also have believed that on balance revolutions produced terrible consequences. (He managed to justify the French Revolution, but that was by rather ingenious special pleading.)[14] Rather the reasons lay in the nature of the act.

To rebel against established authority was not just to challenge some power-holders, but also to destroy the common law under which we stand. It involves reversing the step we took in the social contract, and refusing once again the moral order. 'Revolution under an already existing constitution means the destruction of all relationships governed by civil right, and thus of right altogether.'[15] That is why it can never be justified. It runs against the very principles of right.

We have no right to resist 'even what is apparently the most intolerable abuse of supreme power',[16] and even to call its authority into question can be punishable. The fundamental law can be thought of as divine.

A law which is so sacred (i.e. inviolable) that it is practically a crime even to cast doubt upon it and thus to suspend its effectiveness for even an instant, cannot be thought of as coming from human beings, but some infallible supreme legislator. This is what is meant by the saying that 'all authority comes from God', which is not a *historical derivation* of the civil constitution, but an idea expressed as a practical principle of reason, requiring men to obey the legislative authority now in power, irrespective of its origin.[17]

This passage may seem pretty hard to swallow, and may even be very puzzling to us, coming from the pen of one of the great apostles of freedom and reason in the age of the Enlightenment, who even defined enlightenment in terms of the ability to use one's own understanding without the guidance of another.[18] But Kant is not reversing himself here. This idea of reason is the very cornerstone of morality, the recognition of common law. That is what gives it virtual divine status. It does not enjoy this status at the expense of freedom, but rather as constitutive of it.

---

[14] *Ibid.*, p. 164.   [15] *Ibid.*, p. 162.   [16] *Ibid.*, p. 145.   [17] *Ibid.*, p. 143.
[18] *What is Enlightenment?*, translated in Reiss, *Kant's Political Writings*, pp. 54–60.

III

For this uncompromising refusal of the right of rebellion did not prevent Kant from judging the relative value of different political orders, and from opting for a republican polity as the one most consonant with the idea of law. In fact, the Kantian idea of moral order not only enjoins us to belong to a polity, but also provides the basis for determining what an adequate one would be like. This is the second way in which it shapes Kant's political theory.

The basic moral point of political society is that we stand under commonly recognized law. Law is the common standard of right which holds between us. The law tells us what we can do and what we cannot. It draws the boundaries of our external freedom. And the aim is to draw these boundaries in such a way as to realize our moral freedom, as legislators. This means that they have to be drawn in such a way as to harmonize the external freedoms of the participants according to general principles. Thus we get the formula: 'Right [translating Recht, i.e. the institution of law as such] is the restriction of each individual's freedom so that it harmonizes with the freedom of everybody else (in so far as this is possible within the terms of a general law).'[19]

The basic point of politics is freedom: the regulation of external freedom, in a way consonant with morality, and therefore inner freedom. Not that political structures can hope to realize this latter. That is quite ruled out, as we saw above, since law can never direct motives, and we must never try. But the political structures will come closer to the idea of law if they organize external freedom in keeping with the basic principle of this idea, that of a moral order of free beings.

This then is the yardstick by which to judge political structures, and not happiness. Kant expresses his fundamental opposition to utilitarian theories. To judge the value of political orders or of policies on utilitarian grounds is to miss the entire point. Of course, a policy which produces happiness is *pro tanto* better than one which does not; but this can never provide the standard of right. The rejection of utilitarian criteria must follow, Kant thinks, from his basic insight.

Human beings are rational agents. As such, what they must be accorded above all is the respect of being treated as ends and and not just as means.

---

[19] *Theory and Practice* (short title of Kant's article 'On the common saying: "This may be true in theory, but it does not apply in practice"'), translated in Reiss, *Kant's Political Writings*, p. 73.

We treat them with respect because they are ends in themselves or, otherwise put, they are the points of origin of ends. But to respect a being as an originator of ends is above all to respect his freedom of action. Now this is a demand laid on us by all rational agents. And so we have an obligation to respect all their freedom of action, i.e. to respect the freedom of each compatibility with that of all the others.

So we can show that politics is concerned with the regulating of freedom according to principles. But we can also show that it ought not to be concerned with anything else. If our goal is to respect the freedom of originators of ends, then the only ground on which we can restrict the freedom of one such agent in our attempt at reconciliation is to harmonize it with the freedom of others. Happiness cannot be a justification of such restrictions. No one else's happiness can be, because to overrule his own goals in the name of those of someone else would be to use him as a means. And his own happiness cannot be, because to restrict him for his own utility would be to determine for him in what his happiness consists. This would be an unacceptable paternalism, one that would constitute a rejection of his status as a free rational agent.

Kant thus rejects a utilitarian criterion of right, partly on the very ground that utilitarians often used to justify their theory against earlier moral views: that in making each man the best judge of his own happiness, they were overthrowing the paternalism of earlier authoritarian societies. Kant pays them back in their own coin, arguing that to justify laws restricting an agent's actions on the grounds of happiness is using him for someone else's good; or else, if the alleged goal is his own happiness, telling him what his own fulfilment ought to be. The only way really to avoid paternalism for Kant is to allow happiness only as a determinant of each individual's plan of action, but exclude it utterly from the realm of political justification.

Political authority is concerned with allowing equal freedom to all agents to seek happiness in their own way, but can never presume to judge whose plan of life is right.

The state intervenes to protect the right of one against the other; and to protect the whole system of rights against exernal threat. Government may, indeed, act for the prosperity of the society. But the goal here should not be to make the people happy, but to secure the state. A certain amount of prosperity may be necessary for 'strength and stability both internally and against external enemies'. But 'the aim is not . . . to make the people happy against its will, but only to ensure its continued existence as a commonwealth'.[20]

[20] *Ibid.*, p. 80.

Whether this distinction between policies aimed at stability and those aimed at happiness can really be sustained is, of course, a moot point. But Kant's intention is clear: the end of politics is the regulation of freedom. This is itself the ground for the existence and preservation of the state.

The principle allows us to trace the lineaments of a good polity, one which would conform as fully as is possible to the idea of law. Kant gives an outline of the proper civil state in his *Theory and Practice* article. He enunciates three principles:

1. The *freedom* of every member of society as a *human being*.
2. The *equality* of each with all the others as a *subject*.
3. The *independence* of each member of a commonwealth as a *citizen*.[21]

The first point expresses Kant's opposition to paternalism. The principle of the state must be freedom, the recognition of everyone's liberty as a human being.

No one can compel me to be happy in accordance with his conception of the welfare of others, for each may seek happiness in whatever way he sees fit, so long as he does not infringe upon the freedom of others to pursue a similar end which can be reconciled with the freedom of everyone else within a workable general law.[22]

A government established on the principle of benevolence, of making people happy, tends towards a condition where subjects are treated 'as immature children who cannot distinguish what is truly useful or harmful to themselves'. A government of this kind 'is the greatest conceivable despotism'.[23]

The second point asserts the equality of all before the law. This is implicit in the principle that we are all subject to one common coercive law. This law is truly impartial between agents; and therefore no one has rights of coercion over others which are not symmetrical with their rights over him, except where he is acting in an official capacity. The head of state can, of course, command us where we cannot command him; but he has this power as the executor of the public law. In their personal capacity, citizens enjoy perfectly symmetrical rights of coercion relative to each other.

Kant believes that this principle rules out as inconsistent with the principles of right any hereditary privilege of rank. Inequalities of wealth or possessions are permissible, because they can be earned by talent and hard work. They are in principle anyone's; everyone can make a bid for

---

[21] *Ibid.*, p. 74, original emphasis.   [22] *Ibid.*   [23] *Ibid.*

them. But the institution of hereditary rank ties certain powers to certain individuals by birth, and prevents others from ever acceding to a similar status. This would violate the principle of equality. No man of privilege may

prevent his subordinates from raising themselves to his own level if they are able and entitled to do so by their talent, industry and good fortune. If this were not so, he would be allowed to practise coercion without himself being subject to coercive counter-measures from others, and would thus be more than their fellow-subject.[24]

The third principle concerns the status of the person as citizen. Kant speaks of this as 'independence', following a basic notion of Rousseau. In so far as we live by a law which we give to ourselves, we are dependent on no other will, but only on ourselves.

The principle flows as well from the idea of a coercive law which is an expression of a moral order. If the subjects are truly to recognize this law as binding on them, then they must give it to themselves.

As Kant puts the point, the public law defines what is just and unjust. It ought not, therefore, to be possible for it to do injustice to anyone itself. But the only way to rule this out is for the law to emanate from the entire people, since 'only towards oneself can one never act unjustly'.[25]

The influence of Rousseau is evident here. But there is also a vital difference. It is not just that Kant seems to see some difficulty in the integral fulfilment of this third requirement, greater even than the other two. A true citizen must be his own master, which means in Kant's view that he must have some property, or at least skill, to support himself. For otherwise his independence will be a sham. Consequently, domestic servants or proletarians cannot be given the franchise. Universal citizenship thus seems to be a difficult goal to achieve. It appears from this passage, however, that Kant sees it as a condition which we ought to approach to through the maximum diffusion of property. He seems to be counting on a process whereby the estates of large feudal landowners will be sold or divided by inheritance 'and thus made useful to more people'.[26]

But – and this is perhaps even more important – Kant does not share Rousseau's commitment to civic humanism, his love of republican institutions as the privileged *locus* of the good life. The value of universal citizenship for Kant is that it approaches the idea of law. But the life of a citizen is not itself the good life. This is because of the most basic principle

---

[24] *Ibid.*, p. 76.   [25] *Ibid.*, p. 77.   [26] *Ibid.*, p. 78.

of Kant's ethical theory, which prevents us from ever equating any pattern of action whatever with morality. This is always a matter of inner motive. No way of life can ever be a sufficient condition of moral goodness, for even the most beneficent actions can be done from interested motives; in which case they are morally worthless.

But the central notion of civic humanism is that men find the good in the public life of a citizen republic. In the definition of this ideal, action and motive are inextricably intertwined. This is utterly incompatible with Kantian dualism. This is one terrain on which Kant could not follow Rousseau, admire him as he might.

IV

But although no civic humanist, Kant was plainly a believer in a liberal republic, guaranteeing negative liberty, dispensing justice equally, without hereditary privilege, and with an ever-widening franchise. We need only to add to this picture an international comity of such republics to complete the sketch of Kant's political vision.

There may be no inconsistency in a strict sense, but many have felt the strain between this political vision on the one hand, and Kant's stern assertion of the duty of obedience on the other. In an age of despotism, privilege and war, how could one be true to the vision without being a revolutionary? This question is a very natural one for us to pose, who are heirs to many revolutions.

It must be said, of course, that Kant was a strong supporter of the French revolutionary cause, even though he had to square this with his theory by some special pleading which avoided classing it as a revolution. But his opposition to rebellion was none the less seriously meant. And he did not see the conflict which looms so large to us.

This conflict was avoided – or the opposition was mediated – in Kant's outlook by two things. The first was his theory of history. Kant saw the human race as developing slowly towards civilization and morality. Men start off as virtual brutes, and it is only after a long and strenuous development that they evolve the culture, the discipline and the moral sense to sustain something like republican politics.

Nor is it mere contingent misfortune that men did not start off capable of effortless comity, and painless adaptation to the demands of civilization. The very nature of the Kantian ideal, free self-determination through reason, is such that we could not attain it by following the bent of instinct alone. Men could be instinctively beneficent, but not instinctively free. Free rationality requires that they win through to self-determination by overcoming the unreflecting bent of nature.

Because of this, the realization of freedom presupposes a history, and one full of struggle and conflict. And we can consider it providential that men are not inclined by nature to harmony, but are marked by antagonism, by 'unsocial sociability'.[27] For this is what goads them ever onward towards the only stable solution possible for human society, a law-governed social order. Meanwhile, as we look over the span of centuries, we can see men driven ever by their own conflicts and tensions towards their destiny.

This long-term – as he saw it – rational hope helped to bridge for Kant the despotic present with the republican future. But there were also some short-term, more immediately observable factors which encouraged him. Despotism was being forced to enlightenment, he thought, by the demands of international commercial and military competition. Rulers were induced to foster economic development and, as a necessary condition of this, freedom of thought and opinion. The growth of an active and influential burger class would in turn restrain galloping military expenditures, and hence gradually put limits on princely adventurism and foster peace. The growing force of enlightened opinion would in turn push governments slowly towards reform, and the polities of Europe would gradually come to conform to the principles of the civil state.

All this may seem charmingly naive to a jaundiced late-twentieth-century reader. But it was not entirely incredible to someone who had lived the greater part of his life in Fredrician Prussia, and who witnessed in his last years the portentous events of the French Revolution. Enlightened opinion had become, by the end of the century, a force that could hardly have been dreamt of at the beginning, certainly in Germany. And that is why the freedom on which Kant insists the most in the contemporary context is the freedom of the pen.[28]

But his own hopes and fears are of secondary importance. Kant's definitions of freedom have made him one of the most important thinkers in the

---

[27] *Idea for a Universal History with Cosmopolitan Purpose*, translated in Reiss, *Kant's Political Writings*, p. 44.

[28] *Theory and Practice*, p. 85: 'The freedom of the pen is the only safeguard of the rights of the people, although it must not transcend the bounds of respect and devotion towards the existing constitution, which should itself create a liberal attitude of mind among the subjects. To try to deny the citizen this freedom does not only mean, as Hobbes maintains, that the subject can claim no rights against the supreme ruler. It also means withholding from the ruler all knowledge of those matters which, if he knew about them, he would himself rectify, so that he is thereby put in a self-stultifying position.'

development of modern culture. On one level his grounding politics on freedom, on respect for the agent as the originator of his own life-plan, remains one of the most powerful formulations of the liberal ideal, and is plainly central to influential contemporary theories, such as those of Rawls and Dworkin.[29]

On another level, Kant's ideal of total rational self-determination, of free self-activity unmixed with merely 'positive' standards, has worked as a ferment, ultimately breaking the bounds of liberalism, and emerging in the revolutionary theories of liberation which are now transforming our world. Fichte, Hegel and Marx helped to mediate this ideal into the traditions of revolution. But the original, rigorous formulation of the standard of radical freedom was Kant's.

---

[29] Cf. J. Rawls, *A Theory of Justice* (Oxford, 1972); R. Dworkin, *Taking Rights Seriously* (London, 1977).

INDEX